Explore
Essential English

GRAM Belfast Metropolitan College **D ENGLISH**

Castlerea...

Mark Slim

A.D.R.(London) Limited England

Belfast Metropolitan College
Castlereagh Campus

Dedication

In memory of my English language teachers who taught me diligently

ADR's Publishing Motto

'A person who searches for knowledge is a student'

British Library Cataloguing in Publication Data

A catalogue record for this book is available from the British Library

ISBN 190 1197 123

First published by ADR in UK 2003

Warning and Disclaimer

Every effort has been made to make this book as complete and as accurate as possible, but no warranty or fitness is implied. The information given in this book is on an "as is" basis. The author and the publisher shall have neither liability nor responsibility to any person or entity with respect to any misunderstanding, loss or damages arising from the use of the information contained in this book.

Direct Order

In case of difficulty, you can obtain a copy from the publisher:

A.D.R.(London) Limited
24 St. Alban Road
Bridlington
YO16 7SS
England

Tel: 01262 605538/400323
Fax: 01262 400323
email: sales@ adrlonodon.ltd.uk
Web Site: http:// www.adrlondon.ltd.uk

Printed in Great Britain by Antony Rowe Ltd, Chippenham, Wiltshire

Contents

Contents

Chapter 4 Adjectives

Chapter 5 Adverbs

Chapter 6 Prepositions

Chapter 7 Determiners & Interjections

Contents   V
****

VI   **Contents**

****

Chapter 11 Sentences

Part 3 Punctuation   **253**

Chapter 12 Punctuation

Contents

****

Part 4 Idiomatic Expressions

Chapter 13 Idiomatic Expressions

Part 5 Writing Skills

Chapter 14 Social Letter Writing

Chapter 15 Business Letter Writing

Examples of Letters:

Glossary
Index

Introduction

. Introduction

Like other languages, the English language can be spoken and written. For both purposes we require vocabulary and grammar. Vocabulary consists of words. Grammar has rules for combining words for meaningful communication in spoken and written English. By vocabulary, we mean all the words in English or any other language. No one knows precisely how many words there are in the English language. One of the main reasons is that it is a dynamic language, which is continuously changing. The other reason is that experts have different views on what constitutes a distinct word, and whether we should include scientific words in the English vocabulary. However, it is generally understood that the English language, excluding scientific words, has about one million words. Some words do become obsolete, and some new words are being continuously included.

It is interesting to imagine for a moment what is required to build a strong and safe brick wall. You will need some bricks. If you just pile these up on top of each other, the wall will not be a strong and safe structure. Therefore, you would require some lime or cement and sand in order to mix these with water to make some mortar. The mortar is used to hold the bricks together. By using the right amount of mortar between bricks, you can create a strong and safe brick wall structure.

Like bricks, *vocabulary (words)* by itself is insufficient for both writing and speaking purposes. To create a language *structure*, such as a phrase or a sentence, what is needed is ***a set of rules of grammar*** (mortar). Like mortar, the correct application of the rules of English grammar can convert a meaningless combination of words into a meaningful structure.

Here, the word *structure* means the way some words are arranged, in accordance with the rules of grammar, into phrases, clauses, etc. There are numerous types of structures such as a human body structure, building structure and so on. We are interested in the *grammatical structure* of the English language.

A particular *style* is a distinct way in which something is organised, arranged or done for whatever purpose. For instance, a manager can be kind, friendly and assertive when dealing with staff in order to get the job done. We can label this manager's style as a 'friendly style of management'. On the other hand, another manager can be nasty, unfriendly and authoritarian. This is an 'autocratic style of management'. These are two distinct styles of management. Similarly, there are many styles of using the language. For example, some people prefer:

- *simple style* – some people prefer a simple style – they use common words, short phrases and sentences mainly in private conversation and personal letters

- *complex style* – some people find simple writing and speaking dull – they use complicated words and *jargon:* words and phrases that are used by some group of people and are difficult for others to understand

- *colourful style* – some people such as toastmasters, writers and speakers who make money by writing and speech making use very *colourful language:* metaphor, alliteration, smile, hyperbole and wordplay

- *colloquial style* – some people use very simple words and phrases. This style is not for formal speech and writing. It is used in private conversation

One can think of many other styles such as a *humorous style*, *prose style*, *archaic style*, etc.

The English language is widely used in the world and therefore it has many different forms. I am concerned with the contemporary English in use in Britain. Despite the fact that there are many regional variations, there is *standard English*. Standard English is the form of the language that is nationally used in Britain. It is the medium of communication at the national level. It is used by institutions including educational bodies, text books, newspapers, broadcasting services, government agencies, etc. Standard English is socially accepted as the most correct form of the English language. Speakers of other languages also learn standard English.

A number of words can be put together without applying any rules of grammar. Let's consider the phrase *'any grammar book'*, in which three words are side by side. We do understand the meaning of the combination of these three words. If you exchange places of two words in this combination, or pattern of words, it will not make any sense. The reason is that we do not say 'book grammar any'. This new combination of words becomes no more than a meaningless jumble of words.

If you ask a number of native speakers of English, they will immediately recognise both the correct and incorrect pattern of these words. They use mental pictures which help them to recognise these groups of words as meaningful or meaningless. It is not only the combination of words that native speakers recognise, but also the meaning associated with that combination of words. They apply their knowledge of the order in patterns of words, and their associated meanings, by using their familiar vocabulary.

****

Native speakers use the language in its complexity from early childhood. They have been using the language up to the present time in their lives, and their knowledge of grammar is stored somewhere in their memories, just like the memory of a computer. Often, they are able to recall it and use it intuitively. They might have forgotten the technical terms needed to explain why the structure, such as a complicated sentence, is unrecognisable, or difficult to understand. Whether you are a native speaker or a student of the English language, you must learn *English grammar* in order:

- to be able to put words into recognised structures, namely phrases, clauses, sentences and paragraphs

- to identify grammatical structures, e.g. sentences, etc.

- to understand the meaning associated with these structures

- to analyse these structures in order to explain them to others, if there is a need for it

What is grammar? Grammar is an umbrella term. In essence, it is concerned with the words of a language and the mechanism, or rules of combining, or joining them together in meaningful phrases, clauses and sentences. It can also mean a person's knowledge and use of a language. For our purpose, the word *rule* means a recognised standard way of constructing structures. Therefore, the rules of grammar are principles for both spoken and written language.

In this age of the World Wide Web, the use of English is expanding exponentially through the Internet, and the correct use of English and its grammar is increasingly becoming highly desirable. Boldly speaking, it can be said that you are only as good as your grammar.

The prime aim of this book is to describe, and explain with the aid of numerous helpful examples, those aspects of English which are essential for both written and spoken standard English. The general objective of this book is to enable readers to improve their knowledge and skills in using the language with confidence. If you are an intermediate or advanced learner of English, or a teacher of English, you will find this book invaluable. The *prescriptive method* of grammar explanation is applied in this book. This approach is concerned with prescribing what is correct. It means discussing how the language should be used.

Diagram 1 shows that the relationship between words and rules is inseparable as indicated by a double arrow between them. The rules of grammar govern words and words are needed to make rules about them. All illustrations are numbered simply as 1,2, etc. within chapters.

The *linguistic* aspects of the English grammar are beyond the scope of this book. In passing, the *linguistics* is the scientific study of language. Linguistic is connected with linguistics. A *linguist* studies languages and works in the linguistic field, mainly in the academic world. In this book, uncommon words, such as *discourse* (for combining sentences) and *lexis* (the words of a language) i.e. linguistic terminology used by linguists, are not included.

A Visualisation of the English Language

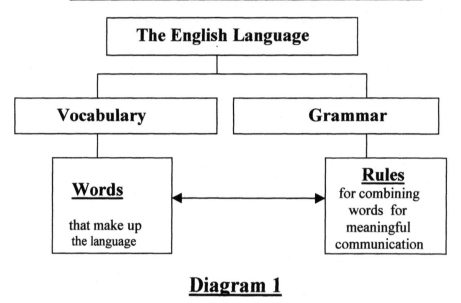

Diagram 1

• How to use this book

This book consists of five parts. Words are the building blocks of language. Therefore, **Part 1** starts with word classes which are also known as parts of speech.

Part 2 is devoted to the construction of phrases, clauses and sentences. This part follows Part 1 so that the reader can fully grasp the importance of each class of words and the role that can be played by different words in phrases, clauses and sentences.

Part 3 deals with punctuation. Punctuation makes communication clear.

Part 4 is about the usage of idiomatic expressions – idioms are in their own class.

Part 5 examines writing skills for global communicators.

It is suggested that Parts 1 and 2 are to be read consecutively. Parts 3-5 may be read in any order.

The glossary contains an alphabetical list of definitions of terms used in this book. The book finishes with an index. These can be used for reference at any time. Illustrations, diagrams and tables are numbered simply as 1,2,3…etc. within chapters.

Part 1

Word Classes

Word Classes at First Glance

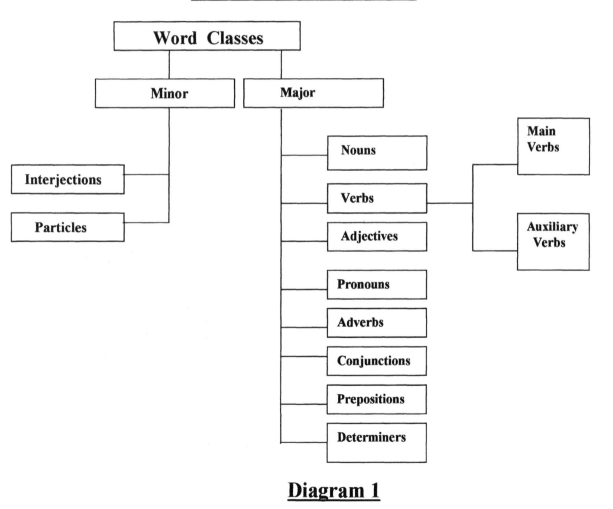

Diagram 1

There are different word classes as depicted in Diagram 1 above. These are also known as parts of speech. You may find that different books have different numbers of word classes. If you see differences in this respect, you have to decide for yourself which classification is the most appropriate and meets your specific needs. Minor word classes have very few words in them, but it is important to recognise them as classes, at least for the sake of clarity.

Diagram 1 is self-explanatory. However, many words can be placed in more than one word class. Even so, the idea of word classes helps us to group words with similar features together, and know exactly how they are used.

<u>*A word* is a single and independent unit of vocabulary</u>. It can be recognised in both speech and writing (or print). Many words have several meanings. A recognised word has the following features:

- it has a distinct sound, which can be a combination of sounds

- it has a meaning, i.e. definition

- a written word is recognisable by its structure, i.e. the number of letters in it and their combination pattern.

Yes, you can have words consisting of not only alphabetic letters but also other elements such as recognised symbols, e.g. £ sign.

For instance, the word *table* consists of five alphabetic letters. To speakers of English, it is recognisable as a combination of five letters when arranged in this given order. Therefore, when this word is used in *speech*, a speaker of the English language knows it by its distinct sound. This sound is produced by the sounds of four letters in it because the last letter 'e' is silent.

When the same word is *written* (printed), a reader of the English language identifies it by the pattern of letters put together side by side to structure it.

We know that a table is a piece of furniture, which has a flat top on legs, trestles or pillars. It can hold things *(meaning/definition)*. When it is a part of a sentence, we are interested in understanding what role *(function)* it plays in the sentence. You know many such words, and most likely you consider them as the building blocks of the English language. Now consider the following sentence:

I am learning to write.

This text has spaces between the words which makes it easy to identify and count the words used there. It has five words. Normally, in English writing, there are spaces between words, but there are occasions when word identification as a single independent unit is not so easy, for example, when two or more words make a single unit.

In written English, there are normally spaces between words, which makes it easy to identify each word. *A compound word* is composed of two or more words.

- It can be written with *a hyphen* (hyphenated word) between words, as exemplified below:

    (1) **. mother-in-law**

    (2) **. man-made fibres such as polyester**

    (3) **. dark-haired**

    (4) **. passer-by**

- It can be written <u>without</u> any spaces between words. This is illustrated below:

    (5) **. teapot** ⟸ two words joined together

    (6) **. housewife** ⟸ two words joined together

- It can be written <u>with or without spaces between</u> words constituting a compound word. For example:

    (7) **. troublemaker or trouble-maker** ⟸ hyphenated word

    (8) **. teamwork or team-work** ⟸ hyphenated word

    (9) **. plant pot** ⟸ a space between them - in speech it is considered as a single
                    word ⟹ **plantpot**

    (10) **. world war** ⟸ a space between them – some people spell it as a single
                    word ⟹ **worldwar**

All these words and many more in terms of meaning are singular words. These and many similar words can cause some confusion to learners of English, as they do not appear to be single words. However, they are considered as single words, meaning something is singular.

Furthermore, *in an idiomatic expression* a word does not usually give its own meaning. This can be a really serious problem to learners of English. For example, **a hard nut to crack** is a group of five individual words forming an **idiomatic expression**.

In this expression, each word does not have its own dictionary meaning. Such an expression is fixed, and its meaning is deduced from the context in which it is used. For instance:

(11) • Financing a stand at this international IT exhibition will be **a hard nut to crack** for us.

                                          ----

                                            an idiomatic expression ⏎

In this context, it means that we will find it difficult to finance a stand at this international exhibition. Here, each underlined individual word does not render its dictionary meaning. The idiomatic expression "a hard nut to crack" means a difficult problem, but its real sense is deduced from the context in which it is used. An idiomatic phrase by itself often does not make sense to those whose mother tongue is not English. The same is true about idioms in other languages.

All major word classes shown in Diagram 1 are discussed next in Part 1 in considerable depth with the aid of scores of helpful and practical examples. Each major word class has its own chapter. The other two minor word classes are discussed under other relevant chapters. You will find a discussion on **interjections** in Chapter 7. This class is so small that it is usually not discussed separately.

• **Particles class** is a very small word class. Particles are used with a verb to make a phrasal verb (e.g., multi-word verb). For instance:

(12) • She tore up his letter.   *tore up* $\Rightarrow$ *phrasal verb*

(13) • He fell off the stairs.   *fell off* $\Rightarrow$ *phrasal verb*

(14) • Our car broke down.   *broke down* $\Rightarrow$ *phrasal verb*

In these sentences, *up*, *off* and *down* are particles. These three words are actually adverbs as well as prepositions. When you use them with verbs to make phrasal verbs such as *tear up*, *fall off* and **break down**, these are then known as particles. Many writers do not discuss particles class as a word class in its own right, because there are few words in it.

• Some writers classify numerals as a separate class. In this book, numerals are discussed as determiners. See Chapter 7 on Determiners & Interjections.

• Determiners, pronouns and conjunctions are much smaller classes than verbs, nouns, adjectives and adverbs.

Chapter 1
Nouns

. Introduction

A large number of words are used as **names** of such things as:

- **People** - Anne, Blair, Clinton, John, Jane　(someone unique)

- **Places** - London, Frankfurt, Stockholm, Singapore, Manchester　(a specific place)

- **Objects** - printer, table, book, pen, motor, computer　(an artefact)

- **Animals** - cow, horse, donkey, fox, rabbit

- **Nature** - star, earth, moon, sea, sky, flowers

- **Abstract** – love, unhappy, communism, belief, bravery, truth, beauty, staff morale
       These are ideas, concepts, qualities, state of mind or intangible things.

The word **noun** is derived from the Latin word *nomen*. In Latin, it means *name*. Therefore, when a word is used as a name, it is called a **noun**. Nouns make up the biggest category of word classes. Every thing is given a name. Nouns are at the heart of our language as they are frequently used in speech and writing. For instance, in the following simple sentences:

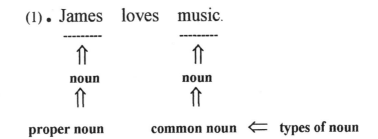

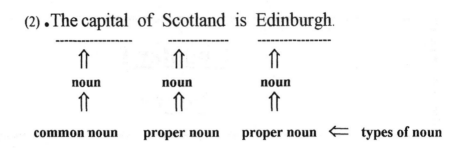

. Types of Nouns

The above two examples illustrate that there are two types of nouns, **proper nouns** and **common nouns**. James, Scotland and Edinburgh are proper nouns. They are also proper nouns for the following reasons:

     • words **Mary White** refer to ⟹ someone **unique**

It is true to say that more than one person can be called **Mary White**, but still that particular person *Mary White* is unique.

         • the word **Scotland** refers to   ⟹ a specific country

         • the word **Edinburgh** refers to ⟹ a particular city

Music and capital are **common nouns**.

. Why is it so?

         • the word **music** by itself does not refer to any unique music

         • the word **capital** by itself does not refer to a particular capital city of the world

There are many different types of music and a large number of capital cities in the world.

. Concrete and Abstract Common Nouns

Common nouns may be classified as concrete and abstract. This classification is based on the idea of tangible and intangible. One can see and touch tangible things. Such things may be concrete nouns. On the other hand, there are intangible things, which cannot be seen or touched, but they exist as ideas, concept and qualities. Such non-material things may be abstract nouns. The following list shows some nouns of both types.

Some concrete and abstract nouns

Concrete Nouns	Abstract Nouns
park	democracy
horse	freedom
floppy disc	falsehood
hammer	Buddhism
bed	anger
tree	liberty
officer	truth
woman	socialism
book	action

List 1

- ## How can you know whether a word is a proper noun or a common noun?

The following guide will help you to decide whether a noun is a proper noun or a common noun.

A Guide to proper & common nouns

Proper Nouns	Common Nouns
• Begin with a capital letter in writing Examples:	• Initial capital letter is not essential in writing unless they begin a sentence. Examples:
Birmingham, Cairo, Thomas, Friday*, July*, Christmas, India * see next page	coffee, bread, car, concept, method *(continued on next page)*

----

* see next page (continued on next page)

****

• Specific or unique names
  Examples:

    Einstein, Johnson,
    Cliff Richard, France

• Group or member of group names
  Examples:

    girl, woman, man, people, animal, train

* Exception to the above rules:

    Seasons : *spring, summer, autumn and winter do not begin with a capital letter,*
               <u>unless they start a sentence.</u>

•<u>Noun Gender</u>

Another feature of common and proper nouns is that they have gender. In the English language, gender classification is based on a man and woman as natural creation. In accordance with this idea, a **woman** is classified as **feminine** and a **man** as **masculine.** The third gender class **neuter** is reserved for artefacts, such as a computer.

<u>Examples of proper nouns and their respective genders</u>
⇓

Masculine	Feminine	Neuter
John Webb	Barbara Cartland	Russia
Robin Taylor	Rachel Berios	British Airways
Adam Shaw	Anne Kling	Microsoft
Daniel Shaw	Silvia Plew	Sweden

<u>Examples of common nouns and their respective genders</u>
⇓

Masculine	Feminine	Neuter
king	queen	table
boy	girl	magazine
lion	lioness	banana
conductor	conductress (on a bus collects money)	post

• <u>**Are there any nouns which do not fall into any of these gender groups?**</u>

Yes, indeed, a few nouns have their own gender class known as **dual gender**. For instance:

- **teacher** man or woman ⇐ dual gender

- **singer** man or woman ⇐ dual gender

- **adult** man or woman ⇐ dual gender

- **player** man or woman ⇐ dual gender

- **student** man or woman ⇐ dual gender

. Compound Nouns

A compound word is made of two or more words. Here are some examples:

- **milkman** ⟹ **milk + man** - is a compound noun

- **headache** ⟹ **head + ache** - is a compound noun

- **postman** ⟹ **post + man** - is a compound noun

- **Some compound words are written as hyphenated words** – there are no exact rules about whether two or more specific nouns or words are hyphenated or not.

Some Compound Nouns

Single Words	Hyphenated words	A pair of words
postman	daughter-in-law	teddy bear
sportswoman	Anglo-American	blood bank
clergyman	non-fiction	shoe brush
housewife	major-general	blind spot
businesswoman	waste-bin	health food
policeman	window-shopping	wine bar
doorstep	father-figure	magic carpet
gamekeeper	ultra-modern	black box
standpoint	flight-recorder	court martial
teapot	X-ray	package holiday

List 2

A compound noun can be written as a single word, hyphenated word or as a pair of two words. Some compound nouns are shown in List 2 below.

Some compound words may be written in one dictionary as a hyphenated word and in another as one word or as a pair of two or more words. <u>When some compound nouns are formed with **noun + gerund** (stamp-collecting) and **verb + adverb** (take-off) are hyphenated.</u> Sometimes words which have prefixes such as **non, pre, anti, semi** and **ultra** are also hyphenated. Here are four examples: **pre-packed** sandwich, **anti-aircraft** missiles, **non-committal** reply, and **ulta-modern** design. It is best to be consistent with your own spellings and consult a dictionary when in doubt (sometimes two dictionaries may differ).

. <u>Singular and Plural Nouns</u>

As a noun is a name, it can be used for a single thing **(singular)** or a number of the same things **(plural)**,but Plural nouns differ from singular nouns in their endings. <u>A large number of plural nouns end with 's' as exemplified in Table 1 below:</u>

<u>Examples of plural nouns with 's'</u>

Singular	Plural	Singular	Plural
boat	boats	border	borders
bolt	bolts	bridge	bridges
candidate	candidates	car	cars
chop	chops	competition	competitions
corner	corners	date	dates
delay	delays	diplomat	diplomats
director	directors	dot	dots
effect	effects	effort	efforts
exhibit	exhibits	eye	eyes
farm	farms	fool	fools
friend	friends	gap	gaps
heart	hearts	jacket	jackets
jug	jugs	length	lengths
lip	lips	pedestrian	pedestrians
map	maps	shop	shops
reader	readers	spoonful	spoonfuls
student	students	traveller	travellers

<u>Table 1</u>

The following examples illustrate how in most cases plural nouns are formed:

• boat $\Rightarrow$ singular and • boats $\Rightarrow$ plural

• cake $\Rightarrow$ singular and • cakes $\Rightarrow$ plural

• chair $\Rightarrow$ singular and • chairs $\Rightarrow$ plural

• shop $\Rightarrow$ singular and • shops $\Rightarrow$ plural

• **A large number of singular nouns end with a letter (-s, -ss, -sh, -tch, -x, -o) other than 'e' but their plural nouns end with 'es' as exemplified in Table 2.**

Examples of plural nouns end with 'es'

Singular	Plural	Singular	Plural
boss	bosses	box	boxes
cargo	cargoes	bus	buses
crash	crashes	coach	coaches
loss	losses	sandwich	sandwiches
gas	gases	pass	passes
patch	patches	scratch	scratches
sex	sexes	blemish	blemishes
stitch	stitches	trench	trenches
torpedo	torpedoes	tomato	tomatoes
watch	watches	wish	wishes

Table 2

• **Singular nouns which end with ' e' also form their plural with 'es'.**

Some examples of such nouns are given below:

• cabbage $\Rightarrow$ **cabbages**

• cable $\Rightarrow$ **cables**

• cause $\Rightarrow$ **causes**

• house $\Rightarrow$ **houses**

16   **Nouns**   **Word Classes**

****

- shade $\Rightarrow$ shades

- vegetable $\Rightarrow$ vegetables

- **Many plural nouns end with 'ies' as exemplified in Table 3**

If you carefully study Table 3, you will learn that all singular nouns end with **a consonant + y**. Therefore, their corresponding plural nouns are formed by changing the last letter **y** to **ies**.

Examples of plural nouns end with 'ies'

Singular	Plural	Singular	Plural
body	bodies	category	categories
cavalry	cavalries	cemetery	cemeteries
community	communities	country	countries
currency	currencies	duty	duties
energy	energies	entry	entries
family	families	glory	glories
hobby	hobbies	humanity	humanities
itinerary	itineraries	liberty	liberties
penalty	penalties	story	stories
remedy	remedies	territory	territories

Table 3

- **All singular nouns, which end with a vowel (a, e, i, o, u) and 'y', do not always form their plural with 'ies'.**

Here are some examples of such singular nouns and their corresponding plural nouns:

- way $\Rightarrow$ plural noun $\Rightarrow$ ways

- turkey $\Rightarrow$ plural noun $\Rightarrow$ turkeys

- ray $\Rightarrow$ plural noun $\Rightarrow$ rays

- journey $\Rightarrow$ plural noun $\Rightarrow$ journeys

- toy $\Rightarrow$ plural noun $\Rightarrow$ toys

- holiday $\Rightarrow$ plural noun $\Rightarrow$ holidays

- essay $\Rightarrow$ plural noun $\Rightarrow$ essays

. Irregular Nouns

There are some smaller groups of nouns, which form their plurals in some different ways. These are illustrated below.

Examples of a smaller irregular group of nouns which form their plural by replacing their 'f' with 'ves' (v+es)

Singular	Plural	Singular	Plural
scarf	scarves	leaf	leaves
hoof	hooves	knife	knives
life	lives	loaf	loaves
thief	thieves	scarf	scarves
wife	wives	wolf	wolves

Table 4

Examples of another smaller irregular group of nouns which form their plural in some peculiar ways

Singular	Plural	Singular	Plural
child	children	criterion	criteria
goose	geese	foot	feet
man	men	mouse	mice
penny	pence **or** pennies	stimulus	stimuli
tooth	teeth	woman	women

Table 5

A small group of nouns can be troublesome to some writers, as they have their own peculiarities. In this group, some singular nouns have no plural. On the other hand, some nouns are used only as plural. Furthermore, some nouns can be used in singular or plural forms. These forms are illustrated below:

Examples of nouns surrounded by inconsistencies

Noun	Singular verb	Plural verb
economics use as singular	The economics of the Third World is in need of help from the First World.	
premises use as plural		The premises were locked up when we arrived.
mathematics use as singular or plural	Mathematics is the science of numbers, quantity and space.	Her mathematics are good.
litter use as singular	Her room was a litter of dirty crockery and old clothes.	
Media it is often used as singular, but some people think it should be used as plural only.	The media has shown keen interest in this murder trial. (The Internet is the modern **medium** of communication - here medium is **singular**)	The media have shown keen interest in this murder trial. **(debatable use)**
news plural form but its use is singular	No news is good news.	
jeans plural and its use is singular with 'a pair'	He was wearing a pair of blue jeans.	
scissors plural and its use is singular with 'a pair'	Here is a pair of steel scissors for you.	
wrinkle use as plural		He is beginning to get wrinkles around his eyes.

Table 6

• **A very small group of nouns has two forms of plural. These plural are formed in their own specific way as shown in Table 7.**

Examples of nouns which have two plural forms

Singular	Plural	Singular	Plural
appendix	appendixes appendices	formula	formulae formulas
focus	focuses foci	trauma	traumas traumata

Table 7

• Countable Nouns

A noun is considered as countable if it meets the following requirements:

(a) • **It has both singular and plural forms**

For instance:

dog ⟹ **singular form**   dogs ⟹ **plural form**

ship ⟹ **singular form**   ships ⟹ **plural form**

(b) • **It is countable, i.e. can be counted (how many)**

For example:

three men, two problems, ten books, etc.

(c) • **It can be preceded by such determiners as listed below:**

the, a, an, every, many, one, two, three, four, etc.

****

<u>Here are some examples:</u>

- a company $\Rightarrow$ two companies   • a computer shop $\Rightarrow$ many computer shops

- an egg $\Rightarrow$ two eggs   • a student $\Rightarrow$ a group of ten students

- a coach $\Rightarrow$ a fleet of coaches **or** 10 coaches **or** many coaches **or** every coach, etc.

- a singular form agrees with a singular form of the verb $\Rightarrow$ a dog **is** in their factory yard.
                                     ----

                singular form of the verb ↵

- a plural form agrees with a plural form of the verb $\Rightarrow$ Two dogs **are** in their factory yard.
                                     -----

                plural form of the verb ↵

• <u>Uncountable (Uncount or Mass) Nouns</u>

These nouns have the following attributes:

(a) • they cannot be counted – refer to qualities , mass

(b) • they do <u>not</u> have a plural form – use a singular form only

(c) • they can be used with or without a determiner

(d) • some uncountable nouns are preceded by a **<u>PARTITIVE</u>** phrase or words. A partitive phrase or word refers to a part or quantity of something. For instance:

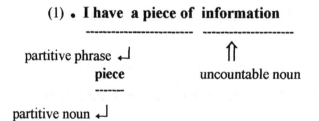

          (1) • **I have a piece of information**
                     ------------------------   --------------------

partitive phrase ↵   ⇑
           piece   uncountable noun
           ------

partitive noun ↵

The reason is that information is not countable. However, you can refer to any amount

Word Classes   **Nouns**   **21**

****

of information as a part of the whole mass of information. It may be that you want to refer to the whole mass of information (no matter how little is the whole mass of information).

Here are some examples of uncountable nouns:

(1) • There is still *some* milk in the jar.   ⇐ some is a determiner

singular form of the verb ↵   ⇑

            Since it is not counted as an individual thing, it is preceded by **some**.

(2) • There are *three items of* equipment for you.

       ⇑   ⇑

   plural form of the verb   uncountable noun

Since equipment is not counted as an individual thing, it is preceded by *three items of*

                                       partitive phrase ↵

(3) • Chemistry is her favourite subject at school.

      ⇑

   uncountable noun

In this sentence, there is no need to precede the uncountable noun with any determiner.

(4) • It is common knowledge already.

         ⇑

      uncountable noun ⇒ it is not preceded by '**a**'

(5) • The tutor spoke in praise of her class.

        ⇑

      uncountable noun ⇒ it is not preceded by '**a**'

****

● <u>**Sometimes, in accordance with the context, a noun may be either countable or uncountable.**</u>

The following examples illustrate this feature of nouns:

(1) ● In the hall, all lights are switched on.

⇑

in this context lights is a **countable noun** ⟹ preceded by *all*

(2) ● Have you got a light?   (Someone may ask you for a light for a cigarette.)

⇑

here the noun light is **countable** ⟹ preceded by *a*

(3) ● This box contains a bedside **light**.

⇑

in this example the noun light is **countable** ⟹ here it means one lamp

(4) ● Light travels faster than sound.

⇑

In this sentence light is used as **uncountable**

(5) ● Would you like to have *two pounds of* sugar?

Partitive phrase ↵   ⇑

uncountable noun

(6) ● Do you take *one* sugar or more?

determiner ↵   ⇑

countable noun

(7) . There is no personal *sympathy* between John and Jill.

in this context **uncountable** noun ↵ - here *sympathy* = **understanding**
between people with similar interests

(8) . Sandra has no **sympathy** for Barbara; it was her wrong idea.

⇑ - here *sympathy* = **the feeling of being sorry for someone**
in this context **countable** noun

(9) . You can have *two slices* of bread.

partitive phrase ↵   ⇑

uncountable noun   ⇒ preceded by *two slices of*

. <u>Collective Nouns</u>

A collective noun is a singular word, but it refers to a group of things. These things or objects in a group can be people, animals, animated things, ideas or concepts. <u>In most cases, a collective noun takes a singular verb.</u>

. <u>**Some examples of collective nouns agreeing with singular verbs:**</u>

(1) . **Our team has 10 members in it.**

⇑   ⇑   ⇑

collective   singular   more than one person
noun   form of   in this group
        the verb

(2) . **The council has 30 elected members.**

⇑   ⇑   ⇑

collective   singular form   more than one person
noun   of the verb   in this group

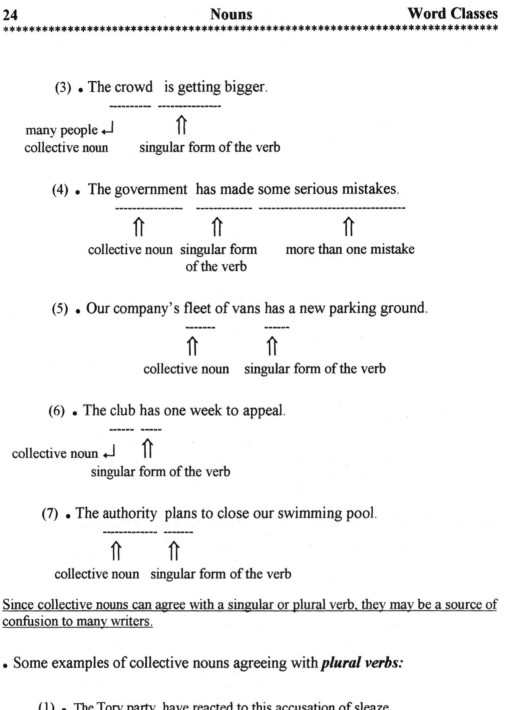

(3) • The crowd is getting bigger.

many people ↵   ⇑
collective noun   singular form of the verb

(4) • The government has made some serious mistakes.

collective noun singular form   more than one mistake
                 of the verb

(5) • Our company's fleet of vans has a new parking ground.

collective noun   singular form of the verb

(6) • The club has one week to appeal.

collective noun ↵   ⇑
                singular form of the verb

(7) • The authority plans to close our swimming pool.

collective noun   singular form of the verb

Since collective nouns can agree with a singular or plural verb, they may be a source of confusion to many writers.

• Some examples of collective nouns agreeing with ***plural verbs:***

(1) • The Tory party have reacted to this accusation of sleaze .

collective noun↵   ⇑
                plural form of the verb

****

(2) • The government are unhappy about the steady decline of taxes collected.

collective noun↵   ⇑
                    plural form of the verb

(3) • The staff have accepted new terms of employment.

collective noun↵   ⇑
                    plural form of the verb

(4)   • The police have caught the thief.

collective noun↵   ⇑
                    plural form of the verb

(5) • Your goods have arrived.

collective noun↵   ⇑
                    plural form of the verb

'Goods' may be one thing, but it is used as a plural noun. For instance, a parcel may contain one item only. We still say, **_goods have arrived_**.

• When should you use either singular or plural verbs with a collective noun?

Usually, when one is thinking of the whole group or body of objects as a single unit, the singular form of the verb is used. On the other hand, if one refers to individuals or components, which make up the body or group, the plural form of the verb is applied.

(1) • The jury has/have returned a verdict of guilty.

collective noun↵   ⇑
                    either singular or plural form

• How can you test that a word is a noun?

The following tests can help you to determine whether a word is a noun:

• A noun has a determiner in front of it. If you can justify placing one of the determiners such as **a**, **an**, **any**, or **the** in front of the word, then you know that it is a noun. For instance:

(1) • She was walking with *a* dog.
---

determiner ↵

The determiner is in front of the word dog. This indicates that the word **dog** is a noun.

• When you can justify placing one of the partitive words or phrases in front of a word, you can conclude that the word is a noun:

(2) • I have *three pieces of* information that might be of some use to you.
----

partitive phrase ↵

Here the partitive phrase before the noun points to an uncountable noun **information**.

• Nouns can point to ownership. For instance:

(3) • I do not know about his *sister's* marriage.

⇑

This indicates ownership/possession.

The word **sister's** is a *possessive form*. Now, isolate the word marriage and then place the determiner in front of it to read: **a marriage**. This is indeed another noun in this sentence.

. Possessive Forms

When we add an -*'s* to a singular noun, we change its form to the possessive form. Here are some more examples:

(1) • brother ⇒ this is my brother's hat   brother's ⇒ possessive

(2) • team ⇒ our team's brilliant victory is good news   team's ⇒ possessive

(3) • shop $\Rightarrow$ someone has smashed our shop's front glass door   shop's $\Rightarrow$ possessive

(4) • car $\Rightarrow$ this is my wife's car .   wife's $\Rightarrow$ possessive

• When proper nouns end with –**s**, you have a choice of adding apostrophe s, or placing an apostrophe after the '**s**'. For instance:

   (1) • I have been invited to stay in the *Jones's* new home for the weekend.

   (2) • They went to *James'* office to see a demonstration of new office equipment.

• When a common plural noun ends with –**s**, just add *an apostrophe* to convert it into its possessive form. For instance:

   (1) • Our history tutor often does not remember his *friends'* names.

   (2) • You can use our *customers'* car park until 17.00 hours every day.

   (3) • The idea of socialism was to make ordinary *workers'* lives easy.

• See $\Rightarrow$ Noun Phrases

In summary, nouns are words that we use to give names to people, animals, natural and man-made objects. They are also used to name abstract things. Common and proper nouns are the main groups of nouns. The other two groups of nouns are collective and abstract nouns. In order to use nouns correctly in both written and spoken English, it is important to understand noun gender (male, female and neuter) and number (singular or plural) of the same gender.

Chapter 2

Pronouns

. Introduction

A word used instead of a noun or a noun phrase is called a pronoun. Diagram 1 contains types of pronouns. Personal pronouns occur more frequently than any other types of pronouns. In fact, pronouns do the work of a noun in naming a person or a thing. They take the place of a noun.

Diagram 1

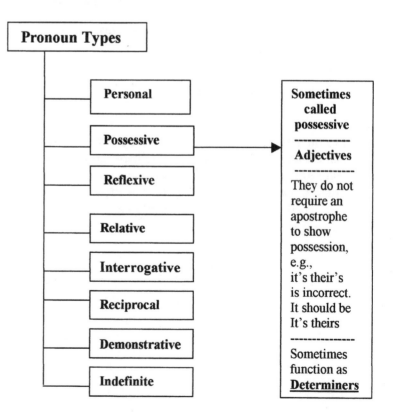

. Personal and Possessive Pronouns

Consider the following examples:

(1) . **I** would like a cup of tea.

  ⇑

personal pronoun – refers to ⟹ *first person*

I stands for a single <u>first person</u> who would like (action) a cup of tea. The first person is used by a writer or a speaker about himself/herself. It is the **subject** of this sentence, and for this reason, it is called a **subjective pronoun**. The subjective pronoun occupies the subject position in a sentence. <u>The subjective pronoun comes before the verb.</u>

(2) . **You** went home at about 11 p.m.

  ⇑

personal pronoun – the second person

You is the <u>second person</u>. The second person in a sentence is the person to whom he/she writes or speaks. **You** can be singular or plural. Here, **you** is in the subject position. It also comes before the verb. Therefore, it is the **subjective pronoun** in this sentence.

(3) . John has already informed **me**.
  -----

personal pronoun ↵
----
objective form ↵

me represents a single person. Here, **me** is the **object** of this sentence. Thus it is known as an **objective pronoun**. <u>Note that the pronoun **me** occurs after the verb informed.</u>

. **It is worth mentioning that an objective pronoun may be in the subject position. This can happen in informal writing, as shown by the following example:**

(4) • **Me** and John have reconciled all payments with customers' accounts.

⇑

objective pronoun used in the subject position in this sentence

This is not recommended as it is not standard English.

(5) • **They** want to go to the cinema in **my** car.

⇑   ⇑ - also called <u>possessive adjective see page 28</u>
personal pronoun   **possessive pronoun** - indicates that the car belongs to
plural form   the person who writes or speaks this sentence.

In this example, the possessive pronoun **my** comes before the noun **car**. Here, the possessive pronoun is used with a noun. <u>If a possessive pronoun is used with a noun, then it is in the **dependent form**.</u> In this example, *my* is a possessive pronoun in the dependent form.

They is in the <u>third person plural</u> form. A <u>third person</u> is the person or thing/object/abstract idea about which the first person speaks or writes. A third person can mean things, or objects or abstract ideas, as well as persons.

(6) • Here are two copies of 'The Sunday Times' newspaper.
One is **mine** and the other is **hers**.

⇑   ⇑
possessive pronoun   possessive pronoun - independent form
indicating noun's **gender** ↵

In this example, the possessive pronoun **hers** is used <u>without</u> any noun. In fact, it is independent of any noun. <u>When a possessive pronoun is used instead of a noun phrase then it is in the **independent form**.</u>

(7) • **Theirs** is the red car parked in row A. **Ours** is parked in row C.

⇑   ⇑
possessive pronoun - plural   possessive pronoun - plural
independent form   independent form

The classification of pronouns is given in Tables 1 and 2. Reflexive pronouns are in Table 2.

Classification of Personal & Possessive Pronouns

	Subjective Pronouns	Objective Pronouns	Possessive Pronouns*	
Singular			Dependent form used with nouns	Independent form used instead of nouns
1st person	I	me	my	mine
2nd person	you	you	your	yours
3rd person	he, she, it, they	him, her, it, them	his, her, its	his, hers, its
Plural				
1st person	we	us	our	ours
2nd person	you	you	your	yours
3rd person	they	them	their	theirs

Table 1

* An apostrophe is not required in writing a possessive pronoun. For instance, it is wrong to write **your's**.

- **Is there any exception to the rule?**

  Yes, there is one exception worth mentioning:

(1) • One must look after ***one's*** elderly parents. Here one's implies people in general.

- The above examples illustrate that personal and possessive pronouns perform a number of **functions** in a sentence:

  (a) ***show the person:***

   first person - person (s) speaker (s) or writer (s)

second person - the person or thing being addressed. It does not refer to the speaker or the writer

third person - it is the person or thing about which the first person is writing or speaking

(b) indicate the gender of the noun which it renders
(c) denote the number – singular or plural
(d) substitute for the proper noun, e.g. Johnson
(e) point to the case of a sentence, e.g. possessive case
(f) identify a belonging , or belonging to, or a possession, e.g. our

.<u>Reflexive Pronouns</u>

A reflexive pronoun refers to the subject. Consider the following examples:

(1) • **I** cut **myself** last night with a kitchen knife.

personal pronoun   reflexive pronoun

Here *myself* is a reflexive pronoun because the subject's action comes back on the person (pronoun) concerned. In this example, the person concerned is **the subject - I**, personal pronoun – singular.

(2) • **John** has found new employment at a local computer shop **himself**.

⇑   ⇑
Noun   **reflexive pronoun**

(3) • **They** earn a great deal of money for **themselves**.

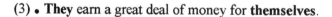

personal pronoun   **reflexive pronoun**

refers back to the subject **they** ⟹ plural

- These examples illustrate that a reflexive pronoun refers back to the subject of a sentence, which may be a noun or a pronoun. In Table 2, you can find all reflexive pronouns.

- Sometimes a reflexive pronoun is used for emphasis or clarification. When a reflexive pronoun is used for this purpose, it is labelled as an **intensifying pronoun.** This is illustrated below:

(4) • I designed my web site **myself**.

⇑

functioning as an **intensifying pronoun** placing emphasis

(5) • Did you see the accident **yourself** ?

⇑

functioning as an **intensifying pronoun** for clarification

(6) • The parked car started rolling down the hill **itself**.
------

functioning as an **intensifying pronoun** ↵ – indicating no interference

Reflexive Pronouns

	Singular	**Plural**
First Person	myself	ourselves
Second Person	yourself	yourselves
Third Person	himself, herself, itself, themself *	themselves

Table 2

> **The following style is not recommended in this book. It is incorrect grammatically.**
>
> * **Themself** is not recognized in standard English. It is used when someone does not want to specify the sex of the person, or when the gender is unknown. In this case, the word **they** is treated as a singular personal pronoun without any sex-marking. Its reflexive pronoun is derived from them and self as **themself**. It is a modern idea, which is disliked by many people. Its use is illustrated below:
>
> (7) • If any of you are bored, **he or she** can quietly leave the room now for ten minutes
> for some fresh air for himself or herself.
>
> <u>In order to avoid the use of he or she in the above sentence, it is stated as:</u>
>
> (8) • If any of you need some fresh air, **they** can quietly leave the room now for ten   ⇐ correct = **you**
> minutes for some fresh air for **themself**.   ⇐ correct = **yourselves**
>
> (9) • Somebody has forgotten their umbrella. They must collect it
> **themself** from my office.   ⇐ correct = **themselves**
>
> If you write **they** and **themselves** for a singular personal pronoun, most of your readers will find this use repellent.

. <u>Relative Pronouns</u>

A relative pronoun is a word, which links a subordinate clause to a main clause. These words are *that*, *who*, *whose*, *which*, and *whom*.

The following examples illustrate their application:

(1) • He inherited a great deal of money, *which* he has used to set up a new business.

(2) • This is the same person *who* sent us so many threatening letters.

(3) • Joan is the lady *whose* son was tricked by the perpetrator.

(4) • The car *that* I was to purchase was in poor condition.

(5) • He is a man *whom* you can trust.

> **See ⇒ Clauses**

****

. <u>Interrogative Pronouns</u>

Interrogative pronouns are used to ask questions. These words are also called **wh-words**. There are only five of them. These are exemplified below in ***bold*** characters:

(1) . ***Who*** are you?

(2) . ***Which*** of these bicycles do you wish to order?

(3) . ***What*** is your prime aim now?

(4) . ***Whose*** are those birds in a cage left in our front garden?

(5) . By ***whom*** were you interviewed last week?

These interrogative pronouns also function as relative pronouns.

. <u>Reciprocal Pronouns</u>

Reciprocal pronouns express a mutual relationship. They are like a two-way communication mode: one message going in one direction and one coming back from another direction. There are only two such pronouns: ***each other*** and ***one another.*** Here are some examples:

(1) . They wrote to ***one another*** for a number of years. ⇐ each person wrote to the <u>other person</u>

(2) . Jack and Jill always help ***each other.*** ⇐ each member in this group of two helps the <u>other person</u>

(3) . They can use **each other's/ one another's** computers without any password.
----

       use in possessive form ↵- apostrophe is before the –s in the possessive form

(4) . Sometimes they stay at **one another's/each other's** country homes.
----

       use in possessive form ↵ apostrophe is before the –s in the possessive form

In general: more than two persons ⇒ **one another**, - if they = two person ⇒ **each other**

. <u>Demonstrative Pronouns</u>

Demonstrative pronouns are those pronouns which indicate, show, or point to things.

They are also used to refer to a particular person or people. These pronouns consist of :

- **this** $\Rightarrow$ singular demonstrative pronoun - indicates something within close reach
- **that** $\Rightarrow$ singular demonstrative pronoun - points to something further way
- **these** $\Rightarrow$ plural demonstrative pronoun - shows something nearby
- **those** $\Rightarrow$ plural demonstrative pronoun - refers to something further away

The following examples illustrate their usage:

(1) . **This** is our car.

⇑

indicates <u>here</u> near the speaker <u>now</u>

(2) . **These** chairs are no longer needed in this room.

⇑

shows a <u>present</u> situation in a <u>nearby place</u>

(3) . **These** are our friends from Germany: Anne and Wolfgang.

⇑

refers to people <u>now</u> and <u>nearby</u>

(4) . In my view **that** contract should be renewable.

⇑

refers to people's action <u>backward in time and space</u> (a contract is between people)

(5) . **These** are slightly faulty goods for our summer sales next month.

⇑

refers to things <u>forward in time and space</u>

****

(6) • **That** was Margo sitting at the end of the second row.

⇑

refers to a <u>person</u> <u>farther away in time and space</u>

(7) • **That** was our sales forecast revealed by our sales manager this morning.

⇑

refers to a <u>thing</u> <u>farther away in time and space</u>

(8) • **Those** suitcases were found unattended by the airport police.

⇑

refers to <u>things</u> <u>farther away in time and space</u>

(9) • Sarah hasn't written to us from Sweden during the last six months.
    This is a worrying situation.

⇑

<u>refers</u> to a person's action (Sarah's action) mentioned earlier on ⇒person's action rather than just a person

(10) • The motorways were very busy. **That**'s why our coach arrived two hours late.

⇑

refers to 'traffic' on the motorway to tell why their coach arrived late

(11) • I'd like to say *this*. Our team displays enthusiasm but lacks a real talent to win tonight. -----

⇑

use this when you are going to explain something

This way you **refer forward**. <u>Note **that** is not used this way.</u>

<u>In the above sentences, the meaning is relative to the context. The reader can understand the meaning from the **context** of each sentence.</u>

- During a conversation, the speaker can also point to something without mentioning the noun or noun phrase. The following examples illustrate that the meaning is relative to the **speaker** who points to things <u>without mentioning the noun or the noun phrase:</u>

  (12) • I will take **this**. $\Rightarrow$ a speaker picks up a basket of strawberries
  without mentioning it – leave out the noun phrase

  (13) • She prefers **those**. $\Rightarrow$ a speaker points to a pair of shoes in a shoe shop

  (14) • Was **that** John on the telephone? $\Rightarrow$ it is used here to refer to a particular
  person $\Rightarrow$ John

  (15) • **These** will do. $\Rightarrow$ a speaker buys a bunch of flowers

•Indefinite Pronouns

Indefinite pronouns are those words which do not refer to any particular person or thing. There are a large number of words which can be used as indefinite pronouns. The following is a list of some commonly used indefinite pronouns.

Some commonly used indefinite pronouns

all	anyone	either	everything	little	nobody	several
any	anything	enough	few	many	none	somebody
another	both	everybody	least	much	no one	someone
anybody	catch	everyone	less	neither	nothing	something

- Some of these indefinite pronouns have exactly the same meaning. This is illustrated by the following examples:

(1) • In this room, *everyone* is aware of the class test this afternoon. $\Rightarrow$ it means all persons

(2) • In this room, *everybody* is aware of the class test this afternoon. $\Rightarrow$ it means all persons

****

- **Therefore:**   **everyone = everybody** $\Longrightarrow$ all persons or all the people (concerned here)

  ----

(3) . *Someone* has removed my spectacles from the table. $\Longrightarrow$ it means a person

(4) . *Somebody* has removed my spectacles from the table. $\Longrightarrow$ it means a person

- **Therefore:**   **someone = somebody** $\Longrightarrow$ a person

  ----

(5) . *Nobody* has given me any message for you. $\Longrightarrow$ it means no person

(6) . *No one* has given me any message for you. $\Longrightarrow$ it means a person

- **Therefore:**   **nobody = no one** $\Longrightarrow$ no person

         ----

          ⇑

it is more common than **nobody** in written English

Note that **no one** is usually written as a two-word pronoun. Some people may write it with a hyphen. All other indefinite pronouns listed above are compound words.

. **Numerals**

Numerals often function as pronouns. These are discussed under determiners.

In summary, pronouns are substitutes for nouns.

Chapter 3

Verbs

. Introduction

The word verb is derived from the Latin word *verbum*. In Latin, it means 'the word'. A verb is a central part of speech and writing. A verb can be a word or a group of words. The reason for its pivotal importance is that as a word or a group of words, it is required to construct a sentence. Generally speaking, people think of a verb as a *doing* or *action* word. Indeed, most readers would have learnt this idea of a verb at school. In fact, verbs are also used to describe the *state* or *condition* of something. Now, consider the following two sentences:

(1) . Andrea *received* a large bouquet of fresh roses.

              ⇑
            verb

Here the verb clearly shows the physical action of Andrea , **'doing'**. Many verbs are used for this type of **action** of doing something.

(2) . John *believes* in her good character.

              ⇑
            verb

In this example, the verb indicates '*John's state of mind*', which is not his physical action of doing something. There are many such verbs in English that indicate a state or a condition. If a word can be marked by inflection for *tenses*, then the word is a verb. This is the major difference between verbs and any other classes of words. Tenses are discussed under tenses in Chapter 11. Like nouns, many verbs have more than one form. The verb is at the heart of sentences and clauses, and thus it is the most important part of speech.

• Verb forms

Verbs have the following forms:

      • *Base form*   • *s-form*   • *Participle*   • *Past Participle*

• Base Form

Verbs in a dictionary are listed in their base forms. The base form is also known as ***bare infinitive***, ***root form*** or ***stem***. It is without the particle *to*. The following verbs are in their base forms:

      be, sing, dance, laugh, work, run, wonder.

Sometimes, the bare infinitive is preceded by *to*, e.g. *to wash, to wish, to go*, etc. For instance:

      (1) • I wanted *to wash* my hands.

      verb ↵   ⇑ = to +verb

      verb ⟹ *to-infinitive form* of the verb ⟹ *wash*

      (2) • I promised *to send* some flowers to Anne.

      verb ↵   ⇑ = to + verb

      verb ⟹ *to- infinitive form* of the verb ⟹ *send*

When a verb is preceded by the word *to*, it is known as ***to-infinitive***. The word ***to*** is used as ***to-infinitive marker.*** It also functions as an adverb and a preposition. See ⟹adverbs.
See ⟹Prepositions.

• s-form

The bare infinitive form is inflected in relation to the third person singular of the subject by adding –*s/es* to the verb. This is discussed under concord or agreement. Here are some of such verbs, e.g. *looks, runs, sees, plays, smiles* and *jumps*. The following examples demonstrate the use of the s-form of the verb:

(1) • She *looks* happy.

       ⇑

s- form of the bare infinitive ⟹ *look*

(2) • Frank *loves* Elene.

       ⇑

s- form of the bare infinitive ⟹ *love*

• Participle –ing Form

It is that part of the verb which ends in *-ing*, e.g. *going, coming, seeing, missing, jumping,* etc. Its use is illustrated below:

(1) • I am *writing* a letter.

       ⇑

-ing participle form of the verb ⟹ *write*

(2) • Alexander is *playing* with his toys.

       ⇑

-ing form of the verb ⟹ *play*

• Past Participle Form

It is that part of the verb which ends in *-ed* in <u>regular verbs</u>, e.g. *happened, disappeared,* etc. For instance:

(1) • I *joined* him at London Victoria Station.

       ⇑

simple past tense form of the verb ⟹ *join*

(2) • They have **worked** for us.

⇑

present perfect tense: past participle form of the verb ⟹ *work*

• In irregular verbs the past participle ends with *-en'* or **some other endings**, e.g. *fallen*, *struck*, *undergone*, *laid*, etc. For instance:

(3) • She *became* his wife.

⇑

simple past tense: past participle form of the verb ⟹ *become* (irregular verb)

. Inflection

Inflection means changing the ending of a word or spelling of it in accordance with its grammatical function. In English, many words have inflected forms. As shown above, verbs are inflected. Here is another example of an inflected verb:

(1) • Prince Charles has *made* an enthusiastic speech tonight.

⇑

verb inflected from ⟹ *make* (present perfect tense)

. Regular and Irregular Verb Forms

Verbs are divided into regular and irregular verb forms. The forms of regular verbs are determined in accordance with the changes they undergo in order to explicit tense (time) or mood. These verbs are also known as weak verbs. The reason for calling them weak is that they follow rules to express tense, time or mood. The four different forms of regular verbs and how they are formed are shown in Table 1. A vast majority of verbs are regular. In fact, there are thousands of regular verbs.

Irregular verbs are so stubborn that they do not follow any set of rules. Like regular verbs, irregular verbs also change their shapes, but unexpectedly as shown in Table 2. There are

44   **Verbs**   **Word Classes**

****

three forms of irregular verbs, as you can see in Table 2. Due to their stubbornness, they are also known as <u>strong verbs.</u> A good thing is that most verbs are regular. The total of irregular verbs comes nowhere near to the total of regular verbs. In fact, there are about 300 irregular verbs. You may find all these listed towards the end of your quality English Dictionary.

. <u>Moods of the Verb</u>

In both speech and writing, verbs enable us to express the *'mood'*. There are three types of moods in English, namely:

- **Indicative** - to make a statement, state a fact or ask a question.

- **Imperative** - to give a command or an order. The command or order can also be of a polite nature, e.g. *forgive me*.

- **Subjunctive** - to express a possibility, uncertainty, condition, wish, hope, etc.

The word 'mood' is a derivative of *'modus'*, a Latin word. The following examples illustrate their use.

Indicative Mood	Imperative Mood	Subjunctive Mood
Spring is already here.	Go away.	He wished he were rich.
Am I allowed to ask a question?	Sit down.	I would have liked to go.
He is writing a letter to his bank.	Excuse me.	It is conceivable that he could have met us here.

     ⇑   ⇑   ⇑

Verbs in these sentences are in the indicative mood   Verbs in these phrases are in the imperative mood   Verbs in these sentences are in the subjunctive mood

. <u>Tenses and Verb Agreement</u>

The following examples illustrate that verbs help us to express the time when the action or the state or condition of a verb takes place. The present tense means *now*. It enables us to communicate the action or the state of something at the present time. Similarly, the past tense means *then*. It assists us to put into words the action or the state of something which took place in the past. The verb is vital in any sentence.

In English, the verb tense is marked by inflection for only the *present tense* and *past tense*. However, the form of the verb is controlled by the person or thing and number of the subject. The future can be expressed by the present time. The way it is formed is discussed under Future Tense, Future Progressive Tense, Future Perfect Tense and Future Perfect Progressive tense. All these ideas about verbs and tenses are discussed under phrases.

. Tenses $\Rightarrow$ See $\Rightarrow$ Phrases

Now examine the following sentences:

(1) . Janet *hates* no one.

subject - singular third person ↵   ⇑

present tense –s form of the regular verb $\Rightarrow$ *hate*
⇑
state of mind/behaviour/attitude

(2) . She *held* my hand in her soft hand.

subject - singular third person ↵ ⇑

past tense - $\Rightarrow$ - irregular verb $\Rightarrow$ *hold*   (see $\Rightarrow$ page 43)
⇑ - no '-ed' here as it is
action   irregular verb

.Active & Passive Verbs & Voices

Verbs may be classified as active and passive verbs. When the subject performs the action or experiences state or condition, it is called an ***active verb or active voice***.

When the subject is affected by the action or state or condition of the verb, it is called a ***passive verb or passive voice***. For instance:

(1) . The writer *sent* the proposal. ⇐ ***active sentence/active voice***

active verb ↵

Who *sent* the proposal? The writer. Therefore, the *subject - the writer* is doing the action.

    (2) • The proposal *was sent* by the writer. ⇐ *passive sentence/passive voice*

             ----

    passive verb ↵

Who *sent* the proposal ? The writer - doing the action is directed at the proposal ⟹ *subject*

Active sentences are the **active voice**. The active voice means being active or doing something. The active voice in both written and spoken language is considered as a good style. The **passive voice** is just the opposite of the active voice. The passive voice involves the use of the **auxiliary verb** *to be*. This may be stated as:

    Passive voice = auxiliary verb to be + past participle

    (3) • The diploma *was gained* by me from our local university. ⇐ *passive form*

              ⇑

    auxiliary verb + past participle = passive verb

    (4) • I gained my diploma from our local university. ⇐ *active form*

        ⇑

transitive verb functioning as active verb

    (5) • She broke the cup. ⇐ *active form*

    (6) • The cup was broken by her. ⇐ *passive form*

    (7) • Someone has to answer the phone. ⇐ *active form*

    (8) • The phone has to be answered by someone. ⇐ *passive form*

    (9) • He handed me a letter of employment. ⇐ *active form*

    (10) • A letter of employment was handed to me. ⇐ *passive form*

****

Some Regular Verbs

Base Form or Infinitive(bare) or Root or Stem	Present Form -s (/es) added to infinitive form	Participle Form 'ing' added to infinitive form	Past Participle Form 'ed' added to infinitive form
abuse	abuses	abusing	abused
accuse	accuses	accusing	accused
advise	advises	advising	advised
blame	blames	blaming	blamed
blush	blushes	blushing	blushed
bore	bores	boring	bored
cease	ceases	ceasing	ceased
disturb	disturbs	disturbing	disturbed
enter	enters	entering	entered
guide	guides	guiding	guided
help	helps	helping	helped
interview	interviews	interviewing	interviewed
join	joins	joining	joined
knock	knocks	knocking	knocked
laugh	laughs	laughing	laughed
look	looks	looking	looked
love	loves	loving	loved
miss	misses	missing	missed
manage	manages	managing	managed
note	notes	noting	noted
owe	owes	owing	owed
push	pushes	pushing	pushed
rate	rates	rating	rated
scatter	scatters	scattering	scattered
turn	turns	turning	turned
unfold	unfolds	unfolding	unfolded
vanish	vanishes	vanishing	vanished
wash	washes	washing	washed
wish	wishes	wishing	wished
work	works	working	worked
yearn	yearns	yearning	yearned
zoom	zooms	zooming	zoomed

Table 1

Some Irregular Verbs

Basic Form (infinitive)	Past Tense Form	Past Participle Form
arise	arose	arisen
be	was, were	been
become	became	become
begin	began	begun
bet	bet or betted	bet or betted
bid	bade or bid	bidden or bid
catch	caught	caught
choose	chose	chosen
come	came	come
dream	dreamt or dreamed	dreamt or dreamed
drink	drank	drunk
eat	ate	eaten
fall	fell	fallen
feel	felt	felt
forecast	forecast or forecasted	forecast or forecasted
get	got	got
give	gave	given
hang	hung or hanged	hang or hanged
hold	held	held
keep	kept	kept
know	knew	known
lay	laid	laid
mislead	misled	misled
overlay	overlaid	overlaid
overthrow	overthrew	overthrown
put	put	put
quit	quit or quitted	quit or quitted
read	read	read
ride	rode	ridden
saw	sawed	sawn
tear	tore	torn
tell	told	told
undertake	undertook	undertaken
wake	woke or waked	woken
wear	wore	worn
write	wrote	written

Table 2

• Verb Classes

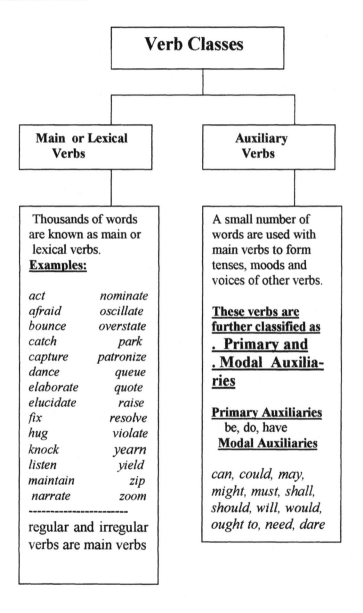

Verb Classes

Main or Lexical Verbs

Thousands of words are known as main or lexical verbs.
Examples:

act	*nominate*
afraid	*oscillate*
bounce	*overstate*
catch	*park*
capture	*patronize*
dance	*queue*
elaborate	*quote*
elucidate	*raise*
fix	*resolve*
hug	*violate*
knock	*yearn*
listen	*yield*
maintain	*zip*
narrate	*zoom*

----
regular and irregular verbs are main verbs

Auxiliary Verbs

A small number of words are used with main verbs to form tenses, moods and voices of other verbs.

These verbs are further classified as
. Primary and
. Modal Auxiliaries

Primary Auxiliaries
be, do, have
Modal Auxiliaries

can, could, may, might, must, shall, should, will, would, ought to, need, dare

Diagram 1

• <u>Auxiliary Verbs</u>

The word 'auxiliary' is derived from the Latin word *auxilium*, which means help. Indeed, this is exactly what the auxiliaries do in a variety of ways.

• <u>**The primary auxiliary 'do'**</u> It is used in specific tenses in the following ways:

• <u>*To ask a question:*</u>

(1) • Where *do* you *live*?

⇑

main verb supported by the auxiliary verb ⟹*do*

• <u>*To emphasise a point:*</u>

(2) • Ursula *does show* a sign of worry.

Auxiliary do in the form of **does** ↵   ⇑ **show** ⟹*main verb*

main verb supported by the auxiliary verb ⟹*does*

• <u>*To state a negation:*</u>

(3) • James *does not care* about Jane.

Auxiliary do is in does form with *not*↵   ⇑

main verb **care** supported by the auxiliary verb ⟹*does*

• <u>*To construct a negative question form:*</u>

(4) • She *didn't* like travelling abroad, *did* she?

negative ↵- past   past form ↵- **question tag** – a short question
                                               added to the end of a statement

****

● *<u>The primary auxiliary 'be'</u>*

In its various forms, the auxiliary *be* is used with a main verb in order to express a wide range of meanings. This is illustrated below:

(1) ● We *are travelling* to France.

'**be**' in the form of **are** ↵   ⇑

           present participle form of the verb ⟹*travel*

Here *are* is a vital part of this sentence. It helps us to indicate the relationship between the action of the verb *travel* and the point of time when the action takes place.

In this case, the auxiliary *are* assists us to understand that the action is not yet complete, but it is still ongoing. The point of time when the action of the verb *travel* takes place, is expressed by a present progressive /continuous tense form *are travelling*.

(2) ● Millions of civilians *were killed* during the Second World War.

    '**be**' in the form of **were** ↵   ⇑

        past participle form of verb ⟹*kill*

This example illustrates the application of the auxiliary *be* in its form *were*. Here it is helpful in showing us the relationship between the action of the verb *kill* and the point of time when the action was complete. In this case, the point of time when the action of the verb *kill* takes place, is expressed by the past participle tense form *were killed*.

Furthermore, this example includes a passive verb phrase '**were killed**' whose subject *millions of civilians* is the recipient of the action 'killed'. See active and passive verbs.

<u>Examples 3-6 illustrate the use of 'be' in order to express a negation (negative meaning):</u>

(3) ● We **are** not *aware* of his whereabouts.

'**be**' in the form of **are** ↵   ⇑

        main verb supported by the auxiliary with 'not' for negation

(4) . The burglar *was not caught*.

(5) . She *isn't coming* tonight.

(6) . She *isn't present* here, <u>is she</u>?   ⇐ the underlined is a **question tag**

a short question added to the end of a statement ↵

. ***The primary auxiliary 'have'*** in its three forms (have, has, had) is used with a main verb in order to construct the past tense. This is illustrated below:

(1) . I *have walked* all the way from Hyde Park to Piccadilly Circus.
                      ----- --------
auxiliary verb ↵   ⇑

        past participle form of verb ⟹ *walk*

The main verb is supported by the auxiliary **have** to construct the present perfect tense. The use of *have* is crucial as it shows that the **action** walk is complete. In this case, the point of time when the action of the verb *walk* took place is expressed by the **present perfect tense**.

(2) . She *has resigned* from her post as head teacher.
                ---- ---------
auxiliary form of have↵   ⇑

        past participle form of verb ⟹*resign*

The use of *has* is decisive as it helps to understand that the action (termination of employment) is complete. In this case, the point of time when the action of the verb *resign* took place is expressed by the **present perfect tense form.**

(3) . I *had passed* secondary school examinations some years ago.
              ----- --------
auxiliary form of have↵   ⇑

        past participle form of the verb ⟹ *pass*

This example illustrates the application of 'have' in the form of 'had'. In this case, the auxiliary indicates that the action of achievement at secondary school is complete. In this example, the point of time when the action of the verb *pass* took place is expressed by the **past perfect tense form.**

. <u>Verb Aspect</u>

The primary auxiliary 'be' and 'have' are used to form the verb aspects. The aspects are subtle meanings expressed by the verb forms as demonstrated below. There are two verb aspects:

- **. progressive aspect** and
- **. perfect aspect**

- <u>The progressive aspect shows that the action is in progress or continuous or ongoing. The progressive aspect can be visualised as:</u>

The progressive aspect = be + present participle

This is exemplified below:

(1) . John *is returning* home today from France.

(2) . Anne *was studying* at Moscow University for one semester.

- <u>The perfect aspect implies that the action has been completed. The perfect aspect can be stated as:</u>

The perfect aspect = have/had + present participle

This is exemplified below:

(1) . Julia has written a letter to us from Norway.

(2) . Sarah has/had no money to buy a cottage in the country.

. <u>*Can you use both the progressive and perfect verb aspects in a sentence?*</u>

Yes, you can. This is demonstrated below:

(1) . *He has been writing* for a living for the last ten years.

(2) . She *had been visiting* her mother.

(3) . Stewart *had been playing* cricket for England until he was 44 years old.

. Modal Auxiliaries

A modal verb reflects a grammatical mood. Modal Verbs, like the primary auxiliaries, also help the main verb to express a range of meanings as exemplified in Tables 1 and 1A.

Examples of Range of Meanings Rendered by Some Modal Auxiliaries (cont. on page 55)

(cont. on page 55)

Modal Auxiliary	Use of Modal Auxiliary	Meaning Rendered
can	He **can** play cricket.	ability
cannot	John **cannot** dance.	ability/negative form
could	Joan **could** swim when she was only six years old.	ability
could not	James **could not** run fast enough.	ability/negative form
can	**Can** I go now? She **can** stay with us for two weeks.	permission permission
could	The nurse on duty said, 'You **could** go out for some fresh air.'	permission
may	**May** I ask you a question?	asking for permission
should	I **should** study hard as I want to gain high grades	obligation
ought to	I **ought to** take a holiday now if I am to get over this sudden loss of business.	necessity/ obligation
must	I **must** return home by 16.00 hours as we are expecting some guests from Paris for the week-end.	necessity

Table 1

Word Classes   **Verbs**   **55**

****

Examples of Range of Meanings Rendered by Some Modal Auxiliaries(cont. from page 54)

Modal Auxiliary	Use of Modal Auxiliary	Meaning Rendered
will	I **will** attend the annual office party this year.	intention
shall	I **shall** spend my long summer holiday in Spain.	intention
would	She **would** have gone to see her mother if she had had a day off from work.	conditional intention/wish
may	I **may** see you tonight at the club if I can finish my work early.	possibility
might	I **might** consider leaving this job if they do not promote me soon.	possibility
could	Your parents **could** at least have written to us about your trip to England	ability
will	I **will** fly to Frankfurt in July providing I can re-arrange my work schedule.	prediction
should	I **should** write to you soon from Japan.	prediction
would	She **would** buy a mansion in Kensington if she had two million pounds in her bank.	condition/ prediction
could	I am so tired of mountaineering that I **could** fall sleep.	prediction/result
could	**Could** you repeat what you have just told us?	strong request/ demand/ instruction
could	You **could** telephone us from the airport.	suggestion
could	**Could** you lend me five pounds until this after-noon?	request
need	**Will** I need to carry with me a full British pass-port when I am in Russia?	necessity/ obligation

Table 1A

From the above examples, you can see that auxiliary verbs enable us to use main verbs in some specific ways in order to express a variety of meanings.

.Transitive and Intransitive Verbs

An intransitive verb does not take an object or a complement. It can stand alone. If necessary, it can be followed by a prepositional phrase. In contrast, a transitive verb is followed by an object because it cannot stand alone. The difference between these types of verbs is exemplified below:

(1) . She *smiles*.
          ----

intransitive verb↵

Without any other words after the verb, this simple sentence makes sense. The action of this intransitive verb is complete. **It is intransitive because it can stand alone.**

(2) . I *speak*.
          ----

intransitive verb ↵

The action of the transitive verb is complete as the sentence makes sense. It can stand alone.

(3) . It *happens*.
          ----

intransitive verb ↵

It is meaningful and there is no need for an object after 'happens'. **It can stand alone.**

- An intransitive verb is not followed by an object, but if it is required, it can be followed by a prepositional phrase. Here are some examples:

(4) . She *smiles* **at** you.
          --------   ---

intransitive verb↵   ⇑
                  prepositional phrase

(5) . Our female staff *complained* **to the manager**.
          ----------------   ----------------------

                ⇑   ⇑
       intransitive verb   prepositional phrase

****

- The action of the transitive verb affects the person or thing. For this reason, it is followed by an object (person or thing). This is exemplified below:

> (6) . He *appointed.*
> -----------
> ⇑
> transitive verb

It does not answer the question: who? or what? Therefore, it does not stand alone to be meaningful. To be meaningful, this sentence must have an object:

> (7) . He ***appointed me*** to this post.
> ----------- -----
> transitive verb ↵   ⇑
>   object

There is no need to add anything after the object as *'He appointed me'* is also perfectly meaningful.

> (8) . I ***enjoyed*** our ***meeting***.
> ---------- --------------
> transitive verb ↵   ⇑
>   object

Without the object, ***I enjoyed*** does not make much sense. The verb ***enjoy*** refers to feelings. There are many transitive verbs, which can express feelings and other aspects besides actions.

- There are many verbs that can be either transitive or intransitive. For instance:

> (9) . He ***played*** cricket.
> -------
> ⇑
> functioning as **transitive** verb

In this context, it requires an object ***cricket*** . Here the action of the subject ***he*** is transferred by the transitive verb to the object ***cricket***. This sentence conveys intended meaning.

****

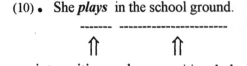

(10) • She *plays* in the school ground.

    ⇑   ⇑

functions as intransitive verb   prepositional phrase

Here there is no object, and thus the action of the verb is not transferred to the object. The prepositional phrase qualifies the verb. See ⟹ Prepositions.

(11) • Our doorbell *rang*.

functioning as intransitive verb ↵

(12) • A caller *rang* our door bell.

functioning as transitive verb ↵

• **The following verbs are among those many verbs that can be transitive or intransitive.**

---

begin, break, breathe, burn, close, cook, continue, divide, drive, end, explode, finish, fly, hang, hurt, increase, join, open, pour, roll, separate, shine, smash, sound, stand, start, stop, tear, unite, weaken.

• Linking or copular or copula verbs

A linking or copular or copula verb links the subject with a complement. The Latin word *copula* means a 'bond', hence its derivative is linking. The basic linking verb is '*be*' with its most used forms: *am, is, are, was* and *were*. There are other linking verbs, which include:

---

appear, become, feel, get, go, look, prove, remain, seem, sound, stay, taste.

The following examples illustrate the role played by the copula verbs:

linking verb + complement

. The following examples illustrate the role played by the copula verbs

⇓

Subject	Linking Verb	Complement
It	is	Monika. ⇐ noun
They	remained	silent. ⇐adjective
She	became	a teacher. ⇐noun phrase
He	proved (may be followed by **to be**)	a helpful person. ⇐ noun phrase
Our aim	proved	right. ⇐adjective
She	appears (**to be**)	intelligent. ⇐adjective
Our journey	looked	very long. ⇐adjective phrase
The old lady	feels	a lot of pain. ⇐noun phrase

. Verbs are also used to describe something other than action of doing something

⇓

His son	grew	tall and handsome. ⇐ adjective phrase
His wife	seems **to be**	a very kind person. ⇐ noun phrase
It	gets	cold and windy. ⇐adjective phrase

. An adverbial phrase after a linking verb also relates to the subject: linking verb + adverbial. Here are some examples:

(1) **.** My chair was here 10 minutes ago.
             ----

     adverbial phrase of place ↵ + time

(2) **.** She felt ill before her meal time.
             ----

prepositional phrase of time ↵   see ⇒ adverbial phrase

. <u>Participles</u>

The idea of present and past participles has been introduced in relation to regular and irregular verbs. You know by now that the **present participle** and **past participle** are two important parts of the base form of the verb. For instance:

- listen   ⟹ *base from of the verb*

- listening   ⟹ *present participle*

- listened   ⟹ *past participle*

Let's examine the following examples:

(1) • I *listen* to you.   (2) • I am *listening* to you.   (3) • I have *listened* to you.

     ⇑   ⇑   ⇑

   base form   auxiliary form + participle-**ing**   auxiliary form + past participle **–ed**
   of the verb

      present participle form ↵   past participle form ↵

<u>Examples (2) and (3) show *present* and *past participle forms*. Both present and past participles forms with the auxiliary verbs are used frequently as verbs.</u>

(4) • I *listened*.

     past tense ↵

Here the verb *listened* is not functioning as the past participle, despite the fact that 'listened' is also the past participle form. To function as a past participle verb, the verb requires an auxiliary verb as illustrated above. Participles cannot work in their own rights as verbs. They can function as <u>***verbals***</u>. This is discussed towards the end of this chapter.

Example 4 demonstrates the difficulty associated with participles that can function in a variety of ways.

. <u>Participles are frequently used in clauses</u>. For example:

Word Classes   **Verbs**   **61**

****

(5) • *Flying in the air*, he conceived the idea of his latest innovation.
      ----

participle clause↵ – phrase does not have a finite verb

(6) • She was at that bus stop for 30 minutes *waiting for him patiently*.
                         ----

                         participle clause ↵

(7) • *Smoking is prohibited* in public places.
      ----

participle clause ↵ - clause has a finite verb

In example 7, smoking is functioning as a noun but it is a participle. When a participle functions as a noun, it is a gerund. It is getting somewhat complicated. Let's discuss gerunds because gerunds and participles are very close to each other.

• Gerunds

When a participle verb formed with *-ing* is used in a clause or a sentence as a noun, it is known as a *gerund*. In other words, a gerund is a verb form that functions as a noun. The following examples show that gerunds can function as the subject, object or form a phrase.

(1) • *Running* keeps you healthy.
      ----

unaccountable noun ↵ - *ing* form of the verb $\Rightarrow$ *run* $\Rightarrow$

In this example, Running is functioning as a noun, subject and *gerund*. In contrast, in example 2 below, running is only a participle(not a gerund).

(2) • He *is running* for his local charity.
      ----

present participle ↵ - *ing* form of the verb $\Rightarrow$ *run*

(3) . *Dancing* is her favourite hobby.
----

gerund ↵ - stands alone as a noun ⟹ *functioning as the subject*

(4) . *Washing* is a burden.
----

gerund ↵ - stands alone as a noun ⟹ *functioning as the subject*

(5) . Antonia loves *laughing*.
----

gerund ↵ – *functioning as a noun* ⟹ **object**

(6) . I enjoyed *having* you.
----

gerund ↵ - *forming a noun phrase*

(7) . I wouldn't mind *waiting* for you.
----

gerund ↵ - *forming a noun phrase* ⟹ **waiting for you**

(8) . Hazel is very good at *cooking*.

⇑

gerund *forming a noun phrase* ⟹ *at cooking*

. It is important to remember that only possessive nouns and pronouns can modify a gerund. This is exemplified below:

(9) . I don't like Barbara's *laughing* at the old lady.

⇑

gerund – Barbara's ⟹ possessive noun modifying gerund
Barbara possesses *laughing*

Barbara laughing is incorrect

(10) ● Hazel's *choosing* the colour won't be a good idea.

　　　　　-----------

　　　　gerund ↵ - Hazel's ⟹possessive noun modifying gerund

Hazel choosing is incorrect

● Verbals

A verbal is derived from a verb. It may look like a verb, but it is never used in a sentence as a verb. In a sentence, it can function as a noun, adjective or adverb. There are three classes of verbals. These are participles, gerunds and infinitives. A gerund has the same form as the present participle. This can be a source of some confusion. Here are some examples of each class of verbals:

(1) ● I find the show *amusing*.

　　　　-----------

　　　　participle ↵ - verbal

It is functioning as an adjective and modifying the noun ⟹ *show*

(2) ● We were given a talk by a very *interesting* speaker.

　　　　　-------------

　　　　　participle ↵ -verbal

It is functioning as an adjective and modifying the noun ⟹ *speaker*

(3) ● It was a *frightening* scene.

　　　　-------------

　　　　participle ↵ verbal as an adjective and modifying the noun ⟹ *scene*

(4) ● We sold our shop as a *going* concern.

　　　　　--------

　　　　　participle ↵ verbal as an adjective and modifying the noun ⟹ *concern*

The above examples demonstrate that when a participle is functioning as an adjective, it is placed next to its noun.

****

• **The *to-infinitive can be used to form noun and adverbial phrases.*** For instance:

(5) • *To take a train* is the easiest means of transport tonight.
  ----
  verbal ↵

Here the verbal is functioning as a noun phrase. It is also the subject of the sentence.

(6) • She wished *to be the beauty queen*.

  Verbal ↵

In this case, the verbal fulfils the function of both the object of the sentence as well as acts as a noun phrase.

(7) • *To take a train*, they didn't know the location of the local rail station.
  ----
  verbal ↵

Here the verbal is functioning as an adverbial phrase. It can also be called an infinitive phrase.

(8) • He telephoned me *to break the news*.
  ----
  verbal ↵ - functioning as an adverbial phrase

These examples may not be easy to grasp. It will help you to understand these if you read about finite and non-finite clauses. See ⟹Clauses.

• **The gerund can be used as a verbal noun.** For instance:

(9) • *Walking* in the evenings is our daily routine.
  ----
verbal noun ↵- functioning as a noun as well as the subject of the sentence

Word Classes   **Verbs**   **65**

****

(10) • *Arriving late at work* is not recommended.

    ----

noun phrase ↵ - verbal use of gerund forming a phrase

(11) • *To run a small business* is difficult.

    ----

noun phrase ↵ - verbal use of infinitive

In this example, the infinitive phrase is functioning as a noun phrase. It is also the subject of the sentence.

(12) • She wished *to get another job*.

    ----

noun phrase ↵- verbal use of infinitive

The infinitive phrase is functioning as a noun phrase. It is also the object of this sentence.

• **Should you always use to-infinitive?** The use of *to* with the base infinitive depends on the grammatical structure. For instance:

. I am pleased *to meet* you.
. I did not see Jane *enter* through this gate.
. She is always lucky *to be winning*.
. She likes to touch flowers. – It means that she likes to touch flowers, as a 'one-off'.
. She likes touching flowers. – it means that she always likes touching flowers, as a 'habit'.

• **Sometimes the omission of *to* is not considered as an error, but an ellipsis. It means shortening.** For instance:

(13) • My husband helped Mrs. Williams(to) *carry* her shopping.

(14) • They wanted us (to) *run* faster than we could.
    to is required ↵ - Without **to**, this is does not make sense.

(15) • It is better if you do it now than (to) *leave* it till tomorrow.

. <u>Split Infinitives</u>

Placing of a word or words between the *to* and the *verb* creates a split infinitive. Some people do not like the idea of split infinitives. In fact, sometimes it is desirable to use a split infinitive as it helps to show the verb is modified. For instance:

(1) . In order **to** *precisely reply* to your letter, I must consult my staff.
                    ----

split infinitive↲- precisely is causing a ⟹ **split**

<u>Adverb *precisely* is modifying the verb *reply*.</u>

(2) . *To fully appreciate* your ideas, I must read your book.
                    ----

split infinitive↲ - appreciate is causing a ⟹ **split**

<u>Adverb *fully* is modifying the verb *appreciate*.</u> The writer of this sentence may consider it rather necessary to use a split infinitive.

. <u>Sometimes the use of split infinitives can result in a clumsy construction of a sentence.</u>

For instance:

(3) . Caroline began *to slowly cry* until she became hysterical.

(4) . The interview panel wanted *to again interview* me.

Examples 3 and 4 are re-written without split infinitives. The following re-constructions are simple and sound better:

(5) . Caroline began *to cry slowly* until she became hysterical.

(6) . The interview panel wanted *to interview* me again.

. There are no rules regarding the use of split infinitives. If you are sure that a split infinitive is needed, split the infinitive. If you think that it may create some ambiguity, re-write the sentence without it.

****

. <u>Misuse or Omission of Infinitive, Participle and Gerund</u>

When we write or talk about verbs, we refer to them as *to drink*, *to eat*, *to love, to go*, etc. Misuse of infinitives, participles and gerunds often happens. Here are some examples:

> (1) . *Watching* from the window, the procession got bigger and bigger.
>
> --------------------------------   --
>
> participle clause ↵   main clause ↵

This construction suggests that *the procession* was watching from the window. This is meaningless. It can cause misunderstanding. The reason for this misunderstanding is that the subject of the main clause is *the procession* which is the implied subject of the participle.

<u>In order to avoid the danger of misunderstanding, we can rewrite it correctly as:</u>

> (2) . Watching from the window, *we saw* the procession getting bigger and bigger.

Here it means: We were watching ....., we saw the ..... bigger.

> (3) . Standing by the bus stop, the car hit a lamp post.
>
> -------------------------------   -----------------------------------
>
> participle clause ↵   main clause↵

This sentence implies: the car was standing .....stop, the car hit...post.

<u>The following re-construction is correct:</u>

> (4) . Standing by the bus stop, *we saw* the car hit a lamp post.

. <u>When using gerunds, writers often ignore the fact that a gerund can only be modified by *a</u> <u>possessive noun or pronoun*</u>. For instance:

> (5) . Annemarie does approve of her husband buying another new car.

<u>The correct statement of this example:</u>

> (6) . Annemarie does approve of her *husband's buying* another new car.
>
> -------------- ----------
>
> possessive noun ↵   gerund↵

- The misuse of an infinitive happens, when it is separated from the word it is expected to modify. Sometimes an infinitive is placed in an inappropriate place in a sentence. For instance:

> (7) • All of us had electrical blankets *to sleep* when camping in the forest.
>   ------------
>   misuse ↵

In this sentence, the infinitive is connected with blankets instead of the subject. This is not the purpose of using it here. The following re-construction is grammatically correct:

> (8) • All of us had electrical blankets enabling us to *sleep* when camping in the forest.

In the following example, the infinitive is incorrectly used:

> (9) • The idea is that you use German *to manage* local branches.
>   -----------
>   inappropriate use ↵

This construction suggests that you use German person or German language which will manage *(action)* local branches. This is ambiguous. This is not the intention. The intended meaning is that you use German language to manage local branches *(action)*. The *action* of the verb is to be performed by the subject. The following sentence is correct:

> (10) • The idea is that you use German language in order *to manage* local branches.
>   -------------
>   the language which enables you to manage ↵

This communicates the intended meaning.

- Some people feel strongly about the use of split infinitives as a contentious issue. This does not mean that you should avoid using them.

In summary, the verb is the most important element in a sentence. Without a verb, we cannot express action (working), and condition, or state (alive).

Chapter 4
Adjectives

. Introduction

Adjectives are words used with a noun or a pronoun to modify the noun or the pronoun. In doing so, they tell us what something is like. There are many thousands of words that are classed as adjectives and function as adjectives only. In addition, many more thousands of words which function as nouns, adverbs and so on also function as adjectives. Adjectives change their forms when a comparison is made. They <u>do not</u> do so for a gender or number (singular or plural). Some adjectives are shown in List 1 below.

Some Adjectives

awful, beautiful, big, busy, cheap, clear, clever, dangerous, dark, difficult, easy, expensive, extraordinary, famous, foreign, gloomy, glorious good, happy, harmful, harmless, huge, inaccessible, inaccurate, incapable, jealous, jobless, jolly, kind, lovely, loving, low, mean, medium, mental, native, nice, noble, nosy (or nosey), obnoxious, obscene, opportune, painful, passionate, popular, quick, quiet, quizzical, recent, relentless, religious, short, smooth, straight, tall, three-quarters, tiny, ugly, unfit, unfriendly, vain, vast, vivid, weary, wedded, wide, yellow, young, youthful, zonal.

List 1

Let's consider first the following two examples:

(1) . I can see a ***tall* man** standing in front of our house.

            ----- -------

      adjective ⌐   ⇑

             noun

In this sentence, the word **tall** gives some information about the man by describing him as tall. Since it is used with the noun **man,** its function is considered as modifying or qualifying the noun **man.** Here the adjective is a modifier. If you wish, you can think of modifying as defining the noun **man.** The adjective in this position in this sentence is giving us information about an attribute (tall) of the noun man.

(2) • I can see a *very tall* **man** jumping up and down.

intensifier ↵   ⇑   ⇑

             adjective   noun

Here **very** is preceding the adjective **tall** and thus functioning as an intensifier. The reason for placing it in front of the adjective is to grade the height of that particular man who is jumping up and down. By placing **very** in front of tall, we have graded the adjective on an imagined scale. **Very** is an adverb of degree that tells us about the measurement on an imagined scale as it does not specify the height in any recognised unit of measurement. This example shows that adjectives are **gradable**.

Here are some more examples:

(3) • She is a *most generous* **person**.

intensifier ↵   ⇑   ⇑

          adjective   noun

(4) • You are *kind* to me.

⇑   ⇑   ⇑

1   **2**   **3**

In this example:

> **1** is personal pronoun – subject form
> **2** is adjective
> **3** is personal pronoun – object form

In this example, the adjective *kind* refers to the personal pronoun *you*. This way, it is modifying the personal pronoun by giving information (kind) about the pronoun.

(5) . It is a *nice new* car for us.

```
         -----  -------
adjective ⌐        ⇑
              adjective
```

In this example, *nice* is modifying the adjective *new*. Adjective *new* is modifying the noun car. When two or more adjectives occur before a noun, their position is fairly fixed as above.

The following examples further illustrate that adjectives modify pronouns:

(6) . *She* was *happy* to hear the news about her son.

(7) . *They* arrived home *hungry* and *angry* due to traffic congestion on the M1 motorway.

(8) . *It* is a *cold*, *wet* and *stormy* night.

. <u>The Position of Adjectives</u>

Most adjectives can occur in two particular positions in a sentence or a clause. Certainly, some adjectives can be placed in one particular position, but not in the other position in a sentence or clause. These rules are explained below:

. <u>**An adjective can occur before a noun**</u>. Here are some examples:

(6) . John lives in an *old* house.

```
                    -----
adjective before the noun ⌐
```

The adjective **old** relates to the house. In fact, it defines or modifies the noun 'house' in terms of its age. The word age as an attribute is giving information about the house. <u>When an adjective modifies or defines a noun, and it comes before the noun, such a word is called **attributive adjective**.</u> This is further illustrated by the following examples:

(7) . We are having a *lovely* time.

```
                   --------
attributive adjective ⌐
```

(8) . It is certainly a *big* day for all of us.
     ------

attributive adjective ↵

(9) . This is an *expensive* property.
     ----

attributive adjective ↵

(10) . I do not like *loud* music.
      ----

attributive adjective ↵

(11) . It was a *memorable* holiday for all of us in France.

(12) . It is a *beautiful* garden to enjoy.

(13) . They have two *lovable* daughters.

. **An adjective can occur in the predicate.** This is demonstrated below:

(1) . This crime is the *worst* in our city's history.
          -------   -------

noun to which the ↵   ⇑
adjective relates   adjective

In this sentence, the adjective occurs between a noun and a verb. Here the adjective is in the predicate.

. See ⇒ Sections on Subject Element and Complement Element for Predicate ⇒ under Clauses

---

In this sentence, **crime** is the subject. The remainder of this statement is the predicate. Since after the subject, the remainder of the sentence describes the **crime** (subject) as the **worst** (adjective), and thus the adjective occurs in the predicate.

****

(2) • The **house** in which John lives **is** **old**.

noun to which the ↵

the adjective relates

verb↵   ⇑

adjective ⟹ occurs in the predicate position

When an adjective occurs in a sentence in the predicate as illustrated above, it is called **predicative adjective**. In each example, the adjective is placed after the noun.

Here are some examples of adjectives that occur only in the attributive position:

(1) • A number of countries of the **former** Soviet Union are now independent countries.

attributive position ↵ - **former** ⟹ attributive only

(2) • The proposed new road will link the **principal** cities in our part of the country.

attributive position ↵ - **principal** ⟹ attributive only

(3) • Her bank overdraft **upper** limit is £2500.

attributive position↵ - **upper** ⟹ attributive only

(4) • I am very sorry that he is **unwell** and will not be able to come to work today.

predicative position ↵- **unwell** ⟹ predicative only

(5) • He lives **alone** in a big house.

predicative position ↵- **alone** ⟹ predicative only

(6) • He was a **contented** person.

predicative position ↵- **contented** ⟹ predicative only   (contented used with nouns)

Some examples of adjective forms

Descriptive (Positive)	Comparative	Superlative
beautiful	more beautiful	most beautiful
black	blacker	blackest
big	bigger	biggest
cold	colder	coldest
difficult	more difficult	most difficult
endearing	more endearing	most endearing
few	fewer	fewest
great	greater	greatest
intelligent	more intelligent	most intelligent
large	larger	largest
long	longer	longest
loud	louder	loudest
lovely	lovelier	loveliest
many	more	most
nice	nicer	nicest
noisy	noisier	noisiest
old	older	oldest
poor	poorer	poorest
quiet	quieter	quietest
short	shorter	shortest
sunny	sunnier	sunniest
tall	taller	tallest
ugly	uglier	ugliest

Table 1

. Comparisons of Adjectives

The only time adjectives change their forms is when a comparison is made. There are three comparative forms of adjectives, namely:

. Descriptive or Positive   . Comparative   . Superlative

These forms are graded by degree, which shows the extent of comparative qualities. The *descriptive form* is the form of the adjective as listed in dictionaries. It is also known as the *positive form*. The **comparative form** is used for comparing two objects, and the **superlative form** is for comparing three or more objects. Objects are people, animals, animated and natural things . The following examples illustrate these forms of adjectives:

    (1) . He is a *tall* person.

           ⇑

descriptive (or basic) **form** of adjective ⟹ no comparison is intended here

    (2) . He is *taller* than you.

         ⇑

comparative form of adjective ⟹ a comparison is made between two persons

    (3) . He is the *tallest* in our group of 10 persons.

         ⇑

superlative form of adjective ⟹ compares a person with more than two other persons

. There are some adjectives that have **_irregular forms._** The adjectives shown in List 2 with their comparative and superlative forms are amongst the most commonly used irregular adjectives:

List 2

Descriptive	Comparative	Superlative
good	better	best
little	less	least
bad	worse	worst
many or much	more	most

. *Intensifiers* are words like *extremely, fairly, incredibly, quite* and *very*. Sometimes an adjective can be preceded by an intensifier to emphasise the quality of the adjective.

****

By means of intensifiers we can strengthen the meaning or the quality of the adjective to a desirable varying low or high degree of comparisons. The following examples illustrate the use of intensifiers:

(1) ● You can say about someone:

> ● He is *very* clever.
>
> ● He is *fairly* clever.
>
> ● He is *quite* clever.
>
> ● He is *extremely* clever.
>
> ● He is *incredibly* clever.

(2) ● You can describe a place as:

> ● It is a *large* cricket ground.
>
> ● It is *quite* a large cricket ground.
>
> ● It is a *fairly* large cricket ground.
>
> ● It is a *very large* cricket ground.
>
> ● It is an *incredibly* large cricket ground.

(3) ● You can compare one person or thing with another:

● James was *more* intelligent than John.

● Today the crowd was *much* bigger than any other crowd I have ever seen.

● His speech proved *less* formidable than yours. ⇐ lower degree comparison

● Europe's Express Coach Network is the *least* expensive travel system in Europe.

                         ------

       lowest degree of comparison ↵ - cheapest mode of travel

● He is the *least* successful in our group in this tournament.

. Absolute Adjectives

There are some adjectives that cannot be graded by degree in the same way as shown above. Such adjectives exist only in their basic form. The following examples demonstrate this characteristic of some words used as adjectives:

(1) . You are *right* this time.
‾‾‾‾‾‾
⇑

descriptive or basic form ⟹ no other forms exist except ⟹ absolute adjective.

It means that you cannot be more or less right if you are right. It is the highest degree of quality implied by this adjective. Just the opposite is wrong. For instance:

(2) . Robert is *wrong* to suggest that John is guilty.
‾‾‾‾‾‾‾‾
⇑

descriptive or basic form ⟹ no other forms exist. It is also an absolute adjective

It means what it implies no more no less. It cannot be graded. It is wrong to say *very wrong*.

(3) . This is a *unique* occasion in our lives.
‾‾‾‾‾‾‾‾
⇑

descriptive or basic form – no other forms.

It means one specific occasion. It is incorrect to grade it as a *very unique* occasion or *more unique* than the other occasions.

(4) . It is *impossible* for you to reach Manchester from here by car in 60 minutes.
‾‾‾‾‾‾‾‾‾‾‾‾
⇑

descriptive or basic form.

You cannot say *less impossible fairly impossible* or add any thing else to it in order to grade it. It is also an absolute adjective.

Therefore, you cannot compare absolute adjectives. The following words are also examples of absolute adjectives:

> absolute, dead, elder, infinite, like, only, perfect, real.

• <u>When can a word function as an adjective?</u>

There are a great many words, which can function as adjectives. A noun can be used as an adjective. Similarly, an adverb can function as an adjective. Pronouns can do the work of adjectives. Furthermore, some words can be used as participles and adjectives. Indeed, you can also create many adjectives by adding suffixes to many words. For the sake of understanding words that can function as adjectives, we can discuss them as follows:

• <u>**Descriptive**</u> - These are descriptive words and easily recognised. For instance:

> handsome, good, beautiful, green, black, ugly, bad, rough, smooth.

• <u>**Demonstrative**</u> – this, these, that and those. They demonstrate/ point out to the noun which they modify. For instance: ***This*** ship, ***those*** books, ***that*** car

ship   ⟹   modified by   ⟹this

books ⟹   modified by   ⟹those

car   ⟹   modified by   ⟹that

    (1) • That car is mine.   ⟸ *that* is used with a noun car to modify it

    (2) • This house belongs to John's sister. ⟸ *this* modifying the noun house

• <u>When *this, that, these* and *those* are used with nouns as shown above, they are known as demonstrative adjectives; otherwise they function as pronouns. This is illustrated below:</u>

    (1) • You can have ***this***.

—————

pronoun ↵ | See ⟹ Pronouns |

• <u>**Interrogative**</u> - What ? Which? These words are used with nouns to ask questions.

For instance:

   (1) . What time was it when you saw her?

      ------ -----

interrogative adjective↵ ⇑
      noun

   (2) . What arrangements have you made for your Easter break?

   (3) . Which newspaper do you normally read?

   (4) . Which car did you buy the other day?

In examples 1 – 4, both **what** and **which** as adjectives are connected with one attribute of a noun that is next to them in each sentence. By asking a question, the speaker is inquiring about the quality/ attribute of a noun. This is how they function as adjectives when they are next to a noun.

- **These interrogative words can perform different functions under other word classes as** illustrated below:

   (5) . *What* went wrong ?

     ----

pronoun↵

   (6) . *What* job will you do first?

     ----

determiner↵

   (7) . I have several products. *Which* do you want?

        ----

       pronoun↵

   (8) . *Which* teacher is your tutor?

     ----

determiner↵

****

In examples 6 and 8 *what* and *which* are before nouns and thus they are functioning as determiners. On the other hand, in examples 5 and 7, *what* and *which* are not used with nouns next to them and thus these are functioning here as pronouns.

- **Adverbs** – Some words can function as adjectives as well as adverbs. For instance:

  (1) • She talks *fast*.
        ------

       adverb ↵ - modifying verb ⇒ talks

  (2) • It is a *fast* train.
        ------

       adjective ↵ - modifying noun ⇒ train

Fast can also function as a verb and as a noun.

  (3) • We will most *likely* miss her now.   (likely means expect or probable)
        ----

       adverb ↵ - modifying verb ⇒ miss   (miss is also a noun)

Note that *likely* as an *adverb* must be preceded by any of these intensifiers: **most**, *more*, or *very*.

  (4) • The most *likely* outcome is a draw.
        ----

       adjective ↵ - modifying noun ⇒ outcome

Note that *likely* as an *adjective* is usually preceded by more or most.

- **Nouns** – Some nouns can function as adjectives. Conversely, adjectives can also function as nouns. The following examples show how this happens in practice:

  (1) • From my *past* experience I'd say it is more likely to happen.
        ----

       adjective ↵ - modifying noun ⇒ experience

  (2) • During the *past* month I was in Italy.
        ----

       adjective ↵ - modifying noun ⇒ month

Word Classes   **Adjectives**   **81**

****

In both examples, past means gone by in time.

> (3) • He often looks back on the ***past*** with a mixture of regrets and joys.
>   -------
>
>   functioning as a noun ↵

> (4) • I have travelled on this route in the ***past***.
>   -------
>
>   functioning as a noun ↵

In examples 3 – 4, past means the time that has passed away, things that you have done in an earlier time. The context of these examples illustrates in what capacity a word is functioning in a sentence.

<u>Sometimes adjectives can function as nouns if they are preceded by a definite article 'the'.</u>

Here is an example:

> (5) • Our government must do more to help the ***homeless***.
>   -------------
>
>   functioning as a noun ↵

> (6) • There have been many failed government attempts to help ***homeless*** people.
>   --------------
>
>   functioning as an adjective ↵

• **Participles** – Some participles (verb + - ing ending) can function as adjectives:

> (1) • The current international political crisis is ***worrying***.
>   ------------
>
>   functioning as an adjective ↵

> (2) • Marion's forthcoming travel to Siberia alone is ***worrying*** her parents.
>   --------------
>
>   functioning as a participle ↵   See ⟹ Participles

• How can you recognise an adjective?

Words such as *cold, good, bad* and *wonderful* are descriptive adjectives. Such adjectives are easily recognisable. The English language has thousands of adjectives. There are some common word endings that help you to recognise adjectives. Some of these word endings, together with some adjectives, are listed below:

– able	breakable , fashionable, desirable, comparable
– al	commercial, brutal, dismal, natural
– ar	circular, perpendicular, popular, solar
– ed	worried, excited, subdued, inexperienced
– ent	intelligent, excellent, urgent, negligent
–ful	joyful, wonderful, harmful, careful
– ible	incredible, sensible, compatible, horrible
– ic	alcoholic, athletic, classic, idiotic
– ing	dying, laughing, charming, encouraging
– ish	Irish, foolish, childish, selfish
– ive	decorative, demonstrative, adhesive
– less	meaningless, harmless, childless, defenceless
– like	childlike, warlike, businesslike, ladylike
– ous	dangerous, courageous, nervous, marvellous
– some	awesome, troublesome, handsome
– worthy	newsworthy, praiseworthy, roadworthy

• A Word of Warning

Words ending with *–ly* and *–y* often cause confusion as many adverbs and adjective have these endings. For instance: *holy* is an adjective but *yearly* is both an adjective and an adverb.

See $\Rightarrow$ Adjective Phrases in $\Rightarrow$ Chapter 9 in $\Rightarrow$ Part 2

In summary, some adjectives only identify the noun as in the phrase *first chapter*. Many adjectives describe nouns as in the phrase *a green coat*. It is telling us about the noun which is of a green colour. There is a widespread tendency to use adjectives, when they do not add any information to the meaning of the nouns they modify (in *serious crisis*, both words mean the same).

****

Chapter 5

Adverbs

. **Introduction**

An adverb is a word that modifies or qualifies another word, which may be a verb, an adjective or another adverb. It can also modify or extend an adverbial phrase, prepositional phrase and conjunctions. Indeed, the adverb has the largest range of functions of any part of speech (Word class and parts of speech mean the same).

Adverbs can be difficult to identify. However, the most common function of adverbs is to modify the main verb in a sentence. Therefore, it is reasonable to assume that this is a reason for giving it this name. There is a large number of adverbs for expressing reason, time, manner, place, order, etc. Some of the adverbs are listed below:

abruptly	*absolutely*	*accordingly*	*afterwards*	*again*
aggressively	*carefully*	*early*	*easily*	*frightfully*
fully	*gently*	*ghastly*	*heavily*	*here*
however	*just*	*nevertheless*	*nervously*	*now*
quickly	*quietly*	*perfectly*	*roughly*	*slowly*
so	*softly*	*sometimes*	*successfully*	*suddenly*
then	*there*	*therefore*	*too*	*truthfully*
unintelligently	*unintentionally*	*vaguely*	*vastly*	*very*
violently	*why*	*wholly*	*widely*	*willingly*
worriedly	*yearly*	*yearningly*	*yesterday*	*yet*

The following examples illustrate the use of adverbs:

(1) . We walked **slowly**.

⇑

adverb of manner – modifying the verb ⟹ ***walked***

It tells us how we walked. The adverb *slowly* has affected the meaning of this short sentence.

(2) . *Soon* we will leave home.

⟰

adverb of time ⟹ *expressing time* ⟹ it tells us about *when* we will leave in the future

(3) . He said *almost* nothing new to protect his reputation.

⟰

adverb of degree – it means here scarcely *(almost nothing = scarcely anything)*

Here *almost* is modifying the quantifier *nothing* (= no single thing = not anything)

(4) . Some people go to bed *early*.

⟰

adverb of time

(5) . Have you anything *else* to do this afternoon?   (else = any other things)

⟰

adverb modifying the question

Here *else* means in addition to something already known.

(6) . If you *ever* wish to visit Berlin, you must come and stay with us.

⟰   (ever = at any time)

adverb of frequency - modifying the verb ⟹*wish*

(7) . You knew where I was. **Moreover**, you knew who had done it. (moreover = in addition)

⟰

adverb – here its function is to support the previous statement

****

(8) • **Somehow**, I do not feel she can convince them of her honesty. (somehow = reason unknown)

⇑

adverb of reason – related to an unspecified reason

(9) • During the boring seminar, he answered the question *drowsily*.

⇑

adverb of condition – indicating sleepy state

(10) • That red car could *easily* be our motor.

⇑

adverb of possibility – indicating possibility

(11) • There was a road accident but *luckily* no one was injured.

⇑

adverb – expressing wish

(12) • Ute-Susanne speaks English *very* fluently.

⇑

adverb modifying another adverb ⇒*fluently*

(13) • That little girl looks *very* pretty.

⇑

adverb modifying adjective ⇒*pretty*

The above examples demonstrate that adverbs are useful words to enhance the meaning of both written and spoken statements. Many adverbs give information about *when, where, how* and *the extent of something* . In addition, there are many other adverbs of other meanings. Some of these are exemplified above and more examples are given later in this chapter.

. Position of Adverbs

You can see in the above examples that adverbs can be positioned at the beginning, in the middle or at the end of a sentence. However, if you place an adverb without thinking about which word the adverb should modify, you can change the meaning of the sentence unintentionally. For instance:

(14) ● John spoke to us *clearly* in English.

⇑

adverb modifying verb ⇒ *spoke*   *In this position: clearly = distinctly*

Here the adverb clearly is functioning as an adverb of quality.

It is specifying how distinctly/clearly John spoke to us in English.

(15) ● *Clearly*, John spoke to us in English.

⇑

adverb of certainty   *In this position: clearly = certainly*

In this sentence, the adverb is modifying the whole sentence. It refers to the entire context of this sentence. It is implying that without doubt John spoke to us in English.

It shows that an adverb can modify different parts of the sentence. It is, therefore, important to position it correctly in order to avoid ambiguity. You may come across some rules of placing the adverb in a sentence. There are no universally laid down rules. In general terms, you can place an adverb before the word it is modifying. This rule is not workable in many cases. However, before using an adverb, make sure that it does not lead to unnecessary ambiguity of meaning.

. Adverb Forms

1. Many words exist as adverbs

These adverbs are not related to adjectives or any other classes of words. Many adverbs of this group are commonly used. Some adverbs of this category are listed below:

| again | almost | always | ever | ever-more | else | here | however | moreover | perhaps |
| quite | soon | somehow | there | therefore | today | tomorrow | very | yesterday |

2. <u>Many adverbs have the same form as adjectives</u>

The following words can function as adjectives and adverbs:

Adjective	Adverb
backward(s)	backward(s)
early	early
enough	enough
fast	fast
forward(s)	forward(s)
full	full
further	further
hard	hard
late	late
long	long
next	next
only	only
straight	straight
weekly	weekly
well	well

<u>Some examples of words used as adjectives and adverbs</u>

Word used as adjective	Same word used as adverb
• It is a ***straight*** street.	• I went ***straight*** home as we were expecting a guest.
• You must cook it for a ***further*** 3 minutes.	• I had walked ***further*** than I had planned.

(Cont. on page 88)

Some examples of words used as adjectives and adverbs (Cont. from Page 87)

Word used as adjective	Same word used as adverb
• It is *hard* work for me.	• You must try *hard* to pay back my money.
• From London to Edinburgh by coach is a *long* journey.	• You can stay here as *long* as you like.
• How far is it to the *next* underground station?	• Who will jump *next*?
• He was the *only* person at the scene of the accident.	• I *only* arrived a few minutes before the the meeting started.
• Since the car accident, she is not a *well* woman.	• Nothing was going *well* without him.

3. Many adverbs are formed from adjectives as:

$$adverb = adjective + ly$$

The following examples illustrate how adverbs are created by applying this rule:

Adjective $\Rightarrow$	Adverb derived from adjective + ly
articulate	articulately
bold	boldly
certain	certainly
descriptive	descriptively
excessive	excessively
glorious	gloriously
jealous	jealously
memorable	memorably
quick	quickly
serious	seriously

- In addition to the above, the following spelling rules for converting adjectives into adverbs are applied:

4. To form an adverb from an adjective ending in a consonant + y:

insert i after the consonant and replace y by ly

The following examples illustrate how adverbs are generated by applying this rule:

Adjective	⇒ Adverb derived from adjective - ily forn
bloody	bloodily
bloodthirsty	bloodthirstily
cheery	cheerily
drowsy	drowsily
dry	drily (also dryly)
easy	easily
gloomy	gloomily
haughty	haughtily
hearty	heartily
lazy	lazily
lucky	luckily
patchy	patchily
risky	riskily
shy	*shyly* (exception as it does not obey the rule)
sly	*slyly* (another adverb formed against the rule)

It is worth mentioning that the adjective **gay** has a vowel 'a' before 'y'. It becomes an adverb **gaily** in the same way as adverbs derived above. This is another exception to the above rule.

5. To form an adverb from an adjective ending in a consonant + le , replace e with ly.

The following examples illustrate how adverbs are created by applying this rule:

Adjective	$\Rightarrow$	Adverb derived from adjective – ly form
agreeable		agreeably
able		ably
ample		amply
credible		credibly
debatable		debatably
equable		equably
humble		humbly
laughable		laughably
probable		probably
possible		possibly
reasonable		reasonably
simple		simply
subtle		subtly
terrible		terribly
understandable		understandably
vulnerable		vulnerably

5. To form an adverb from an adjective ending in -ic, add -ally to the word.

The following examples illustrate how adverbs are created by applying this rule:

Adjective	$\Rightarrow$	Adverb derived from adjective + ally form
apologetic		apologetically
artistic		artistically
basic		basically
bureaucratic		bureaucratically
characteristic		characteristically
dramatic		dramatically
frantic		frantically
heroic		heroically
historic		historically

(continued on next page)

****

Adjective	⇒ Adverb derived from adjective – ally form
idiotic	idiotically
intrinsic	intrinsically
optimistic	optimistically
organic	organically
periodic	periodically
prosaic	prosaically
symbolic	symbolically
sympathetic	sympathetically
systematic	systematically
telepathic	telepathically

Here is an example of an exception to the above rule: *public* ⇒ *publicly*

7. To form an adverb from an adjective ending in l, just add -ly to the word.

The following examples illustrate how adverbs are created by applying this rule:

Adjective	⇒ Adverb derived from adjective + ly form
awful	awfully
beautiful	beautifully
boastful	boastfully
careful	carefully
eventual	eventually
material	materially
meaningful	meaningfully
medical	medically
punctual	punctually
respectful	respectfully
successful	successfully
wonderful	wonderfully

8. To form adverbs from adjectives ending in -ll, just add -y to the word.

For instance:

>   (1) • full $\Rightarrow$ fully (also full)

>   (2)   • shrill $\Rightarrow$ shrilly

There are not so many adjectives which end in double *-ll*.

. Adjunct Word or Phrase

An adverb or phrase that adds meaning to the verb in a sentence or part of a sentence is called an adjunct. When additional information is given by the adjunct in a sentence, it is called modifying or qualifying. For instance:

(1) • He came *fast*.   (2)   • He telephoned us *in a great hurry*.

    -----   -------------------

    ⇑   ⇑

fast is an adverb and adjunct (adjunct verb)   adjunct phrase

Both the adverb and the phrase add further information to the verbs *came* and *telephoned* respectively.

. Functions of Adverbs

• The most common function performed by many adverbs is to **modify the verb.**

Here are some examples:

>   (1) • She drives *safely*.

>   -------

>   ⇑

>   adverb modifying the verb drives by adding further information $\Rightarrow$ *safely*

safely enhances the central meaning conveyed by this statement.

Word Classes   **Adverbs**   **93**

****

(2) • He walks *gently*.

⇑

adverb modifying the verb walks

Here the adverb adds further information by way of highlighting *how* this particular person walks.

(3) • We are *very* pleased to meet you.

⇑

adverb modifying the verb pleased

Here the adverb *very* places emphasis on the meaning of the whole sentence.

(4) • Due to noisy people in the room, I could *hardly* hear you.

phrase ↵   ⇑

adverb modifying the verb hear

In this sentence, the adverb *hardly* adds meaning to the verb in the clause(part of a sentence).

(5) • She was seen *recently*.

⇑

adverb modifying the verb was seen

Here the adverb adds further information to the meaning of this statement by pointing out the time when she was seen.

• An adverb modifies another adverb:

This is exemplified below:

(1) • Police arrived at the accident scene *very quickly*.

first adverb ↵   ⇓

second adverb

In this sentence:

    . quickly $\Longrightarrow$ adverb modifies verb $\Longrightarrow$ *arrived*

    . very $\Longrightarrow$ adverb modifies second adverb $\Longrightarrow$ *quickly*

In this case, the adverb *very* acted as an intensifier. It is one of the adverbs of degree. Its use in this sentence has graded the adverb *quickly*, and thus placed greater emphasis on the meaning of the other adverb.

    (2) . He has performed *unexpectedly well*.

            ---------------- ------

     first adverb ↵   ⇓

               second adverb

In this sentence:

    . well $\Longrightarrow$ adverb modifies verb $\Longrightarrow$ *performed*

    . unexpectedly $\Longrightarrow$ adverb modifies adverb $\Longrightarrow$ *well*

Here the adverb *unexpectedly* is a descriptive adverb. Its function is similar to that of adjectives modifying nouns. It adds an extra layer of meaning to the central meaning of this statement.

    (3) . He left home *most resentfully*.

           ------ -----------

     first adverb↵   ⇓

           second adverb

    . resentfully $\Longrightarrow$ adverb modifies verb $\Longrightarrow$ *left*

    . most $\Longrightarrow$ adverb modifies adverb $\Longrightarrow$ *resentfully*

    (4) . We visited John *quite* often.

           ------- -------

     first adverb ↵   ⇓

           second adverb

    . often $\Longrightarrow$ adverb modifies verb $\Longrightarrow$ *visited*

    . quite $\Longrightarrow$ adverb modifies adverb $\Longrightarrow$ *often*

Here the adverb *quite* adds extra meaning conveyed by *often* which is an adverb of time.

(5) • Sarah answered questions *more fully* than Jane did. (comparative use)

first adverb⌐   ⇓
                  second adverb

• fully ⟹ adverb modifies verb ⟹ *answered*

• more ⟹ adverb modifies adverb ⟹ *fully*

In this example, *more* is acting as an intensifier by placing emphasis on the meaning of the adverb *fully*.

• <u>An adverb can modify an adjective:</u>

The following examples show this action:

(1) • He is *fairly happy*.

adverb ⌐   ⇓
              adjective

• fairly ⟹ adverb modifies happy ⟹ *adjective*

The adverb *fairly* is placed before the adjective *happy* in order to intensify the meaning of this adjective.

(2) • This suitcase is *really nice.*

adverb ⌐   ⇓
              adjective

• really ⟹ adverb modifies adjective ⟹ *nice*

The use of the adverb *really* adds further information to the meaning of the adjective *nice*.

(3) • This car is *too long.*

adverb ⌐   ⇓
          adjective

 • too $\Rightarrow$ adverb modifies adjective $\Rightarrow$ *long*

(4) • You're **absolutely right**.

     ------------ ------

     adverb ↵   ⇓

                adjective

 • absolutely $\Rightarrow$ adverb modifies adjective $\Rightarrow$ *right*

(5) • This is a **quite small** office.

     ------ --------

     adverb ↵   ⇓

            adjective

 • **quite** $\Rightarrow$ adverb modifies adjective $\Rightarrow$ *small* modifies $\Rightarrow$ noun $\Rightarrow$ office
<u>when quite is used with an adjective, before a noun , it must be preceded by a, or an as above.</u>

• <u>An adverb can modify a preposition:</u>

This is exemplified below:

(1) • He is *sitting* **right beside** his father.

     ------- -------

     adverb ↵   ⇓

          preposition

 • *right* (right = exactly) $\Rightarrow$ adverb modifies preposition **beside** (beside = next to)

(2) • The car **just in front of** me stopped suddenly causing this accident.

     ----- -----------

     adverb ↵   ⇓

         preposition

 • *just* (= exactly) $\Rightarrow$ adverb modifies preposition

 • *in front of* (= ahead but near)

(3) • When you called, I was **really in** the garden shed without my mobile phone.

     ------- ---

     adverb ↵   ⇓

         preposition

****

. *really* (= truly or in reality) $\Rightarrow$ adverb intensifying the meaning of the preposition *in*

(4) . They are *always at* home in the evenings.

    adverb ↵   ⇓
            preposition

. always (= at all times) $\Rightarrow$ adverb modifies preposition *at*

(5) . He entered the hall *quietly from* the back door, which was unlocked.

    adverb ↵   ⇓
            preposition

. *quietly* (= without any sound or noise) $\Rightarrow$ adverb modifies preposition *from*

. Adverbs can also modify prepositional phrases: See $\Rightarrow$ phrases.

. Types of Adverbs

The prime function of an adverb is to support the central meaning of a statement by supplying further information. Indeed, the inclusion of an adverb in a sentence can enhance the meaning of a statement. The examples given above illustrate this role played by adverbs in sentences. The following types of adverbs cover a wide range of functions performed by adverbs:

. Adverbs of Manner

The adverbs of manner describe *__how__* something happened or was done. This is exemplified below:

(1) . Andrew approached Jane *calmly.*

        adverb of manner ↵

It gives us information about **how** Andrew approached Jane. It answers the question:

. **How** did Andrew approach Jane?   It modifies the verb $\Rightarrow$ *approached*

(2) • He drives *smoothly*.
        ----
adverb of manner ↵

It answers the question: • How does he drive? *smoothly*. It modifies the verb ⟹ *drives*

(3) • Tell us *frankly*, what's the matter with you.
        ----
adverb of manner ↵

• How did she tell him? **frankly**. It modifies the verb ⟹ *tell*

• **Most adverbs of manner end in *ly* as illustrated by the above examples. Some adverbs of manner do not end in *ly* as demonstrated below:**

For instance:

(4) • Cars were running *fast* on the motorway.
        ------
adverb of manner ↵

• How were cars running? *fast*.   - modifying the verb ⟹ *were running*

(5) • Robert walks *straight*.
        ----
adverb of manner ↵

• How does Robert walk? *straight*.   - modifying the verb ⟹ *walks*

• **Sometimes the adverb of manner can be without ly.** For instance:

(6) • She told him the *loudest* in front of their guests that she didn't love him.
        ----
adverb of manner ↵- modifying the verb ⟹ *told*

• **Louder, loudest are used in *informal style*.**

(7) • You should walk *slowly*.

           ------

adverb of manner ↵ - modifying the verb ⟹ *slow*

. Adverbs of Time

Adverbs of time state *__when__* something or some action has taken place or will take place. The following examples illustrate how adverbs of times can be used:

(1) • We enjoyed a group discussion *afterwards*.

           ----

adverb of time ↵ - modifies the verb ⟹ *enjoyed*

It answers the question: •When did you enjoy group discussion? *afterwards*

(2) • We discussed this matter *yesterday*.

           ----

adverb of time ↵ - modifies the verb ⟹ *discussed*

(3) • She is ill *now*.

           -----

adverb of time ↵ - modifying the verb ⟹ *ill*

(4) • This news programme is broadcast *nightly*.

           ----

adverb of time ↵ - It modifies the verb ⟹broadcast

(5) • *Soon* I will finish this job.

           ------

adverb of time ↵ - it modifies the verb ⟹ *finish*

. Adverbs of Place

Adverbs of place tell us *__where__* something occurs or happens. The following examples show the use of adverbs of time:

(1) • We will meet *here*.
‎   ------

adverb of place ↵ - it modifies the verb ⟹ *will meet*

(2) • They live *upstairs*.
‎   ----------

adverb of place ↵ - it modifies the verb ⟹ *live*

(3) • We parked our car *somewhere*.
‎   --------------

adverb of place ↵ - it modifies the verb ⟹ *parked*

(4) • Silvia is *abroad* for her friend's wedding.
‎   ----------

adverb of place ↵ - it modifies the verb ⟹ *is*

(5) • The bad weather kept us *indoors* over the weekend.
‎   ---------

adverb of place ↵ - it modifies the verb ⟹ *kept*

• Adverbs of Reason and Purpose

Adverbs of reason and purpose inform us why an action or something has happened. The following examples show their application:

(1) • He said it *deliberately*.
‎   ----------------

adverb of purpose ↵ - it modifies the verb ⟹ *said*

It tells us the reason why he said it and thus answers the question: •Why did he say it? *deliberately* – it means intentionally.

(2) • *Inevitably*, our journey was cancelled because of late payment.
‎   -------------

adverb of reason ↵

****

- **Why?** *inevitably* means something certain to happen or occur. The cause is given in this statement.

        (3) • I broke it *accidentally*.
            ----

        adverb of reason ↵

        (4) • You made it difficult for us *purposely*.
            ----

            adverb of reason ↵

        (5) • I did not hurt your feelings *intentionally*.
            ----

            adverb of reason ↵

• Adverbs of Frequency

Adverbs of frequency tell us about the repetition or occurrence of something. Some adverbs of frequency are used in the following examples:

        (1) • The class *always* begins at 9.15.
            ----

    adverb of frequency ↵ - How often ? *always*

        (2) • I come to this park *often*.
            ----

        adverb of frequency ↵ - How often? *often*

        (3) • It's *usually* the manager's responsibility.
            ----

    adverb of frequency ↵ - How often? *usually*

        (4) • I eat rice *rarely*.
            ----

    adverb of frequency ↵ - How often? *rarely* (seldom = rarely)

(5) • Nothing *ever* happens in this place for young people.
        ------

adverb of frequency ↵

Ever is used with negative statements and questions. It expresses doubt or condition. It usually comes before a verb as shown above.

. Adverbs of Degree

Adverbs of degree show the **extent** to which something has happened. These adverbs include
words like: *easily*, *enough*, *forever*, *somewhat*, and *twice*. The following examples show how
to use such adverbs:

(1) • He visited us *fairly* recently.
                     -------   ---------
                        ⇓   ⇓

            adverb of degree   adverb of time

            modifying *recently* ↵ - intensifying the meaning of the adverb

(2) • I *hardly* knew his intention.

           ⇓

adverb of degree modifying the verb ⇒ *knew*

(3) • This pair of shoes is *rather* expensive.
                            -------   ----------
                               ⇓   ⇓
                    adverb of degree   adjective

        modifying *expensive* ↵

(4) • She fell *right* to the bottom of the stairs.
                -------   ----
                   ⇓   ⇓
        adverb of degree   preposition

    modifying *to* ↵

      (5) ● The lecture hall was *half* full.
                   ------

       adverb of degree ↵ - modifying adjective *full*

Adverbs of degree can also be a fraction (half) or percentage, e.g. thirty percent wrong.

● <u>Adverbs for other Functions</u>

In addition to the above types of adverbs, there are adverbs for indicating the following wide range of functions:

● *<u>Adverb of Viewpoint</u>* expresses a particular view concerning a particular state or situation. Some adverbs of viewpoint are: *financially*, *economically*, *personally* and *strictly*.

Here are some examples:

      (1) ● This trip is *financially* bearable.
                     ----

      adverb of viewpoint ↵ - expressing financial state

      (2) ● *Economically*, the USA is the strongest country.
               ----

adverb of viewpoint ↵ - expressing economical status/state

● *<u>Adverb of Focus</u>* is used to highlight the word or a phrase which the writer or the speaker wants to focus on. Some adverbs of focus are: *also*, *even*, **especially**, and *only*. Their use is exemplified below:

      (1) ● I *only* visited him once in London.
             ------

adverb of focus ↵ - focusing on the verb *visited*

<u>Only</u> is the word the writer wanted to focus on.

      (2) ● She *especially* loves his wealth.
            ----

adverb of focus ↵ - focusing on the phrase ⟹ *his wealth*

****

- *Adverbs of different attitudes* relate to a comment on someone's behaviour, feeling, truth, falsity and similar attitudes. Some relevant adverbs are: *curiously, fortunately, honestly, possibly, naively , surprisingly* and *wisely*. Here are some examples:

   (1) • He was in the lecture hall, but *curiously*, I did not see him.

   ⇑

   adverb of attitude

In this sentence, the adverb *curiously* (= strangely*)* indicates the truth the writer/speaker knows.

   (2) • She *naively* trusted the caller.

   ⇑

   adverb of attitude – indicating behaviour

   (3) • *Honestly,* I have no idea where he has gone for his lunch.

   ⇑

   adverb of attitude – emphasizing that what I am saying is true

   (4) • *Possibly*, they will reject our invitation.

   ⇑

   adverb of attitude – predicting feelings of some people

- *The linking adverb* relates to the previous sentence or clause. Some linking adverbs are: *anyway, besides, further, furthermore, however, moreover, nevertheless*. For instance:

   (1) • You say the balance is zero. *However*, I think one invoice is still unpaid.

   ⇑

   adverb of *linking* – linking the previous sentence/statement

   (2) • We are late for the meeting. *Anyway,* we must attend it.

   ⇑

   adverb of *linking* – linking the previous thought/statement

- *<u>The comparison of adverbs</u>* is similar to the comparison of adjectives. Some adverbs have the same form as adjectives. Adverbs take the comparative and superlative forms with such endings: *er/est, more/most, farther / farthest, further, furthest* and *better/best*.

For instance:

(1) • Tomorrow you should start your work ten minutes *earlier* than usual.
                                     ----

                           comparative form of adverb ↵

(2) • She likes him *more* than his wife.
                     ----

comparative form of adverb ↵

(3) • Friday is the *soonest* I can contact you by telephone.
                 ----

superlative form of adverb ↵ - it means here as soon as possible

(4) • Which car do you like *best*?
                 ------

superlative form of adverb ↵ - superlative of *well*

(5) • The railway station is *farthest* from where our car is parked.
                 ----

superlative form of adverb ↵ - superlative of *far (farthest = very long distance)*

(6) • His complaint is *worst* than I thought.
                 ----

superlative form of adverb ↵ - superlative of *badly (badly, worse, worst)*

As you have already noticed adverbs are single words. In addition, there are many groups of words that can function with and without adverbs as *<u>adverbial elements</u>*. These adverbials form phrases and clauses. These are discussed and exemplified in Part 2. For instance:

Yesterday morning, I saw him. In this sentence, the adverbial element is highlighted. In fact, it is an adverbial phrase as it has no finite verb. **See ⟹ Phrases.**

• <u>When is a word an adjective or an adverb in a sentence?</u>

Both adjectives and adverbs have some common features and differ in some respects. In order to understand adverbs as a word class, it is vitally important to appreciate their specific characteristics. Certainly, there are many adjectives and adverbs, which perform the same function of describing something in a sentence. However, from the context of a sentence you can find whether it is an adjective or an adverb.

For instance:

(1) • She had a *long* wait at Heathrow due to an industrial strike.

      ------

adjective ↵ - *long* is placed before a noun ⟹ modifying the noun ⟹ wait

(2) • She had to wait *long* at Heathrow due to an industrial strike.

      ----

adverb ↵ - *long* is positioned after the verb wait modifying the verb ⟹wait

Sometimes, it can create some confusion in recognising when a word is an adjective or an adverb. Furthermore, this may lead to the incorrect use of a word.

In summary, adverbs can enhance the overall meaning of a statement. Even so, most of the time, they are not essential components for structuring sentences. You can construct a meaningful and grammatically complete sentence or statement without any adverb. However, there are occasions when the inclusion of an adverb in a sentence is vital.

Chapter 6

Prepositions

• Introduction

A preposition is a word or a group of words used before a noun, pronoun or noun phrase. It also shows the relation of a noun, pronoun, noun phrase or clause to the rest of a sentence. There are many simple words and groups of words which act as prepositions. Some of these are listed below:

> ***Simple prepositions***: *about, above, across, along, among, at, bar, before, behind, beside, by, circa, down, during, except, for, from, in, inside, into, minus, near, notwithstanding, of, on, out, over, per, plus, pro, to, since, towards, under, with, without(it is listed as one word in some dictionaries)*
>
> ***Group prepositions***: *according to, ahead of, apart from, because of, due to, instead of, near to, as far as, in accordance with, in addition to, for the sake of, in favour of, in front of, in a hurry, in terms of, in view of, on behalf of, with reference to, with regard to*

As shown above, the basic form of a preposition is just one word. This form is known as a *simple preposition*, e.g. *at*. A *group* or *compound* or *complex preposition* consists of two or more prepositions, e.g. *in accordance with*. It is worth mentioning here that sometimes two or more simple prepositions merge together to form a complex word preposition, e.g. *onto*. See above. The following examples illustrate their specific feature of coming before a noun, pronoun or noun phrase:

     (1) • **Anne left the office** *before* **lunch.**

                       -------- ------

     preposition before a noun ↵   ⇑

                           noun

In this sentence, the preposition *before* joins the first part of the sentence (highlighted) with its second part. This is how it shows the relationship between these two parts of the sentence. It also meets the specific requirement of a preposition, e.g. a preposition comes before a noun ⇒ *lunch*. Similarly:

(2) • **They shouted my name** *across* the road.

preposition ↵   ⇑

noun phrase

preposition occurred before a noun phrase ↵

(3) • We live *next to* him.

preposition ↵   ⇑

personal pronoun

Prepositions express a variety of relationships between a noun, pronoun, noun clause or noun phrase and the rest of a sentence. They cover a wide range of meanings. The most typical are the relationships of *place* and *time*. Some of these relationships are illustrated below:

. Prepositions of Place

This is illustrated by the following examples:

(1) • You will find it *near* the door.

preposition of place ↵   ⇑

noun phrase ⇒ *near* refers to a place/door

(2) • I will meet you *at* Piccadilly Circus.

preposition of place ↵   ⇑

noun phrase ⇒ *at* refers to a place/Piccadilly Circus

(3) • Anne saw me *opposite* the main post office.

preposition of place ↵   ⇑

noun phrase ⇒ *opposite* refers to a place

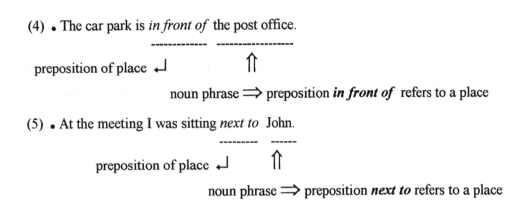

(4) ● The car park is *in front of* the post office.

preposition of place ↵

noun phrase ⟹ preposition *in front of* refers to a place

(5) ● At the meeting I was sitting *next to* John.

preposition of place ↵

noun phrase ⟹ preposition *next to* refers to a place

In example 5, John is a person who was sitting in a certain place. Thus, *next to* refers to the place where John was sitting.

● <u>Prepositions of Time</u>

We use prepositions of time in a variety of ways. Here are some examples:

(1) ● We arrived here *on* Monday.

preposition of time ↵

noun ⟹ time – the preposition *on* refers to the time/today
Preposition *on* joins both parts of the sentence.

(2) ● Roads were deserted *during* the World Cup matches.

preposition of time ↵

noun phrase

Preposition *during* refers to a period of time⟹ the World Cup matches - <u>a definite time</u>

(3) ● We have lived in France *for* ten years.

preposition of time ↵ - *for* indicates the length of time – how long

(4) ● You should arrive *before* the weekend.

preposition of time ↵ - *before* refers to the time ⟹ <u>no later than</u> the weekend

(5) • My contract will not expire *until* the end of next month.

preposition of time ↵ - *until* refers to the time ⟹ when an event or

something ends ⟹ *contract*

• **A sentence can have both place and time prepositions.**

This is exemplified below:

(1) • We will meet you *at* breakfast *in* our hotel.

preposition of time ↵   ⇑   ⇑   ⇑
refers to breakfast   noun preposition noun phrase
⇑   └refers to a place ⟹ *our hotel*
it is at a particular time

(2) • We have been living *for* three years *in* this house.

preposition of time ↵   ⇑
refers to a period of time   *preposition of place* - refers to a place ⟹*this house*

(3) • We lived *close to* their shop *in* 1995.

preposition of place ↵   ⇑
refers to a place = shop   *preposition of time* - *in* refers to time ⟹ *1995*

• Prepositions of Other Meanings

Here are some other prepositions related to other meanings. These are discussed under some appropriate headings below.

• Prepositions of cause, reason & purpose

These are described below with the aid of the following examples:

(1) • I am happy **because of** a return to normal working hours.

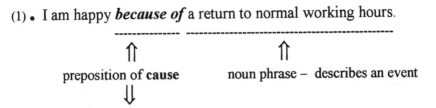

preposition of **cause**   noun phrase – describes an event

indicates the effect of an event described by the noun phrase on *I (subject)* as ⟹ *happy*

(2) • His lateness was **due to** a traffic jam in the town.

preposition of **cause**   noun phrase – describes an event

indicates the effect of an event stated by the noun phrase on *his lateness* ⟹ *subject*

Note that *a cause* produces *an effect*, e.g. an event or something that happens. On the other hand, a reason has a much wider scope. For instance, you can give a reason for something which is done. A reason can be a justification for something happening. The following examples illustrate the use of some *prepositions of reason*:

(3) • The brutal crime was committed *without* a motive.

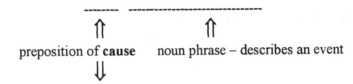

preposition of **reason** ↵   ⇑
                       noun phrase

The preposition *without* is followed by the noun phrase, which points to *a motive* ⟹ *reason*

(4) • Our Prime Minister is anxious *about* the predicated unfavourable election result.

preposition of **reason** ↵

• It is worth mentioning that the word *purpose* means an intention or determination to do something. Here are two examples of using prepositions of purpose:

(5) • *Despite* the rain, we will travel to London for Jane's wedding ceremony.

⇑

preposition of **purpose**

Here the preposition *despite* points to travel without being deterred by rain.

    (6) • She went to work *contrary to* her doctor's advice.
                  ----

   preposition of **determination** ↵ preposition *contrary to* ⟹ shows the
                                   determination to work against her doctor's advice

• <u>Prepositions of exception, addition, support, opposition, etc.</u>

Consider the following examples:

    (7) • We have paid the loan *except* for the commission and interest charges.
                 ----

     preposition of **exception** ↵ Preposition *except* refers to an exception.

<u>It can also be a verb meaning *exclude* or *exempt*.</u>

    (8) • All guests have left *except* John Smith from England.
                 ----

    preposition of **exception** ↵ - implying that only John Smith is still here

    (9) • We have no close friends in this area *other than* Jack and Jill.
                       ----

      preposition of **exception** ↵ - implying *only or except*

Here is another example to demonstrate its further use:

    (10) • Jane seldom seems *other than* cheerful.
                    ----

    preposition of **exception** ↵ - implying *only or except*   (*seldom = not often*)

    (11) • She is beautiful, *apart from* her height

                   ⇑

    preposition of **exception** ⟹ *apart from* implies that the height is excluded

****

(12) • I have completed all orders *apart from* the one received just now.

⇑

preposition of **exception** ⟹*apart from* implies the order just received is not yet completed

• In examples 10 and 11, *apart from* = *except for*. In examples 12 and 13, *apart from* has a different meaning. In these examples: *apart from* = *in addition to* = *as well as*

(13) • *Apart from* his inherited wealth, he has built up his own large enterprise.

⇑

preposition of **addition** ⟹ *apart from* means here in addition to something.

(14) • *Apart from* his well-paid full-time job, he also has a part-time job.

⇑

preposition of **addition** ⟹ *apart from* means here in addition to something.

(15) • Our trainer was *with* us throughout the race.

preposition of **support** ↵ - or preposition of ⟹*possession*   *(Also see example 18)*

(16) • His age is *against* him for this travel salesman's job.

preposition of **opposition** ↵

• Among the most common prepositions are *of* and *with.* These are used to denote possession or belonging as demonstrated below:

(17) • Sarah is a young pianist *of* rare talent.

preposition of **possession** ↵

(18) • I saw Eric walking *with* a girl *with* red hair.

preposition of **accompaniment** ↵

preposition of ⟹ **possession**

Example 18 shows that sometimes prepositions can express different meanings. In this sentence 'with red hair' means 'who has red hair'.

• **There are prepositions for almost all kinds of meanings.** Here are some examples:

(19) • You can pay for your travel *by* cheque or *by* credit card.

preposition of **manner**   implies 'any card'

(20) • Some parents stay together *despite* their differences *for the sake of* their children.

preposition of **concession**   preposition of **reason/purpose**

• **Some prepositions are not easy to recognise, e.g. via and vis-à-vis.**

These are exemplified below:

(21) • We came to know about your success *via* your sister.

preposition of **manner** ↵

(22) • It is claimed that Microsoft has an unfair commercial advantage *vis-à-vis* other software companies in the world.

this is of French origin↵

preposition of **comparison**

The preposition *vis-à-vis* means in comparison with or in relation to something. Here is another example of its use:

(23) • Nurse's earnings *vis-à-vis* the national average are very low.

⇑

preposition of comparison/relation

• Prepositional Idioms

Many prepositions are used with idioms. You have to learn the use of idioms. Here are a few examples of prepositional idioms.

(24) • John and Jill began to argue loudly, and I thought it was time I *stepped in*.

----

prepositional idiom ↵

idiom⟹ *step in = to intervene*

(25) • She is *at heart* a very kind person.

----

prepositional idiom ↵ idiom ⟹ *at heart = really*

(26) • He thanked us *from the bottom of his heart* for all our help.

----

prepositional idiom ↵ idiom ⟹ *from the bottom of one's heart = very sincerely*

(27) • The manager wants to talk to all of us *one by one*.

----

prepositional idiom ↵ idiom ⟹ *one by one = individually*

(28) • The resolution was passed by the board of directors *on the nod*.

----

prepositional idiom ↵

idiom ⟹ *on the nod = all agreed without taking a vote*

• When is a word a preposition, adverb or conjunction?

A word can function as a preposition, adverb or conjunction. The main feature of a preposition is that it is followed by a pronoun, noun or noun phrase. If you apply this rule to a sentence, you should be able to find any preposition in a sentence. The following three examples illustrate the use of the word *before*.

(1) • John had left home *before* his wife's arrival.

Preposition of time ↵   ⇑
                        noun phrase

• The adverb modifies a verb, an adjective, another adverb or an adverbial phrase.
  For instance:

(2) • That happened *before*.

adverb of time ↵ - modifying the verb *happened*

• The function of a conjunction is to join clauses to form compound and complex sentences.
  For instance:

(3) • It may be a long time *before* we meet again.

clause 1 ↵   conjunction ↵   clause 2 ↵

clause 1 + conjunction + clause 2 = complex sentence

You have to examine the context in which the word is used in a sentence to determine if the word is a conjunction, adverb or preposition.

In summary, prepositions have a wide range of meanings and many different uses. They can be a source of confusion. For example, *by* can express time, place, manner and action. For instance: The computer was repaired *by* me.(Preposition of *action*). It must arrive *by* next day. (Preposition of *time*). It is laying *by* the table. (Preposition of *place*). They went away *by* taxi. (Preposition of *manner*). By is also an adverb. For example: Time goes *by* so quickly. Here *by* is an adverb.

• See ⇒ Phrases and Clauses in ⇒ Part 2

Chapter 7

Determiners & Interjections

• Introduction

A determiner is a word that comes before a noun or a noun phrase. It is used to determine which person (s) or thing(s) are being referred to in a statement. Let's consider two examples:

(1) • *The* chancellor.

----- -------------

determiner ↵   noun↵

There are chancellors' posts in many countries. In this sentence, it refers to a unique chancellor in one country. Here the determiner indicates a unique position.

(2) • *The* House of Commons.

------ ----------------------------

determiner ↵   noun phrase↵

The United Kingdom has only one place called the *House of Commons*. This is the only recognised place of this name in the country. In this case, the determiner refers to a unique status for a unique building.

The above examples show that some words are called determiners because they determine how nouns and pronouns are being used. In the above examples, it determines how the noun the *chancellor* and phrase *House of Commons* are used. A determiner by itself does not make much sense, but when it is used with nouns and noun phrases it amplifies their meaning.

• Groups of Determiners

In order to identify different determiners, in Table 1 the most commonly used determiners are listed under major groups.

Determiners

Definite Determiners	Indefinite Determiners
• **Definite article:**	• **Indefinite articles:**
the	a, an
• **Possessive determiners:**	• **Indefinite determiners:**
my, your, his, her, their, our - when qualifying nouns or pronouns these are **determiners** - When standing in for nouns they are **pronouns**: mine ,his, hers, yours, ours, theirs	all, almost, another, any, both, each, either, enough, every, few, fewer, fewest, little, less, least, many, more, most, much, no, neither, other, several, some
• **Demonstrative determiners:**	• **Interrogative determiners:**
this, that, these, those	what, which, whose

•**Numerals:**
 	
  - **cardinal:** one, three, ten,…
  - **ordinal:** third, fourth seventh …
  - **fraction:** a quarter of, a seventh of…	

Table 1

• The Definite Article

Its use is exemplified below:

(1) • It is *the* house where I was born.
　　　　　　‑‑‑‑
　　　　　　⇑

the definite article before a noun ⟹ *house* - indicates the uniqueness of the house

<u>Here its function is to place emphasis on the noun (house) which comes after it.</u>

(2) • I will buy a **car** tomorrow. *The* **car** will make my travel to work easy.
　　　　　　　　　　　　　‑‑‑‑‑

　　　　definite article ↵ before a noun ⟹ *car*

In this example, definite article *the* <u>makes reference to a noun a *car* already mentioned in the</u> <u>previous sentence.</u> Here its function is to attach an attribute to a car: " *will make my travel to* *work easy"*

(3) • We developed interactive timetable software. *The* software is licensed to schools.
　　　　　　　　　　　　　　　　‑‑‑‑‑

　　refers back to the software mentioned previously↵

(4) • Some members of *the* Royal Family attended the celebration tonight.
　　　　　　　　　　　‑‑‑‑

denoting a distinct family ↵

(5) • *The* French nation was pleased when France won *the* World Cub.
　　　‑‑‑‑‑‑　　　　　　　　　　　　　　　　‑‑‑‑
　　　⇑　　　　　　　　　　　　　　　　　　⇑

pointing to a distinct group of people　　　　specifying the unique award

(6) • The promised letter is in *the* post.
　　　　　　　　　　　　‑‑‑‑‑
　　　　　　　　　　　　⇑

　　indicating that the noun *post* is a communication organisation

Here the *post* is not thought of as a particular post office, but as an organisation in the com-munication business.

(7) • *The* highest mark in the psychology examination was gained by Anne.

⇑ - noun phrase

the precedes the superlative adjective ⟹ *highest* in an underlined noun phrase

Here *the* is modifying the superlative adjective *highest*.

(8) • June 21ˢᵗ is *the* longest day each year.

⇑

the preceded the superlative adjective *longest* in this noun phrase

In this example, *the* is modifying the superlative adjective *longest*.

(9) • Margaret Thatcher has been *the only* female prime minister in Europe.
----

the preceded the adjective **only** in this noun phrase ↵ - modifying the adjective *only*

(10) • Now is the turn of *the next* person.

⇑

the preceded **next** in the noun phrase ⟹ *the next person*

In this case, *the* **is modifying the adjective** *next.*

(11) • It was *the* summer of 2000, when I went to Poland.
----

phrase of time ↵

It is not preceded by an adjective but by *the*.

• A phrase of time containing a noun begins with *the* as illustrated above. The condition is that the noun must not be preceded by an adjective. Some more examples to illustrate this rule are:

(12) • We visit our parents at *the* weekend.

----

phrase of time without an adjective before the noun ↵

(13) • They married *the* following Saturday.

----

the preceded the phrase of time ↵

• Use *the* <u>before the name of a country, if its name ends with kingdom or republic:</u>

For instance:

(14) • This book was published in *the United Kingdom*.

(15) • *The Republic of Ireland* is in Europe.

• Use *the* <u>before a plural name of countries:</u>

For example:

(16) • In 1958, *the Netherlands* became a founding member of the EEC.

(17) • *The United States of America* consists of 50 administrative states.

• <u>If the name of a region is not modified by another word (an adjective), *the* comes before it:</u>

For instance:

(18) • Birmingham is situated in *the Midlands.*

• <u>The definite article can be used to express how something is measured:</u>

This is illustrated below:

(19) • In these days, potatoes are sold by *the* **kilogram**.

• *The* **definite article precedes the names of entertainment places, trade and similar centres, galleries and museums.** Here are a few examples:

    (20) • We met in *the* **Tate Gallery** some years ago.

    (21) • *The* **World Trade Centre** is situated near London Bridge.

                    ----

           the is not needed before this name ↵

Many bridge names are without *the*, but there are exceptions to this rule. For example, the River Humber in East Yorkshire, England, has a bridge over it. This bridge is called *The Humber Bridge*.

    (22) • I have been to *the* **Albert Hall** several times.

           ----

an entertainment hall in London ↵

    (23) • *The* **Dorchester** is a well-known hotel.

• **A definite article comes before a noun, if it indicates a unique position/status:**

    (24) • As *the* **secretary** of this club, I am responsible for administration.

• *The* **is used with an unaccountable noun, providing an unaccountable noun refers to some particular person(s) or object(s).** For instance:

    (25) • *The* **petrol** in the United Kingdom is more expensive than in France.

          ----

unaccountable noun↵ - preceded by *the* ⟹definite article

    (26) • Their cat loves *the* **music** played on radio.

          ----

    unaccountable noun↵- preceded by *the* ⟹definite article

• *The* **is used with a plural noun when a noun refers to some specific meaning:**

For instance:

(27) . Michael Jackson and *the children* were shown together in a documentary programme.
         ----
        plural noun↵ - here it means some particular children

(28) . *The books* we received from Poland are not in English.
     ----
plural noun↵ - refers to some specific books

. Indefinite Articles

The indefinite article has two forms: *a* and *an*. Their functions are exemplified below:

(1) . Yesterday was *a bit* warmer day.
                    --- -------------------
    indefinite article↵   ⇑
                        noun phrase

. When a noun phrase describes something or a person, the indefinite article *the* precedes the noun phrase as shown above.

In example (1) the indefinite article *a* is required. On the other hand, in example 2, *an* is essential as explained below.

. The article *an* precedes the noun if a singular noun begins with a *vowel (a, e, i, o, u)*.

For instance:

(2) . *An* elephant from India has ears like *the* map of India.
      -----------------   -----
            ⇑   ⇑
      indefinite article   definite article

In example 2, four nouns (elephant, India, ears, map) are mentioned five times. Only on two occasions indefinite and definite articles are used respectively. On the other three occasions, there is no need to insert any of these determiners. <u>Both examples show that the indefinite article stands for *one* or in other words, **a** and **an** function as one.</u>

(3) • She is *a* nice girl, isn't she?

indefinite article ↵   ⇑

     noun phrase with a singular noun ⇒*girl*

(4) • My son is *a* student.

indefinite article↵ - preceded a singular noun ⇒*student*

• <u>**A phrase of time begins with *a* if a noun is preceded by an adjective.**</u>

This is illustrated below:

(5) • *A* very cold winter day is here. Or :   *A* very cold winter day!

      ⇑   ⇑

phrase indicating time   phrase of time forming no sentence

winter ⇒ noun is preceded by the adjective ⇒*very*

. *very* is both an adjective and an adverb. Here it is functioning as an adjective of degree

. *cold* is both an adjective and a noun. Here it is used as an adjective   **See ⇒ adjective**

---

(6) • *A* wonderful day when England won the World Cup.

phrase of time ↵ - day ⇒ noun preceded by the adjective ⇒*wonderful*

(7) • *A* remarkable *day!*

****

In this phrase, the noun is preceded by the adjective. For this reason, the indefinite article *a* started this phrase.

- **The indefinite article comes before a noun if it does not indicate a unique position/status:** For instance:

> (8) • As *a* member of this union, I am entitled to free admission.
> -------------------------------
> essential in this phrase ↵

Since a union has many members, the status of a member is not unique.

- **The indefinite article a/an precedes a noun expressing prices and similar rates:**

For instance:

> (9) • Bananas are eighty pence *a* **kilogram**.
> ---------------
> essential in this phrase ↵

- **The indefinite article can come before a noun in place of *one*.** For example:

> (10) • I would like to buy *a* car.
> ---
> here a = one ↵

- **The indefinite article is used to indicate someone's job or profession or any attribute that describes the person:** For instance:

> (11) • Jane is *a* **belly dancer** in Cairo.
> --------------------
> *a* is essential here ↵

> (12) • Before he joined the Labour Party, he was *a* **communist**.
> --------------------
> *a* is essential ↵

- **The indefinite article can be used instead of *any*.** For instance:

     (13) • Just buy **a book** on psychology.
              ----

    a book = any book ↵

- **Many idiomatic phrases embody both definite and indefinite articles.**

    Here are some examples of idiomatic phrases:

        • *an* angel of mercy   • *a* bag of nerves   • *a* fair crack of the whip

        • *the* top brass   • *the* iron curtain   • *the* golden rule   See ⟹ idioms.

• <u>Possessive Determiners</u>

Possessive pronouns function as determiners if they ***qualify a noun***.

The following examples illustrate their function as determiners.

(1) • This is *my* book . Possessive determiner *my* qualifies a singular noun ⟹ ***book***

(2) • This is *his* car. Possessive determiner *his* qualifies a singular noun ⟹*car*

(3) • That house is *our* property. Possessive determiner *our* qualifies a noun ⟹ ***property***

               ⇑

    plural form of the possessive determiner

(4) • This is *her* handbag. Possessive determiner *her* qualifies a singular noun ⟹ ***handbag***

(5) • Where is **your** horse? Possessive determiner *your* qualifies a singular noun ⟹*horse*

(6) • It is *their* homeland. Possessive determiner *their* qualifies a singular noun ⟹*horse*

• <u>Indefinite Determiners</u>

Indefinite determiners function as determiners if they modify a noun. The following sentences exemplify their use.

****

(1) . *All things* work well here.
       -----

indefinite determiner ↵ – *qualifies* ⟹ *things* ⟹ a plural noun

(2) . Can he be *another* Ali in boxing?
           ----

indefinite determiner ↵ – *qualifies* ⟹ *Ali* ⟹ a singular noun

(3) . He doesn't eat *any* meat.
          ------

indefinite determiner ↵ – *qualifies* ⟹ *meat* ⟹ an unaccountable noun

The determiner **any** is usually used with negative sentences.

(4) . *Both* students are brilliant.
      ----

indefinite determiner ↵ – *qualifies* ⟹ *students* ⟹ a plural noun

Strictly speaking, the word *'both'* functions as adjective, adverb and pronoun.

(5) . *Each* article is priced.
      ----

indefinite determiner ↵ – *qualifies* ⟹ *article* ⟹ a plural noun

(6) . *Either* place is suitable for our purpose.
      ----

indefinite determiner ↵ – *qualifies* ⟹ *place* ⟹ a singular noun

(7) . You can take a seat on *either* side of the table.
                 ----

indefinite determiner ↵ – *qualifies* ⟹ *side* ⟹ a singular noun

Note that *either* is also a pronoun and an adverb. It is often used with *or* as *either ...or* to indicate a choice between two alternatives.

(8) • I have recorded *every* item I found.

(9) • *Several* men refused to show their passes.

(10) • *Few* players have shown an interest in this tour.

⇑

qualifies ⟹ *players* ⟹ a plural noun

The word *few* (= not many). It also functions as an adjective and pronoun. Its attributes are fewer and fewest. See ⟹ pronouns.

• <u>Demonstrative Determiners</u>

A demonstrative pronoun becomes a demonstrative determiner <u>only if it precedes a noun</u>. You can leave out a noun, if you think that a sentence makes clear sense. The following examples illustrate how a possessive word becomes a demonstrative determiner:

(1) • Please come to my office to see *this* invoice from the wine suppliers.

⇑

demonstrative determiner precedes ⟹ *invoice* (= noun)

This indicates that the invoice is near the speaker. *These* is the plural form of '**this**'. Its use is exemplified below:

(2) • *These* **bags** are full of bank notes.

demonstrative determiner ↵ - precedes bags ⟹ a plural noun

On the other hand, *that* and *those* imply that a person(s) or thing (s) are not so near but further away:

(3)• *That* **man** looks suspicious.

precedes man ↵ - a singular noun

(4) . *Those* **eggs** were hardly boiled.

⁣⁣⁣⁣⁣--------

⇑

precedes eggs ⟹ a plural noun

. <u>**Demonstrative determiners can also be used to imply space of time in terms of:**</u>

now = near in space of time indicated by ⟹ *this* and *these*

then = further away in space of time indicated by ⟹ *that* and *those*

These are exemplified below:

(5) . I will be in France *this* **month**.

‎-----

⇑

precedes month ⟹ a singular noun *this* = now at present

(6) . The only thing I do in my spare time *these* **days** is reading.

‎-------

⇑

precedes days ⟹ a plural noun

(7) . During 1999, I lived far from here. I travelled to work by car in *those* **days**.

‎--------

⇑

precedes days ⟹ a plural noun

(8) . When you telephoned me *that* **time**, I was having a shower.

‎——

⇑

that/ those = *then* ⟹ some time elapsed. *Those* is used with a plural noun.

. <u>Interrogative Determiners</u>

What*, *which and ***whose*** function as interrogative determiners if they precede a noun. Their use is shown by the following examples:

- <u>**The word *that* as an interrogative determiner is used when one wants to ask someone to specify something from an indefinite number of possibilities.**</u>

   For instance:

   (1) • ***What*** time is it?

   ⇑

   interrogative determiner preceded the noun ⟹ ***time***

   (2) • ***What*** politician did you see at Harrods of Knightsbridge?

   ⇑

   interrogative determiner preceded the noun ⟹ ***politician***

- <u>**The word *which* as interrogative determiner is used when one wants to ask someone to specify or identify something from a limited number of possibilities.**</u>

   Examples 3 and 4 show this use.

   (3) • ***Which*** lecturer did you see in our department?

   ⇑

   Interrogative determiner preceded the noun ⟹ ***lecturer***

   (4) • ***Which*** library do you often visit in this area?

   ⇑

   interrogative determiner preceded the noun ⟹ ***library***

• *Whose* **is an interrogative determiner of** *whom* **when it comes before a noun**.

Here are some examples:

(5) • *Whose* book is this?   *interrogative determiner preceded the noun* $\Rightarrow$ *book*

(6) • *Whose* car is parked in my place? *interrogative determiner preceded the noun* $\Rightarrow$ *car*

(7) • *Whose* idea is this ?   *interrogative determiner preceded the noun* $\Rightarrow$ *idea*

• Numeral Determiners:

As shown in Table 1 in this chapter, numerals are divided into:

• *Cardinal numbers* are: 1 one   2 two   3 three   4 four   20 twenty
                                100   hundred   400 hundred   1000 thousand etc.

The following examples show how cardinal numbers are written in words and numbers:

(1) • I have ordered *ten* bottles of French quality red wine.

(2) • They have bought *two* new cars in the last *12* months for their family.

(3) • *5 million* people voted for our party at the last local election.

(4) • In *1999*, I met her in London.

• The following phrases illustrate the use of commas in cardinal numbers:

(4) • **3,580** full-time students and **500** part-time students.

        ⇑

three thousand five hundred and eighty

(5) • *1,000,000*   read it as $\Rightarrow$ *a million* or *one million*.

(6) • **123,000,590** people.

Read it as: one hundred and twenty three million five hundred and ninety.

• <u>**You can make phrases with cardinal numbers:**</u> For instance:

(7) • *Three* of us together.   ⇐ *Cardinal number used in a phrase*

(8) • *approximately* two thirds full. ⇐ *approximately modifying the number - about 2/3*
                                          full not exactly 2/3

(9) • *Over* 100 guests.   ⇐ *over modifying the number – more than 100*

• <u>*Ordinal numbers*</u> are:

> *1st first   2nd   second   12th   twelfth*
> *20th   twentieth   100th   hundredth etc.*

    Here are two examples:

(10) • On my *60th* birthday, I invited my parents for a meal at the Bombay Restaurant.

(11) • **1st and 2nd** prizes were won by two brothers.

• <u>*Fractions*</u> are : *quarter, half, third, fourth, two and a third, etc.* If the number is less than one, the noun phrase is preceded by *of*. For instance:

(12) • *One third of* our products is for export to the USA.   ⇐ 1/3 = one third

(13) • It is only *four fifths* full.   ⇐ 4/5 = four fifths

(14) • It should be *four and three quarter metres* long.

(15) • The length of this stick is *only three quarters of a metre.*

(16) • She was *an hour and a half* late.   <u>*OR alternatively:*</u>

(17) • She was *one and a half hours* late.

In summary, the most common determiners are the definite and the indefinite articles. Other parts of speech such as adjectives and pronouns also function as determiners.

• See ⇒ adjectives • See ⇒ pronouns.

. <u>Interjections (Exclamations!)</u>

Interjections are considered as a minor class of words. These are exclamations. Interjections are useful for expressing feelings such as excitement, surprise, etc. They are not essential for the construction of sentences. Some of these are listed below:

Aha! Alas! Damn! Gosh! Hey! Ooh! Ouch! Phew! Ugh! Wow! Yuck!

Here are some examples:

(1) . ***Oh!*** How is he now?

            ⇑

Here it is used to show someone's reaction to something that has been said. It also indicates that one did not know it before.

(2) . ***Phew***, *it is stuffy in here!*

            ⇑

It shows disapproval as the place is warm in an unpleasant way and without enough fresh air.

. Some of the most commonly used exclamatory phrases are as follows:

(3) . Good heavens!   (4) . Oh dear!   (5) . Marvellous!   (6) . Great!

. <u>You can see from the above examples that some interjections are made from other</u> words. There are some interjections in which verb forms are used. For instance:

(7) . Watch out!   (8) . Cheers!

(9) . Look out!   (10) . Shut up!

(11) . What lovely flowers !   (12) . How warm it is today!

(13) . Thanks a lot! ⇐ sarcastic remark ⇐ opposite to what you mean

. **<u>An exclamation mark(!) is also discussed under punctuation.</u>** See ⇒Punctuation.

Chapter 8

Conjunctions

. Introduction

A word that joins other words, phrases, clauses or sentences is known as a conjunction.
For instance:

(1) . She is called Mary *and* she is my student.

     ⟰   ⟰   ⟰
    clause 1   conjunction   clause 2

Commas are omitted between short main clauses.

In this case, *and* joins two main clauses or two simple sentences into a compound sentence.
This is a simple conjunction. It has no other function except to combine parts of a sentence.
In this example, clause 1 and clause 2 can exchange places without altering the meaning of
this sentence. We can classify conjunctions into the following two classes:

> . *coordinating conjunctions* or *coordinators*
>
> . *subordinating conjunctions* or *subordinators*

. Coordinating Conjunctions or Coordinators

There are only the following coordinators:

and, but, or, so, nor.

Nor is the negative counterpart of **or** coordinator. It is less used than other coordinators. A
coordinating conjunction is a linking element. For this reason, it comes between two clauses.
It cannot be placed anywhere in the sentence. It performs the following functions:

- <u>To join two or more clauses of equal status in a sentence. The use of the coordinator generates a compound sentence in which clauses are independent.</u>

This is illustrated below:

(1) • Ralf cleaned the car *and* Silvia prepared lunch.

⟰   ⟰   ⟰

clause 1 + coordinator + clause 2   = *compound sentence*

This is a compound sentence. It consists of two main clauses joined together by the *and* coordinator. The clause on the left of the coordinator *and* is of the same status. We can analyse clauses in this sentence as shown below:

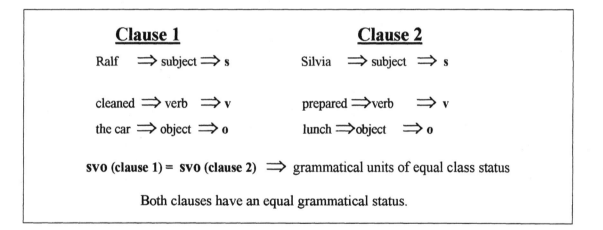

Clause 1	**Clause 2**
Ralf ⟹ subject ⟹ **s**	Silvia ⟹ subject ⟹ **s**
cleaned ⟹ verb ⟹ **v**	prepared ⟹verb ⟹ **v**
the car ⟹ object ⟹ **o**	lunch ⟹object ⟹ **o**

svo (clause 1) = **svo (clause 2)** ⟹ grammatical units of equal class status

Both clauses have an equal grammatical status.

We can reverse the order of clauses in this sentence without changing their meaning or the meaning of the sentence. Thus, the sentence becomes:

(2) • Silvia prepared lunch *and* Ralf cleaned the car.

coordinator is still between the two clauses ↵

It should be noted that *and* does not add any new information to the meaning, except that it tells us that there are two parts in the sentence. The sentence consists of two independent clauses. Since it is not a long sentence, the use of a comma between the clauses is unnecessary.

If you prefer to place a comma, in accordance with the rules of punctuation for a main clause, you can do so. See ⟹ punctuation.

(3) • Anne did the gardening *and* cooked a meal.
       ------

coordinator ↵ - the second clause has the same subject ⟹ *Anne*

In this sentence, both clauses have the same subject *Anne*. Examples 4-5 below show the use of the coordinator *but*:

(4) • Barbara likes to travel abroad (/Barbara/she)* *but* hates flying.

                                                      ⇑

coordinator /coordinating conjunction – same subject in both clauses ⟹ *Barbara*

(5) • She was in the car (she)* *but* was unhurt.
                               -----

coordinator ↵ - same subject in both clauses

( )* - When two clauses have the same subject ( ) as in examples 4 and 5, there is no need to repeat the subject in the second clause. No comma is required when the linked clauses are short.

The coordinator *but* suggests that there is an obvious contrast between the meaning of clauses on both sides of it.

(6) • The shop was closed *so* I could not buy anything.
       -------------------------- --- --------------------
clause 1 ↵   ⇑   ⇑
                              coordinator clause 2

in this context it means *'therefore'*↵

(7) • I was tired last night *so* I went to bed early.
       -------------------------- ---- -------------------------
clause 1 ↵   ⇑   ⇑
                              coordinator clause 2

here it means *'therefore'*↵

So as a conjunction is used to indicate a reason or result of something. In these two examples, it is pointing to the reason given in clause 1 and the result in clause 2. In fact, it is coordinating the verb in clause 1 with the verb in clause 2. Both clauses are units of equal

grammatical status $\Rightarrow$ **SVO**clause (1) = **SVO**clause (2)

The word *so* also functions as an *adverb* and *noun*.

The coordinator *or* introduces an alternative to the meaning conveyed by the first main clause. For instance:

(8) . You mustn't stay *so* near the fire *or* your trousers will catch fire.

                ⇑   ⇑

            1*   coordinator

1* '*so*' is functioning here as an adverb of degree. See $\Rightarrow$ adverbs. See $\Rightarrow$ phrases.

Both clauses are of the same/similar grammatical status $\Rightarrow$ **SVO**clause (1) = **SVO**clause (2)

Another example of the use of *or* :

(9) . You can collect it tonight *or* your son can collect it now.

            ⇓   ⇓

    SVOclause (1)   =   **SVO**clause (2)

• Correlative conjunctions or coordinators operate in pairs. These are used to join:

    • units of equal status – clauses in compound sentences

    • words and phrases.

Some common correlative coordinators
⇓

---

both ... and, but ... also, either ... or, neither ... nor, whether ... or.

The use of correlative coordinators is exemplified below. Also see pages 144-145 for more examples.

(10) • *Either* you will drive the car to London *or* we will travel by coach.

⇑   ⇑

first word in a compound sentence   implies an alternative to the first suggestion in main clause 1

main clause 1 ↵   *main clause 2* ↵

Another example of the use of *either ---- or* :

(11) • *Either* you do the gardening this week *or* we ask our local nursery to do it.

⇑   ⇑

occupies first position in the first main clause   coordinating – suggests an alternative to the proposal
                                                    given in the first clause of this compound sentence

Examples 10 and 11 illustrate that *either* comes at the start of the first clause in a compound sentence. It is also shown that the pair of *either...or* joins clauses of similar status in a compound sentence.

• **In order to render negative meaning, we can use *neither ...nor* in phrases.**
For instance:

(12) • *Neither* the public library *nor* the main post office were open.

⇑   ⇑

noun phrase   noun phrase

(13) • Due to heavy snowfall, we could turn *neither* north *nor* south.

noun phrase/single word phrase ↵   ⇑

                                        noun phrase/single word

• Subordinating Conjunctions or Subordinators

Like the coordinators, subordinating conjunctions also join parts of a sentence. They perform the following functions:

- • to link two clauses of unequal status in complex sentences

- • to introduce subordinate clauses   (often adverbial clause)

- to indicate the relationship between a subordinate clause and a main clause

- to link sentences - many subordinators can do so

<u>Complex sentences</u> have clauses of unequal status. Subordinating conjunctions such as *when, although, if, until, etc.* join subordinate clauses to a main clause in compound sentences.

Therefore, they link unequal grammatical units in compound sentences. Sometimes, a subordinator can add meaning of its own to the overall meaning of a subordinate clause. A subordinating conjunction introduces a subordinate clause, which is a less important component of a compound sentence than its main clause. There are many subordinating conjunctions. There are also multi-word subordinators. These include: ***so that, as long as, in order that, etc.*** Some of these are listed below: See ⟹ Clause. See ⟹ Sentences.

<u>Some Subordinating Conjunctions</u>

after, although, as long as, as quickly as, as soon as, as if, as though, as to, assuming that, because, before, even if, even though, except, except that, excepting that, if, in case, in order to, lest, more ... than, rather ... than, provided that, since, so that, sooner than, such, such as, till, unless, until, when, whenever, where, whereas, wherever, whether ,while

- Coordinating conjunctions **and**, **but** *and* **so** can also be used as subordinators.

The following examples illustrate the use of some main subordinators:

(1) ● Our train arrived ***after*** the other train had left the platform.

main clause ↵   ⇑   ⇑

            subordinator   subordinate clause introduced by the subordinator
            indicating time

Here the clause introduced by the subordinator is an ***adverbial clause of time*** (See ⟹clauses). The use of the subordinator has linked two clauses in this compound sentence. Furthermore, it has established a relationship between these clauses which helps us to understand the meaning of the whole sentence. Without the subordinator, the meaning of the sentence would not be clear. The subordinator ***after*** has preciously enhanced the intended meaning of this sentence by indicating the time factor between the arrival of one train and the departure of the other train.

(2) ● You must have lunch with us *before* you leave.

subordinator indicating time ↵   ⇑

subordinate adverbial clause introduced by

the subordinator ⟹ *before*

(3) ● She is upset *as* her son hasn't won the first prize.

subordinator of cause ↵   ⇑
pointing to a cause/reason   subordinate clause

(4) ● He ran fast *because* the last bus was about to depart.

main clause ↵   ⇑   ⇑
              subordinator   subordinate clause
          of reason – pointing to a reason

(5) ● *Because* the last bus was about to depart, he ran fast.

⇑   ⇑   ⇑
subordinator   subordinating clause   main clause

Here the subordinator started the sentence. It has enhanced the meaning of the sentence by expressing the reason for *running fast*. This way, it has established the relationship between the main clause and its subordinate clause.

(6) ● *If* you eat too much, you will get fat.

subordinator ↵   main clause ↵

In this example, the subordinator is indicating a condition and a predictable outcome.

(7) ● *If* you come late, you will not be allowed to enter the lecture hall.

subordinator ↵   ⇑   main clause ↵
indicating   subordinate clause
predictable possibility

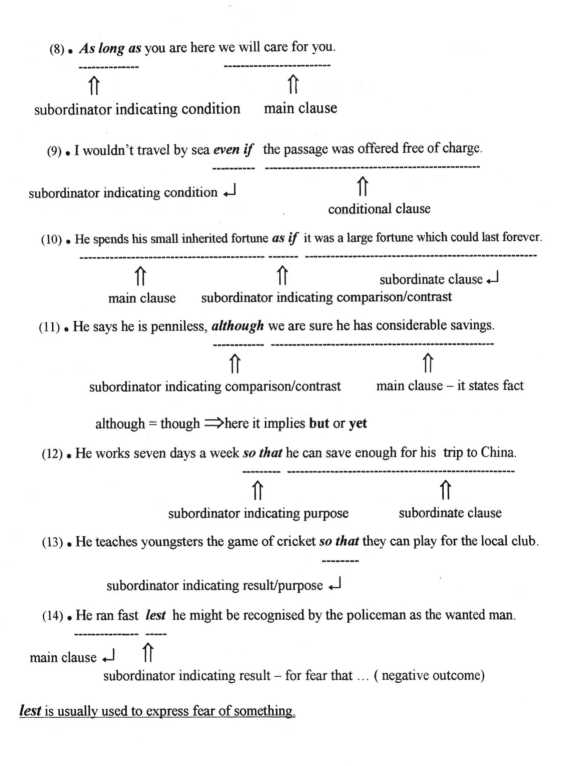

(8) • *As long as* you are here we will care for you.

⇑   ⇑

subordinator indicating condition   main clause

(9) • I wouldn't travel by sea *even if* the passage was offered free of charge.

subordinator indicating condition ↵   ⇑

                                           conditional clause

(10) • He spends his small inherited fortune *as if* it was a large fortune which could last forever.

⇑   ⇑   subordinate clause ↵

main clause   subordinator indicating comparison/contrast

(11) • He says he is penniless, *although* we are sure he has considerable savings.

⇑   ⇑

subordinator indicating comparison/contrast   main clause – it states fact

although = though ⇒ here it implies **but** or **yet**

(12) • He works seven days a week *so that* he can save enough for his trip to China.

⇑   ⇑

subordinator indicating purpose   subordinate clause

(13) • He teaches youngsters the game of cricket *so that* they can play for the local club.

subordinator indicating result/purpose ↵

(14) • He ran fast *lest* he might be recognised by the policeman as the wanted man.

main clause ↵   ⇑

         subordinator indicating result – for fear that ... (negative outcome)

lest is usually used to express fear of something.

(15) • I have written to some friends in Paris *in order to* invite them to the wedding.

          subordinator indicating purpose ↵   ⇑

                                            subordinate clause

(16) • Our television works *except that* the picture is poor.

subordinator indicating exception ↵   ⇑

                            subordinate noun clause ⇒ see Clauses

(17) • She would visit the hospital *except* she has little time to spare.

                    ⇑

             subordinator indicating exception

(18) • I'd prefer to walk to my hotel *rather than* travel in his car.

                  ⇑

           subordinator indicating preference

(19) • You should find out *where* the car was stolen.

                ⇑

           subordinator indicating place

(20) • He travels by car *wherever* he goes for his business in Europe.

               ⇑

          subordinator indicating place

(21) • We will decide tomorrow *whether* we can place an order for a new car.

                ⇑

          subordinator indicating possibility

(22) • I don't know *whether* I will be able to fly from Humberside Airport to Berlin.

         subordinator ↵ - indicating possibility/alternative

(23) • Our sales will decline *unless* we advertise our products.

⇑

subordinator indicating negative possibility

(24) • Their house doesn't have a back garden *unless* you call a backyard a back garden.

main statement ↵　　　　　　　　⇑　　　　　　　　⇑

subordinator adding　　　afterthought stated
an afterthought to the main statement

(25) • You can send it by e-mail *so that* they can receive this message now.

sentence 1 ↵　　　　　　⇑　　　　　　⇑

subordinator　　　sentence 2
linking two sentences

(26) • Can we have lunch together? *If* you wait until my lunch hour starts.

sentence 1 ↵　　　　⇑　　　　⇑

subordinator　　　sentence 2
linking two sentences

• **Some subordinating conjunctions also function as prepositions and adverbs.**
For instance:

(27) • I haven't seen you *since* last December.

⇑

functioning as preposition of time

(28) • I haven't seen you *since* you moved away .

⇑

functioning as subordinating conjunction

****

(29) • You have moved away and I haven't seen you *since*.
   ----

functioning as adverb ↵

(30) • You should have asked for it ***before***.
   ----

functioning as adverb ↵

(31) • The matter was brought ***before*** the tribunal.
   ----

functioning as preposition ↵

(32) • You must do it ***before*** you forget.

⇑

functioning as subordinating conjunction

- **<u>Examples of coordinators joining words of equal status:</u>**

   (1) • Slow ***and*** steady.

   ⇑

   coordinator ⇒ joins two words together

   (2) • fast *or* slow.

   ⇑

   coordinator ⇒ joins two words together

   (3) • The room was narrow *yet* long.
      -----

   coordinator joins two words ↵ - equal status ⇒ adjective with adjective

- ***Or*** has its negative counterpart ***nor***. One can use ***nor*** to coordinate clauses providing the first clause in a compound sentence relates to a negative idea or thought. It can also coordinate words as well as phrases. A phrase may be only a single word. See ⇒ phrases

For instance:

      (9) • She can't dance *nor* can she speak.

                               ------

coordinates negative clauses ↵

      (10) • The car could not move backward *or* forward.

                                        -----

                       coordinates words/phrases ↵

• **The pair *neither* ... *nor* does not join clauses but phrases**

For instance:

      (1) • Unfortunately, he *neither* hears *nor* speaks.

      (2) • She is *neither* rich *nor* poor.

• **The correlative pair of *but* ... *also* shows a mutual relationship**

For instance:

      (1) • ***Both*** Jack ***and*** Jill are likely to be present at the wedding.

            ------   ----

          ⇑   ⇑

correlactive pair of coordinators ⇒ equal grammatical status ⇒ ***noun with noun***

      (2) • He was a great Prime Minister, ***but also*** the winner of the Nobel Prize for Peace.

           ---------------------------   --------   --

                ⇑   ⇑   ⇑

             phrase 1   correlactive coordinator   phrase 2

In summary, conjunctions are widely used in phrases, clauses and sentences. There are ample examples of their usage in the next three chapters.

  • See ⇒ phrases. See ⇒ Clauses. See ⇒ Sentences

Part 2

Phrases, Clauses & Sentences

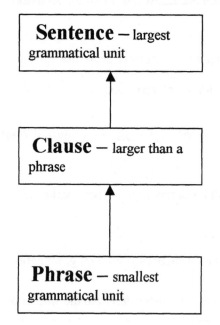

Chapter 9
Phrases

.Introduction

A phrase consists of words without a verb and a tense, but functions as a grammatical unit. On the other hand, a clause may be a distinct component of a sentence, or a separate group of words with a subject, verb and any compulsory elements. Table 1 contains some examples to illustrate the difference between these two groups of words, namely phrases and clauses:

Table 1

Phrases	Clauses
(a) • your book	(f) • My book is written by my friend.
(b) • in the car	(g) • He bought this car in London.
(c) • fine wine	(h) • You like that red wine from Wiesbaden in Germany.
(d) • a white pure silk scarf	(I) • He bought a white pure silk scarf.
(e) • all these overseas students in my class	(j) • All these overseas students in my class are clever.
⇑	⇑

• a phrase consists of a small group of words*   • a clause has a subject, and predicate

• a phrase does not have a finite verb   • a clause has a finite verb – key element

Strictly speaking, in grammar, a phrase may consists of one word or a group of words. However, the word phrase means to most people a group of words.

• Types of Phrases

A phrase has an internal structure. This is illustrated below:

(1) • my *book*

　　　　⇑

key word in this phrase is *book* ⇒ *noun* known as **headword**

(2) • very *old*

　　　　⇑

　　　headword ⇒ *old* ⇒ *adjective*

(3) • may have *gone*

　　　　⇑

　　　headword ⇒ *gone* ⇒ *verb*

(4) • very *slowly*.

　　　　⇑

　　　headword ⇒ *slowly* ⇒ *adverb*

(5) • *in* the house.

　　　⇑

　　　headword ⇒ *in* ⇒ *preposition*

These examples illustrate five different types of internal phrase structures. In each example, the internal structure is analysed in terms of its headword and its modifier. Let's consider another example:

(6) • certainly *nobody.*

--------- -------

⇑   ⇑

1   **2**

$\left\lceil 1+2 = \text{phrase} \right\rceil$

1 = adverb used to modify the pronoun nobody   2 = The headword ⇒ *nobody* ⇒ *pronoun*

• In these examples, each headword is either a noun or pronoun. Because of this noun or pronoun, each phrase is identified as a **noun phrase**. In fact, there are the following five main types of phrases:

          (1) • **Noun phrase**

          (2) • **Verb phrase**

          (3) • **Adverb phrase**

          (4) • **Adjective phrase**

          (5) • **Prepositional phrase**

• <u>How can you identify the type of phrase?</u>

As shown above, the headword is a key word, which enables us to identify the phrase type. If you know the class of the headword, you can identify any of the above types of phrases. Indeed, there are some exceptions to this rule. One exception to this rule is that a noun phrase does not always have a noun as a headword. This exception is exemplified by examples 4-6 above. The other exceptions are discussed with examples at the appropriate place in this chapter. The following examples show each type of phrase first.

      (1) . Joan likes *James* as a doctor.

             ⇑

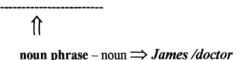

        noun phrase – noun ⇒ *James /doctor*

You can identify a phrase in a sentence. A sentence may have more than one phrase.

(2) • Our journey has finished.

                   ⇑

verb phrase - verb ⟹ ***has finished*** (see verb phrase for detail)

(3) • He returned quickly from the office.

                   ⇑

adverb phrase - adverb ⟹ ***quickly***

(4) • I am *very* pleased to see you.

                 ⇑

adjective phrase - adjective ⟹ ***very***

(5) • I have been thinking of you all day.

                 ⇑

prepositional phrase - preposition ⟹ ***of***

• <u>Noun Phrases</u>

Now, consider examples in Table 1 above:

example a: there is only one main word, which is *a **noun** ' book* '

example b: the main noun is preceded by ***a determiner*** ⟹ *the*

example c: there is only one main word, which is *a **pronoun*** ⟹ *you*

example e: the determiner, 'these' is preceded by another ***pre-determiner*** ⟹ *all*

In example 1 above the ***modifier*** is added after the main noun (James) to modify/qualify it ⟹ *as a doctor (modifier)*. The phrase is a noun phrase because the ***headword*** is a noun.

These examples illustrate that:

- a noun phrase will include **one headword** which may be a noun or pronoun, e.g.,

London $\Rightarrow$ noun or she $\Rightarrow$ *pronoun*

In fact, only one noun by itself is enough to make a noun phrase. A noun phrase is so called, as it has a noun or pronoun. In addition to this headword (noun or pronoun), a noun phrase may include:

- *a determiner* before the headword, e.g., *a* book, *the* map, *an* apple, *this* computer, *that* hat, *these* chairs, *those* ladies, *my* coat. Determiners occur at the beginning of a noun phrase <u>only</u>. See $\Rightarrow$ determiners.

- *a modifier* before the headword is used to modify the noun. A modifier may be another noun, an adjective, a verb used adjectivally (in 'kitchen knife' the word kitchen is used adjectivally) or a participle(a word formed from a verb, ending in -ing e.g., seeing $\Rightarrow$ participle). Here are some examples:

(6) • the *beautiful* women.

⇑

adjective used as $\Rightarrow$ *pre-modifier*

- When a modifier comes before the headword, it is called a *pre-modifier*. It is possible to **have more than one modifier as illustrated below:**

(7) • a *delicious hot* meal.
---------- ----
pre-modifier adjective 1 ↵   ⇑
                   pre-modifier adjective 2

In this example, the headword *meal* is pre-modified by both adjectives $\Rightarrow$*delicious* and *hot*

(8) • a *British insurance* company.
-------- -----------
pre-modifier adjective ↵   ⇑
                   pre-modifier noun

The headword *company* is pre-modified by:

an adjective $\Rightarrow$ ***British*** and a noun $\Rightarrow$ ***insurance***

• It is important to note that when the headword is pre-modified by more than one type of modifier, the pre-modifying noun comes near to the headword/noun. Therefore, 'an insurance British company' would be <u>incorrect</u>.

(9) • a really workable plan.

                      ------   -----------

pre-modifier adverb ⌐   ⇑

                 pre-modifier adjective

In this case, there are two pre-modifiers before the headword ***plan*** (= noun). Here, the noun is pre-modified by the adverb and the adjective.

• Examples 7, 8 and 9 demonstrate that you can have more than one adjective to pre-modify a the headword/noun. It is also possible to have an adverb and a noun to pre-modify the headword. For instance:

(10) • Indeed a police station

                      ---------   -------

pre-modifier adverb ⌐   ⇑

               pre-modifier noun

• <u>How many adjectives are permissible before the headword?</u>

There is no restriction on the number of adjectives which can come before the headword. However, if you use too many adjectives, their meanings may become blurred due to adjectives contrasting with each other. It is best to avoid using more than three adjectives before the headword. For instance:

(11) • a brave, dangerous, ruthless incursion.

              ------- --------------- --------- --------------

                ⇑   ⇑   ⇑   ⇑

         adjective adjective   adjective headword/noun

Here, the head noun is pre-modified by three adjectives.

• A participle can pre-modify the headword:

>   (12) • a running total.
>   ---------
>   ⇑
>
>   pre-modifier ⟹ *participle*   (running is also an adjective and a noun)

Running total means a total of expenses or whatever which includes each item as it occurs.

• The headword may be ***post-modified***. Post-modifiers come after the headword. These may prove to be more complex than pre-modifiers are. The reason for this complexity is that a variety of elements can function as a post-modifier. This is illustrated below:

>   (13) • a new bookshop in our shopping precinct.
>   -- ---- ----------- ---------------------------------
>   ⇑ ⇑   ⇑   ⇑
>   1   2   3   post-modifier/qualifier
>   **prepositional phrase** – here *in* is a preposition of place
>
>   **1** = determiner   **2** = pre-modifier - adjective   **3** = headword/noun

After the headword/noun, a prepositional phrase is added to qualify or pre-modify the headword. There can be more than one pre-modifier:

>   (14) • a new bookshop in our shopping precinct which is a good idea.
>   ----------- --------------------------- -------------------------
>   ⇑   ⇑   ⇑
>   **headword** ↵   **prepositional phrase**   **relative clause**

Example (14) is expanded by adding a relative clause. Thus, the headword is pre-modified by a prepositional phrase and by a relative clause.

>   (15) • the small shop on the corner from where I buy newspapers.

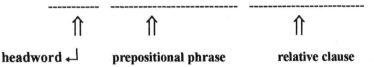

>   ⇑ ⇑   ⇑   ⇑   ⇑   ⇑
>   **1** **2**   **3**   **4**   **5**   **6**

****

1 = pre-determiner

2 = determiner – adjective modifying the noun $\Longrightarrow$ *shop*

3 = headword - *shop*

4 = adverb phrase modifying the noun $\Longrightarrow$ *shop*

5 = prepositional phrase of place modifying the noun $\Longrightarrow$ *shop*

6 = clause modifying the noun $\Longrightarrow$ *shop*

- This example shows that the headword/noun can be post-modified by both phrases and clauses. In addition, it illustrates that several phrases can be joined together. This example has three phrases put together to make one long phrase.

How big can a phrase be?

The size of a phrase is not restricted. The idea is not to make it too long. If you do so, your reader or listener may not receive it well. It is worth mentioning here that the largest unit of construction is a sentence. The second largest unit of construction is a clause. As a unit of construction, then, the smallest unit of construction is the phrase. The fact is that phrases are formed from words and clauses are formed from phrases. Therefore, the clause as a unit of construction is larger than the phrase. Phrases constitute clauses. All three constructions are units of syntactic (connected with grammatical rules and structures) constructions.

- Possessive pronouns both proper and common can also be used as determiners:

(16) • James's son-in-law from the USA.
```
     ----------  -------------  -------------------
         ⇑              ⇑                 ⇑
    determiner     headword     another phrase functioning as qualifier/post-modifier
possessive ⤶
proper noun
```

(17) • *the children's* birthday party.   (note: not childrens, but the children's)
```
     ----------------  ----------  ------
          ⇑               ⇑          ⇑
     determiner       qualifier   headword
possessive ⤶
common noun
```

• Noun phrases can function as the subject and the object of a sentence:

(18) • *The policeman* arrested the suspect.

⟰

Noun phrase functioning as the *subject* of this sentence.

(19) • I asked *the traffic warden*.

⟰

Noun phrase functioning as the *object* of a sentence.

• A *complement is* an adjective or a noun which comes after a *linking* or *copula* or *copular verb*. A linking, a copula and a copular verb all mean the same. See ⟹ copular verbs.

The noun phrase can function as a complement that is as an *object*. For instance:

(20) • He seemed **to be** *an expert in mathematics.*

copula verb ↵ ⟰

describing the subject   *noun phrase* functioning as ⟹ *object*

When the complement is a noun phrase, and the copula is 'seem' or 'look', use *to be* in order to describe or identify the subject:

(21) • He looks to be *a perpetrator*.

⟰

noun phrase functioning as ⟹ *object*

One can leave out '*to be*', if the noun phrase gives some other kinds of information instead of identifying the subject.

• A noun phrase may be followed by another noun phrase. In such cases, the purpose of a second noun phrase is to give explanatory information about the headword/noun. The second phrase is termed as an *apposition* to the first phrase. Here are two examples:

(22) • York city, in north-east England, is visited by 3 million tourists a year.

⇑   ⇑

first phrase   second phrase

(23) • Gamal Abdel Nasser, once president of Egypt, nationalised the Suez Canal.

⇑   ⇑

first phrase   second phrase

• <u>Verb Phrases</u>

The headword of a verb phrase is a verb. A verb phrase may have only one base verb. Here are two verb phrases. Each has only one word, which is the base/basic form of the verb given in a dictionary:

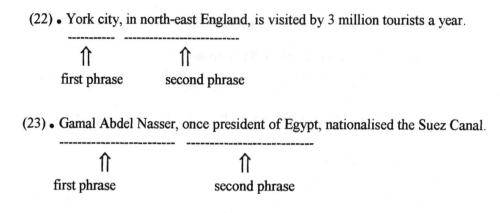

(1) • Go   (2) • See

⇑   ⇑

headword *go* ⇒ *base verb form*   headword *see* ⇒ *base verb form*

• The headword (main verb) of a verb phrase may be one of the following forms:

• *the base form* – arise, catch, know, show:

    (3) • I *arise* at 6 am.

    (4) • They *know* me well.

• *the present 's' form* – writes, talks, sees, goes, loves, washes:

    (5) • Anna *writes* to me regularly.

    (6) • She *loves* both her children.

• *present participle –ing form* - dancing, running, singing, talking, writing walking:

(7) • We *are talking* about your success.

(8) • She *is singing* her own song.

• *Past participle -ed form* (both regular and irregular verbs) - driven, felt,
ran, sung, striven, talked, torn, understood, written:

(9) • I *have written* to her today.

(10) • She *has understood* you.

• Verb Tense

A verb phrase always has a verb as its head. A verb always has a tense. Therefore, it is important to understand the relationship between tenses and phrases. First, consider the following examples:

(1) • Janet **laughs** a lot.

present tense - verb **laughs** ⟹ present tense –s form of the regular verb **laugh**

(2) • I **work** here.

⇑

present tense - the verb **work** ⟹ present tense – **base** form of the regular verb **work**

(3) • I **proved** that he was wrong.

past tense - the verb proved ⟹ past tense **-ed form** for the irregular verb **prove**

(4) • Jane **left** the office a few minutes ago.

past tense - the verb **left** ⟹ past tense **-ed form** for the irregular verb **leave**

****

These two examples illustrate that verbs are used to express time when the action of a verb takes place. The word *'tempus'* is a Latin word, which means time. The word *tense* is a derivative of this Latin word. Therefore, the **present tense** means the present time (now). Similarly, the **past tense** means the past time (then).

- The tense is a form of a verb as shown above. It is either the present or past tense.

- In English, the verb tense is marked by *inflection* (change in the form of a word, especially the ending) for the *present tense* and *past tense* only.

- There are other tenses, which are marked by other means. All sixteen tenses are summarised in Table 1 in this chapter. Before we discuss tenses, it is desirable to understand what we mean by verb concord or verb agreement.

.Verb Concord or Agreement

Verb concord or agreement is a rule, which states that the form of the verb is dictated by the person and number of the subject. Let's apply this rule to the following examples:

(1) • I *travel* today.

       ⇑ ⇑
       1 2

1 is a subject   *I* ⇒ first person and single (number)

2 is a verb   *travel* ⇒ It is the *base/infinitive* form of the verb.

In this example, in accordance with the verb concord, the verb form is agreed with the person and number of the subject.

(2) • She *speaks* German well.

      ⇑   ⇑
      1   2

1 is the subject *she* ⇒ third person and single (number)

2 is a verb $\Longrightarrow$ It is –*s* **inflection** which marks the third person singular of the ***present tense*** as demonstrated above. This way, the verb form agrees with the <u>third person singular.</u>

(3) • They ***work*** in a restaurant.

1 is the subject ***they*** $\Longrightarrow$ third person and plural

2 is a verb $\Longrightarrow$ it is the ***basic/infinitive*** present form of the verb. Here, the verb agrees with the third person and is plural (number).

(4) • I ***lived*** in London some years ago.

⇑ ⇑
1 **2**

1 is a subject ***I*** $\Longrightarrow$ first person and singular

2 is a verb $\Longrightarrow$ it is the *-ed **past or participle form*** $\Longrightarrow$ *regular form*

(5) • You ***left*** England yesterday.

⇑ ⇑
1 **2**

1 is the subject ***you*** $\Longrightarrow$ second person and singular

2 is a verb $\Longrightarrow$ it is the *-ed **past or participle form*** $\Longrightarrow$ **irregular form**.

Here, the verb agrees with the person and number of the subject. ***Past tense***.

• <u>The essence of concord is that the subject controls the form of the verb. This rule is applied in all sixteen tenses discussed later in this chapter.</u>

.Finite and Non-finite Verbs

- In the following examples, the verb is marked for tense. When a verb is marked for tense, it is called a *finite verb or* a *finite verb phrase*. A finite verb may be the only verb in a sentence. You can have a finite verb in both main and sub-ordinate clauses.

See ⟹ Clauses.

Here are some examples:

(1) ● He *breeds* ducks.

⇑

finite verb - present tense form

- The relationship between the verb *'breeds'* and the subject *'he'* is in concord (agreement).

(2) ● Anne *travels* to Russia twice a year.

⇑

finite verb - present tense form

- The relationship between the verb *'travels'* and the subject *'Anne'* is in concord (agreement).

(3) ● I always *buy* some flowers for my wife.

⇑

finite verb - present tense

- The relationship between the verb *'buy'* and the subject *'you'* is in concord (agreement).

(4) ● We *love* their new cottage in the country.

⇑

finite verb - present tense

- The relationship between the verb *'love'* and the subject *'we'* is in concord (agreement).

(5) . I *joined* your book club.

⇑

finite verb - ***past tense***

- The relationship between the verb *'joined'* and the subject *'I'* is in concord (agreement).

(6) . You *interviewed* her the other day for a job.

⇑

finite verb - ***past tense***

- The relationship between the verb *'interviewed'* and the subject *'you'* is in concord (agreement).

(7) . We *went* to Switzerland last year.

⇑

This verb phrase contains a finite irregular verb

The finite irregular verb ***go*** changes its form for the past tense by becoming ***went***.
This is equivalent to the past participle **-ed** form. There are many such irregular verbs.
See ⇒Verbs.

- The relationship between the verb *'went'* and the subject *'we'* is in concord (agreement).

- A sentence must have one finite verb. See ⇒ Clauses also Sentences.

- A non –finite verb is not marked for tense. The non-finite verb phrase can contain one of the following verb forms:

  - ***infinitive*** - the base form of a verb   - ***gerund*** - the –ing form of a verb

  - ***participle*** – it has two forms:

    (1) . the -ing from = the present participle or

    (2) . the – ed from = the past participle

The non-finite phrase does not give information in the same way as the finite phrase gives on tense (time). It does not take a subject. All verbs except modal auxiliaries have non-finite forms. See Modal Auxiliaries. Here are some examples of non-finite phrases:

(1) • serious to study

              ⇑

         to- infinitive form ⟹ non-finite phrase

(2) • slow going

              ⇑

         gerund form ⟹ non-finite verb

(3) • appearing on screen

              ⇑

         participle form ⟹ non-finite verb

• With an auxiliary verb, a non-finite verb can express a tense. For instance:

• The past participle '–d' form, depending on the context, can function as finite and non-finite:

(4) • Some young hooligans attacked Maria in the street.

                        ⇑

                    finite verb ⟹ *past tense*

(5) • We saw Maria attacked by some young hooligans in the street.

                        ⇑

         non-finite participle verb – it has no subject and tense

• A sentence can have both finite and non-finite phrases. Here are two examples:

(5) • We *wished to travel* together.

finite verb phrase⌐   ⇑

                  non-finite verb phrase

(6) • The doorman *asked* us *to show* our tickets.

finite verb phrase⌐   ⇑

           non-finite verb phrase

Now we can examine tenses in some detail.

1. <u>Present Tense or Simple Present Tense</u>

The present tense is used to express a present action or state that exists now. Let's first examine the following examples:

(1) • I *walk* all the way.   this sentence has a subject ⟹ *I singular first person*

⇑

verb phrase indicating present tense formed from the base form of the verb ⟹*walk*

(2) • You *talk* to him.   here subject ⟹*you second person singular/plural*

⇑

verb phrase indicating present tense formed from the base form of the verb ⟹*talk*

(3) • He/she *runs* fast.   here subject ⟹ *he/she third person singular*

⇑

verb phrase indicating present tense formed by an **-s inflection** in the third person singular

on verb ⟹*run*

(4) . They *sing* nicely.   **here** the subject $\Rightarrow$ *they third person plural*

           ⇑

verb phrase indicating present tense formed from the base verb $\Rightarrow$ *sing*

- These examples illustrate that the base form of the verb is used for all persons, except the third person singular. For the third person singular the verb form changes by – *s inflection.* Here are some more examples of the present tense used in verb phrases:

  (5) . He *lectures* on Russian literature $\Rightarrow$ *indicates recurrence of event*

  (6) . We *arrive* the next day $\Rightarrow$ *indicating future*

  (7) . He *loves* his family very much $\Rightarrow$ *indicating feelings/state*

  (8) . This car *belongs* to my brother $\Rightarrow$ *indicating relation/state*

  (9) . Water *is* essential for our survival $\Rightarrow$ *indicating fact true at all times*

  (10) . I *think* it's a great idea $\Rightarrow$ *indicating opinion/state*

2 . Present Progressive/Continuous Tense

The present progressive tense indicates that the action is continuous. It is still happening. The present continuous can also be used for present states which last for some time. For permanent states, use the simple present tense. The following examples demonstrate the use of this tense in verb phrases:

  (1) . I *am working* hard to pass my examinations. $\Rightarrow$ *indicating action over a period of time*

  (2) . She *is cooking* our lunch. $\Rightarrow$ *indicating someone in the middle of doing something*

  (3) . They *are coming* to stay with us tomorrow. $\Rightarrow$ *talking about some future*
                                              arrangements – stay

  (4) . We *are* always *dining* in that restaurant every Friday.

           ⇑

      always shows that something has been happening for some time

(5) • After answering a telephone call, she *is feeling* depressed. $\Longrightarrow$ *indicating a temporary state of one's mind*

(6) • This afternoon our car sales *are looking* poor. $\Longrightarrow$ *temporary state of business*

In order to construct the present progressive tense, place the present form of the auxiliary **be** before the participle form '**ing**'. It is easy to remember it as:

. *The present progressive tense = present form of be + participle form 'ing'*

3 • Past Tense

The Past tense describes an event which has already happened or a state of something which existed at a particular time **(then)** before the present time**(now)**. The following examples illustrate the construction of verb phrases indicating the past tense, which is also known as the *__simple past tense__*.

(1) • I *walked* to Chelsea.

⇑ ⇑   ⇑
1   2   3

Here:

1 = subject first person singular. Also I is a *pronoun*

1 = *verb phrase* indicating the past tense formed from the past participle – ed (-ed inflection) the regular verb $\Longrightarrow$*walk*

3 = *noun phrase* The preposition *to* can occur before a noun.

(2) • Robin *managed* his family business well. **here** the subject $\Longrightarrow$*Robin third person singular*

⇑

verb indicating past tense formed from the past participle -ed form (-ed inflection) the regular verb $\Longrightarrow$***manage***

(3) • You *led* your team successfully.   **here** the subject $\Longrightarrow$ second *person singular*

⇑

verb indicating the past tense formed from the past tense form of the irregular verb $\Longrightarrow$*lead*

(4) • We *bought* a cottage in Wales.   **here** the subject $\Rightarrow$ first *person plural*

⇑

verb phrase indicating past tense formed from the past tense form of the irregular verb $\Rightarrow$***buy***

- Examples 1 and 2 demonstrate that the past participle form 'ed' inflection of regular verbs is used to form the past tense.

- Examples 3 and 4 show that the past tense form of the irregular verbs is also used to form the past tense.

- Some examples of using the past tense in verb phrases:

    (5) • She *said* that she *was* an actress. $\Rightarrow$***reported speech***

    (6) • They announced that our train *arrive*d on time. $\Rightarrow$***reported speech***

    (7) • We *went* to school everyday by car. $\Rightarrow$***describes past event***

    (8) • Once upon a time we *lived* in that house. $\Rightarrow$***describes past circumstance***

    (9) • Was he unconscious when you *arrived* at the scene? $\Rightarrow$***inquires about the past condition/state of a person***

    (10) • There *was* no rain. $\Rightarrow$***describes state or environmental condition***

4 • <u>Past Progressive Tense</u>

The past progressive/continuous tense is used to express what was happening at some point in time in the past. In order to express the past continuous state such as feelings, normally the simple past tense is used. Sometimes for a temporary state, one can use the past progressive tense. The following examples illustrate the use of this tense:

    (1) • I *was swimming* in the sea. $\Rightarrow$ indicating action over a period of past time

    (2) • He *was working* every day seven days a week. $\Rightarrow$indicating action over a whole period

    (3) • We *were training* our staff when the fire broke out. $\Rightarrow$ indicating sudden occurrence when in the middle of doing something

    (4) • Due to an industrial strike, we *were working* from home that day. $\Rightarrow$ indicating temporary action for a short period

(5) . She *was crying*. $\Longrightarrow$ indicating temporary feeling.   (she cried = past tense)

To summarise:

- **The past progressive tense = past form of be + participle form'ing'**

5. <u>Future Tense</u>

The future tense expresses actions or states which will happen in the future. It also describes the future in the past. The future tense is formed using an auxiliary verb with the bare infinitive form of the verb. We can summarise the construction of *<u>simple future tenses</u>* as:

- <u>Future tense = auxiliary will or shall + bare infinitive verb form</u>

<u>Traditionally</u>

shall $\Longrightarrow$ *was used for the first person subject*

will $\Longrightarrow$ *was used for the second and third person subject*

<u>Present-day</u>

For the first person subject $\Longrightarrow$ *use either shall or will*

For other subjects $\Longrightarrow$ *use will*

See $\Longrightarrow$ Shall and Will

Here are some examples of verb phrases with the future tense:

(1) . I *shall visit* you soon in Germany. $\Longrightarrow$ *will* may be used with first person singular subject

(2) . He will help you.

(3) . They *will come* to see us next year.

(4) . *We'll telephone* you on our arrival.

(5) . It *will go* by airmail tonight.

****

• The future in the past is expressed by the future tense by using *would* form of the auxiliary *will*:

(6) • Angelica *told* Thomas that he *would arrive* on time.

           past tense   **future in the past**

(7) • You *promised* that we *would write* this article together.

           past tense   **future in the past**

The future can also be expressed in some other ways. Here we are discussing tenses rather than the future.

6 • <u>Future Progressive Tense</u>

The future progressive expresses an action that is continuous over a period in the future. It is constructed as:

> ***Future Progressive tense = shall/will + be + participle form – ing form***

Here are some examples of the future progressive tense showing the relationship between the information conveyed by the verb phrase and time/tense, when these were uttered:

(1) • I *shall/will be going* to see my mother soon.

(2) • We shall/will be drinking in that pub over there.

(3) • Everyone *will be cheering* when you appear on the stage.

(4) •They *will be serving* us as soon as we take our seats.

7 • <u>Perfect or Present Perfect Tense</u>

The perfect or present perfect indicates that the action or state is complete in the near past up to the present time. This is just the opposite to the simple past, which denotes that the action or state ended in the past.

(1) • Our guest *arrived*.

⇑

It means that the action was completed in the past.

• When did they arrive?

The only conclusion we can draw from this statement is that they arrived in past time. It does not tell us that the past was a day ago, a month ago or whenever. Thus, the action of arrival finished in the past.

(2) • Our guests *have arrived*.

⇑

It means that the action was completed in the near past that is up to the present time.

• When have they arrived?

It means that our guests have arrived presently and that they are here now. (⟹ present time)

(3) • She *felt rotten* for leaving her children behind.

⇑

The action was completed in the past. We do not know when in the past.

(4) • She *has felt rotten* for leaving her children behind.

⇑

It implies that the action was completed in the near past up to the present time.

The construction of the present perfect tense can be visualised as:

• Present perfect = present of auxiliary verb have + past participle

This is further illustrated below:

(1) • He *has sheltered* his manager from criticism.

----

present perfect ↵

In accordance with the concord, the verb is in agreement with the subject *he*. '**has**' is the singular form of the primary auxiliary verb **have**.

(2) ● We *have written* to them for a copy of the contract.

present perfect ↵ - irregular verb ⟹ *write* its past participle form ⟹*written*

(3) ● Our hosts *have shown* us the area by car.

present perfect ↵ - irregular verb ⟹ *show* its past participle form ⟹*shown*

8 ● <u>Present Perfect Progressive Tense</u>

The present perfect continuous/progressive is used to express an action over a period of time in the past and is continuing up-to the present time. Its method of construction can be outlined as:

● *<u>Present perfect progressive tense = present of have + been + participle form ing</u>*

The following examples illustrate the application of this mode of expression:

(1) ● She *has been working* with us for four years.

present perfect continuous ↵ - shows repeated action - working up to now/present time.

(2) ● We *have been living* in this building since it was built.

present perfect continuous ↵ - shows repeated action

(3) ● They *have been singing* on stage for a living for the last five years.

present perfect continuous ↵ - shows repeated action

● The present perfect continuous is not used to express state ('I believe you.' believe = state).

9. Past Perfect Tense

The past perfect tense is used to express an action or a state that happened or existed some time ago in the past. It is constructed as:

- ***Past perfect tense = past of auxiliary verb have + past participle***

The following examples exemplify the use of the past perfect tense:

(1) . I *had received* many such requests before.
   ----

past perfect ↵ - shows an action in the distant past

(2) . This was a request for money. I *had received* such requests before.
                           ----

    past perfect ↵ - relates to action occurred in the distant past

(3) . They *had planned* their trip some time ago.
   ----

   past perfect ↵ - action before a past time

(4) . They *had thought* about their own families.
   ----

past perfect tense ↵- points to a state that existed in their minds in the distant past

(5) . We *had admired* their courage.
   ----

past perfect tense ↵- shows a state ⟹ approval in the distance past

(6) . We had had a new car then.
   ----

   past perfect tense ↵- shows a state ⟹ownership/own in the distant past

• Note that sometimes the past perfect is called **the pluperfect (Latin: Plus quam Perfectum)**

10 . <u>Past Perfect Progressive Tense</u>

The past perfect progressive is used to indicate a continuous action over a period of time in the past. It is described as:

   • *<u>Past perfect progressive tense = past of have + been + participle form - ing</u>*

This is illustrated below:

(1) • I *had been travelling* all day.
            ----

past perfect progressive ↵

It indicates a continuous action(travelling) in the past continuous it happened in the distant past.

(2) • We *had been running* early in the morning to get fit for this race.
            ----

past perfect progressive ↵

(3) • In those days, our business *had been doing* very well.
                  ----

                  past perfect progressive ↵

(4) • When I met her, she *had been shopping* at Harrods of Knightsbridge London.
                ----

            past perfect progressive ↵

• This does not mean that I met her during her shopping at Harrods, but after her shopping. If you wish to say that you met her during her shopping period/time, use the ***past progressive tense*** as shown below:

   • When I met her, she was shopping at Harrods of Knightsbridge London.
                  ----

   past progressive tense ↵

---

(5) . When our guests arrived, I *had been cooking* for them.

----

        past progressive tense ↵ - points to an ongoing action ⟹ in the distant past

. In all these cases, it implies a continuous action in the distant past. The continuity in the distant past is at the heart of the past perfect continuous tense. A few more examples are:

(6) . We were in France. We *had been enjoying* our long weekend in Paris.

(7) . She *had been studying at Warsaw University* when I moved to Poland.

(8) . When we saw Robin last time, he *had been distributing* leaflets for another
        musical show on the doorstep of the Carlton Club.

These examples illustrate that the past perfect continuous tense is used only in the past context.

11 . <u>Future Perfect Tense</u>

The future perfect tense is used when the speaker or the writer is thinking about the future, and then looks back when something will be completed at a specific point in the future time. It is constructed as:

. ***future perfect tense = will/shall + have + past participle(- ed/en/ other ending)***

For example:

(1) . By next month, they *will have submitted* our report to the director.

    thinking about the future   saying by next month (specific point in future time)

                                     report will be submitted ⟹ looking back into the future

(2) . Three days' stay is enough in Berlin, as you *will have seen* its main attractions within
                                                                        this time.

    projecting into the future   saying in three days (specific point in future time) all main

                                     places will be visited ⟹ looking back into the future

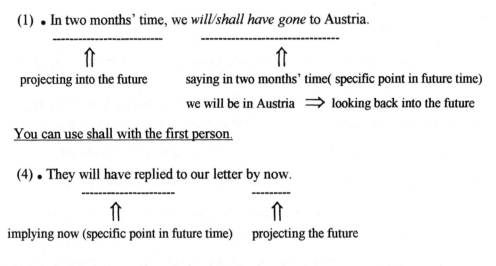

(1) • In two months' time, we *will/shall have gone* to Austria.

       ⇑   ⇑

   projecting into the future   saying in two months' time(specific point in future time)

                           we will be in Austria ⟹ looking back into the future

<u>You can use shall with the first person.</u>

(4) • They will have replied to our letter by now.

       ⇑   ⇑

implying now (specific point in future time)   projecting the future

12 • <u>Future Perfect Progressive Tense</u>

The future perfect progressive tense is used when the speaker or the writer is thinking about something and then looks back when something will be completed at a specific point in the future time. It is constructed as:

• *<u>future perfect progressive tense = will/shall + have +been + participle –ing ending</u>*

    (1) • At the end of January, *I shall/will have been living* in London.

    (2) • Tomorrow night, we *will have been crossing* the English Channel by a night ferry.

    (3) • She wants us to marry next summer, as we *will have been living* in our new home.

    (4) • You will have been staying with us in three weeks' time.

• <u>It shows continuity in the future.</u>

Tenses show that there are many facets of verb phrases. When an **auxiliary verb** is added to the **lexical verb** (main verb) to construct a verb phrase, the auxiliary verb helps us to make a statement. Indeed, tenses contain verb phrases. Tenses enable us to express an extensive range of astonishing meanings. In Table 1, you can see at a glance the full working of all tenses. It is a summary of the information embedded in each statement, and the relationship between the **information** and the **time** (tense) when it was enacted or spoken.

13 . Future in the Past

The future in the past is looking forward to the future from the past. You can imagine it as your intention of doing something in the future but in the past time. For instance:

(1) . I *should/ would travel* to France to see Paris. ⇐ simple future in the past
    (travel in the future ahead of the present time but in the past time)

(2) . I *should/ would be travelling* to France to see Paris. ⇐ future progressive in the past

(3) . I *should/ would have travelled* to France to see Paris. ⇐ future perfect in the past

(4) . I *should/ would have been travelling* to France to see Paris.⇐ future perfect
                                                    progressive in the past

A Summary of Tenses

Present Simple	Past Simple	Future Simple	Simple future in the Past
I go	I went	I shall/will go	I should/would go
Present Progressive	**Past Progressive**	**Future Progressive**	**Future Progressive in the Past**
I am going	I was going	I shall/will be going	I should/would be going
Present Perfect	**Past Perfect**	**Future Perfect**	**Future Perfect in the Past**
I have gone	I had gone	I shall/will have gone	I should/would have gone
Present Perfect Progressive	**Past Perfect Progressive**	**Future Perfect Progressive**	**Future Perfect Progressive in the Past**
I have been going	I had been going	I shall/will have been going	I should/would have been going

Table 1

. <u>Adverb Phrases</u>

An adverb phrase may consist of only a headword, which is an adverb. It may be a group of words, in which the headword is an adverb. It does not contain a finite verb. On the contrary, an adverb clause contains a finite verb. See $\Rightarrow$ Clauses.

An adverb phrase contains an adverb, and can modify an adjective or adverb.

Let's examine some examples:

(1) . She walks *slowly*.

               ⇑

adverb phrase of manner ***headword*** $\Rightarrow$ ***slowly*** -   (describes how she walks)

Here, the adverb phrase consists of only the headword. <u>*The headword or the main word is an adverb*</u>.

(2) . You can enter the main library ***through this doorway***.

                                   ⇑

adverb phrase of place consists of three words ***through*** $\Rightarrow$ ***adverb***

(3) . He left our home ***fairly quickly***.

                     ⇑

adverb phrase of time consists of two adverbs $\Rightarrow$ ***fairly*** and ***quickly***

The **adverb fairly** *is pre-modifying the other* <u>**adverb quickly**</u> *by intensifying the meaning of the adverb quickly. See* $\Rightarrow$ *Intensifiers.*

(4) . We found travelling by buses in that country ***incredibly slow***.

                                     ⇑
                          adverb phrase of time

The **adverb incredibly** is pre-modifying the <u>adjective slow</u>. Thus, the pre-modifier **incredibly** intensifies the meaning of the **adjective slow**. Here, it functions as an intensifier.

(5) • This reason is not *really sufficient* to secure a loan.

⇑   ⇑

adverb   adjective

adverb is modifying the adjective ↵

This is an example of an adverb phrase of *degree*. An adverb of degree can be used before some adverbs and adjectives. By degree, we mean an extent, or a measure of something. In this case, the *adverb really* is used to express the actual fact or truth about something. Here, it is about the reason to secure a loan. The adverb *really* is pre-modifying the *<u>adjective sufficient</u>*.

(6) • The cake is *quite tasty*.

adverb phrase of degree ↵

In this context, the *adverb quite* means somewhat, to some extent, not very or fairly. The *adjective tasty* is premodified by the *adverb quite*. In fact, *quite* intensifies the meaning of the *adjective tasty*. It attaches to this cake's quality a medium degree(a measure of taste). The word *delicious* is another adjective. When *quite* is used with delicious, it expresses a different meaning. For instance:

(7) • The cake is *quite delicious*.

adverb phrase of degree ↵

In this example, the *adverb quite* is pre-modifying the *<u>adjective delicious</u>*. Depending on the meaning of the *adjective delicious*, the adverb quite means completely to the full extent.

(8) • My son speaks German *fluently*.

adverb of manner ↵

(9) • You must take action *quickly*.

adverb of manner ↵

• An adverb of manner modifies a verb.

In examples 8-9, the *adverbs fluently and quickly* are modifying the *verbs speaks* and *must take* respectively.

Most adverbs of manner are formed from adjectives. Often they end with *-ly*. Of course, there are a few adverbs of manner without *-ly* endings (e.g. fast, loud). The following two examples show the use of adverbs of manner <u>without</u> *-ly* endings: See ⟹ Adverbs ⟹ Chapter 5.

(10) • You should do your best to do it *right* next time.
          ----
          adverb of manner ↵ – it answers the question *how*?

(11) • She often arrives *late* by train.
          -----
          adverb of manner ↵ – it answers the question *when* ? - **late** <u>or</u>
                                                        how? - **by train**

• It is unusual to postmodify the head adverb with an another adverb. For instance:

(12) • Indeed I visit them *sometimes*.
          ----
          adverb of time ↵
sometimes ⟹ adverb post-modified by another adverb ⟹ *indeed*

The pre-modifier adverb **indeed** intensifies the meaning of the adverb **sometimes**. This is rather formal. See ⟹ Prepositional Phrase and Clauses and for pre-modifiers.

• Adjective Phrases

An adjective phrase may consist of only a headword, which is an adjective. It may be a group of words in which the headword is an adjective. <u>An adjective phrase does not contain a finite verb</u>. It has an adjective. These phrases are similar to adverb phrases. Like adverb phrases, adjective phrases can also be modified. Like an adverb phrase, sometimes, it has an adverb of degree.

Here are some examples:

(1) • He is ***brave***.

⇑

adjective phrase

headword ⟹ *adjective* ⟹ ***brave*** *- just a single word*

(2) • *It is **easy** to carry it.*

⇑

adjective phrase *headword* ⟹ *adjective* ⟹ ***easy***

(3) • He is ***very brave***.
      ----

adjective phrase ↵ - ***very*** ⟹ adverb of degree before an adjective

This adjective phrase consists of one adjective and one adverb.

headword ⟹ *adjective* ⟹ *brave* is pre-modified *very* ⟹***adverb***

• When ***very*** is used before an adjective, it is an adverb.

(4) • This is ***good enough*** for me.
      ----

adjective phrase ↵

headword ⟹ *adverb* ⟹ *enough* is pre-modified by adjective ⟹***good***

(5) • We went to see a film, but the cinema was ***almost empty***.
                                                  ----

adjective phrase ↵

headword ⟹ *adjective* ⟹ *empty* is pre-modified by adverb ⟹***almost***

• ***Almost***, ***nearly*** and ***practically*** are adverbs of degree with similar meanings. For instance:

****

(6) • The hall is *practically/nearly/almost full* with the audience.
----
adjective phrase ↵

headword ⟹ *adjective* ⟹ *full* is pre-modified by adverb ⟹*practically/nearly /almost*

(7) • He was finding his living without a job *so difficult* that he sold his car.
----
adjective phrase ↵

headword ⟹ *adjective* ⟹ *difficult* is pre-modified by *adverb* ⟹*so*

(8) • It was *extremely noisy* when the police arrived at the party.
----
adjective phrase ↵

headword ⟹ *adjective* ⟹ *noisy* is pre-modified by *adverb of degree* ⟹*extremely*

• Prepositional Phrases

What you have seen so far is that all four types of phrases have one thing in common, which is a headword. Indeed, in these types of phrases the headword can stand alone. In prepositional phrases, the headword cannot stand alone. *Why is it so?*

The headword, in a prepositional phrase, is a preposition. The headword and the prepositional complement together form the prepositional phrase. Without the prepositional complement, the prepositional phrase is incomplete. Thus, the headword in a prepositional phrase cannot stand alone. Usually, the *prepositional complement* is a noun phrase. The typical structure of a prepositional phrase may be represented as:

Prepositional phrase = headword + prepositional complement

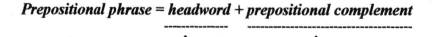

       ⇑   ⇑

     preposition   *noun phrase*

• A prepositional phrase may be complemented by certain types of clauses. See ⟹ Clauses.

• A preposition can be a single word or a group of words. *See* ⇒ *Prepositions*.

Here are some examples of prepositional phrases:

(1) • Sarah sat *next to her husband Robin*.

⇑   ⇑

headword/group preposition(two words)   prepositional component ⇒ *noun phrase*

⇑

meaning in a position right beside her husband Robin

In fact, the preposition *next to* is complemented by the noun phrase *her husband Robin*.

In this example, according to:

prepositional phrase = *preposition(headword)* + *noun or noun phrase*

the prepositional phrase is *next to her husband Robin*.

(2) • You can walk *along the footpath*.

⇑   ⇑

Preposition + noun phrase = prepositional phrase

Here, the preposition *along* is complemented by the noun phrase *the footpath*.

(3) • Rachel was walking *towards Tesco supermarket*.

⇑   ⇑

Preposition + noun phrase = prepositional phrase

(4) • Everything must be ready *before this evening's seminar*.

Preposition + noun phrase = prepositional phrase

Some more examples of prepositional phrases are shown in italics:

(5) • She looks nothing *like her sister*.   *like(means similar)* ⟹ *preposition*

(6) • Our house is situated *behind the church*.

(7) • He has been my best friend *since my childhood*.

   (The word *since* also functions as a conjunction and an adverb.)

(8) • I want to go out *for ten minutes*.

• <u>A prepositional phrase can function as the complement of a verb or adjective:</u> For instance:

(9) • She is *in a rush*.

            ⇑

   Prepositional phrase ⟹complement of verb ⟹*is*

(10) • It is big *for my family*.

                ⇑

   Prepositional phrase ⟹complement of adjective ⟹*big*

Here are some more examples:

(11) • You do not have to be sorry *for us*.

(12) • We have spent a lot *of money*.

(13) • He was singing *on the stage*.

(14) • They were running *towards a bus stop*.

• <u>A prepositional phrase can function as post-modifier:</u>

(15) • He is a *heavyweight boxer of great achievements*.
          -------------------------- ---------------------------
               ⇑   ⇑
          noun phrase   preposition phrase

The headword of noun phrase $\Rightarrow$ **boxer** *is pre-modified by an adjective* $\Rightarrow$ **heavyweight**
and *post-modified by the prepositional phrase* $\Rightarrow$ **of great achievements**

In this sentence, '*of great achievements*' cannot be placed in a different position.

(16) . There is **a nice *girl in a red uniform.***

         --------------   ------------------------

            ⇑   ⇑

    noun phrase   preposition phrase

The headword noun of noun phrase $\Rightarrow$ **girl** *is pre-modified by an adjective* $\Rightarrow$ **nice** and
post-modified by the prepositional phrase $\Rightarrow$ **in a red uniform**

● Prepositional phrases can occur in clusters in extended sentences :

   This is exemplified here:

(17) . There is **a girl** *in a red uniform* **with her mother**.

        -------   -------------------- --   ---------------------

         ⇑   ⇑   ⇑

       noun   prepositional prepositional

      phrase   phrase   phrase

(18) ● She lives in **a cottage** *with her mother* **in a village** *near Stuttgart* **in south Germany**.

         --------   ---------------   -----------   -------------------   ----------------------

         ⇑   ⇑   ⇑   ⇑   ⇑

       noun   prepositional prepositional prepositional prepositional

      phrase   phrase   phrase   phrase   phrase

(19) ● I saw a herd of reindeer with long antlers on a country road in Finland.

       -- ----- -------- ----------------   -----------------------   -------------------------   ---------------

     ⇑ ⇑   ⇑   ⇑   ⇑   ⇑   ⇑

     1 2   **3**   **4**   **5**   **6**   **7**

184   **Phrases, Clauses & Sentences**   **Phrases**

****

We can analyse the above sentence as follows:

> **1** is a noun phrase
> **2** is a verb phrase
> **3** is a noun phrase. In this noun phrase: the following prepositional phrases occur:

> **4** of reindeer   = *preposition* + *noun phrase* ⟹ *Prepositional phrase*
>
> **5** with long antlers   = *preposition* + *noun phrase*⟹ *Prepositional phrase*
>
> **6** on a country road   = *preposition* + *noun phrase* ⟹ *Prepositional phrase*
>
> **7** in Finland   = *preposition* + *noun phrase*⟹ *Prepositional phrase*

In prepositional phrases marked 4 to 7, you cannot change the position of any of these prepositions in their respective phrases because each preposition is the integral part of the prepositional phrase.

- <u>Sometimes, you can change the position of phrases or a phrase within the sentence without altering the meaning.</u> For instance, we can re-write example 19 as:

  - On a country road, in Finland, I saw a herd of reindeer with long antlers.

  - In Finland, on a country road, I saw a herd of reindeer with long antlers.

- **<u>A prepositional phrase can be embedded in another:</u>**

For instance:

(20) • I was waiting *in* a bus shelter *opposite* a bakery *for* my wife.

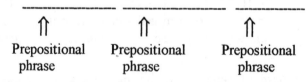

| Prepositional phrase | Prepositional phrase | Prepositional phrase |

The following phrasal analysis in detail shows how these prepositional phrases are embedded in one another. The headword in each phrase is highlighted.

[*in* a bus shelter *opposite* a bakery *for* my wife] ⟹*prepositional phrase* [a bus **shelter** *opposite* a bakery *for* my wife] $\Rightarrow$ *noun phrase*

[*opposite* a bakery *for* my wife] $\Rightarrow$ *prepositional phrase*

[a **bakery** *for* my wife]] $\Rightarrow$ *noun phrase*

[*for* my wife] $\Rightarrow$ *prepositional phrase*

[*my* **wife**] $\Rightarrow$ *noun phrase*

(21) • You must telephone **John** *after* lunch *about* the meeting *with* Simon *in* my office.

⟰   ⟰   ⟰   ⟰

pp   pp   pp   pp *

* prepositional phrase

In this sentence, prepositional phrases are also embedded in one another as shown below. **The headword in each phrase is highlighted.**

[**John** *after* lunch *about* the meeting *with* Simon *in* my office] $\Rightarrow$*noun phrase*

[**after** lunch *about* the meeting *with* Simon *in* my office] $\Rightarrow$ *prepositional phrase*

[**lunch** *about* the meeting *with* Simon *in* my office] $\Rightarrow$ *noun phrase*

[*about* the meeting *with* **Simon** *in* my office] $\Rightarrow$ *prepositional phrase*

[the **meeting** *with* Simon *in* my office] $\Rightarrow$ *noun phrase*

[*with* Simon *in* my office] $\Rightarrow$ *prepositional phrase*

[**Simon** *in* my office] $\Rightarrow$ *noun phrase*

[*in* my office] $\Rightarrow$ *prepositional phrase*

[my **office**] $\Rightarrow$ *noun phrase*

• Phrases in Apposition

When in a sentence or clause, two *noun phrases* come one after the other and both refer to the same thing, then phrases are in apposition. In the following examples, phrases in apposition are shown in *bold*.

(1) • Most tourists in London visit *Buckingham Palace*, *the London Office of the Queen*.

(2) • She has shown me a letter from her *English tutor, a university lecturer*.

• **Sometimes, the second phrase is used to place emphasis on the adjacent noun phrase.**
  For instance:

(3) • You must visit *Windsor Castle, The Queen's residence near London*.
   ----

placing an emphasis on the adjacent noun phrase ↵

(4) • *Nelson Mandela, the most famous African leader*, was imprisoned for 27 years.
   ----

emphasizing the meaning of the first phrase ↵

In examples 3-4 each second phrase is giving additional information about its adjacent noun phrase. In all three cases, a comma is needed to separate adjacent phrases.

• **When the purpose of the second noun phrase is to identify the first one, there is no
  need for a comma to separate them**. Here are two examples:

(5) • *Prince Charles the Prince of Wales* is heir-apparent to the throne.
   ------------------   --------------------
         ⇑   ⇑
first noun phrase   second noun phrase

(6) • What today's newspapers have revealed about *Mr John Major a famous
      politician* is disgusting.

Here the second phrase is identifying Mr Major.

• Coordination of Phrases

Coordinating and subordinating conjunctions are discussed in the last chapter 8. In grammar,
coordination means joining together two elements of the same status. These two elements can
be phrases or clauses. The coordination is achieved by using coordinating conjunctions. Let
us examine the following sentences:

(1) • We visited Frankfurt city *and* Stuttgart city on the same day.

     -------------------- ------ ------------------

    noun phrase⤶   ⇑   ⇑

               coordinating noun phrase
               conjunction

(2) • She likes to eat soup made from *fresh cauliflower and fresh cabbage*.

(3) • Anne can write *in German or in English*.

(4) • He *cleaned and polished* his shoes.

     ----

verb phrases coordinated ⤶ - cordinating conjunction ⇒*and*

• <u>**You can join other types of phrases as well.**</u> Here are some examples:

(5) • We drove in heavy snowfall *slowly and safely*.

     ----

    adverb phrases coordinated ⤶

(6) • He was *successful and happy*.

     ----

adjective phrases coordinated ⤶

(7) • He was sitting *in the waiting room in Thomas Hospital*.

     ----

    prepositional phrases coordinated ⤶

Both coordination and apposition help us in explaining the meaning by merging words, that is using fewer words. For instance: the above example without the apposition might have been written or uttered as:

He was sitting in the waiting room and he was in Thomas Hospital.

In summary, words are the smallest unit of language. The next category in the hierarchy of units is phrases. We can analyse a phrase in terms of the headword and its modifier(s). Phrases form both clauses and sentences. The next classification in the hierarchy of linguistic units is clauses. These are discussed in the next chapter.

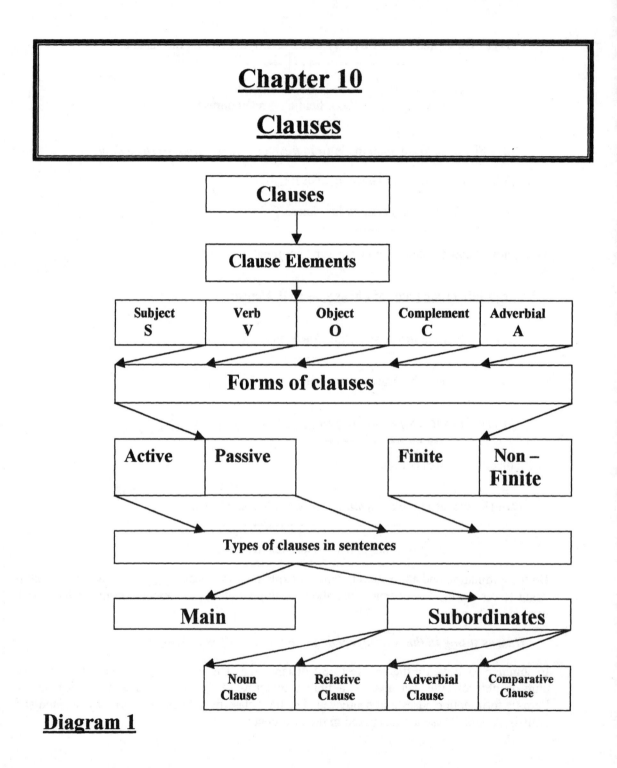

Diagram 1

. Introduction

A clause consists of some words that include a subject and a verb. A clause in its own right is a sentence. It can also be a part of a sentence. *A sentence* may consist of just one clause, or it may have two or more clauses. A sentence may be a simple, compound or complex sentence. *A simple sentence* has at least one clause. *Compound* and *complex sentences* consist of a number of clauses. Both clauses and sentences have their own particular internal structures. Diagram 1 gives a summary of the topics which are discussed in this chapter in order to understand the structures, types and functions of clauses and sentences.

. A Clause or a Sentence

Let's examine first some clauses:

(1) . Wolfgang went home.

subject ↵   ⇑   ⇑

finite verb object ⇒noun

(2) . Annemarie has written a letter.

subject ↵   ⇑   ⇑

verb group   object ⇒noun phrase

Both examples make sense without any further information added. Each example includes *subject* and *verb*. In fact, these are two clauses as well as two sentences. When the structure of a sentence can not be broken down into smaller sentences, the sentence is a *simple sentence*. A simple sentence has only one verb or verb group. Since these two sentences cannot be broken down into smaller sentences, they are simple sentences.

Both verbs in these examples are finite and active. The meaning or action (something changing or happening) of each verb is indicated by the non phrase. These clauses do not require any further information to be grammatically complete. These clauses can stand alone. Any clause which can stand alone is *a main clause*. Since a main clause makes sense without the aid of any further information or clause, and is grammatically complete, it is also known as an *independent clause*. In terms of grammar, it makes syntactical sense on its own.

Here are some more examples of main clauses. *The verb is shown in italics in each clause*:

> (3) • Karen *telephoned*.

> (4) • Mr. Taylor *will come*.

> (5) • The Prime Minister *has arrived*.

> (6) • Our guests *have left*.

- These are also examples of simple sentences as a simple sentence must have one subject element and one verb element. The structure of these examples based on the subject (abbreviated as **S**) followed by the verb (abbreviated as **V**). <u>*SV* is the minimum clause structure</u>. Clause structures and elements are discussed later.

> (7) • I opened the door **and** Anne entered the room.

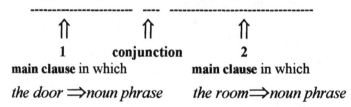

- Example 7 consists of two main clauses joined together by a conjunction **and** to form one sentence. We use **and, or, but** as **coordinating conjunctions** to join main clauses, which have
  the same status in a sentence.

- This is, in fact, a **compound sentence**. Unlike a simple sentence, a compound sentence can be broken down into smaller sentences or clauses. Example 7 meets this criterion.

- In this sentence, both clauses can stand alone. It implies that the meaning of the verb in each clause is completed by its respective noun phrase. Thus, both clauses are main clauses.

- If we change Example 7 to read as in Example 8:

> (8) • *When I opened the door*, Anne entered the room.

This sentence still has two clauses. Clause 1 begins with a ***subordinating conjunction,
when***. This clause is now dependent on clause 2 (⇒ main clause) in order to make syntactical (grammatical) sense. Therefore, any such clause is a ***dependent clause.*** The function of a
dependent clause is to support the main clause as its subordinate. This is why it is also known
as a ***subordinate or sub clause***. A ***complex sentence*** can have a number of clauses. One
clause must be a subordinate clause. Example 8 shows a complex sentence, as it has both
main and subordinate clauses. See ⇒Sentences. See ⇒subordinate clauses.

. Typical Clause Structure

Now examine the structure of the following declarative statement:

(9) . Robin Taylor ***has made*** a big profit.

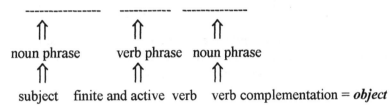

noun phrase   verb phrase   noun phrase

subject   finite and active verb   verb complementation = *object*

We can analyse this structure as:

- verb is preceded by the subject ⇒Robin Taylor

- the essence or the action of the verb is given by the verb complementation -
  noun phrase ⇒ a big profit

- this statement makes a declaration about the subject's action, that is giving
  information about the subject

- all three structural elements (subject phrase, verb phrase and verb
  complementation) are core or ***obligatory elements***

- the removal of any of these obligatory elements would make this clause
  syntactically incomplete.

This example typifies the structure of clauses. Since this structure relates to a declarative
statement, it is known as a ***declarative structure***.

In this example, the verb complementation is an object (abbreviated as **O**), *a big profit* <u>The object follows the <u>verb element</u></u>. The clause structure displayed by this example is an **SVO.** It is widely used in English.

- Indeed, you can add information to the SVO structure by adding some non-obligatory items. For instance, we can re-write the above example as:

(10) . *Most certainly*, Robin Taylor has made a big profit *by selling shire horse*s.

Here, the information in *italics* is adverbial. The adverbial elements usually provide detailed information. This is not essential as, without it, the clause is syntactically complete.

.Clause Elements

Clauses are constructed by combining certain clause elements. There are five clause elements, each of which has a particular function and renders a specific meaning. These clause elements are listed below with their abbreviations pointed by arrows.

. **subject**	$\Rightarrow$**S**
. **verb**	$\Rightarrow$**V**
. **object**	$\Rightarrow$**O**
. **complement**	$\Rightarrow$**C**
. **adverbial**	$\Rightarrow$**A**

A clause may have some or all of these elements. All clauses contain subject and verb elements. Furthermore, the meaning of the verb has to be complete. For this reason, the verb element is followed by an object or complement. Usually, the object and complement elements follow the SV in a clause. There may be some adverbial elements.

. Subject Element

The subject usually comes in the *subject position* which is usually before the verb element.

The following examples illustrate the positions of the subject and other elements in clauses:

(1) • Alison likes flowers very much.

⇑	⇑	⇑
s	v +	other element(s)

⇑
predicate (see below)

(2) • I bought some books.

⇑	⇑	⇑
s	v +	other element(s)

⇑
predicate

(3) • There will be a university bookshop.

⇑	⇑	⇑
s	v +	other element(s)

⇑
predicate

(4) • Berlin is the capital of Germany.

⇑	⇑	⇑
s	v +	other element(s)

⇑
predicate

(5) • Morning was really lovely.

⇑	⇑	⇑
s	v +	other element(s)

⇑
predicate

(6) • It seems our train is running late.

⇑	⇑	⇑
s	v +	other element(s)

⇑
predicate

• All the above examples show that the subject controls the verb in terms of singular or plural.

• Examples (1), (2), (4) and (5) illustrate that normally the subject element is a ***noun phrase***.

• Examples (3) and (6) indicate that in the subject position, sometimes, there can be *it* or ***there***. In fact, these words do not relate to any specific thing. When *it* or ***there*** is used in the subject position, it is called an ***empty subject*** or a ***dummy subject***.

Let's re-write example (3) as: *A university bookshop will be there.*
No doubt, this is a possible construction. Therefore:

• **There will be a university bookshop** = *A university bookshop will be there*.

Usually, a phrase that contains some new information begins with *a* or *an* as in this case. Normally, such a phrase does not start a sentence. It is the dummy or the empty subject, which starts the sentence.

• When the verb *be* is followed by *some* , *a*, or *an*, it is not preceded by a real subject. In such a case, an empty subject *"there"* is placed in the subject position. This is the reason for starting the phrase with an empty subject *there*.

Similarly, we can re-write example (6) as: Our train seems to be running late. Thus:

It seems our train is running late = *Our train seems to be running late*

The re-written clause is not so usual. It is preferred to begin the phrase with an empty subject *it*.

• The following examples also show the use of an empty subject:

  (7) • *It* was a cold night.   (a cold night it was ⇒ unusual construction)
       ---

an empty subject ↵

  (8) • *There* is a bank round the corner.   (a bank is round the corner ⇒ unusual)
       ----

an empty subject ↵

• The verb is controlled by the subject. The following examples illustrate this rule:

  (9) • She is a cook.   (10) • We are listening.
       ---- ---   ---- ----

3rd person singular ↵ ⇑⇑   1st person plural subject ↵ ⇑⇑
  subject   singular verb   plural verb

  (11) • They are at home.   (12) • I am going to Austria.
        ------ ----   --- ----

3rd person plural ↵ ⇑⇑   1st person singular subject ↵ ⇑⇑
  subject   plural verb   singular verb

(13) • You are working very hard.   (14) • You were wrong at that time.
       ----- ----   ------ ------

2nd person singular⌐ ⇑   2nd person plural ⌐   ⇑
    subject   plural verb   plural verb

Both second person singular and second person plural take the plural form of the verb.

- The subject of a clause is an important element. Indeed, it can be said that it is the subject which gives the clause its theme or topic.

- In examples (1) to (6), you can see that *V+ other element(s)* are marked as **_predicate_**. The predicate is a traditional grammatical term for verb and any other element(s) that follow the verb. Traditionally, the clause was divided into two parts, namely the subject and the predicate. Here is another example:

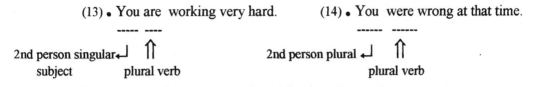

(15) • Denmark *is a small country*.
             ---------- ---------------------

theme of this clause subject ⌐   ⇑

information about the theme or the subject ⟹*predicate*

- In summary, the predicate includes all other elements except the subject element of a clause.

•Verb Element

The verb element is considered as the focal point of the clause. Let's first examine the following examples:

(1) • A guest *has written* to the hotel manager.

              ⇑

verb element ⟹*verb phrase*   (auxiliary verb + transitive verb)

- A guest ⟹*subject* is the topic

- *has written* to the hotel manager ⟹ this is the information about the subject which

  the writer/speaker wants to say ⟹*predicate*

(2) • She *walks*.

verb element ↵ - *verb phrase*

Here the verb *walks* is intransitive, the predicate ends at walks. walks ⇒*predicate*

(3) • Romania *is* a country in Europe.

verb element ↵ - *verb phrase*   (copular/linking verb)

Here *is* a country in Europe ⇒*predicate* what the writer/speaker wants to say about Romania

If you remove the verb phrase, the clause will not make any sense. Furthermore, it will be grammatically incomplete. As the subject sets the theme, there must be something about it. It is the verb in the form of a verb phrase which tells us about the action or the state relating to the subject. It is suggested that you browse the chapters on verbs and phrases, where you can see more relevant information on the verb element.

• Object Element

The object element comes after the verb in a clause. Here are some examples:

(1) • John ate *a cake*.   (2) • He enjoyed *the visit*.

⇑ ⇑ ⇑   ⇑ ⇑ ⇑
s v o   s v o

object ⇒ *noun phrase*   object ⇒ *noun phrase*

• In these examples verbs are transitive. The transitive verbs take an objective. Here are some more examples in which the verbs are also transitive:

(3) • He likes **history books**.   (4) • Someone rang *the door bell*.

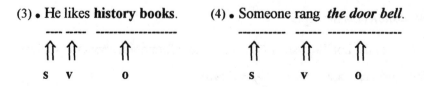

⇑ ⇑   ⇑   ⇑   ⇑   ⇑
s v   o   s   v   o

• **A clause can have two objects with some verbs as illustrated below:**

(5) • Mary gave *[to]* Margaret some seeds.

object 1 ⟹ *indirect object* ⏎   ⇑

object 2 ⟹ *direct object*

In this case, the action of the verb *gave [to]* directly affects *some seeds (primary effect)* as these were given to Margaret. Margaret is also indirectly affected *(secondary effect)* by the action of the verb as she received *some seeds*. Also note:

Margaret ⟹ *noun*   *some seeds* ⟹ *noun phrase*

(6) • Alex has written a letter **to his mother-in-law.**

object 1 ⟹ *direct object* ⏎   ⇑

object 2 ⟹ *indirect object*

• *It should be noted that both objects are* **noun phrases** <u>but</u> *to his mother-in-law is a* **Prepositional phrase**. *(Remember that a phrase can be just one word.)*

(7) • I bought some perfume **for** my wife.

object 1 ⟹ *direct object* ⏎   ⇑

object 2 ⟹ *indirect object*

for my wife ⟹ *Prepositional phrase*

Both objects are noun phrases.

The primary effect of the verb *bought* is on perfume. For this reason it is the first object. Of course, the second object is also affected to the extent that the perfume is for my wife. Thus, the secondary effect of the verb *bought* is on the second object.

• **As shown above, the object is usually a noun phrase. Sometimes a clause functions as an object.**

(8) • No one believed that *he was alive*.

⇑

finite clause functioning as an object

(9) • We look forward *to our weekend in Prague*.

⇑

non- finite clause functioning as an object

• In a clause, an object can be either **direct** or **indirect**. The difference between the direct and indirect object is that:

   • the primary effect of the verb is on the direct object

   • the secondary effect of the verb is on the indirect object

   • the indirect object can be preceded by **to** or **for**
   (by converting a noun phrase into a prepositional phrase as in examples 6-7)

•Complement Element

A complement is a word or a group of words in a clause or a sentence. It is used after

   • linking (copular) verbs and

   • some transitive verbs, which take *an object* and *object complement*.

Often in constructing a clause or a sentence, a complement is an essential grammatical requirement. A complement which follows a linking verb is known as **subject complement**. A complement which comes after a transitive verb and an object is called **object complement**. For instance:

(1) • It looks very pretty.

------   -------------

copular verb↵   ⇑

subject complement – tells us more about the subject ⟹*it*

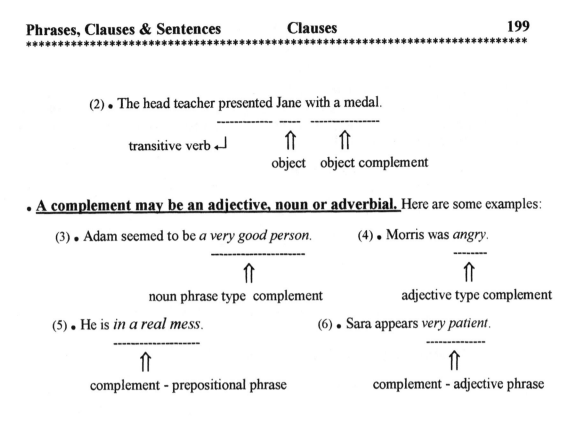

(2) • The head teacher presented Jane with a medal.

transitive verb ↵   object   object complement

• **A complement may be an adjective, noun or adverbial.** Here are some examples:

(3) • Adam seemed to be *a very good person.*

noun phrase type complement

(4) • Morris was *angry.*

adjective type complement

(5) • He is *in a real mess.*

complement - prepositional phrase

(6) • Sara appears *very patient.*

complement - adjective phrase

In examples (3) to (6), the complement refers to the subject of the clause (Adam, Morris, he and Sara). Without the complement, the linking or copular verb cannot function in a clause.

When the complement relates to the subject of the clause, it is also known as the ***subject predicative***, which is the ***subject complement*** . The linking or copular verbs are useful for describing the subject's attributes such as ***patient (attribute)*** or ***state*** in which one finds oneself, i.e. ***in a real mess***.

The weakness of linking verbs is that they cannot take an object and object complement. Furthermore, a clause containing a linking verb cannot be turned into a passive clause. However, the most used copula/copular verb *be* can be utilised to denote the association between the object and ***the object complement***. The object complement is also known as ***the object predicative.*** This is exemplified below:

(7) • Our guests made my mother very happy.

subject ↵   verb   object   object complement or object predicative

adjective phrase type ↵

Since *very happy* is an adjective phrase, the object complement is considered as the adjective phrase type. In this case, the complement is related to the object instead of the subject. For this reason it is the ***object complement*** or ***object predicative***. Here are some examples of object complement (object is in **bold**):

(8) • Students Union elected **her** *treasurer*.
                                 ----

         object complement - noun ↵

(9) • The chairman has declared **the meeting** *open*.
                                                ----

         object complement – object ↵

(10) • They consider **their captain** *as the best team leader*.
                                       ----

      object complement = as + noun phrase ↵

(11) • The Lottery money helped **me** *to retire from work*.
                                       ----

              object complement ↵ – noun-finite clause with *to-infinitive*

(12) • Our trainer kept **us** *practising for another hour*.
                              ----

         object complement ↵ – noun-finite clause with *-ing* participle

(13) • John helped **Dolly** solve this puzzle.
                           ----

      object complement ↵ - non- infinitive clause with **bare** infinitive

• <u>Adverbial Element</u>

The adverbial element is often an adverb phrase or prepositional phrase. It functions as an adverb. A clause can also function as adverbial. An adverbial element can occur anywhere in a clause. The following examples illustrate the adverbial element in clauses:

(1) • Anne works *very hard*.
                 ----

         adverbial ↵ - an adverb phrase functioning as adverbial

(2) • *Currently*, my boss is away in London.
       ----

adverbial ↵ - an adverb phrase functioning as adverbial

(3) • At present, he is having a shower.
       ----

adverbial ↵ - prepositional phrase acting as adverbial

(4) • My wife will not return from Russia *until* tomorrow.
                                       ----

adverbial ↵ -prepositional phrase acting as adverbial

(5) • I am not *against* his brilliant idea.
       ----

adverbial ↵ - prepositional phrase acting as adverbial

(6) • He talked slowly *because of* his recent illness.
       ----

adverbial ↵ - prepositional phrase functioning as adverbial

• Adverbial elements are often optional. For instance, examples (2) and (3) can still make sense without any adverbial element. These examples will also be grammatically complete without adverbs.

• An adverbial element may not contain an adverb, but it still functions like an adverb. For instance:

(7) • Adam is in London *to visit his sister*.
       ----

non-finite verb phrase ↵ ⟹ *to-infinitive*

Example (7) answers the following adverbial questions:

(8) • *Where* is Adam ? - Adam is in London   (9) • *Why* is Adam in London? - to visit his sister
       -------   -----

adverb ↵   adverb ↵

Example (7) does not have any adverb. Since it answers adverbial questions, it contains an adverbial element. This is the reason for calling the adverbial element by this name.

. Forms of Clauses

There are four different forms of clauses based on the verb used in each form of clause. Their specific features are listed below in Table 1, so that they can be compared at a glance.

Table 1

Forms of Clauses

Finite clause	Non -Finite clause	Active clause	Passive clause
. it has a finite verb	. it has a non-finite verb	. It has an active verb form which shows the agent's activity -	. it has a passive verb form indicating something is done
. the verb is marked for tense	. the verb is to- infinitive or bare infinitive, present participle *-ing* form, and past participle *-ed* form		
. it has a subject which precedes the verb	. usually it is a part of the finite clause	doing something/ something happening	to the agent -subject
		. agent is grammatically	. statements with transitive verb can
. the subject may be left out to avoid	. by itself it does not seem grammatically correct	the subject	be converted to passive clauses
repetition	. it may not include a subject	. it is extensively used as it is typical voice	. it sounds formal
	. all verbs except modal auxiliaries have non-finite forms		

● Here are some examples of **finite clauses**:

> (1) ● Daniel *works* for our company.
> ‒‒‒‒‒‒‒‒
>
> finite verb ↵ – *present tense*

(2) • Adam *is walking* towards Hyde Park.

⇑

finite verb – *present continuous tense*

(3) • He is very pleased *that everything has worked well*.

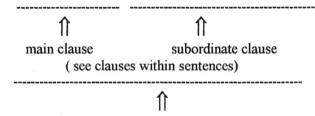

main clause   subordinate clause
(see clauses within sentences)

⇑

both clauses have finite verbs

• <u>You can see that all three above examples contain subjects .</u> **In fact, often a finite clause has no subject as illustrated below:**

(4) • Sylvia corresponds with us and *(she)* visits us regularly.

main clause ↵   you can leave it out ↵   finite clause ↵- subordinate clause

This sentence has two clauses: namely main and subordinate. These are discussed later. Both clauses have finite verbs.

Here are two more examples of a finite clauses *(in italic bold style)* <u>without subjects</u>:

(5) • She is very busy at work and *cannot go out with you*.

(6) • The weather was terrible and *caused some train cancellations*.

• Here are some examples of **non-finite clauses**:

(1) • **We went to Agra** *to see the Taj Mahal*.

to-infinitive verb form↵   ⇑
object

In the structure of this sentence, the main clause is shown in **bold style**. The subordinate clause has a *"to-infinitive verb"*, which is not marked for tense. Thus, it is a non-finite clause. <u>It is without the subject.</u>

- In this sentence, when you read the non-finite clause only, you can see that by itself it does not seem grammatically correct. For this reason, the non-finite clause is usually a part of a sentence which also has a finite clause. In this sentence, "we went to Agra" is a finite clause, because it has a finite verb **went** – past tense form of the verb **go**

(2)• **The plan was** *to take a night train.*

to-infinitive verb form↵   ⇑
                                 object

<u>The non-finite clause *(in italics)* is without the subject.</u>

(3) • He eats a variety of vegetables *to reduce his weight.*

subject of the non-finite clause↵   ⇑   ⇑

                        non-finite verb   object of the non-finite clause

Here, the non-finite clause *(in italics)* has a subject.

(4) • Antonia wanted *Ivan to marry her.*

subject of non-finite clause ↵   ⇑   ⇑
                        non-finite verb object of the non-finite clause

In Examples 3 and 4, each noun-finite clause *(in italics)* has its subject.

(5) • Jane assisted *John to develop a CV.*

subject of non-finite clause ↵   ⇑   ⇑
                        to- infinitive object of the non-finite clause

(6) • We wanted *to eat* **the Indian food**.

to- infinitive verb ↵   ⇑
         object of the non-finite clause

infinitive clause in **bold italics** ↵

In Example 6, the non-finite clauses *(in italics)* is without the subject.

• <u>Active and Passive Clauses</u>

Here are some examples of **active clauses**:

(1) • Frank *is driving* the car.

    ⇑   ⇑

agent doing something / activity/ action taken by the agent ⟹ is driving = active verb

Therefore, it is an *active clause* with present continuous tense. The active clause structure is considered as the primary structure. From it, the structure of the passive clause is derived as:

(2) • The car *is being driven* by Frank.

  ⇑   ⇑   ⇑
 agent something is *adverbial element (= optional information)*
     done to the car ⟹agent

(2 A) • The car *is being driven*.

passive clause grammatically complete ↵

• A comparison between Example 1 and Example 2 reveals that the object in Example 1 is now in the subject position in Example 2 ⟹ the passive clause

• The verb phrase, "*is driving*" in Example 1 has been modified to become, "*is being driven*" in Example 2.

The reason for doing so is that the verb phrase in the active clause indicates the present continuous tense. The passive clause must also express the present continuous tense by using the passive verb form:

is being driven.
---------- -------

present continuous form of the verb *be* ↵   ⇑

passive participle

- In example 2, the agent, ***Frank*** is preceded by the adverb ***by***. Thus, ***by Frank*** is the adverbial element added to the passive clause. It is an optional piece of information.

- The adverbial element is not necessary as without it, the passive clause "The car *is being driven.*" is grammatically complete. See Example 2A in a box above.

- In Examples 2 and 2A, since the agent *(= the car)* is receiving the action *(=affected)*, it is a passive clause expressing present continuous tense.

Here are some examples of both active and corresponding passive clauses:

(3) ● She loved her children. ⇐ *active clause*

(4) ● Her children were loved (by her). ⇐ *passive clause*

(5) ● They ***should count*** the money. ⇐ *active clause*

            ⇑

model + infinitive = active verb

(6) ● The money ***should be counted***.   ⇐ *passive clause*

             ⇑

model+ infinitive = active verb

(7) ● We admire your sincere desire ***to help*** the aged. ⇐ *active clause*

             ⇑

active to-infinitive

(8) • Your sincere desire *to help* the aged is admired (by us). ⇐ *passive clause*

                         ⇑

active to-infinitive converted to passive to- infinitive

(9) • There is something *to do* this afternoon. ⇐ *active clause*

                    ⇑

active to-infinitive

(10) • There is something *to be done* this afternoon. ⇐ *passive clause*

                     ⇑

active to-infinitive changed to passive infinitive

(11) • They left without *eating* their lunch. ⇐ *active clause*

                  ⇑

active gerund

(12) • They left without the lunch *being eaten*. ⇐ *passive clause*

                     ⇑

active gerund converted to passive gerund

• Subordinate Clauses

A subordinate clause supports the main clause. Subordinate clauses are categorized as:

• Noun or Nominal Clauses

• Relative Clauses

• Adverbial Clauses

• Comparative Clauses

This categorization is based on the function of clauses in relation to the main clause. When a subordinate clause is linked itself to the rest of the sentence, it performs its specific function as discussed here.

.Noun or Nominal Clauses

A noun clause can act as an object, subject or complement of the main clause. You will see that a noun clause functions in the same manner as a noun phrase does. Usually, a noun phrase commences with **that**, **if** or with a **wh-question** word such as **what**. It can also come after a preposition, adjective or a noun. The following examples illustrate their characteristics:

> (1) • We believe *that the business will grow*.
>
> ⇑   ⇑
>
> main clause   noun clause acting as an object

> (2) • The teacher didn't think *that she was an able girl*.
>
> ⇑   ⇑
>
> main clause   noun clause acting as an object

• Without **that** the above clauses will still convey the same meaning and are grammatically correct.

Examples 1 and 2: The following comparison illustrates the similarities between noun phrases and noun clauses.

. the business ⇒ noun phrase   . the business will grow ⇒ noun clause

. she ⇒ noun phrase (grammatically: just one word can be a phrase)

. She was an able girl ⇒ noun clause

Here are some more examples of a noun clause acting as an object:

> (3) • We were thinking *whether you would come*.
>
> noun clause acting as an object ↵

> (4) • I wonder *if you would stay with us*.
>
> noun clause acting as an object ↵

(5) • We told the police *that we were strangers in London.*

⇑   ⇑

direct object – noun phrase   indirect object – noun clause

It demonstrates that a noun clause can be an indirect object.

• The following examples illustrate that a clause can function as a subject:

(6) • ***Whether I'll be able to attend a meeting*** depends on the transport.

noun clause acting as subject ↵

• When a noun clause is the subject, it does not start with *if*.

(7) • *That my son returned from the war* was the most memorable day.

noun clause acting as subject ↵

(8) • *What you* say is nonsense.

noun clause - subject ↵

• A ***wh- question*** word begins a question with any of the nine question words: *what, when, where, which, who, whom, whose, how* and *why.*

(9) • *Who* can come with me?   ***Possible answer*** ⇒   *Someone can come with me.*

⇑   ⇑

noun clause begin with *wh-question* word   declarative sentence/statement

If the word order in an interrogative sentence is the same as in a declarative sentence/ statement as shown above then there is *no* inversion (change) of the normal word order in the wh-question.

• Here are some examples of noun clauses when a noun clause can function as a complement of the main clause.

(10) • Our problem is *how we are going to reach the airport on time by public transport.*

noun clause acting as the complement of the main clause ↵

(11) ● The fact is *that they are happily married*.

----

complement of the main clause *the fact is* ↵

● The following examples illustrate that noun clauses can come after some adjectives and nouns.

(12) ● I am *afraid* that I shan't see you tonight.

------   ------------------------------------

adjective ↵   ⇑

noun clause

(13) ● I am *confident* that she will soon recover from her illness.

-----------   ---

adjective ↵   ⇑

noun clause

(14) ● I am *glad* that Joan has returned home safely.

-----   --

adjective ↵   ⇑

noun clause

● You can leave out *that* in the above examples and similar cases.

(15) ● Your *belief* that she is rich is only imagination.

------   --

noun ↵   noun clause ↵ - **do not leave out** ⟹ *that*

(16) ● What gave you the *idea* that Rachel is abroad?

----   ----------------------------

noun ↵   noun clause ↵ - **do not leave out** ⟹ *that*

(17) ● The news that he is already married has shocked Monica.

-------   ---

noun ↵   noun clause ↵ - **do not leave out** ⟹ *that*

● A noun clause can occur after a preposition as illustrated by the following examples.

(18) . Our jobs depend *on* what management decide(s)* today.

                 --- --

                 preposition ↵   noun clause ↵

*The word management is a countable group noun. It can be singular or plural.

(19) . We were amazed (*at**) how colourful and bright the Christmas lights were.

               --- --

               preposition ↵   noun clause ↵

* You can also say *by* instead of *at* or no preposition at all.

. Relative Clauses

A clause introduced by any of the relative pronouns or a relative phrase, which refers to an earlier noun or a noun phrase, is a relative clause. It acts as a post-modifier of the noun or the noun phrase. For instance:

(1) . The lady **who** *bought some tea bags* is my aunt.

           ----

          relative clause ↵ - *post-modifying the noun phrase* ⟹ *the lady*

. The word *who* is **a relative pronoun** which joins the relative clause to the **main clause** *the lady is my aunt*. The noun or the noun phrase which is post-modified (or refers back) is called the ***antecedent of the relative clause***. Here, ***the lady*** is the **antecedent**.

(2) . The cricket team *who were in red outfits* won the game.

          ----

          relative clause ↵

who ⟹ relative pronoun links relative clause to main clause ⟹ *the cricket team won the game*

You may think that the word team is not a person. On the contrary, it consists of persons. It is a countable group noun, which can agree with a singular or plural verb.

. In examples (1) and (2), there is no need to place a comma before and after the relative clause.

The reason for omitting commas is that both relative clauses are acting as **identifying (restrictive) clauses**. The purpose of the information given by an identifying clause is to identify the earlier noun in the main clause. The following examples illustrate this rule as well:

(3) • The footballer *who had short blonde hair* was not from Scandinavia.

----

relative clause ↵ - *who* ⟹ *relative pronoun* (*linkage*)

Here, the head word *footballer* in the main clause is post-modified by a relative clause which begins with the relative pronoun *who*.

(4) • The lady *who is wearing a white dress* is married to our mayor.

----

relative clause ↵ - *who* ⟹ *relative pronoun*

• The pronoun *whose* denotes possessive meaning. For instance:

(5) • Our neighbours *whose daughter lives in Spain* have gone to Spain for a week.

----

relative clause↵ - functioning as identifying clause

(6) • Some motorists *whose vehicles were damaged by the crowd* complained to the police.

----

relative clause↵ - identifying which motorists

(7) • Wolfgang **whose** *car is a black BMW with an open roof* is a German insurance expert.

----

relative clause↵

It tells us which Wolfgang is being talked about.

• When the relative clause functions as an identifying clause, the determiner *the* is usually used before the noun instead of any possessive pronoun *my, your, her etc.* For instance:

(8) • James is driving **the** car *that he bought from me.*

----   -------------------------------

determiner preferred ↵   relative clause ↵ - *that* ⟹ *relative pronoun refers to car*

Here, the head word *car* in the main clause is post-modified by the relative clause.

(9) • James is driving **his** car *that he bought from me.*
　　　　　　 ----　　 ----------------------------

possessive pronoun is unfit ↵ relative clause ↵ - *that* ⇒ *relative pronoun refers to car*

(10) • She liked *the* car *that she bought last year.*
　　　　　　 ----　　 ------------------------------

determiner preferred ↵　　　　　　　　　⇑

　　　　　　　relative clause used as identifying clause - identifies which car

(11) • She liked *her* car *that she bought last year.*
　　　　　　 ----

possessive pronoun unsuited ↵ - because it implies **which car**

The purpose is to identify the *car* not but not refer to **which car**.

(12) • I went to *the* cottage *that I inherited last year.*
　　　　　　 -----　　 ----------------------------

determiner preferred ↵　　　　　　　　　⇑

　　　　　　relative clause used as identifying clause

(13) • I went to *my* cottage *that I inherited last year.*

Possessive pronoun unfit ↵ - as it refers to **which cottage** instead of identifying the cottage.

• <u>The relative pronouns *who* and *that* are used for both things and people as shown above. On</u> <u>the other hand, the relative pronouns *which* and *that* are usually used for things and ideas.</u>

Here are some examples:

(14) • Flats *which/that overlook the sea* cost a great deal more.
　　　　　　 ----------------------------

　　　　　relative clause ↵ - you can use *which* or *that*

(15) • She doesn't know much about the job *which/that has been offered to her.*
　　　　　　 ------------------------------------

　　　　　　relative clause ↵ - *which/that* ⇒ *relative pronouns*

(16) • It was a dream *which/ that never came true*.

----

relative clause ↵

<u>You can see that the pronoun *that* can be used with any noun.</u>

• A relative clause also functions as ***a classifying clause***. The idea of classifying is to describe the head noun in the main clause by its nature, types or class. <u>Classifying</u> clauses *do not* have commas around them. The following examples illustrate this rule:

(17) • Annemarie does not want **customers** *who waste her business time*.

------------   ---------------------------------

head word/noun ↵   relative clause ↵

Here, the purpose of the relative clause is to say what type of customers.

(18) • They were asking for the **shopping centre** *that has a car park in front of it*.

----------------------   --

head noun ↵   relative clause ↵

(19) • We need some young persons **who** *can do some community work once a week*.

----

relative clause ↵ - classifying the head noun persons

(20) • Motorists **who** *have caused fatal accidents* should be banned from driving.

----

relative clause ↵ - classifies and points to a particular type of driver

• A relative clause can function as ***an adding (or identifying/non-restrictive)clause***. An adding clause provides some additional information about the head word in the main clause. The relative clause is separated from the main clause by two commas. In fact, the <u>punctuation rules regarding the use of comma with subordinate clauses are not universally the same rules.</u> The following examples of relative clauses exemplify how they can function as adding clauses:

(21) • **Buda,** **which** *is a part of Budapest in Hungary*, has many historical buildings.

-------   ---

head noun ↵   relative adding clause ↵ - giving additional information about the noun ***Buda***

(22) •The gentleman, **who** *asked so many questions during the meeting*, is my boss.

head noun ↵   relative adding clause ↵ - additional information

(23) • All football hooligans, **who** *have caused so much disturbance in London tonight*,

should be expelled by their clubs.   ⇑

adding clause giving additional information

about the noun ⇒ *hooligan(s)*

(24) • Nobel, **who** *was the captain of Test Cricket Team 2001*, made 200 runs against Australia.

relative clause adding information about the noun ↵

(25) • Some boxes, **which** *had been missing for two months*, were found hidden under the

staircase.

relative clause adding information about the noun ↵

(26) • Margaret Thatcher, **who** *was the first female British prime minister*, was replaced by

John Major in 1990.

relative clause ↵ - functioning as an adding clause and giving extra

information about Margaret Thatcher

• In examples (21) to (26) you can leave out adding clauses and these sentences still make sense. The information between the commas is not restricted. This is the reason for calling these types of clauses non-restrictive clauses. Usually, **whose** relates to people as shown by examples 6 and 7. Here are some more examples.

(27) • Anne, *whose husband Wolfgang drives a Rolls-Royce*, is a businesswoman.

relative clause ↵ - acting as adding clause

(28) • We wish to interview some students *whose overall performance is above B grade*.

relative clause ↵ - acting as classifying clause

****

(29) • Our neighbours **whose** *house was burgled last night* called the police.

----

relative clause ↵ - identifying clause

(29) • Mahatma Gandhi, **whose** *courage I admire greatly*, was a pioneer and campaigner of a non-violent movement for freedom and justice.

whose *courage I admire greatly* ⟹ relative clause which is functioning as an adding clause

• **Whose** can also refer to an organisation or a country. This is illustrated below.

(31) • Switzerland, **whose** *inhabitants speak four official languages*, is in West Europe.

----

relative clause↵ - giving extra information about the head noun

(32) • IBM, **whose** *ideas have been copied by many PC manufactures*, is a large company.

----

relative clause ↵- giving extra information about the head noun

Organisation ⟹*group/collective noun* -considered as singular noun but it renders plural meaning.

The relative pronoun *whose* indicates that something belongs to something (possessiveness). When it relates to things (entities), it is a group noun as in examples (31) and (32). It can refer to people as shown below.

• We can use relative pronouns *which* and ***that*** for constructing identifying and classifying clauses. This is exemplified below.

(33) • The city **which** *I have marked on this map* is a large place in Scotland .

----

relative clause ↵

(34) • This schedule **which** *our supervisor submitted to the manager* has been rejected.

----

relative clause ↵

(35) • These are imported garments **which** *cannot be exhibited as made in England.*

----

relative clause ↵

(36) • A passage to India was her big ambition **that** *was fulfilled.*

                            ----

                           relative clause ↵

(37) • It is a home-made cake **that** *is delicious.*

                   ----

                relative clause ↵

• **When should you use *which* or *that* as a relative pronoun?**

In examples 33 to 37 both *which* and *that* are possible relative pronouns in order begin a relative clause. In these examples, you can replace *that* with *which* or *vice versa* without altering meaning rendered in each case. The use of *that* is generally recommended with any noun, but *which* with ideas and things. For instance:

(38) • Your silly plan **which/that** *has ruined our trip should not have been accepted.*

                  ----

                      relative clause ↵

(39) • I have developed a database system **that/which** *generates my mail shot.*

                 ----

                relative clause ↵

• Some people consider the use of *which* as somewhat formal when it relates to only head noun. On the other hand, when *which* relative pronoun refers to the whole clause instead of head noun, *which* relative pronoun is used. This is illustrated below:

(40) • The Indian touring cricket team drew the final test mach, **which** *ended the current*
                                                                        test series in a draw.

--   ---------------------------------

whole clause ↵ referred by the relative clause   relative clause ↵ adding information

(41) • Our coach driver suddenly felt a sharp pain in his chest, **which** *caused this*
                                                                           terrible accident.

--   ---------------------------------

whole clause ↵ referred by the relative clause   relative clause ↵ adding information

****

- In informal English, often the relative pronoun is omitted when it is not the subject of the relative clause. This is exemplified below:

    (42) • The book *I am reading* is really useful for my work.
    ⟰

    relative clause without *which/that* ⟹ relative pronoun

    (43) • The big man *my brother is talking to* is a well-known boxer.
    ⟰

    relative clause without *whom/whom* ⟹ relative pronoun

    (44) • The urgent letter *I posted to Anne last Friday* still hasn't reached her.
    ⟰

    relative clause without *which* ⟹ relative pronoun

- When a relative pronoun is the subject of the relative clause, the relative pronoun cannot be discarded. The following examples illustrate this rule:

    (45) • The lady **who** *was wearing a flowery hat* was his grandmother.

    relative clause ↵ - *who* ⟹ subject

    (46) • A student **who** *gave a talk on morality* lives in our area.

    relative clause ↵ - *who* ⟹ subject

    (47) • I have a number of software packages **that /which** are used for administrative work.

    relative clause ↵ *that or which* ⟹ subject must be used

- A relative clause can have either an active or a passive participle without a relative pronoun. Here are some examples:

(48) • Some overseas students *taking part in the debate tonight* are Asians.
----

relative clause ↵ – *who are* (= relative pronoun + auxiliary) omitted

Note: *taking* is *active participle* here *as it relates to some overseas students and their on-going activity.*

(49) • Anne spotted the car *coming fast from the opposite side of the road.*
----

relative clause ↵ – *which was* (= relative pronoun + auxiliary) omitted

coming ⟹ *active participle*

(50) • Projects *submitted today* will be assessed and returned to you by 30ᵗʰ June.
----

relative clause ↵ – *which were* (= relative pronoun + auxiliary) omitted

Note: *submitted* is *a passive participle* here *as it relates to projects given – the activity performed by other persons.*

(51) • Some sweets made in Bridlington *presented to the Kling family* were eaten up fast by us.
----

relative clause ↵

which were (= relative pronoun + auxiliary) omitted

presented ⟹ *passive participle -* sweets were given by someone to the Kling family.

• Use of *whom* and *which* pronouns with prepositions

• The relative pronoun **whom** is not used very often in spoken English. Its use in the relative clause after a **preposition** is rather formal. For instance:

(52) • The Plew family **with whom** *I stayed in Germany* is visiting us.
----

relative clause ↵ - *with* ⟹ preposition comes before the pronoun

(53) • We will telephone John Russell *to whom we supplied a red car.*
----

relative clause ↵ - *to* ⟹ preposition placed before the pronoun

- In identifying and classifying relative clauses the relative pronoun **whom** can be the object pronoun. In such cases, it is not usually used. Instead of whom you can use **that** or **who**. Often, the relative pronoun is altogether omitted in identifying and classifying relative clauses. For instance:

(54) • John Smith **who/that** *I interviewed yesterday* has been appointed.

           relative clause ↵

(55) • Robin Taylor **who/that** *I telephoned today* was pleased to accept our invitation.

           relative clause ↵

(56) • Yvonne **[who/that/whom]** *I met in France* will visit us soon.

           relative clause ↵ − [the relative pronoun can be omitted]

- In spoken English the use of **whom** is not common. It is preferred to use who and place the preposition at the end of the sentence. For instance:

(57) • You are not telling me **who** *you went out last night* **with**.

           relative clause ↵ - preposition **with** at the end of the sentence

(58) • Please let me know **who** *you address the letter* **to**.

           relative clause ↵ - preposition **to** at the end of the sentence

. In adding clauses the relative pronoun **who** is often used instead of **whom**. In such cases, you cannot leave out the relative pronoun as exemplified below.

(59) • James Berg, **who** *we liked as a tutor*, is a science journalist for "The Times."

           relative clause ↵ - adding extra information

(60) • Our Russian colleague, **who** *we bought a wedding present for*, is a father now.

           relative clause ↵ - giving extra information about the colleague

Note that in examples 59 and 60 the use of that instead of who or whom is not allowed.

• Like **whom** we can also put the preposition before the relative pronoun **which**.

    (61) • My long overseas trip **for which** *I saved for so many years* was memorable .
                              ----

                             relative clause ↵ - identifying trip

    (62) • The current upheaval **for which** *we are not prepared* is very harmful.
                              ----

                          relative clause ↵ - identifying trip

In both examples, the preposition is put before the preposition ⟹ *for*

• <u>Adverbial clauses</u>

An adverbial clause in a complex sentence functions in the same way as an adverb in a simple sentence. It modifies the main clause by adding information about time, place, manner, cause, etc. An adverbial clause may be in the first position, in the middle position or in the end position in a sentence. So, it can occur anywhere in the sentence. The adverbial clause is joined to the main clause by a conjunction.

• <u>A comma is inserted between the adverbial clause and the main clause when the adverbial clause is in the first position in a sentence.</u> The following examples illustrate adverbial clauses.

    (1) • They can visit us *if they wish*.
                       ----

         adverbial clause ↵ - *indicating a condition*   *if* ⟹ *conjunction*

Here, the adverbial clause modifies the main clause, "*They can visit us*" by giving additional information.

    (2) • *If she likes it*, she can have it as a present.
        ----

adverbial clause ↵ - relates to a condition   *if* ⟹*conjunction*

    (3) • We'll go out for a walk by the sea *as soon as I finish my gardening*.
                             ----

               adverbial clause of time ↵   - *as soon as* ⟹*conjunction*

(4) • *Since you are not coming with me*, I don't want to travel alone.

    adverbial clause of reason ↵   - *since* ⟹ *conjunction*

(5) • *Where an Indian restaurant is*, there is a Chinese take-way at the corner.

    adverbial clause of place ↵   - *where* ⟹ *conjunction*

(6) • I went to Germany *in order to attend an international book fair*.

    adverbial clause of purpose ↵   - *in order to* ⟹ *conjunction*

(7) • *If we meet at Heathrow*, we can discuss the final draft.

    adverbial clause ↵ - here if is used with the present simple for future time

(8) • *As far as I can remember*, she was with her husband at that time.

    adverbial clause ↵ - expressing truth   - *as far as* ⟹ *conjunction*

(9) • How can she be happy *as though nothing had happened in her family*?

    adverbial clause of manner ↵   - *as though* ⟹ *conjunction*

You can also say *as if* instead of *as though*. In passing, note as follows:

    instead ⟹ *an adverb* but *instead of* ⟹ *a preposition*

(10) • You should rest tomorrow *so that you can recover after your long journey*.

    adverbial clause of purpose ↵   - *so that* ⟹ *conjunction*

• There may be several adverbials in a clause.

Let's consider the following questions and answers in relation to example 11:

    • How did they arrive ? ⟹ *happily*

• Where did they arrive ?   ⇒ *at the airport*

• Why did they arrive at the airport?   ⇒ *to fly home*

• What was the purpose of flying home?   ⇒ *for a wedding ceremony*

---

(11) • We arrived *happily* *at* the airport *to* fly home *for* a wedding ceremony.

⇑	⇑	⇑	⇑
adverbial	*adverbial*	*adverbial*	*adverbial*
⇑	⇑	⇑	⇑
adverbial phrase	*prepositional phrase*	*non-finite phrase*	*prepositional verb phrase*

The above analysis shows that a clause can have a number of adverbials. Furthermore, it demonstrates that not all adverbials consist of adverbs, but adverbial phrases. Adverbial phrases do not always contain an adverb as illustrated by this example.

• <u>Comparative Clauses</u>

These clauses express comparison. Some comparative clauses involve the use of the subordinating conjunction *than*. On the other hand, some comparative clauses introduce the second part of the comparison by means of correlative subordinators *as .... as*. Here are some examples of comparative clauses relating to different situations:

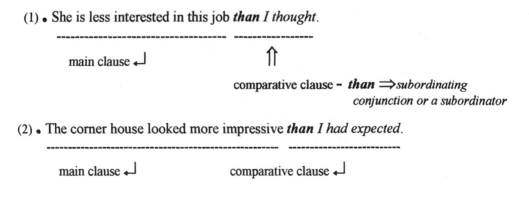

(1) • She is less interested in this job *than I thought*.

    main clause ↵   ⇑

               comparative clause - *than* ⇒*subordinating*
                             conjunction or a subordinator

(2) • The corner house looked more impressive *than I had expected*.

    main clause ↵   comparative clause ↵

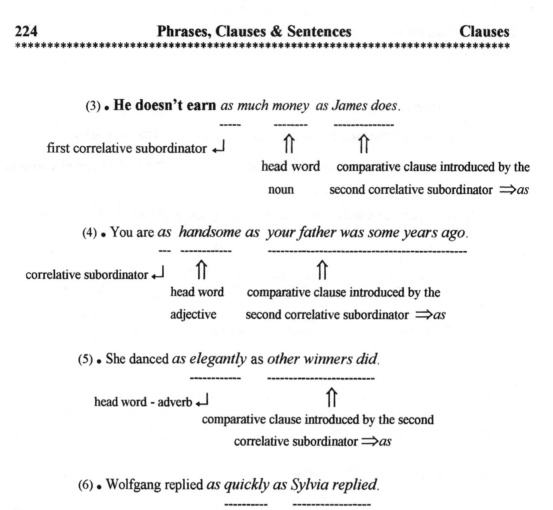

(3) . **He doesn't earn** *as much money as James does*.

first correlative subordinator ⤶

head word   comparative clause introduced by the

noun   second correlative subordinator ⟹*as*

(4) . You are *as handsome as your father was some years ago*.

correlative subordinator ⤶

head word   comparative clause introduced by the

adjective   second correlative subordinator ⟹*as*

(5) . She danced *as elegantly* as *other winners did*.

head word - adverb ⤶

comparative clause introduced by the second

correlative subordinator ⟹*as*

(6) . Wolfgang replied *as quickly as Sylvia replied*.

head word - adverb ⤶

comparative clause

These examples illustrate that comparative clauses premodify the head word. The head word may be a noun, pronoun, adverb or adjective.

This chapter begins with an introduction to clauses and sentences. Since a sentence consists of at least one clause, the idea of clauses is explained and exemplified in some depth. A sentence is the biggest unit of syntactic structure. For this reason, the next chapter is devoted to sentences. A classification of sentences is drawn for the purpose of understanding the meaning, types and structures of sentences.

Chapter 11

Sentences

. Introduction

In the last chapter, the idea of sentences is introduced and discussed in relation to clauses. For the sake of understanding the structures, types and intended meaning conveyed by sentences, a classification of sentences is shown in Table 1. This forms the basis of our discussion in this chapter.

Table 1

A Classification of Sentences

Meaning	Types	Structure
Positive	Declarative	Simple
Negative	Interrogative	Compound
Active	Imperative	Complex
Passive	Exclamative	

. Positive and Negative Sentences

A positive sentence expresses positive meaning. A negative sentence communicates a negative idea. A positive sentence can be converted to a negative sentence and vice versa. These are discussed below:

• Often a negative sentence is formed by using the word *not* or its short version *n't* after the auxiliary. If there is no auxiliary, the *dummy do* or *does* auxiliary is inserted. For instance:

****

(1) • She *has* spoken to me about this matter.   ⇐ *positive statement/sentence*

(2) • She *has not* spoken to me about this matter.   ⇐*negative statement/sentence*

(3) • Angelica *will* call you tomorrow evening. ⇐ *positive statement/sentence*

(4) • Angelica *won't* call you tomorrow evening. ⇐*negative statement/sentence*

⇑

the auxiliary *will* and *n't* (not) are written as one word ⇒ *won't*

(5) • Frank likes a hot drink in bed. ⇐ *positive statement/sentence*

(6) • Frank *does not/ doesn't* like a hot drink in bed. ⇐ *negative statement/sentence*

⇑

dummy auxiliary as the positive sentence is without the auxiliary in Example 5.

(7) • They were running in that direction. ⇐ *positive statement/sentence*

(8) • They *were not/ weren't* running in that direction. ⇐ *negative statement/sentence*

(9) • You *should have* done this work.⇐ *positive statement/sentence*

(10) • You *should not have/shouldn't* have done this work. ⇐ *negative statement/sentence*

⇑   ⇑

not comes after   *n't* placed after first auxiliary
first auxiliary

(11) • The gold medal *had been* stolen. ⇐ *positive statement/sentence*

(12) • The gold medal *had not/hadn't been* stolen. ⇐ *negative statement/sentence*

(13) • Andrea *might have* told you about it. ⇐ *positive statement/sentence*

(14) • Andrea *might not/ mightn't* have told you about it. ⇐ *negative statement/sentence*

(15) • Ralf knew that I was visiting him. ⇐ *positive statement/sentence*

(16) • Ralf *did not/didn't* know that I was visiting him. *negative statement/sentence*

- You can include an appropriate *negative word* in a positive sentence to turn it into a negative sentence. There are many such words. A few are used in the following examples:

    (17) • The teacher says *never* to do it again.
    ``-------``

    negative word ↵ - means not ever

    (18) • My parents allow *no* one to visit me after 20.00 hour.
    ``----``

    negative word ↵ - means not any person

    (19) • She says *nothing* about her long holiday in Australia.
    ``-----------``

    negative word ↵ - meaning not any thing

    (20) • We tried hard but *nowhere* could we find him.
    ``----------``

    negative word ↵ - means not anywhere

    (21) • Our old house *no longer* exists.
    ``------------``

    negative words ↵ - not any more/ not any longer

- Adverbial phrases with a *negative word* create negative sentences. The adverbial starts the sentence in order to emphasize the negative meaning. It also requires inversion of the subject and verb. Here are some examples:

    (21 A) • Before in my life, I have experienced such a terrifying road accident.
    positive sentence

    (22) • *Never before in my life* have I experienced such a terrifying road accident.
    ``----------------------------`` ``-------``

    adverbial with a negative word ↵   ⇑

    inversion of subject and verb   *negative sentence*

    (23) • You should telephone her today.   *positive sentence*

(24) ● *Under no circumstances* **should you** telephone her today.
　　　------------------------------　---------------

negative adverbial phrase ↵　　　　⇑
　　　　　　　　　　　　inversion of subject and verb　　　*negative sentence*

● An adverbial phrase with a *negative word* in a place other than the beginning of the sentence does not cause any subject and verb inversion.

　　　　(25) ● Sylvia *calls* us.　　　　　　⇐ *positive sentence*

　　　　(26) ● Sylvia *hardly ever* calls us.　　⇐ *negative sentence*
　　　　　　　　　　---------------

negative adverbial phrase ↵ - here it means *almost not*

　　　　(27) ● We always **agree** where to lunch.　⇐ *positive sentence*

　　　　(28) ● We *rarely agree* where to lunch.　⇐ *negative sentence*
　　　　　　　　---------------------

negative adverbial phrase ↵ - it means *not very often*

　　　　(29) ● You can pay *either* today *or* tomorrow. ⇐ *positive sentence / alternative*

　　　　(30) ● Their car is *neither* big *nor* small　⇐ *negative sentence*
　　　　　　　　　　---------　-----
　　　　　　　　　　⇑　　　　⇑
　　　　　　　　　　1　　　　2

In Example 30, **1** and **2** together show that two attributes (big and small) of a car are compared. It is true that the car is not small and not big. The negative statement is true for both attributes.

● An adverbial phrase can be used with a negative word for the emphatic negative.

　　　　(31) ● We *do not* see your point of view *at all*.
　　　　　　　--------　　　　　　　　------
　　　　　　　　⇑　　　　　　　　　　⇑
　　　　　　　negative　　　　it means *in any way* - emphasizing negative meaning

(31) • We haven't yet finished our journey, *not by any means / by no means*.

       ⟰   it means *not at all* ↵ - emphasizing
     negative   negative meaning

(32) • There is *absolutely nothing* more we can do to help you.

    emphasizing ↵   ⟰
negative meaning   negative word means *not a single thing*

The word <u>*absolutely*</u> means something is completely true. In this example, it stresses that it is true that there is not a single thing we can do to help you.

(33) • We are *not in the least* hungry.

  negative word ↵   ⟰
          to underline negative meaning - it means *not at all*

• <u>Active and Passive Sentences</u>

In the last chapter, under active and passive clauses, a number of examples were given to explain the meaning of active and passive and their differences. Here are some more examples:

> "The Principal chaired the emergency staff meeting. At this meeting, the staff were addressed by the principal, who outlined current financial circumstances facing the college. The staff were also informed by the principal about the circular the college received from the Government concerning lower grants during the new financial year, which was to commence next month. The staff were told about the current unfilled vacancies and a cash shortage to pay wages. The staff, who were already under the stress of their workload, feared job threats, and greeted the announcement with dismay and anger ."

The above paragraph contains five reported sentences. We can identify each sentence in terms

of active and passive: The Principal .... meeting. ⇐ *active sentence*

Because the principal (**subject**) which is the agent did something, that is chaired (**active verb**) the meeting. For this reason, it is an active sentence. As the verb element in this sentence is active, you can say it is *active voice*.

- *At the meeting.........facing the college.* ⇐ *passive sentence*

The action (**were addressed**) is a **passive verb** directed at the subject (**the staff**). We can say something was done to the staff. As the verb element in this sentence is passive, you can consider it as *passive voice*. By applying the same rules:

- *The staff ----------next month.* ⇐ *passive sentence*

- *The staff --------- pay wages.* ⇐ *passive sentence*

- *The staff -------- and anger.* ⇐ *active sentence*

- An active sentence has a topic and some new information which is of some interest. The topic of the sentence is the *agent*, which is at the front of the sentence. When a sentence contains a transitive verb, you can convert it into a passive sentence. For instance:

(1) • A young neighbour has ridden our motorcycle. ⇐ *Active sentence with an agent*

      --------------------------   --------------------

          ⇑   ⇑

    agent – the **topic** of the sentence   point of interest – **new information** in the sentence

- **What has the agent done?** - has ridden our motorcycle. Thus, the active sentence contains some new information in relation to the topic of the sentence.

- You can convert this sentence into a passive sentence as shown below:

(2) • Our motorcycle has been ridden by *a young neighbour*. ⇐ *Passive with an agent*

     ------------------   --------------------------

        ⇑   ⇑

    topic of the sentence   new information in the sentence of some interest

In Example 2, the topic is now what is the new information in Example 1. It is also at the front of the sentence. The *topic* in Example 1 became *new information* in Example 2. It is now a part of the phrase which is at the end of the sentence.

- You can have a passive sentence *without an agent*. The presence of an agent in a passive sentence is relevant only if it provides some new information about the topic. For instance:

    (3) • Motorcycles are ridden. ⇐ Passive without an agent.

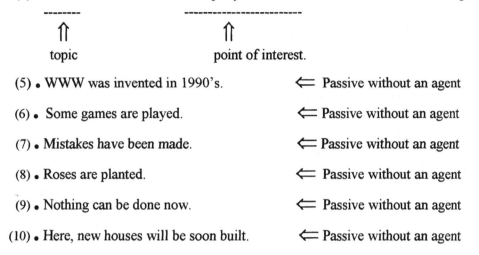

(4) • The car should be driven *carefully at all times*. ⇐ Passive without an agent

           ⇑   ⇑

     topic   point of interest.

(5) • WWW was invented in 1990's. ⇐ Passive without an agent

(6) • Some games are played. ⇐ Passive without an agent

(7) • Mistakes have been made. ⇐ Passive without an agent

(8) • Roses are planted. ⇐ Passive without an agent

(9) • Nothing can be done now. ⇐ Passive without an agent

(10) • Here, new houses will be soon built. ⇐ Passive without an agent

- <u>The following sentences cannot be in passive voice because each sentence has an intransitive verb element:</u>

    (11) • I always *sleep* well.

               ⇑

         intransitive verb

    (12) • It happened.

               ⇑

         intransitive verb

    (13) • The hall has warmed up.

- <u>The passive voice is less common. It is considered as rather an impersonal and official style of writing. However, sometimes, you have to use it.</u>

Now is the time to discuss sentences by their types listed above.

. <u>Declarative Sentences</u>

Declarative sentences are by far the most common sentences in the English language. In a declarative sentence, the subject is followed by the verb, and its complement.

The following examples illustrate this point further:

    (1) • Ari is a father.

        ⇑ ⇑ ⇑
        S V O

    (2) • Frank was a programmer.

        ⇑ ⇑   ⇑
        S V   O

In these two examples **SVO** elements are obligatory. If you remove any one of these elements, the sentence will <u>not</u> be grammatically correct. On the other hand, the good news is that you can expand this basic structure in order to convey a wide range of information. This is illustrated by the following examples:

    (1) • *Joan has studied at London University.*

        ⇑   ⇑   ⇑
        S +   **V**   **+ verb complement (C)** ⇒ **prepositional phrase (PP)**

• This sentence has just one clause. This clause consists of *SVC* structural elements.

• The verb element in this clause **has studied** is **finite and active**.

• The absence of any of these structural elements will make this sentence grammatically incomplete.

• This sentence makes *a **statement*** which conveys some information. It is a typical example.

• In fact, this sentence or a clause will not render the intended meaning, if you remove any of **SVC** structural elements from the sentence. On the other hand, you can extend this sentence so that it can give additional information. For example:

    (2) • *Joan has studied **at** London University **for** her PhD qualification.*

        ⇑   ⇑   ⇑
        S +   **V**   **+**   verb complement (C) consists of two
                                  prepositional phrases (PP)

- There are many different uses of declarative sentences for making statements. A statement may give just some information about something as illustrated above. Alternatively, it may give some information, which leads to an action or doing something. For instance:

(3) • I will copy this document and send it to you by post today. ⇐ *indicating action*

The following examples of declarative sentences demonstrate a variety of statements.

(4) • I am ever so grateful for your help in this matter. ⇐ *thanking someone*

(5) • Police ordered the crowd to clear the road immediately. ⇐ *giving an order*

(6) • There were no injuries in this serious car crash. ⇐ *giving an account of an accident*

(7) • Everything seems to be in order. ⇐ *indicating approval*

(8) • One of the capital cities, in the European Union, on both sides of the River Thames,

is London. ⇐ *describing a place*

(9) • I'm sorry to learn about floods, which have caused so much misery

to your family. ⇐ *conveying sympathy*

(10) • Please let me know your decision by tomorrow. ⇐ *seeking information*

(11) • They'd like me to have lunch with them today. ⇐ *giving invitation*

Each sentence is conveying some information in the form of a statement or a declaration.

• Performative Verbs

Usually, a declarative sentence is constructed to make a statement as illustrated above. Some verbs in the first person present tense and in a declarative context indicate the action they perform. For instance: **'blame'** in 'I blame you'. For this reason, these verbs are called performative verbs. Here are some examples of performative verbs.

---

accept, advise, agree, apologise, blame, demand, forgive, guarantee, inform, insist, name, order, predict, promise, pronounce, propose, protest, recommend, request, suggest, swear, thank, warn.

The following statements illustrate the use of some performative verbs.

(12) • I promise to be there at the agreed time. ⇐ *promising*

(13) • The accused swears to tell nothing but the truth. ⇐ *swearing*

(14) • I thank you for the invitation. ⇐ *thanking*

(15) • No one can predict the outcome of this General Election. ⇐ *predicting*

• A model verb may be preceded by the performative verb in order to make it sound some what polite. Here are some examples:

(16) • We'd require a guarantee in the form of a small deposit. ⇐ *guaranteeing*

(17) • They'd like us to confess any wrongdoing. ⇐ *confessing*

(18) • I have to *declare* that you are no longer a member of this club. ⇐ *declaring*

       ----

    formal use ↵

• Some performative verbs such as *declare*, *order* and *warn* are used in formal writing and speaking. The following examples show their use:

(19) • I *warn* (or I'm warning) you for the last time, not to come late for work
                       any more.

    ----

both forms are possible↵

. Interrogative Sentences

The basic use of interrogative sentences is to ask for information. The interrogative sentences or questions can generate answers in the forms of *yes/no* or some *specific information*.

• The interrogative sentences which lead to yes/no answers are known as <u>*yes/no questions*</u>.

Examples of such questions are given below:

(1) • Have you seen John this morning?   *answer* ⇒ *yes/no*

(2) • Has your wife returned from her shopping trip?   *answer* ⇒ *yes/no*

(3) • Have you ever had such an enjoyable outing to London? *answer* ⇒ *yes/no*

****

(4) • Do you sell fried chicken? *answer* ⟹ *yes/no*

It is possible that answers to any of the above questions may be given more fuller than just
yes/no. For instance, the answer to example **(1)** can be given as *Yes, I have seen him/John.*
Even so, it is still a yes/no question.

• The interrogative sentences which generate some specific information are known as *wh –*
   questions. The following examples illustrate this type of interrogative sentences
   and answers.

(5) •Where were you yesterday at about 2 p.m.?   *answer* ⟹ *I was at home.*

(6) • When will we go for a long walk by the sea? *answer* ⟹ *We will go now.*

(7) • Who can give me a lift by car to the station this afternoon? ? *answer* ⟹ *I can.*

(8) • What's the matter with you?   *answer* ⟹ *I lost my hat.*

(9) • Why were you late this morning? *answer* ⟹ *My car broke down on the way to work*

(10) •Whose is this car in my place? *answer* ⟹ *It is my car.*

• The structure of an interrogative sentence differs from the structure of a declarative
   sentence. The subject and the verb in an interrogative sentence do not occur in the same
   positions as in a declarative sentence. This is illustrated below:

(11) • You live in this area.   ⟸ *declarative sentence*

      ⇑   ⇑   ⇑
      S   V   C

(12) • *Do* you live in this area?   ⟸ *interrogative sentence*

   ⇑ ⇑ ⇑   ⇑
   Aux S   V   C   Aux = Auxiliary Verb
   ⇑

Primary auxiliary verb *do* is used to express simple present tense

(13) • We worked all night to finalise the annual accounts. ⟸ *declarative sentence*

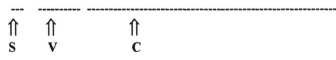

   ⇑   ⇑   ⇑
   S   V   C

****

(14) • Did we work all night to finalise the annual accounts? ⇐ *interrogative*
    ⇑ ⇑ ⇑   ⇑   *sentence*
   Aux S V   C
    ⇑

Primary auxiliary verb *did* expressing simple past tense

• In simple tenses the auxiliary *do* is used to form a question. It comes before the subject.
  If you compare example 11 with example 12 and example 13 with example 14 you can see
  there is *inversion* (changing word order) of the subject and auxiliary.

• In example 15, *be* is used on its own as an ordinary verb. This example is converted to a
  question. This question is example 16. This example demonstrates that there is an inversion
  of the subject and *be* as an ordinary verb. Examples 17 and 18 also illustrate the same rule.

(15) • She is somewhere in the town centre now. ⇐ *declarative sentence/statement*
    ⇑ ⇑   ⇑
    S   V   C

(16) • Is she somewhere in the town centre now? ⇐ *interrogative sentence*
    ⇑ ⇑   ⇑
    V S   C
    ⇑

be is used as an ordinary verb on its own

(17) • He was in Germany last week. ⇐ *declarative sentence/statement*
    ⇑ ⇑   ⇑
    S   V   C

(18) • Was he in Germany last week? ⇐ *interrogative sentence*
    ⇑ ⇑   ⇑
    V S   C
    ⇑

be functions here as an ordinary verb on its own

• If there is more than one auxiliary verb, then there is inversion of the first auxiliary verb and the subject. Examples 19 and 20 illustrate this rule:

(19) • I could have finished that job by now. ⇐ *declarative sentence/statement*

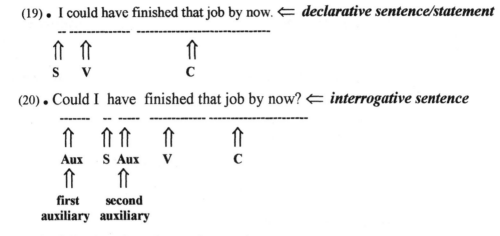

(20) • Could I have finished that job by now? ⇐ *interrogative sentence*

• There are the following nine *wh-question* words:

$$\textit{what, who, whom, which, whose, where, when, why, how}$$

• A question word may be the subject, object, complement or adverbial in a sentence as demonstrated below.

• Examples 21 and 22 illustrate that the *wh-question* word generates the subject *John Smith* in the declarative sentence. There is no inversion.

(21) • *Who* will lunch with you today? ⇐ *wh-question sentence*

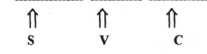

wh-question↵

(22) • *John Smith* will lunch with me today. ⇐ *declarative sentence/statement*

```
---------------  -----------  ------------------
     ⇑              ⇑              ⇑
     S              V              C
```

• Examples 23 and 24 show that the *wh-question* word generates the object *five boxes (object)* in the declarative sentence. *There is no inversion.*

****

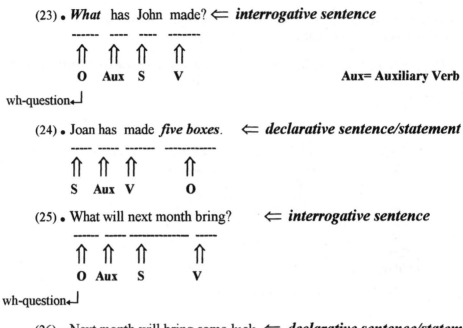

(23) . *What* has John made? ⟸ *interrogative sentence*

O   Aux   S   V   Aux= Auxiliary Verb

wh-question⤶

(24) . Joan has made *five boxes*.   ⟸ *declarative sentence/statement*

S   Aux   V   O

(25) . What will next month bring?   ⟸ *interrogative sentence*

O   Aux   S   V

wh-question⤶

(26) . Next month will bring some luck. ⟸ *declarative sentence/statement*

S   Aux   V   O

- Examples 25 and 26 exhibit that the *wh-question* word relates to the object *some luck* in the declarative sentence. <u>There is inversion of the subject *next month* and the model auxiliary *will*</u>.

- Examples 27 and 28 exemplify that the **wh-question** word refers to the object *my car* in the declarative sentence. <u>There is inversion of the subject and auxiliary verb.</u>

(27) . Whose is this car in this place? ⟸ *interrogative sentence*

O   V   S   ad ⟹ adverbial element

wh-question⤶

(28) . This is my car in this place.   ⟸ *declarative sentence/statement*

S   V   O   Ad ⟹ adverbial element

Here the preposition *in* is before the noun *place*. Therefore, it is a prepositional phrase of place and an adverbial (or adverbial element). See⇒ adverbial

- Examples 29 and 30 illustrate that the *wh-question* word refers to the adverbial element in the declarative sentence. <u>There is inversion of the subject *you* and model auxiliary *will*.</u>

(29) • When will you come home?   ⇐ *interrogative sentence*

        ⇑   ⇑   ⇑   ⇑   ⇑

      ad Aux S   V   O

wh-question⏎

(30) • You will come home at 11 p.m. tonight.

   ⇑ ⇑ ⇑   ⇑   ⇑

   S Aux V   O   ad ⇒ adverbial element

- Examples 31 and 32 illustrate that the *wh-question* word refers to the object musical play Cats in the declarative sentence. <u>There is no inversion, except that the wh-question word is</u> placed to the front in example 32.

(31) • Annemarie Kling likes romantic short story most.

          ⇑   ⇑   ⇑   ⇑

          S   **V**   **O**   **ad ⇒ adverbial element**

(32) • Which short story does Annemarie Kling like most?

       ⇑   ⇑   ⇑ ⇑

       O   **S**   **V   ad ⇒ adverbial element**

wh-question⏎

• <u>Interrogative Sentences without Inversion</u>

An interrogative sentence has the same word order as in a declarative sentence. This happens in informal conversation when the question follows on from what was said before. Here are some examples:

(33) • I may leave you. **You are leaving now?**   ⇒ *Not just yet*

(34) • I must visit my mother to see how she is now.

   Your mother is not well?   ⇒ *yes*

(35) • My friend met me at the airport.

   Anne Kling met you ?   ⇒ *yes, she did*

(36) • I bought a new house.

   The house is which type?   ⇒ *It is a semi-detached house*

(37) • I have not completed this task.

   You haven't completed this task yet?   ⇒ *no*

(38) • We had a nice holiday in France.

   You had a nice holiday in France?   ⇒ *Yes*

(39) • Rachel and Ari became parents.

   Rachel and Ari became parents?   ⇒ *Yes*

Negative interrogative sentences are also exemplified below.

• You can include an appropriate **_negative word_** in an interrogative sentence. This is exemplified below.

   (37) • Did he tell you *never* to do it again?
                    ----

          negative word ↵

   (38) • Why does your father allow *no* one to visit you?
                              ----

          negative word ↵

   (39) • Does she say *nothing* about her previous marriage?
                       ----

          negative word ↵

. <u>Imperative Sentences</u>

The imperative is the base form of the verb. A sentence with an imperative verb element is an imperative sentence. An imperative sentence enables us to make an earnest request, give an order or a command. In fact, you can use it to make someone act on your wishes whether it is under any prevailing condition or without any condition. You can also use the imperative to offer someone your good wishes. It is always in the present tense and refers to the second person, singular or plural form. Normally, an imperative does not have a subject. Here are some examples:

(1) . *Take* a seat, please. ⇐ *an earnest request for an action resulting in sit down*

imperative form of the verb

It refers to second person singular *(= you)*. There may be several persons, but each person is requested to take a seat.

(2) . *Through* this entrance, please. ⇐ *an instruction*

(3) . *Be* careful. ⇐ *an instruction/advice*

(4) . *Do be* quiet. ⇐*/strong order/more emphatic*

(5) . *Do sit down.* ⇐ *an order/more emphatic*

In examples 4 and 5, the auxiliary *do* helps to soften the effect of the imperative on the listener. In other words, the use of *do* sounds less authoritative.

(6) . **Don't** talk so loudly. ⇐ *an order*

In example 6, the auxiliary *do* is essential in order to construct the negative imperative.

(7) . *Stop*. ⇐ *an order – remember traffic/road sign*

(8) . *Don't* talk. ⇐ *an order*

(9) . *Don't be* absurd. ⇐ *emphatic*

(10) . *Come* in. ⇐ *permission* **But** (10A) . *Do* come in. ⇐*more emphatic*

242   **Phrases, Clauses & Sentences**   **Sentences**

****

(11) . *Go* away. ⇐ *an order* – rather impolite

(12) . *Shut* the door at once ⇐ *a strong command/order*

(13) . *Get out* of here. ⇐ *an order* - sounds rude

(14) . If you can't afford to pay, *don't* come. ⇐ *conditional instruction*

(15) . If you *are coming* late, **take** your keys.   ⇐ *conditional instruction*

(16) . If you drive to London, *don't drink* for a day. ⇐ *conditional order*

(17) . *Enjoy* your meal.   ⇐ offering of good wish

(18) . *Let's* have lunch. ⇐ *a suggestion to perform an action together*

      ⇑

imperative form of the verb ⇒ *let + us = let's*

It implies that the speaker and the listener perform the action together. It is in plural form.

(19) . *Let's not* keep arguing about it. ⇐ *negative form of the order*

. You can also construct the negative imperative with *do let's*.

(20) . *Don't let's* lose any of our clients. ⇐ *negative form of the order (informal)*

. When there are two persons, *you* can be the subject

(21) . *You be gentle* when she meets you. ⇐ *an emphatic advice*

      ⇑
     subject

(22) . *You watch* the traffic, I climb the ladder. ⇐ *an emphatic instruction*

. Exclamative Sentences

The purpose of exclamative sentences is to express a variety of feelings. These can be joy,

****

sorrow, anger, shock, surprise or any other emotional feeling. The construction of exclamative sentences is based on *how* and *what* wh-words. An exclamation mark is placed at the end of the sentence instead of a full stop. Exclamative sentences are not as flexible as other types of sentences. We use them for the sole purpose of expressing emotions. The following examples demonstrate their construction and usage:

(1) • How *intelligent* your son is!

It means that your son is very intelligent. It expresses the writer's or speaker's feelings about the degree of intelligence.

• Examples 2 - 8 show that the wh-word can be followed by an adjective. The adjective can be with an article *a* or *an*:

(2) • How *wonderful* the scene is!

(3) • How *lucky* you were!

(4) • How *kind* those people are!

(5) • What *a lovely* person your wife is!

(6) • What *a simple* style it is!

(7) • What a *memorable* show we watched!

(8) • What *an enjoyable* weekend we had!

• Examples 9 -17 illustrate that an exclamative can be a phrase. The phrase can also be just a short phrase:

(9) • How *generous*!

(10) • How *foolish*!

(11) • What *a charming* evening!

(12) • What *a mess* !

(13) • What *fun*!

(14) • *Oh*!

****

(15) • *Look out*!

(16) • *Excellent*!

(17) • *Well done*!

• <u>Examples 18 - 19 demonstrate that the wh-word can be followed by an adverb/adverbial:</u>

(18) • How *slowly* Elena talks!

(19) • How *carefully* Yuonne handled the glass!

• <u>Examples 20 –21 demonstrate that the wh-word can modify the verb:</u>

(20) • How they *run*!

(21) • How the girls *giggled*!

• <u>Simple Sentences</u>

In the last chapter, a distinction between simple, compound and complex sentences is made. In this section, we examine each type of sentence in detail. Some points made in the last chapter are repeated here in order to develop each topic further.

• <u>**A simple sentence has at least one clause.**</u> Here are some examples:

(1) • *Margaret enjoyed her meal.*
　　　----------　----------　------------
　　　　⇑　　　　⇑　　　　⇑
　　　　S　　　　V　　　　O
transitive verb type↵

(2) • It was a warm afternoon.
　　　--　-----　----------------------
　　　⇑ ⇑　　　　⇑
　　　S　V　　　O
transitive verb type↵

****

- the structure of each sentence is stated in terms of SVO

- each sentence has a finite form of the verb

- each sentence can not be broken into smaller sentences because each sentence has just one verb

- each sentence has just one clause

- each sentence is grammatically complete

Each sentence is a ***simple sentence***. It can be said that each sentence has a **main clause** with a *finite verb* in each sentence. Now consider the following examples:

(3) . *She laughs.*

---- --------

⇑   ⇑
S   **V**

(4) . *Susan comes.*

------ --------

⇑   ⇑
S   **V**

In examples (3) and (4):

- each sentence has an **SV** structure

- each has an intransitive verb – can not take an object

- each sentence can not be broken into smaller sentences because each has one verb element

- each sentence is grammatically complete irrespective of its size

Each sentence is a ***simple sentence***. It can be said that each sentence has a *main clause* with a *finite form of the verb*.

- A structure may have a clause but it is still not a simple sentence. For example:

(5) . *Since John passed his driving test.* ⇐ this is **incomplete** sentence

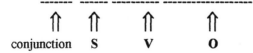

------- ------ ---------- --------------------

⇑   ⇑   ⇑   ⇑
conjunction   S   V   **O**

****

This sentence contains a clause, but it is not a simple sentence. It begins with a conjunction, which requires further information. Thus, this is not a simple sentence as it is grammatically incomplete. If we can remove the adverbial *since* from this sentence, it will become a simple sentence containing a main clause as shown below.

(6) • *John passed his driving test.*

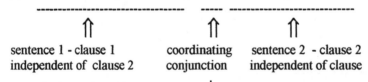

       S   V   O

(7) • It has been very cold all day. ⇐ *simple sentence*

. <u>Compound Sentences</u>

This above sentence has only one verb. It can not be split into smaller sentences. It is a clause as well as a simple sentence. See clauses. We can re-write this sentence and add to it some other structural parts as shown below:

(8) • It has been very cold all day **and** *I have stayed at home.* ⇐ *compound sentence*

        ⇑   ⇑   ⇑

sentence 1 - clause 1   coordinating   sentence 2 - clause 2
independent of clause 2   conjunction   independent of clause

points both clauses have the same status ↵

Example 8 consists of two shorter sentences or clauses joined together with a conjunction *and*. In this example, each clause can stand on its own. In other words, grammatically, these clauses are of *equal status*. For this reason, this sentence is a compound sentence. A compound sentence can have two or more clauses of equal status. In fact, each clause is a main clause in its own right, and thus can stand alone. In order to form compound sentences by linking clauses, we use the following:

- **<u>coordinating conjunctions/ coordinators</u>:** *and*, *or* and *but* are mainly used. See examples 8 – 17. *For* is seldom used. See examples 18-19.

- **<u>coordinating coordinator *or* with *not*</u>:** n*or* can be used with the negative first clause. See Examples 20 – 21.

- **<u>correlative coordinators</u>:** *either --- or* are used for emphasizing an alternative course of action. See Examples 22-24.

****

- Conjunctions ***and, or*** and ***but*** <u>must be placed between the two clauses (short sentences). In fact, you can not place them anywhere except between the clauses.</u> Here are some more examples of compound sentences:

  (9) • Jane wants to work in England, **but** *she doesn't like to be away from home.*

  ```
  ------------------------------------   ----   -----------------------------------------
              ⇑                            ⇑                         ⇑
          clause 1              coordinating conjunction          clause 2
  ```

  (10) • I like fried chicken ***but*** my wife likes grilled chicken.

  (11) • They went out to go swimming ***and*** we walked to the local shopping precinct.

  (12) • I wanted to travel to Paris ***but*** there is no direct train to Paris from here.

- <u>When the subject is the same in both main clauses, we don't have to repeat it in the second clause. When an element of a clause is left out, it is called an</u> ***ellipsis***. The reason is that the left out element can be inferred from the meaning and grammatical context of the sentence. The following examples illustrate the use of ellipsis:

  (13) • You can take a taxi to Heathrow <u>*or*</u> go by airbus from Victoria.

  (14) • I may travel to France by car <u>*or*</u> may fly to Paris by Air France.

  (15) • Police caught John breaking the speed limit on the M1 ***and*** charged him.

- <u>A compound sentence can have more than two clauses. The coordinating coordinators **and** and **or** are used to link more than two main clauses in a compound sentence.</u> For instance:

  (16) • You can borrow my umbrella <u>*or*</u> buy a new one <u>*or*</u> you don't care about it.

  (17) • You asked for some money ***and*** I had no money ***and*** the bank was already closed.

- The <u>coordinating coordinator ***but*** can not join more than two main clauses.</u> The reason is that it is used only when two main clauses are expressing contrasting meaning in a compound sentence. See examples 9 –11 above.

- Now we can examine the use of ***for*** through the following examples:

  (18) • We were dancing ***for*** the music was played.

  ```
  ----------------------   -----   ----------------------------
           ⇑                 ⇑                 ⇑
     main clause 1       coordinator       main clause2
  ```

The coordinator occurs in the same position where **and** coordinator is placed in a compound sentence. Indeed, *for* coordinator functions just like **and** in a compound sentence.

(19) . We couldn't hear very well *for* it was noisy.   ⇐ For = because

<u>In examples 1-19, sentences are too short to place a comma between these two main clauses.</u>

- When the first clause in a compound sentence is conveying negative meaning, **nor** coordinator is used as the negative complement of *or* to link clause 1 to clause 2.

(20) . He could **not** understand the question, **nor** did the teacher repeat the question.

       -----   -----

       ⇑   ⇑

   in clause 1   joining clauses 1 and 2

(21) . I wasn't able to turn left or right on the motorway, **nor** were other motorists.

- We can use *either* — *or* in a compound sentence to express an alternative. The coordinator *or* begins the second clause. Here *or* places emphasis on the alternative – second part of the compound sentence. This is illustrated below:

(22) . *Either* Team A bat first *or* Team B bowl first.

       --------   ---

       ⇑   ⇑

  starts first clause   joins second clause with the first clause

<u>No comma is between these two clauses, as it is a short sentence.</u>

Here are two more examples to confirm that *Either* can commence first clause:

(23) . *Either* you fix it as per our agreement, *or* we employ another joiner to do it.

(24) . *Either* Frank will drive the car back home from the pub, or Elina will drink wine.

<u>Warning!</u>

Two pairs of correlative coordinators *neither ... nor* and *both ... and* can grammatically link phrases but not clauses. Therefore, these can not form part of compound sentences.

.Complex Sentences

Like the compound sentence, a complex sentence also has two or more clauses. The difference between the complex and the compound sentences is that in the complex sentence clauses are **not** of the same equal status (main clauses). In a complex sentence, one clause is a main clause with one or more subordinate clauses. For instance:

(25) • *I came home immediately* **when** *I received this good news.* ⇐ *Complex sentence*

--------------------------------   ------   ------------------------------
⇑   ⇑   ⇑
main clause   conjunction   subordinate clause
clause 1   *clause 2*

In example 25, the main clause can stand alone. For this reason, it is also called an ***independent clause***. It is not dependent on the subordinate clause, which begins with the adverbial element **when**. Clause 2 cannot stand alone. Therefore, it is a ***dependent clause***. Dependent clauses are subordinate clauses. See ⇒ Clauses.

(26) • *When Antonia visited us,* **we made some Hungarian food.** ⇐ *Complex sentence*

---------------------------   ---------------------------------
⇑   ⇑
subordinate/dependent clause   main /independent clause

begins with an adverbial ⇒*when*

The presence of the subordinate clause makes this sentence complex. Here are some more examples:

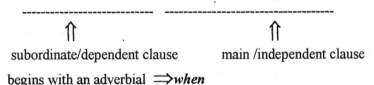

(27) • Soon after we arrived home, *our grandmother greeted us with a smile and kisses.*

------------   --
adverbial ↵   main clause ↵
⇑
starts subordinate clause

In this complex sentence, the subordinate clause begins with a multi-word subordinator *soon after*, an adverbial element.

(28) • *He found himself in a hospital bed* **because** he was involved in a car accident.
\-   \-\-\-\-\-\-\-\-\-   \-

  main clause ↵   adverbial element ↵   subordinate clause ↵

• As shown above, we can start a subordinate clause with **when** and *because*. Similarly, *if* and some other adverbials can do the same. See the last chapter on adverbial clauses.

(29) • *He will help you* if you approach him gently.
\-   \-\-\-   \-

        ⇑   ⇑   ⇑

  main clause adverbial   subordinator clause begins with ⟹*if*
               subordinator

• <u>The following examples demonstrate that a complex sentence can have more than one main and subordinate clause.</u>

(30) • *I remember* that you visited us some years ago **and** spent Christmas with us.
\-\-\-\-\-\-\-\-\-\-\-\-\-\-\-   \-\-\-\-\- \-   \-\-\-\-   \-

        ⇑   ⇑   ⇑   ⇑   ⇑
  main clause conjunction   subordinate clause 1 conjunction   subordinate clause 2

Here *that* starts a subordinate clause 1. Clause 2 is started with *and*. In subordinate clauses 1 and 2, the subject (*you*) is the same. We can leave out the subject in clause 2.

In each of the next three examples, there is one main clause in *bold style* and two subordinate clauses.

(31) • *Although* she was out of work, *she made a return trip to Switzerland because* her mother paid for it.

(32) • *Liz Taylor was married to Richard Burton who* died some years ago *because of* his heart failure.

(33) • *I went to Germany* *and* stayed with some family friends *because* it was interesting.

(34) • *A thief,* who brandished a gun and raided a bank, got away with a lot of money.

In this example:

- *A thief* got away with a lot of money   ⟹ *main clause*

- who brandished a gun   ⟹ *subordinate clause -1*

- and raided a bank   ⟹ *subordinate clause -2*

(35) • Ursula thought *that* Ralf was a millionaire **when** she saw him *coming* in a chauffeur driven Rolls Royce, *but* she was mistaken.

We can analyse this sentence into the following clauses:

- Ursula thought ⟹ *main clause 1*

- that Ralf was a millionaire *subordinate clause 1* ⟹ noun clause

- when she saw him ⟹ *subordinate clause 2* ⟹ adverbial clause

- coming in a chauffeur driven Rolls Royce ⟹ *subordinate clause 3* ⟹ participle clause

- but she was mistaken ⟹ *main clause 2 - but* joins two main clauses

This is how main clauses can be joined together, when there are two subordinate clauses between them.

(36) • She was very tired when she returned from Poland, but went to work the next day, *where* she caught the flu, as it was a very stormy, cold, winter's day.

We can analyse this sentence as follows:

- She was very tired   ⟹ *main clause 1*

****

- when she returned from Poland   ⟹*subordinate clause 1*

- but went to work the next day   ⟹*main clause 2*

- where she caught the flu   ⟹*subordinate clause 2*

- as it was a very stormy , cold, winter's day   ⟹*subordinate clause 3*

- <u>Here are two more examples of complex sentences with non-finite clauses:</u>

(37) • Sarah wishes to return home by car *because* there is no train service tonight.
    ----------------------------------   --

            ⇑   ⇑

       main clause   **subordinate clause**

(38) • I wanted to travel by air but it was not possible to fly from the nearest airport.
    ------------------------------   ----------------------------   --------------------------------------

        ⇑   ⇑   ⇑

    main clause 1   **main clause 2**   **sub clause**

In summary, a sentence does not have to be short to be simple. What makes it simple is the presence of a single clause which is grammatically complete.

A compound sentence has two or more clauses of equal status. A complex sentence has at least one main and one subordinate or sub clause. Both compound and complex sentences can be broken down into smaller sentences or clauses. We often use the same tense in the main and subordinate clauses in both compound and complex sentences. Very long sentences should be avoided for the sake of clarity.

Punctuation   **253**

****

Part 3

Punctuation

• Introduction

Punctuation enables the writer to clarify the meaning of a piece of writing. Punctuation has a set of rules and corresponding marks. These marks are inserted in writing in accordance with these rules. Punctuation also denotes specific points of grammar in a piece of writing. The misuse of punctuation marks or absence of punctuation can lead to misreading and ambiguity. The following punctuation marks with their rules of usage are discussed in this chapter:

• **apostrophe**	• **dash**	• **paragraph**
• **asterisk**	• **ellipses /three dot**	• **question mark**
• **brackets**	• **exclamation mark**	• **quotation marks**
• **capital letters**	• **footnotes**	• **semicolon**
• **colon**	• **full stop**	• **slash/ bar/ diagonal/ oblique mark**

• **comma**	• **hyphen**	• **word-processing marks -**
		     bullets, bolds, *italics*,
		     underlining and arrows, etc.

• <u>The above punctuation marks are not discussed in this chapter in a strict alphabetical order.</u>

You may come across some other punctuation marks which are not listed above. On the other hand, you may find that some of these punctuation marks are not discussed in some other books. For instance, some people do not consider the paragraph formation and capitalisation as punctuation marks. In this book, these are considered as equally important punctuation marks and their application is outlined.

Chapter 12
Punctuation

• Apostrophe '

An apostrophe has the following two major functions:

- to indicate possession or genitive case

- to mark contractions or show contractions or omissions of letters or syllables in the spelling of some words

Each of these functions is exemplified below:

1. To indicate the possessive or genitive case or possession in the following ways:

• When a noun is singular, an apostrophe and *s* are added to the noun.

For instance:

(1) • The *accountant's* office   (2) • *Anne's* wedding dress   (3) • *Robin's* car

(4) • The *company's* management team   (5) • *London's* red buses

(6) • My German *friend's* name is Plew

(7) • It is *John's* chair.

• An apostrophe and *s* is also added to indefinite pronouns that *do not* end in *s.*

(8) • This is *nobody's* fault.

----

indefinite pronoun ↵- *nobody = no one*

(9) . *Someone's* car is parked in my driveway.

⇑

indefinite pronoun ⟹ *someone = somebody or*
                       a person unknown or not mentioned by name

(10) . We hope that this year *everyone's* dreams come true.

⇑

indefinite pronoun ⟹ *everyone = all persons = everybody*

• **An apostrophe is added to plural nouns ending in _s_.** This is demonstrated below:

(11) . This is a *students'* computer laboratory.

(12) . Our *doctors'* surgery hours are between 6 –8 p.m. on Fridays.

(13) . Our *neighbours'* dog barked all night.

(14) . Primary school *teachers'* trade unions help new teachers.

(15) . Our car is parked in *Tesco's customers'* car park.

's with the singular proper noun ↵   ⇑
 to indicate possessive case   an apostrophe is added to a plural noun to show possession

(16) . *The hostages'* release at Frankfurt Airport came unexpectedly.

• **An apostrophe and _s_ are added to plural nouns that do _not_ end in _s_.**

Here are some examples:

(17) . There is the young *women's* hockey club.

(18) . She reads *children's* short stories.

(19) . I think *people's* opinions are important to politicians.

(20) • No one other than parents are allowed in a ***children's*** playground.

• **An apostrophe can be used to show the possessive form without mentioning the noun to which a reference is made.** For instance:

(21) • I met John outside the ***barber's*** (shop).

(22) • Julie works for a local ***optician's*** (practice).

(23) • We would like to have an Indian meal at ***Taj's*** (Restaurant).

You do not have to mention the nouns shown in brackets. Here are some more examples:

(24) • I saw Janet at **Lyon's** *(sport club)*.
                                ----

omitted ↵

(25) • We have our current account at the **TSB-Lloyd's***(bank)*.
                                                      ----

omitted ↵

• **An apostrophe is used with some units of measure to denote possession.** For instance:

(26) • I think in a ***week's*** time she will arrive here.

(27) • My father retired after ***forty years'*** service as a Civil Servant.

(28) • Just imagine how you will look in ***twenty years'*** time.

(29) • I must take a ***fortnight's*** *holiday* before 31 December.

(30) • I don't think this shirt is ***ten pounds'*** worth.

• **When a genitive (possessor) consists of more than one noun, the apostrophe is marked on the last noun.** A genitive shows possession. For instance:

(31) . *The British Prime Minister's* country residence is not too far from London.

(32) . *The Lord Chancellor's office* is in the Palace of Westminster.

(33) . *The Duke of Edinburgh's* Award Scheme, to foster the leisure activities of young people, began in 1956.

- **When possession is shared by more than one noun, the apostrophe and s are added to the last noun.** This is illustrated below:

(34) . *Webster and Lancaster's* books can be seen on ADR web site.

(35) . *Brinkman and Blaha's* Data Systems And Communications Dictionary is a well known book.

- **When possession is not shared by more than one noun, the apostrophe and s are added to each noun.** This is exemplified below:

(36) . *Earnest's* and *Klieg's* insurance training manuals are in our library.

(37) . I have *Hornby's* and *Webster's* dictionaries.

- **Use an apostrophe and s with personal names ending with s or z.** For instance:

(38) . **Prince Charles's** ideas on the environment are serious.

(39) . According to *Leibniz's Law,* if A is identical with B, then every property that A has B has, and vice versa.

- **An apostrophe and *s* are used with nouns which are preceded by the word *sake.***

For instance:

(40) . *For God's sake*, you must not lie during the interview.

(41) . *For pity's sake,* help your aged and sick parents.

(42) . *For heaven's sake*, allow her a day off with pay.

In examples 40 – 42, *bold words (idiomatic expressions)* are used to emphasize that it is important to do something. *God, pity* and *heaven* are singular nouns.

- **An apostrophe can be used with plural nouns which are preceded by the word *sake*:**

(43) • *For old times' sake*, Anne forgave him and invited him for a meal.

If you do something for *old times' sake (idiomatic expression),* you do it because it is connected with something good that happened to you in the past.

- **Use an apostrophe with abbreviations functioning as verbs.** For instance:

(44) • I submitted my application for a day off and my boss *OK'd* it.
                                                                                 ‾‾‾‾‾

                                                          Ok'd =okayed ↵   (OK! in present tense)

In this context, it means my boss officially agreed to let me have a day off work. It is rather an informal expression.

(45) • He was *KO'd* in the first round.
            ‾‾‾‾‾‾‾

KO'd = knocked out ↵ - *it is connected with boxing.*

- **Usually business names do not include an apostrophe in their business titles.**

For example:

(46) • I work at *Sainsburys*.   ⟹ *should be Sainsbury's*

(47) • My wife used to work for *Browns*.   ⟹ *should be Brown's*

(48) • I bought this CD from *Victorias*.   ⟹ *should be Victoria's*

Sainsbury, *Brown* and *Victoria* are business names.

Punctuation   **259**

****

• **In hyphenated compound words the apostrophe is added to the last word.** For instance:

    (49) • My wife's *brother-in-law's* home is not far from our home.

    (50) • A *well-dressed lady's* car is parked in your place.

2 • To mark contractions or indicate omissions in spelling certain words. For instance:

        (51) • *We'll* see you soon.

we will = we'll ↵

        (52) • She *won't* go there today.

will not = won't ↵

        (53) • It is a lovely spring morning, *isn't* it?

                        is not = isn't ↵

        (54) • *I'd* love to come with you.

I would = I'd ↵

        (55) • We arrived here at the beginning of Spring *'02*.

                           2002 = '02 ↵

        (56) • He left home at 8 *o'clock*.   ⇐ *omitting of the*

        of the clock = o'clock ↵ - use it only for telling the time in an exact hour

It is <u>not</u> used with a.m. and p.m.

****

It means that he left home at exactly 8 as shown or reckoned by the clock.

● **The following examples also show the use of an apostrophe *with a pronoun + an auxiliary verb* to contract them**. For instance:

(57) ● I'm = I am   (58) ● We're = We are

(59) ● They're = They are   (60) ● She's = She is **or** She has

● **An apostrophe is also used with *auxiliary verb + not* to contract them.**

Here are some examples:

(61) ● haven't = have not   (62) ● wouldn't = would not

(63) ● mightn't = might not   (64) ● couldn't = could not

(65) ● oughtn't = ought not   (66) ● needn't = need not

● **An apostrophe is used to indicate the omission of figures in dates.** For example:

(67) ● They wanted to stay with us in *'02*.
-----
referring to the year 2002 ↵

(68) ● Thank you for your letter of 9th Jan. *'03*.

● **An apostrophe is not used with the possessive pronouns.**

● *its*   ● *ours*   ● *yours*   ● *theirs*

● **An apostrophe is not used when referring to wars, plans, projects and similar notions related to a specified length of time.**   This is exemplified below:

(69) ● *Six-Day War*   (70) ● *Hundred Years' War* (this does not obey the rule)

    (71) • *Five –Year Plan*   (72) • *Ten –Year Projected Savings*

There are exceptions to the above rule as shown by example 70.

• **An apostrophe is not used with abbreviations and numbers which create plurals:**

  For instance:

        (73) • *the 1980s. For instance:*

        (74) • *In the 1950s, she was very young and pretty.*

Some writers place it before adding 's', e.g. ⇒ In the 1950's.
There is some controversy surrounding it.

• **Sometimes the insertion or omission of an apostrophe is surrounded by uncertainty.**

  For instance:

        (75) • 12 **St. James's** Square London SW 11.

        (76) • *St. John's Wood* Underground station is in London.

        (77) • He was seen in the *Earls Court* area yesterday afternoon.

An apostrophe is usually used with names of places, when possession is involved. See (75) and (76). However, this rule does not always apply. See example (77).

• Brackets

There are several types of brackets. In British English for writing purposes the round brackets ( ) which are known as parentheses are used. Square brackets [ ] are used in the USA. Of course, other types of brackets are used for mathematical and scientific work.

• Round Brackets or Parentheses ( )

Round brackets can perform the following functions:

        • to enclose some additional or optional information without affecting the
          flow and meaning of a sentence, a paragraph or a piece of writing

• to show alternatives

• to include abbreviations and refer to something by figures or letters

For instance:

(1) • Gandhi *(1869-1948)* was the foremost spiritual and political leader of the
twentieth century. He was called the Mahatma *(Great Souls – in Sanskrit)*.
Gandhi was a pacifist and a great champion of non-violence.

The removal of parentheses and their contents will not affect the flow and meaning of this
paragraph. Here are some more examples:

(2) • Any *student(s)* who would like to join this trip must see me today.

(3) • Only 2 *(two)* delegates are allowed free of charge during the book fair.

(4) • (1) Introduction
(2) Objectives
(3) Who should attend

In this book, examples are numbered as (1) •. The purpose of this "•" is to highlight each
example for the ease of readers. You do not have to adopt this method.

• <u>Square Brackets</u> [ ]

Square brackets are used to supplement or append to an original text some information which
may be a correction, an explanation or some translation by a person other than the author.

For instance:

(5) • During the Second World War, the British Prime Minister **[Churchill]** made
great and memorable speeches.   --------------

additional information appended by the editor ↵

(6) • In Germany, during the Second World War, the Führer **[leader, Hitler]** also
made highly nationalistic speeches.   -------------------

translation and additional information by another person ↵

Punctuation   **263**

****

(7) . The first woman party leader in British politics **[Margaret Thatcher]** became

----

added to the original text by the editor ↵

the longest serving 20th century female Prime Minister in 1988.

. Capital Letters

The use of capital letters is governed by the following punctuation rules:

. Use a capital letter at the beginning of a sentence.

For instance:

(1) . Punctuation enables us to write clearly.

(2) . Use punctuation to improve your writing.

. Use a capital letter after a colon.

In the following examples, direct speech is within the inverted commas:

(3) . The British Prime Minister, Margaret Thatcher, said:
  'I am extraordinarily patient, provided I get my own way in the end.'

  (The Observer 4 April 1989)

(4) . Once Mahatma Gandhi said:
  'There is enough for the needy but not for the greedy.'

(4A) . Once Goethe (German poet, novelist, and dramatist) said:
  'Boldness has genius, power and magic in it.'

. The pronoun I is written as a capital.

For instance:

(5) . I'm pleased to meet you.

(6) . It's a pity I missed your birthday party.

• <u>Use a capital letter to begin a proper noun:</u>

This is exemplified below:

(7) . Anne Kling is here from Germany. ⟸ *both names began with capital letters*

(8) . Mrs Johnson has arrived.

• <u>A title of a person and proper names begin with a capital letter.</u>

It is demonstrated below:

(9) . Dr Robertson is our General Practitioner.

   ⇑   ⇑   ⇑   ⇑

title   proper name   first word + second word = **title**

(10) . Mrs Taylor will see her doctor today.

   ⇑   ⇑

title   it is not functioning as a title here but as a common noun

(11) . Aunt Kay lives in Nottingham.

   ⇑

title (Auntie or Aunty is informal for aunt)

(12) . My **aunt** lives in Nottingham but Uncle Tom King died some years ago.

   ⇑   ⇑

aunt is not a title but a common noun   it is the title of Tom King

****

Words like doctor, aunt, grandfather are titles only when they are used with proper nouns.

• **Nouns for religions, scriptural books and related titles begin with a capital letter.**

For instance:

(13) • Islam means submission to Allah. A Muslim is someone who has submitted to
Allah, believing in Muhammad as a prophet of Allah. Allah is God in Islam.
The Holy Qur'an (also known as the Koran) is the holy book of Islam.

(14) • Christ, the Holy Bible, the Prophet Muhammad, Buddha, Judaism, the Talmud,
Hindu and Hinduism are all connected with different religions.

In examples 13 –14, Islam, Muslim, Allah, Muhammad, God, the Holy Qur'an, the Koran, the
Prophet Muhammad, the Holy Bible, Buddha, Judaism, the Talmud, Hindu and Hinduism all
began with capital letters. Here these are considered as proper nouns. However, in the phrase
'as a prophet', prophet is a common noun, not a title. For this reason, it does not begin with a
capital letter.

• **Capitals are used to begin the names of places, rivers, mountains, books, newspapers,
plays, films, trains, ships, spacecraft, aircraft and other such things.**

These are exemplified below:

(15) • London, Berlin, Moscow and Paris are all capital cities in Europe.

(16) • The longest span bridge in the world is Akashi-Kaiyo. It is in Japan.
Its length is 1990 metres.

(17) • The longest railway tunnel in the world is Seikan. It is 54 km long.
The second longest railway tunnel in the world is the Channel Tunnel
UK- France. It is 50 km long.

(18) • The largest desert in the world is the Sahara in northern Africa.

(19) • The highest mountain in the world is Everest in Asia.

(20) • The longest river in the world is the River Nile in Africa.

****

(21) • The largest country in the world by area is **R**ussia.

(22) • The largest city by population in the world is **T**okyo, in **J**apan.

(23) • The **H**imalayas are the highest mountain range on **E**arth. They are in **A**sia.

(24) • The distance from the **E**arth to the **S**un is about 150 million km.

(25) • "The **T**imes" is a daily newspaper for well-informed readers in the **UK**.

(26) • "The **D**iamond **S**ūtra" is the oldest surviving printed book in the world. It is a **C**hinese translation of **B**uddhist scripture, printed in AD 868.

(27) • The **O**rient **E**xpress is a famous train.

(28) • Apollo 11 made the first lunar landing.

(29) • The actress **E**lizabeth **T**aylor played the title role of the 1963 film "**C**leopatra."

(30) • "Java Simplified"is a computer programming book from ADR.

• <u>**Capitals are used for abbreviations of names of some organisations and countries. These are formed from the first letter of each word in the name.**</u>

Here are some examples:

(31) • **UN** is an abbreviation for the **U**nited **N**ations.

(32) • **UK** is a short name for the **U**nited **K**ingdom.

(33) • **EU** stands for the **E**uropean **U**nion.

(34) • **BBC** is an abbreviation for the **B**ritish **B**roadcasting **C**orporation.

(35) • **BP** is short for the **B**ritish **P**etroleum company.

The correct use of both capital and small letters has been muddled by the arrival of the Internet. Often proper names are written either in capital or small letters and joined together. This practice is not recommended in this book.

A Word of Warning

(1) • The Hilton Hotel / Hilton Hotel ⟹*correct*

(2) • a Hotel ⟹*wrong* – it should be ⟹ *a hotel*

(3) • River Indus ⟹*correct*

⇑
first part of this name

(4) • There are many Rivers in England.

⇑
incorrect – it should be <u>r</u>ivers

(5) • Hyde Park is in London. ⟹*correct*

⇑
correct because it is the <u>second</u> part of this name

(6) • There many Parks in London.
----
incorrect ↵ - it should be <u>p</u>arks

Colon

A colon is used for the following functions:

• <u>**To introduce a list or a series of items.**</u>

Here are some examples:

(1) • The following students must register their proposals today before 16.00 hours: James Walker, Joan Smith, Elizabeth Wood and John Baker.

(2) • We can travel to London by any of the three means of travel: by car, by train or by coach.

(3) • These are unused product code numbers: BA 00012C, CC 18919X and CC 18920 X.

• <u>**To identify a speaker in direct speech and quotations.**</u>

For instance:

(4) • Joy said: 'It was my handbag.'

(5) • Silvia shouted: 'Leave my home now!'

(6) • Tony Blair promised: 'Education, education, education.'

(7) • She asked me immediately: 'Who told you about my illness?'

- **Use a colon for introductory remarks.**

For example:

(8) • Ladies and gentlemen: allow me to present tonight's guest speaker.

- **To add information to a clause so that it is elaborated.**

This is exemplified below:

(9) • This group has students from six countries: Germany, Russia, India, China, Ireland and the United Kingdom.

(10) • We specialise in selling technical books: engineering, computing and physical sciences.

(11) • The inner city has been neglected by the authority: derelict buildings, dirty streets, lack of public transport, hardly any footpaths and ill-equipped hospitals are some of the things that local residents reported to the media.

- **To supplement information to a phrase so that it is expanded.**

For example:

(12) • Lots of books: computing, engineering, gardening, short stories and other topics.

- **To start a clause which contains an explanation of the previous clause.**

This is demonstrated below:

(13) ● Today our town is very busy: there is an annual festival and a procession along the promenade.

(14) ● Our train was full of overseas visitors: many passengers were travelling to London Heathrow Airport.

● **To introduce a subtitle.**

(15) ● Essential English: Grammar, Structure and Style of Good English.

----
subtitle ↵

(16) ● C++ Simplified: A practical C++ Programming Manual.

----
subtitle ↵

● **To form numerical ratios and other number systems.**

For instance:

(17) ● Profit and expenditure ratio **4:1**

(18) ● Our train left London Victoria at 15:30 sharp.

● **Another use of the colon is in office memos:**

For instance:

(19) ● From: John Smith   To: James Taylor
        Subject: Delivery by car   Dated: 12.01.2003

Colons are also used in mathematical, scientific and engineering expressions.

● Comma

The comma and full stop are the most common punctuation marks in the English language. The correct use of the comma is not a mystery. Its usage is fairly well documented and

****

understood, yet there is a tendency either to use too many commas or to use too few commas in a piece of writing. Indeed, there is a wide variation in the use of commas. Sometimes, a comma as a separator is essential. There are occasions when the use of a comma may be considered as optional for the sake of clarity. The following discussion illustrates its use for some specific aims:

. List Items

. To separate items in a list of three or more items. These item may be words, phrases or clauses. Here are some examples:

(1) . Anne, Wolfgang, Elena, and Frank went to Austria for a skiing holiday.

---

a comma before a conjunction ↵ - it is debatable - see ⟹ a comment below

(2) . You can have one more portion of potatoes, peas, or cabbage.

---

a comma before a conjunction ↵ - see ⟹ a comment below

(3) . John is energetic, ambitious, and rich.

---

a comma before and ↵ - it is debatable - see ⟹ a comment below

In examples 1-3, a comma is placed before the coordinating conjunction. These coordinating conjunctions come before the last item in each list. The placing of a comma before the coordinating conjunction which indicates the start of the last item is often called the '**Oxford comma**'. However, there is a growing trend towards the omission of the comma before the last coordinating conjunction. On the other hand, when the last item in the list has **and** in it, the comma is necessary to avoid ambiguity. For instance:

(4) . My children used to enjoy watching television game shows, children's programmes, and the *Little and Large* comedy show.

essential comma ↵   compound noun↵ - joined by *and* ⟹conjunction

(5) . He went to Fulham, Putney, and *Kensington and Chelsea* by bus.

a comma is essential here ↵ compound noun ↵

****

If the list ends with such phrases as *etc., and the like* and *so on*, a comma is needed to indicate continuity of the same thing. For instance:

> (6) • Gull, golden eagle, finch, duck, ***and the like*** creatures with feathers and two legs are birds.

> (7) • Tesco, Safeway, Morrison, etc. stores have been attracting customers of small corner shops to their own big retail outlets.

• <u>Main Clauses</u>

• <u>To join main clauses if they are linked by the coordinating conjunction *and, but* or *so*.</u>

For example:

> (1) • Our staff room is situated on the first floor, and the students' room is on the third floor.

> (2) • You can attend our meeting today, but you must not come more than five minutes late.

> (3) • She has declined our invitation, yet there is still plenty of time for her to accept it.

The comma can be omitted when the clauses are short. This is exemplified below:

> (4) • She cooks and I clean.

> (5) • We ran very fast but still missed the last bus.

> (6) • Susan is married yet she is known by her maiden name.

• <u>To separate a subordinate clause or phrase from the main clause, the use of a comma may be justified to avoid misunderstanding. The comma is more desirable and helpful, when the sentence is long.</u>

For instance:

****

(7) . After three hours of the skiing session, they returned to their hotel for a hot meal.
----

           adverbial phrase↵

(8) . At the end of the long working day, I didn't receive my wage.
----

           adverbial phrase↵

(9) . As soon as they left home, we had to cook our evening meal.
----

subordinate clause ↵

The use of a comma is less common, when the subordinate clause follows the main clause. For this reason, the comma is enclosed within the [ ] to indicate that its use is optional. This is illustrated below:

(10) . I did not travel with my wife to London **[,]** *because I had to attend an important meeting at work.*
    subordinate clause ↵

(11) . She wrote short stories as well **[,]** so that she could support her family.
----

           subordinate clause ↵

(12) . We left home in the morning **[,]** soon after our breakfast.
----

           subordinate clause ↵

. **Use commas to separate an adding /non-restrictive/non-identifying clause from the main clause.**

   For instance:

(13) . My son, who is a soldier , has left the army.

          ⇑

    adding/non-restrictive/non-identifying clause

Punctuation   **273**

****

If you remove the adding/non-restrictive/non-identifying clause from the sentence, it will still make sense.

    (14) • Miss Jones, who is our store manager, grew up in a foster home.

In examples 13 and 14, both relative non-adding clauses are specifying the head nouns.

• <u>No commas are needed to separate identifying (restrictive) and classifying clauses</u>

  from the main clause. See ⟹ Clauses for examples.

• **<u>Use commas to separate the speaker from the direct speech.</u>**

  For instance:

    (15) • The head teacher said, ' No one is allowed to use a mobile phone in class.'

         ----

        direct speech within single quotation marks ↵

    (16) • John Smith shouted, 'You are breaking speed limits. Reduce your speed now.'

<u>Note the use of single quotation marks. Single quotation marks are often used to report direct speech. You can use double quotation marks.</u>

For instance:

    (17) • "Ian, I don't agree with you," he said angrily, "you are not thinking clearly."

    (18) • Franklin D. Roosevelt said, "The only thing we have to fear is fear itself."

• **<u>Use commas to separate a question tag from the rest of the sentence:</u>**

Here are some examples:

    (19) • This is your new car, isn't it?

    (20) • Your wife is a doctor, am I right?

274   **Punctuation**

****

(21) • Your complaint was dealt with by me to your satisfaction, wasn't it?

• **Use commas to separate parenthetic remarks from the rest of the sentence.**

Words and phrases such as

> *indeed, certainly, oh, by chance* and *incidentally (adverbial elements)*

are not necessarily essential parts of a sentence in order to render its intended meaning. Indeed, they give additional information. Such words and phrases are also known as parenthetical remarks or parenthetic remarks. In a sentence, these are marked by commas, brackets or dashes. Here are some examples:

(22) • *Indeed,* she came with her two children.

(23) • I promise you, *sir,* I will pay back my tax by monthly instalments.

(24) • *By the way*, do you know where John lives?

(25) • *Now*, what can I do for you?

(26) • *Lords, ladies and gentlemen,* allow me to present our honourable guest
-------- ------------------- speaker, the Lord Mayor of Westminster.

         (12)   ⇑

within a pair of commas   *within a pair of comma*
as it is in the middle   *as it is in the middle of a sentence*
of a sentence

⌊in both cases, a pair of commas is functioning as parenthesis⌋

• **Use commas with numbers in accordance with the following rules.**

• Write non-technical numbers, by placing a comma after every three units, commencing from the right of the number: For instance:

(27) • 10,000   105, 111, 456   88,000,789

(28) • The population of Bridlington is around 65,000.

   • **The comma is not used in numbers smaller than 10,000.**

Punctuation   **275**

****

<u>**The following three numbers show the misuse of a comma in each number:**</u>

(29) .   1,267   2,345   9,999

           --   --   --

comma not allowed ↵   comma not allowed ↵   comma not allowed ↵

<u>Reason:</u> *<u>Commas are used with numbers 10,000 and above.</u>*

- **When dealing with the British currency, the whole pounds should be written with the pound symbol £.**

     For instance:

          (30) . £1   £5,349   £24   £1,009

                             --   --

       coma is essential here.↵   coma is essential here.↵

- **When the British currency involves both pound and pence, write pence in numbers after the decimal point. The comma is also used if the number is £1,000 or greater.**

     For instance:

         (31) .   £34 . 05   £467.99   £ 9,789. 75

                     --   ---

         decimal point ↵   two places after decimal point for pence ↵

When the amounts is in pounds and pence, do not use the symbol/abbreviation *p* for pence. Mixed currency is extended to two places after the decimal point. See example 32. When the amount is less than the whole pound, it is written as:

(32) . 66p   99p   5p   1p **Or write as** ⟹ .66   .99   .05   .01

- **Large amounts involving a million or a billion or a trillion can also be written with their respective symbols/abbreviation or without it:**

For example:

                       . **m**   is an abbreviation or a symbol for million
                       . **bn**   is an abbreviation or a symbol for billion
                       . **trillion** is written as trillion

(33) • 1,000,000   or   1 m   1,000,000,000 or 1 bn

178,000,000   or   178 m   1,500,000,000   or 1.5 bn

We say **a, one, two** or **several** billion or million. <u>There is no need to say millions or billions</u>. We say these without the final 's'. For example:

(34) • At the end of the first six months of this year, our sales reached between 2.6 m and 1 bn.

<u>When there is no quantity or a number before million or billion, we say millions or billions.</u>

For example:

(35) • Millions/billions of pounds were invested in the London Dome.

The following examples on the use of million give further information.

• You can say:

(36) • Our government has wasted *tens of millions* on advertising their failed policies.
                                      ----
                                      plural numbers ↵

• <u>**Always use a plural verb with million or millions and billion or billions:**</u>

For instance:

(37) • One million *pounds* were spent on this building project.
              ----
              plural form ↵

(38) • Three million *pounds* have been deposited in his bank account.
              ----
              plural form ↵

(39) ● Some gangsters make *their millions* by selling drugs and stolen goods.

----

make their millions = all their money ↵

●*Currency in the USA*

Money is written in the same way as pounds and pence in the UK, except with the dollar sign. For instance:

(40) ● $ 5,567 $1.6m $ 10.66   50¢

●**Dash** –

The prime function of a dash is to separate a part of a sentence from the rest of a sentence. There may be one or more dashes in a sentence. The dash is used for a variety of aims. Some of these are exemplified here:

● **In the following examples, dashes have added *some excitement and informality*:**

(1) ● Annabel loved Rex so much – and she left her husband.

(2) ● Here is a bouquet of flowers – my sweetheart.

● **In examples 3 and 4, the dash is used to place emphasis on a phrase towards the end of a sentence:**

(3) ● He only has one thing on his mind – his girlfriend.

(4) ● Their car is just six months old – and rather expensive.

● **In examples 5 and 6 dashes are used to separate list items:**

(5) ● All the team members – John, Carl, Carol, Barry, Derek, Elaine and Eva – left.

(6) • Today we have sold – 20 copies of C++, 20 copies of Java, 54 copies of XHTML – and taken orders for 45 copies of English Grammar – the forthcoming title.

• **In example 7 a dash is used to comment on a phrase which preceded it:**

(7) • Frankfurt, Vienna and Budapest –   these cities are well served by fast trains
                                                                                throughout the year.

-----------------------------------   ---

phrase ↵   comment on the phrase ↵

• **Examples 8 -10 demonstrate that when the dash is used parenthetically, a pair of dashes must be used:**

(8) • The Himalayas – the highest mountains in the world – are the ultimate challenge.

(9) • Martin Luther King Jr – the US civil-rights campaigner, black leader, and Baptist minister – was awarded the Nobel Peace Prize in 1964.

(10) • Muhammad Ali – three times World Heavyweight Champion – was the most recognised person in the 20th century in the whole world.

In these examples, a pair of dashes is used instead of brackets in order to enclose the information. This parenthetic use of dashes is equivalent to brackets. For the parenthetic use, a pair of brackets is preferred as information within the brackets stands out better and makes a stronger impression on a reader. Therefore, it is suggested that you avoid using a pair of dashes for brackets.

• **Examples 11 and 12 show the use of dashes to separate the additional clause from the main clause:**

(11) • Berlin is smaller than London – *where underground trains are too crowded*
       -----------------------------------   *during the rush hours.*

main clause ↵   additional clause telling more about London/head noun ↵

(12) • Charlie Chaplin was a film actor and director – who made his reputation as a
-- tramp with a smudge moustache,

main clause ↵ bowler hat and twirling cane.

We usually separate the additional clause with commas.

• **Examples 13 and 14 demonstrate the use of a dash to indicate different types of ranges:**

(13) • World War I 1914 – 1918 caused the death of an estimated 10 million people.

(14) • World War II 1939 – 45 caused the loss of an estimated 55 million lives
----

last two digits ↵

When on both sides of the dash the dates are in the same decade, it is conventional to write only the last two digits on the right side of the dash.

(15) • Queen Victoria 1819 – 1901

Here full dates are given on both sides of the dash because there is a change of century.

(16) • See pp 210 – 220 **or** See pages 210 – 220

(17) • A – K

(18) • volumes I – V

Some writers use dashes to imitate spoken English, to place emphasis, to indicate a missing word or words (maybe a rude word or phrase), incompleteness or uncertainty. Comic writers and tabloid journalists use dashes frequently. In formal writing and in academic work, commas and round brackets (parentheses) for parenthetic use are generally preferred. It should be noted that after a dash, only a proper noun begins with a capital letter.

• Ellipses(dot dot dot)

Ellipses (singular ellipsis) are a series of usually three full stops, or points, or dots. In essence, ellipses indicate:

- omission of one or more words from a sentence

- a sentence or paragraph is missing from the writing

- withholding of something for whatever reason

These are exemplified below:

(1) • They were thirsty, but also ... and penniless. ⇐ *a word (**hungry**) is omitted*

(2) • You must tell the panel nothing but ... ⇐ *a phrase **(the truth)** is omitted*

In example 2, <u>ellipses occurred at the end of the sentence. When ellipses are utilised at the end of a sentence, there is *no* need for the fourth dot or full stop.</u>

- On the contrary, in example 3, the ellipses are used to separate two complete sentences. In this case, <u>there is a need for the fourth dot</u>. Here ellipses indicate that at least one complete sentence has been withheld. The missing or withheld sentence or further sentences should have been where ellipses are shown.

(3) • I have never said that **...** . I don't use that sort of language.

------------------------- ⇑ --------------------------------------

complete sentence 1↵   ellipses   complete sentence 2 ↵
                                      and a full stop

(4) • They visited us in 1996,1997, 1998 ... ⇐ *omission of some subsequent years*

• Exclamation Mark !

The exclamation mark is represented by !. It is a terminator just like the full stop; but it is used for the following specific purposes.

• To denote strong emotional feelings – *anger, happiness, sorrow*, etc.

For instance:

(1) • You are a bloody fool!

Punctuation 281

****

(2) • How wonderful the party was!

(3) • Didn't they cry!

(4) • We won! Hurrah!

• To mark emphatic phrases - *scorn, insult, swearing, irony, command* , etc.

(5) • She must be silly!

(6) • You're a mess!

(7) • Get out of my class! And wait outside until I call you back!

(8) • Get lost!

(9) • You have no money! And you buy a new BMW !

• To mark the end of interjections

(10) • *Cheers!*

(11) • *Blimey!*

(12) • *Be quiet!*

(13) • *Ow!*   (*Ow! That hurt me!*)

(14) • *Ouch!*   (*Ouch! That hurt me!*) See $\Rightarrow$ Interjections

• To indicate the importance of a specific statement

(14) • What a difficult journey she faced!

(15) • Didn't I call your name? Sorry!

(16) • John is only twelve!

• Some other uses of exclamation marks

Sometimes people use multiple exclamation marks in order to make a piece of writing more interesting. Unless you are writing comic material or working for the tabloid press, try not to use them.

In mathematics, the exclamation stands for the factorial sign. e.g., five factorial = 5!. As a matter of interest, its value works out as: **5!** = (5x4x3x2x1) = 120.

<u>There are other less common uses of exclamation marks. For instance (!) and [!]. These are used in the publishing world.</u>

. <u>Footnotes</u>

A footnote is written below the text at the bottom of the page. It may be an explanation, a comment, some additional information or reference. The most common symbol used for footnotes is the Arabic numeral written as a superscript figure. A superscript number/figure is written above the normal line of writing. For instance:

> "Object Oriented Programming (OOP) is not new. What is
> new is the application of its concepts in modern programming
> languages such as C++ and Java."[1]

> 1 Java Simplified, Adam Shaw, ADR, 1999.

Some people use some other symbols such as asterisks and oblique.

. <u>Full Stop</u>

The full stop is the most commonly used punctuation mark. It is also known as a *full point*. In the United States of America, it is called a *period*. It is a terminator that is used for a variety of situations as exemplified below:

(1) • Rose is engaged to Russell.   ⇐ **full stop at the end of a sentence**

(2) • Would you kindly leave this room now.   ⇐ **at the end of a polite request**

(3) • What you should do is to listen to your mother. ⇐ **at the end of a polite request**

(4) • May I ask you to show me your current pass. ⇐ **at the end of a polite   request**

Example 2-3 are not questions but polite requests and thus a full stop is placed at the end of each statement.

• <u>Use a full stop at the end of indirect speech that sounds like a question.</u>

****

For instance:

(5) • I would very much like to know where your manor in Yorkshire is.

(6) • The office manager wanted to find out why the monthly report was delayed.

• **Many abbreviations end with a full stop.**

For example:

(7) • Joan Smith Ph.D.

(8) • Dr. A .Williams is away this week.

There is a tendency not to place full stops after initials. Some people do not use the full stop at the end of any abbreviation. For instance:

(9) • Jan ⇐ *January*

(10) • e.g. ⇐ *for example*

It is derived from the Latin words *EXEMPLI GRATIA*. For instance: e.g. red colour.

(11) • et al. ⇐ and other people or things

It is derived from the *Latin 'et alii or alia' or 'aliae* . It is usually used after names.

For instance: discovered by John Major et al., 2001

(12) • etc. ⇐ *for showing that in the list there are other items that could have been included.*

It is an abbreviation **for** *et cetera or et ceteri* For instance: Colin, Robin, Jane, etc.

(13) • www.adrlondon.ltd ⇐ **in e-mail address** (*known as 'dot')*

(14) •Mr and Mrs Blair have arrived.   Or ⇐ Mr. and Mrs. Blair have arrived.

(15) •The **UN** offices in the **UK** are in London.⇐ the U.N. offices in the U.K. are in London.

● <u>**Use full stops for both British and American currencies.**</u> For example:

(16) ● £45.76   ⟸ pounds . pence   (17) ● $ 45.90   ⟸ dollars . cents
        ----   ----
        ⇑   ⇑
    seventy-six pence   ninety cents

In both examples, the full stop is used as a ***symbol for the decimal point.*** In the UK, <u>less than a pound is usually written as a number with p.</u> For instance: ***96p***

● <u>No comma is added to abbreviations for metric measurements,</u> e.g. ***cm, mm, kg, l, km,*** etc.

● <u>**Full stops are used between days, months and years when dates are written in numbers.**</u> For example:

(18) ●   01.03.03   (19) ●   31.05.01

● <u>**A full stop is placed between the hours and minutes when time is written in the UK. There is a full stop after m in p.m.**</u> For instance:

(20) ● 3.45 a. m.   (21) ● 8.15 p.m.
     -------   -------

ante meridiem ↵   **post meridiem** ↵

● **ante meridiem** ⟹ before noon. It is from Latin. It starts at 10 a.m.

● **post meridiem** ⟹after noon. It is from Latin. It starts at 3 p.m.

● <u>**A full stop is placed at the end of a footnote irrespective of its grammatical status.**</u>
For example:

(22) ● 1 pp. 12-33.   (23) ● 2 Adam Shaw in Java, pp. 10-12.

<u>Note that **pp.** is an abbreviation for pages. It is written in lower-case letters followed by a full stop. A *lower-case* abbreviation cannot begin a sentence.</u>

. hyphen

It can be said that hyphens are used for two main functions:

- to join two words together

- to split the word at the end of a line of print

In British English, hyphens are more commonly used than in American English. The following examples illustrate some of the purposes for using hyphens.

(1) • He went to see his *mother-in-law* in the Bahamas.

----

hyphen forming a compound noun↵ - compound noun containing a preposition ⇒*in*

. The following examples also demonstrate the use of the hyphen in forming compound words:

(2) • He is a *jack-of-all-trades* who takes on almost any work he is offered.

In example 2, the compound noun is formed by including two prepositions – *of* and *all*.

(3) • You can travel by an *inter-city* train anywhere in France.

(4) • His *ex-wife* is a hairdresser.

(5) • She paid *seventy-seven* pounds for this beautiful dress.

----

hyphen ↵

Compound Numbers

1. The hyphen is used in writing out numbers in words between twenty-one and ninety-nine.
2. Do not use hyphens when writing out numbers in words such as three hundred.
3. In compound numbers hundred, thousand, etc. <u>do not</u> end with –s.

286   **Punctuation**

****

(6) ● Your bill comes to *two hundred* and *thirty-four* pounds.

               ------------------   ------------------

          not hyphenated ↵   hyphenated ↵

● **The following examples show that when a compound word is formed with a verb form, it is written with a hyphen:**

(7) ● John couldn't think of a *put-down* fast enough.

                           ----

a remark to make someone look /feel stupid ↵

(8) ● Natasha gave a *record-breaking* performance last night.

(9) ● It is a *well-thought-out* idea.

(10) ● Barbara is always *well-dressed*.

Some other compound words formed with well + hyphen and verb forms
⇓

---

well-advised, well-aimed, well-behaved, well-born, well-built, well-connected, well-deserved, well-desired, well-documented, well-earned, well-founded, well-groomed, well-heeled, well-informed, well-intentioned, well-known, well-looking, well-made, well-off, well-preserved, well-respected, well-rounded, well-spoken, well-tempered, well-thought-of, well-tried, well-to-do, well-wished, well-won, well-worked-out.

These are compound adjectives (the use of hyphen in compound words is often debatable)

● **The following examples illustrate that some nouns preceded by a letter are hyphenated:**

(1) ● On British motorways a *U-turn* is prohibited.   *U-turn* ⟹ *compound noun*

(2) ● Our hospital is short of chest *X-ray* machines.   *X-ray* ⟹ *compound noun*

(3) • A *T-junction* is a place where one road joins another but does not cross it, so that joining roads form the shape of the letter **T**.   *T-junction* $\Rightarrow$ *compound noun*

(4) • A bend in a pipe or road like the shape of the letter *s* is called an **S-bend**.

compound noun ↵

• **The following examples show that some compound nouns with adverbs or prepositions are usually written with or without hyphens:**

(5) • motorway *or* motor-way

(6) • phone *or* card phone-card

• **The following examples show that in some words with prefixes, hyphens are used to separate the prefix from the root word:**

(7) • Our home telephone number is *ex-directory*.

            ---- ------------

prefix ↵ root word ↵

(8) • A *post-dated* cheque will be treated as payable immediately.

(9) • Please *re-enter* the office from the side entrance.

(10) • There is no *multi-storey* car park in our town.

(11) • At present, there are plenty of *semi-skilled* jobs in our area.

• **The following examples demonstrate that adjective compounds preceded by *self* are hyphenated:**

(12) • The enclosed document is *self-explanatory*.

(13) • In some Indian villages, *self-help* community projects have transformed villagers' lives.

(14) • Last summer, we rented a *self-contained* flat in a small sea-side town in France.

(15) • Don't be too self-critical because such an attitude can be *self-destructive*.

(16) • Professor Burkhardt is a *self-styled* professor of the German language.

(17) • He is a *self-taught* software designer.

(18) • Anne-Marie always seems so calm and *self-possessed.*

(19) • You shouldn't allow fear and *self-doubt* to rule your life.

Some other compound words formed with self + hyphen + root word
⇓

---

self-access, self-appointed, self-appraisal, self-assertive, self-assured, self-awareness,
self-catering, self-centred, self-confessed, self-confident, self-congratulation, self-conscious,
self-contradiction, self-control, self-criticism, self-deception, self-defeating, self-defence,
self-denial, self-destruction, self-determination, self-discipline, self-derive, self-educated,
self-employed, self-esteem, self-evident, self-examination, self-fulfilling, self-government,
self-image, self-important, self-imposed, self-indulgent, self-inflicted, self-interest,
self-made, self-opinionated, self-pity, self-preservation, self-reliant, self-respect,
self-restraint, self-righteous, self-sacrifice, self-satisfied, self-seeking, self-service,
self-serving, self-worth.

• **Hyphens are also used in double-barrelled family names as demonstrated below:**

(20) • Mr. and Mrs. *Douglas-Home* are here.

(21) • Lord *Baden-Powell* founded the Boy Scout movement in 1908.

• **Some British names of places are also hyphenated.** For instance:

(22) • *Southend-on-Sea* is in Essex near London.

(23) • *Stratford-upon-Avon* is where William Shakespeare was born in 1564.

• The word after the preposition begins with a capital letter as in Examples 22-23.

.<u>Hyphens at the End of a Line (Word Division)</u>

We are in the age of Information Technology (IT). Typewriters have virtually been replaced by keyboards and word-processors. Generally speaking, word-processing software truncates a word at the end of a line in accordance with its own rule. Increasing numbers of books are created by using word-processing software. It is the word-processor which formats the document, hence inserts the hyphen at the point of a word division at the end of a line. This is shown below:

There are two subject areas, namely *etymology* and *phonetics*, which deserve mention here. *Etymology* is the study of word origin and *phonetics* is the study of speech and sounds. **Etymology** has a set of rules for dividing the word into syllables, prefixes and suffixes. Phonetics suggests the division of a word based on its sounds. If you are keen to explore word division, it is suggested that you pay a visit to your local library to consult reference books or search the Internet for further information on these topics.

.<u>Paragraph</u>

There are no hard-and-fast rules that regulate a paragraph's size and content. In any piece of writing, paragraphs enable the writer to lay the text in its most appropriate order so that the reader is at ease with the text. A paragraph contains a main theme. The main theme may have one or more related points. The whole idea is to place related points in a paragraph so that the reader is helped to grasp what is being written. Of course, the main theme may have several related paragraphs.

For instance, the main theme of the above section is the use of the hyphen. It has two related paragraphs. The first paragraph talks about the way words are divided by a word-processor these days. In the second paragraph, an example is given in order to demonstrate how the word-processor has divided the word *Etymology* at the end of a line (see above).

These paragraphs are short and concise. In fact, the length of a paragraph is dictated by the amount of the text in the main theme and related points. As in this example, the sizes of both paragraphs are based on the amount and flow of the text in each paragraph.

Some people write long paragraphs. For instance, a letter from a solicitor (lawyer) usually has long paragraphs. There are other experts such as philosophers who also construct longer paragraphs as longer paragraphs provide them with plenty of space to develop their ideas and argue their opinions. <u>Nowadays, the widespread tendency is to write shorter paragraphs.</u>

****

Paragraphs are also visual aids. Some writers prefer to leave at least one blank line between two paragraphs. This is the style of this book. Some writers have other preferences. For instance, they start a paragraph by indenting the first word by a number of letter spaces, usually 3 to 5. They do not allow a blank line between two paragraphs. Hardly ever, writers indent and allow a blank line space at the same time. If you are interested in fiction and poetry, consult some relevant reference materials for paragraphing techniques. <u>It is worth mentioning that publishers have their own house style for paragraphing.</u>

Example of paragraphing by indenting the first word

> This is an indented paragraph....
> you said that----------------
> ....
> This is the second indented paragraph.....

Example of paragraphing with a blank line between two paragraphs

> This is a paragraph...............
> -----------------------------------
> -----------------------------------
> This is the second paragraph --------

. Question Mark ?

The question mark (**?**) is a terminator like the full stop. The main purposes for which it is used are exemplified below:

. The following examples indicate that what precedes the question mark is an interrogative sentence:

(1) • Are you related to this woman?

(2) • What are you carrying in that heavy suitcase?

(3) • The policeman asked me first, 'Is this your car?'

(4) • I asked him, 'Where were you at the time of the accident'?

****

The purpose of the interrogative question is to get an answer from the respondent. <u>An interrogative question or a **direct question** always ends with a question mark.</u>

• <u>**Direct *question-like* a statement ends with a question mark(question tag):**</u>

For instance:

(5) • It is a lovely morning, isn't it ?

(6) • She looks very pretty in her wedding dress, doesn't she?

(7) • They look disappointed, don't they?

(8) • Joan's mother is always nagging her, isn't she?

(9) • You are a footballer, aren't you?

(10) • They are always as busy as bees, aren't they?
          ----
          idiomatic expression ↵ - it means very busy

• <u>**The following example shows that instead of asking a full question, you can make it short. The short question also ends with a question mark:**</u>

(11) •

• What is your name?   ⟹ short form   ⟹ **First name please?**

• What is your surname?   ⟹ short form   ⟹ **Surname please?**

• What is your home telephone number? ⟹ short form   ⟹ **Home telephone please?**

• What is your permanent address?   ⟹ short form   ⟹ **Permanent address please?**

<u>The above example illustrates that a short question may only be a word or several words</u>

• <u>**When there is uncertainty about the fact, a question mark is usually used to indicate it :**</u>

****

(12) • Socrates (?470 –399 BC) was a Greek philosopher.

(13) • Friedrich Engels (?1820-95) was a German philosopher who collaborated with Karl Marx on *The Communist Manifesto (?1848)*.

(14) • Albert Einstein was born in Berlin(?).

<u>Often a date or place of birth is doubtful or unverified.</u>

• <u>**The question mark is not used with an indirect question:**</u>

(15) • We would like to know what your thoughts are on capital punishment.

(16) • I was wondering if you could give my wife a lift to the town centre.

(17) • We would like to know what the cost is.

• <u>**The following question words always end with a question mark:**</u>

	Question Word	**Example**
(18) •	What	What is your question?
(19) •	When	When did you order the goods?
(20) •	Where	Where is your mother?
(21) •	Which	Which is your desk?
(22) •	Who	Who won the election in our area?
(23) •	Whom	Whom did you invite?
(24) •	Why	Why were you late this morning?
(25) •	Whose	Whose book is this?
(26) •	How	How are you this morning?

• <u>**In chess, the question mark is used by itself and with other symbols.**</u>

****

For instance:

    (27) • ? means a bad move   (28) • ?? stands for a serious blunder

• **Some writers use two question marks (??) or a question mark with an exclamation mark (?!) to imply scepticism or strong feeling :**

    (29) • Do you really think he is telling us the truth??

    (30) • What made you believe her??

Some people repeat question marks several times with or without the exclamation mark.

The use of more than one question mark is not recommended for formal writing.

• Quotation Marks ' ' " "

Quotation marks are also known as inverted commas, speech marks and quotes. There are single quotation marks (' ') as well as double quotation marks (" ").In Britain, single quotes are preferred. The main purposes of using quotation marks are exemplified below.

• **The following examples illustrate that quotation marks are used in order to enclose direct speech:**

    (1) • 'How do you like the flowers I sent you through Interflora?' Miss Stubbs asked Anne.

    (2) • 'War is always a sign of failure,' said the President of France.

The rule is that the words within the quotes must be exactly those spoken.

    (3) • 'We will always remember Jill as a kind person,' said Mrs. Jones. 'She was ever so friendly and generous to us.'

Example 3 illustrates:

• When a quoted speech is interrupted at the end of a sentence, instead of a full stop a comma is used to mark the end of the sentence.

• The word which resumes the quoted speech begins with a capital letter. See Example 3.

• <u>**Direct Speech**</u> is someone's exact spoken words. When direct speech is reported or quoted, the words actually spoken must be within quotation marks. The writer must also give the precise source of the words actually spoken. The reader should know to whom quoted words are attributed.

• <u>**When words *where, why, yes* and *no* are part of direct speech, these are enclosed within quotation marks (but not in reported speech):**</u>

> (4) • Veronica said to him, 'Yes!'

> (5) • 'Yes,' Tom replied, but Monica shouted, 'No! It is not for me.'

> (6) • Joyce asked, 'Where?'

> (7) • Gary said, 'Why?'

> (8) • When we asked him to come along with us, he replied, 'No.' ⇐ *direct speech*

• <u>**Indirect Speech**</u> is when instead of reporting someone's exact words, the meaning of words is expressed in the third person form using a past tense.

> (9) • When we asked Derek to travel with us, he said no. ⇐ *indirect speech*
> ---
>
> in reported speech *no* is not within quotes ↵

> (10) • She has just left home. She did not say where she was going. ⇐ *indirect speech*

• <u>**When a quotation is within another quotation, double quotation marks are used to enclose the quotes within quotes:**</u>

> (11) • 'What do you mean by "late"?' I asked him.
> ------
>
> a quote within a quote ↵- enclosed within double quotation marks

> (12) • I asked the speaker, 'Could you please give an example of "willy-nilly"?'

In example 12, *willy-nilly* is a quote within a quote. It is an adverb (informal). It means irrespective of whether someone wants to or not, e.g. we were forced willy-nilly by the policeman to turn left. It also means doing something carelessly without planning or thinking, e.g. She spends her money willy-nilly.

- **When the direct quotation has several paragraphs, it is customary to start each paragraph with an opening quotation mark, and place the closing quotation mark at the end of the entire quotation:**

(13) • 'Tagore also believed in learning by doing. For this purpose, a garden and a handicraft shop were part of his school. He had great interest in ecological matters. He used to have tree planting ceremonies.

'Tagore also founded a university. At his university, he established an international faculty in order to teach unity in diversity.'

(Rabindranath Tagore – the first Asian to receive the Nobel Prize for Literature 1913)

- **When a phrase or a word is quoted, it is enclosed within quotation marks:**

(14) • Colin told me 'certainly no deal', which I conveyed to my boss.

(15) • My doctor declared my health was 'excellent'.

(16) • The hyphenated word 'willy-nilly' has two different meanings as explained above.

- **Titles of lectures, book chapters, articles, short stories and short poems, television and radio programmes and musical writing are shown in quotes:**

(17) • The title of our annual lecture is ' The Role of Neighbourhood Watch'.

(18) • 'Fruit Gathering' is one of Rabindranath Tagore's poems.

- **The following rules should be observed for quotes:**

  - **Punctuation marks (comma, full stop, question marks, etc.) connected with quoted words are placed *inside the closing* quotation mark:**

(19) • 'I am fine. How is your wife?' he said to me.

(20) • 'We have been trying to compromise for three days. Can someone suggest another idea which may appeal to all of us? Let's see who has a bright idea. First, let's have a drink!' The chairman remarked.

• **When a statement or a sentence finishes with a quotation that ends with a full stop, or a question mark, or an ellipsis, or an exclamation mark, the full stop to stop the entire statement is not required:**

(21) • She said, 'I sent you my CV yesterday.'

(22) • Sarah shouted, 'It's marvellous!'

(23) • Alan said to his wife, ' I never agreed to your … '

(24) • My teacher asked me, 'How long do you need to finish this essay?'

• **Punctuation marks (comma, full stop, question marks, etc.) connected with the entire sentence are placed outside the closing quotation marks:**

(25) • A few days ago, I read a book ' Napoleon Bonaparte – The French Emperor'.

(26) • I wrote a letter to a friend and told her about 'White teeth by Zadie Smith'.

• Semicolon ;

A semicolon (;) indicates that there are two separate pieces of information in a sentence. It is used for the following purposes:

• **To join two related clauses:**

(1) • Alexander is a well-known local businessman; he is also mayor.

(2) • Anne went to Austria from Frankfurt; she stopped en route in Stuttgart for a few hours.

In these examples, clauses could have been joined by *and* $\Rightarrow$ a coordinating conjunction.

<u>You can also write each example as two separate short sentences, ending each with a full stop. A semicolon, like the full stop, indicates that these are separate but related short sentences.</u>

- **To join clauses that are linked by a conjunction in order to place greater emphasis on the following clause:**

  (1) • All motor cars must be fitted with seatbelts; and both the driver and passengers must fasten their seatbelts correctly.

  (2) • It is not true to say that poverty is man-made; but it is the result of many complicated and inter-related factors.

- **To separate groups within a list which may have a number of commas in each group:**

  (3) • We publish computer programming, Web design and information technology books; we represent American and Australian medical, engineering and science books publishers; we also supply technical, medical and IT periodicals through the post to our regular subscribers both at home and abroad.

  (4) • You should demonstrate both written and spoken working knowledge of German and French; explain how European Union laws are incorporated and implemented at governmental levels in France and Germany; and the way industry and commerce operate in these countries.

In these examples, semicolons have created groups within the list. The elements in each group are separated by commas. In essence, semicolons eliminate the overuse of coordinating conjunctions and refine long sentences by balancing them well.

- **To create a pause when preceded by an adverb or conjunction such as** *nevertheless, moreover, hence, besides, also, consequently, that is to say*:

  (4) • In city centres car speed is limited; moreover, honking your car horn aimlessly is prohibited.

  (6) • She is really self-motivated; hence, she always completes her task on time.

(7) • Elizabeth is friendly, rich and generous ; therefore she has many friends.

• Slash /

A slash functions as a separator. It is also known as bar, diagonal, oblique mark, solidus, and stroke. Some of its uses are as follows:

• To indicate alternatives:

(1)• Tea/Coffee   ⇐ instead of *or* a slash is used

(2) • Dear Sir/Madam (This phrase may be ended with or without a comma)

(3) • We vote now/adjourn the meeting for lunch.

(4) • True/False

(5) • He/she can stand for the election of club secretary.

• To indicate fiscal (connected with the government's financial year), academic, accounting and similar fixed periods of time:

(6) • Tax Year 2003/04

(7) • Academic year 1999/2000

(8) • Balance Sheet for the Period 2001/02

• To form part of certain abbreviations:

(9) • I/O   ⇐ Input – output in the computing world

(10) • A/C No. 1200   ⇐ Account = A/C

(11) • Send it to me c/o John Smith ⇐ c/o = care of

(12) • We must **w/o** these long outstanding bad debts. ⇐ w/o = write off

- The slash is also used for some specific purposes in scientific, technical and Information Technology (IT) fields. It has two forms in IT. These are a forward slash (/) and a back slash(\). Personal Computers and Internet users deal with these types on a regular basis.

. <u>Asterisk *</u>

The symbol for the **<u>asterisk</u>** is a star (*). It is used for the following purposes:

- <u>To indicate a reference, a footnote or an explanation given at the bottom of the text or elsewhere on the same page:</u>

    (1) . First-degree burns affect the very top layer of the skin.*

      * Hazel Courtney with Gareth Zeal in
      500 of the Most Important Health Tips 2001.

Some people prefer to use superscript numbers instead of the asterisk.

- <u>To indicate omission of letters in taboo words:</u>

    (2) . He is really a gentle person who rarely loses his temper. He was understandably annoyed and shouted, 'F *** off!'

- <u>To show the importance of a particular word or phrase:</u>

    (3) . The items out of stock are marked with an asterisk and should be re-ordered by tomorrow:

        ISBN 19011 97808
        ISBN 1901197 883*
        ISBN 1901197 999
        ISBN 1901197 700*

It is also one of the symbols used in some dictionaries to indicate important points.

. <u>Word-Processing Symbols (or Marks) - Bullets, Bolds, Italics, Underlining and Arrows, etc.</u>

We are in the age of IT and increasingly using word-processors. There are many symbols now that were not available on typewriters. These symbols (also known as marks) should be used sensibly.

Bullets have been increasingly appearing in printed materials. In this book bullets are used in order:

- to begin a heading so that it can stand out as the start of another section.

- to form part of a numbering system for examples.

- to show the importance of the text to follow.

- to summarise points made or show conclusions.

- to use bold, italics, underlining techniques, and arrows which can help the reader in the following ways:

Bolds, italics, underlining and arrows are used for the following functions:

- to highlight the importance of a word, phrase or a larger piece of text.

- to pinpoint a particular word, phrase or a clause in a sentence.

  In many places in this book, this technique is applied (see . ⇐ ↵ ⇓).

- to clarify the pinpointed text by giving further information on its nature and function. You can also make the pinpointed text larger so that it can stand out.

These techniques can only be applied if you use a word-processor. They are very useful tools, when the writer wants the reader to easily comprehend the idea being introduced and discussed. These means of marking text are comparatively new and on the periphery of punctuation. With the passage of time, they will be well recognised and used, especially by writers of scientific, technical and text books. Use them if you think they will help you clarify the text.

In summary, punctuation marks enable us to join, separate and manipulate words, phrases, clauses and paragraphs. In addition, these marks can enhance the meaning of a piece of writing, irrespective of its size.

Part 4

Idiomatic Expressions

. Introduction

An idiom is an expression which has an overall meaning different from the meaning of individual words it contains. Idiomatic expressions contain idioms. An idiom is a phrase of its own type, and should be used without changing its format.

Like other languages, the English language also has a large set of idioms. The use of idiomatic expressions can make your style of writing and speaking more lively and interesting. People use idioms in conversation, writing and the media (radio, television, newspapers, etc.).

There are thousands of idiomatic expressions. Often it is not easy to find them in some dictionaries for a variety of reasons. Some of these reasons are as follows:

- Some idioms are listed under their first word. This is not universally adopted for entering idioms in dictionaries.

- Some idioms are shown under their most important word. However, a word that is considered as the most important word in a particular expression, in one dictionary, may not be the same word taken as the most prominent word in another. For this reason, the same expression may be listed in two different places in two different dictionaries.

- Sometimes, in one dictionary, an idiomatic expression is listed under phrasal verbs section of an entry. Therefore, if you are looking under the idioms section of the entry, you will not find it.

- Sometimes, in a dictionary, an idiomatic phrase has its own dictionary entry instead shown under another word entry. In this case, it is not an idiom, whilst the same expression is listed in another dictionary under 'idiom'.

- Sometimes, a phrasal verb is listed as an idiom under idioms in some dictionaries

- Sometimes, it is also difficult to know where an idiom starts and ends.

- Sometimes, the first word of an idiom may be replaced by another and entered in another dictionary under a different first word.

- There is a large number of verbs and adjectives which are used in many idioms. Thus, many idioms containing such words may not be found in the same place in some dictionaries.

- Some dictionaries do not include, or highlight, idiomatic expressions.

- Some dictionaries do not explain adequately the meaning and usage of idioms, and do not exemplify their usage.

Therefore, it is not easy for learners of English to find idioms in English dictionaries, and some other books entitled 'Dictionary of Idioms'. Indeed, some dictionaries include a cross-referencing procedure which is helpful.

There are some restrictions on the use of idioms. These restrictions are also known as the *style* of using idioms. The styles are based on different situations in which different idiomatic expressions can be used most appropriately and correctly. The misuse of such an expression is usually when its usage is irrelevant to the given situation or circumstance. The styles of idiomatic expressions are broadly as follows:

- *formal* ‑ usually serious situations – it is mainly between people who are not closely related. It indicates a distant relationship.

- *informal* ‑ in social situations – conversation and letter writing between relatives and friends.

- *slang* ‑ spoken – it is between specific group of people, e.g., criminals, schoolchildren, young people, etc. Slang is not included in this book.

- *taboo* ‑ swear words used in conversation – excluded from this book.

- *unclassified* ‑ many idioms are in this category ‑ no restriction on their usage is imposed.

Occasionally, you may find some other styles of usage, such as *rude, old-fashioned, journalism, American, British, literary, derogatory, facetious, written, spoken, etc.*

It is worth mentioning that, occasionally, there are some variations in dictionaries when labelling idioms with these styles. In one dictionary, an idiom may be labelled as *formal*, but in another dictionary, it may be *informal or* even reduced to the level of *slang.* However, luckily, this is not a very common practice.

This book has over 520 entries of idiomatic expressions arranged in an alphabetical order under headwords, and exemplified by over 1060 helpful examples. The order of idiom entries is illustrated below.

• **baby** *headword* in alphabetical order ⇐ lexical word – a fixed word in an idiom

• **leave somebody holding the baby** (informal) — *when unexpectedly someone has to*
---   ------------ *tackle a problematic situation because*
              (1)   (2)   *no one wants to get involved, or no*
                                                other person is available to take control
                                                of the situation:
                                               ----
                                                 (3)

In the above:

(1) ⇒ idiomatic expression

(2) ⇒ style of use is given where appropriate

> • Style of use is the restriction on the use of the idiom. For instance, if it is stated as informal, its use should be avoided in formal contexts.

(3) ⇒ meaning is given in *italics*

    (Example number is in brackets) • Example is stated here.

Chapter 13

Idiomatic Expressions

- **ABC** – *it means the simplest or the most basic knowledge about a subject:*

  (1) • She does not claim to know beyond the ABC of gardening.

  (2) • There is a number of books for laymen on the ABC of philosophy.

  (3) • It is as easy as ABC.   See ⇒easy

- **above:**

- **above all** – *it means more important than anything else:*

  (4) • When you are in Russia, above all, make sure you visit Red Square.

  (5) • Above all, we must not forget the elderly in our society.

- **above yourself** – *it means someone is conceited, that is, having too high an opinion of oneself:*

  (6) • Ron has got a bit above himself since he bought a new sports car.

  (7) • We don't understand why Margo's got a bit above herself recently.

- **Above someone's head** – *it means something is too difficult for someone to understand:*

  (8) • The lecture was well above our heads due to many technical terms used.

  (9) • This note will be above their heads and you will not receive any practical help.

- **Ace:**

- **an ace up your sleeve** (informal) — *it means something in your hand which you can use when you need to gain an advantage. In this context, something may be secret information, knowledge or skill:*

    (10) • Luckily, we have one very important ace up our sleeve. Manchester is much closer to the beautiful Lake District than London and that is something we can highlight in our brochure.

- **hold all the aces** — *it means that someone is in a much stronger position and has all the advantages:*

    (11) • Soon corner shops will disappear in many parts of the country because supermarkets hold all the aces.

- **within an ace of something/ of doing something** — *it means very close to winning something or succeeding in doing something:*

    (12) • Only two candidates reached the final interview stage. I was one of them. I came within an ace of getting the job but the other lucky person was appointed.

• Accord:

- **in accord with something /somebody** *(formal)* — *it means in agreement with something /somebody:*

    (13) • We have taken all necessary steps in accord with local authority planning regulations.

    (14) • Your decision to sack him from his managerial post will not be in accord with our human resource strategy agreed by the board of directors.

- **of one's own accord** — *it means one's own free will:*

    (15) • My son studied German of his own accord.

    (16) • She volunteered for this service of her own accord.

- **with one accord** *(formal) - when some people do something at the same time, it means they are in agreement:*

  (17) • When the well-known chief guest entered the room, with one accord we all stood up and clapped.

  (18) • At the meeting, with one accord, all committee members accepted the new guidelines.

• accordance:

- **in accordance with something** (formal) — *It is used to emphasise that something is done by obeying some, agreement, rules or authority:*

  (19) • We always pay our Council Tax by post in accordance with our agreement.

• act:

- **a class act** — *it means someone is really very good at what they do, i.e. support, signing or any other kind of performance or whatever say, work:.*

  (20) • I have seen many political commentators on British television shows, but Robin Day was a class act. He was equally forceful with leaders of all parties to discover their hidden agenda.

- **catch someone in the act** - *it means to discover someone doing something wrong, secret or criminal:*

  (21) • A young shoplifter was caught in the act of stealing a pair of shoes.

  (22) • A bank cashier was caught in the act of embezzling £1000 in cash today.

- **get your act together** (informal) - *someone should organize oneself better to achieve one's objectives:*

  (23) • If you wish to finish your medical training you must start getting your act together.

. get in on the act (informal) – *start doing something which someone has started and you must also do it yourself to benefit from it:*

(24) . Many big businesses have been increasing their sales through E-commerce; now many small businesses are investing in Web sites to get in on the act.

(25) . It is fashionable to work in casual clothes; even medical doctors dressed up this way to get in on the act.

. a hard act to follow – *When someone's activity, ability, skill or performance is is so good that it will be difficult for someone to match it or be as successful:*

(26) . Jordan's father built this thriving enterprise by applying his great ability, persuasion and hard work. Her father will be a hard act to follow.

. put on an act – *when someone is pretending:*

(27) . A shop assistant offered help, but the shoplifter was only putting on an act.

(28) . When he told us his car broke down, we believed him, but he was putting on an act.

. add:

. add fuel to the fire/flames – *to say or do something that will make a bad situation worse and an angry person angrier:*

(29) . When John and Christine were just about to stop arguing Alison added fuel to the fire when she said, "My husband saw you in a pub last night."

(30) . As we were just about to settle our dispute, Tommy added fuel to the fire by unexpectedly raising another matter.

. add insult to injury – *to offend someone further who has already been harmed in some other way:*

(31) . When my bank transferred by mistake £5000 instead of £50 to my club for an annual membership fee, they added insult to injury by charging me interest and a fee on £5000.

(32) • Our next door neighbours quietly moved our garden fence towards us, and to add insult to injury, they trimmed the branches of our climbing rose bush.

• **Add up*** (informal) — *it means something does not seem logical, or make sense :*

(33) • He is an intelligent person, but on this occasion his attitude towards his son is terribly wrong. It just doesn't add up.

(34) • I have known him for many years as a cold, aloof and distant man. Last night he invited all his neighbours to his home: it didn't add up.

  *1. *add up* *is also a phrasal verb. It means to calculate the sum of two or more numbers:*

   • I want to add up 120 and 234 together.

  2. *add up* *as a phrasal verb has another meaning to lead to a particular result, or outcome, or conclusion, or give specific information:*

   • These documents don't add up to a secret file.

• **aegis :**

• **under the aegis of somebody/something** (formal) – *it means with some sort of support and or protection given by a person or authority:*

(35) • We launched our Information Technology programme under the aegis of the Central Government IT Programme for the Manufacturing Industry.

• **air :**

• **hang in the air** — *when some people dodge the question because they do not wish to get involved and it remains unanswered.*

(36) • At the meeting, I asked repeatedly when our street lights would be repaired. The chairman talked a lot but left the question hanging in the air.

• **in the air** — *when people are aware of something which is happening or is going to happen:*

(37) • Mary looked at her daughter and her new boyfriend and said, " There's romance in the air."

****

(38) . Since we have a new management, new opportunities for some of
us are in the air.

. **up in the air** — *it means not yet decided:*

(39) . My travel to Berlin next month is still up in the air.

(40) . Our building extension project is now up in the air due to John's job situation.

. See $\Rightarrow$ breath of fresh air   . See $\Rightarrow$ build castle in the air   . See $\Rightarrow$ clear the air

---

. airs :

. **airs and graces or put on airs and graces** — *when someone pretends they are
better, more refined and more important than they are. It is used when someone's
behaviour is disapproved. It is a derogatory remark:*

(41) . He employs about 100 employees. He has no airs and graces.

(42) . In spite of all his airs and graces he left school without any qualifications.

. aisle:

. **go/walk down the aisle** (informal) — *it means to get married:*

(43) . Don't you think you should both walk down the aisle?

. alarm:

. **alarm bells ring/start ringing** — when *people begin to worry about something, doubt
some outcome, or suspect something is wrong or is going to happen:*

(44) . Alarm bells started ringing, when her doctor suspected breast cancer.

(45) . When she received a credit card statement showing £12,000 spent,
alarm bells started ringing at the back of her mind as to how she got herself into
this financial mess.

. alive:

****

- **alive and kicking** − *it means healthy, energetic, or full of life:*

    (46) . I met Keith last night. He is alive and kicking and still enjoys playing tennis.

- **bring something alive** − *it means making something more interesting:*

    (47) . The last speaker brought the lecture hall alive with his illuminated lecture and enthusiastic group discussion.

- **all:**

- **all in all** − it means when *everything is considered about a particular situation:*

    (48) . It was cold and cloudy, but all in all we very much enjoyed our day trip.

- **answer:**

- **have/know all the answers** (informal) − *it is said about someone who claims to know something but in reality it is not so:*

    (49) . He is talkative and gives the impression that he knows all the answers.

- **not take no for an answer** − *if someone is repeatedly trying to make you agree to something despite your repeated refusal to agree:*

    (50) . Our local furniture store salesman, who wouldn't take no for an answer, delivered a coffee table but we refused to accept it.

- **apple:**

- **the apple of someone's eye** − *it is said about someone who is very fond of another person or thing:*

    (51) . My son is the apple of his grandfather's eye.

- **in apple-pie order** − (informal) *It means a place that is well-organised, neat and tidy:*

    (52) . Their house is always in apple-pie order.

    (53) . The dining area in that restaurant was in apple-pie order but the toilets were filthy.

****

• **upset the applecart** (informal) — *when someone or something does something that creates trouble, problems or spoils progress, plans. etc.*

> (54) • When John recognised that his son would not be able to win party nomination, he upset the applecart by withdrawing his financial support for the party.

> (55) • Our sales were increasing everyday, when suddenly the financial crisis in the Far East upset the applecart by fear of recession.

• arm:

• **cost an arm and a leg** (informal) — *it is used to emphasise that something is really* expensive:

> (56) • If you travel by train from here to London, it will cost you an arm and a leg.

> (57) • A meal in a restaurant in the West End of London costs an arm and a leg.

• **keep (someone) at arm's length** — *to avoid getting too close or friendly with someone:*

> (58) • We say hello to each other, but I keep him at arm's length.

• **the long arm of the law** (informal) — *it means the authority and power of the police force:*

> (59) • Some gangsters are still on the run, but sooner or later, the long arm of the law will catch up with them.

• arms:

• **(be) up in arms(about/over something)** (informal) — *It is said when someone is angry about something and protesting strongly:*

> (60) • When his next door neighbours blocked his drive-way with their car, he was up in arms about it and exchanged angry words with them.

> (61) • Rail workers are up in arms against their union representatives who have accepted a far lower wage increase offered by their employers.

> (62) • Roger is up in arms over the local council's rejection of his application

for re-building a garage.

. See ⇒ open ⇒ with open arms

. avail:

. to little or no avail (formal) − *it means with little or no success:*

(63) . We have done everything to save our business from bankruptcy, but to no avail.

(64) . We made a determined effort to save our marriage, but to little avail.

. of little or no avail (formal) − *when you mean to say of little or no use:*

(65) . Travelling by taxi instead of bus is of little avail as we are already one hour late.

(66) . Your religious speech is of no avail as these young people are already drunk.

. have an axe to grind − *when someone is involved actively in some sort of dispute or cause for some personal reasons:*

(67) . There are many known protesters who regularly take part in demonstrations because they have an axe to grind.

(68) . I had no axe to grind, but made a complaint against the police for treating a refugee inhumanely in a busy street.

<u>B</u>

. baby

. leave somebody holding the baby (informal) − *when unexpectedly someone has to tackle a problematic situation because no one wants to get involved, or no other person is available to take control of the situation:*

(1) . A lorry in front of our car dropped a big new tool box and I was left holding the baby.

(2) . Suddenly our manager collapsed at work and I was left holding the baby.

(3) . Whenever our boss was away, it was me who was left holding the baby.

. **throw the baby out with the bath water** (informal) — *during the process of re-organising, changing, or getting rid of unwanted articles, ideas, or whatever, you lose something that you must keep* *:

(4) . When our regional rail system was re-organised and a number of village stations closed down recently, the rail authority has thrown the baby out with the bath water.

Another use of this idiomatic expression is made when you **warn someone not to reject something completely as it is partly faulty, or spoiled :*

(5) . It is not easy to negotiate with him but we must not throw the baby out with the bath water.

. back:

. **at/in the back of your mind** — *something about which you are not thinking carefully but you are aware of it all the time:*

(6) . My husband is away from home in Africa, but he is always at the back of my mind.

(7) . I left my homeland when I was young, but it is always in the back of my mind.

. **the back of beyond** (informal) — *it refers to a remote place that is far from you or your home or the place where you are:*

(8) . They used to live a few houses away from our home, but now they live in the back of beyond in one of Fiji's islands.

(9) . We have one rail service per day to our village, so you cannot call it the back of beyond.

. **be glad to see the back of someone** (informal) — *when you are pleased that someone/something has gone and that you do not have to deal with them:*

(10) . The landlady was so glad to see the back of her guest who was argumentative.

****

(11) • A man sitting next to me on the train kept using his mobile phone. When he
got off at the last station, I was ever so glad to see the back of him.

• **behind someone's back** − *it means saying something untrue and/or unpleasant without
the knowledge or permission of someone who is not present :*

(12) • Who has been talking about me behind my back?

(13) • As soon as Doris left the office, the other women laughed and started talking
behind her back.

• **have your back to the wall*** (informal) − *it is said when someone is in a very difficult
situation, and cannot do what one wants to do:*

(14) • Undoubtedly many refugees have their backs to the wall as they
have no money, no home and cannot legally find a job.

(15) • When we were in France, we were stopped by a gang at gunpoint. We had
our backs to the wall and handed over all our possessions to them.

* You can also say: **have someone's back <u>against</u> the wall:**

(16) • Jenny has her back against the wall since her husband died in a road accident,
and left behind a wife, two young children and a big unsecured bank loan.

• **by/through the back door** − *succeeding in doing something unfairly:*

(17) • Paul has got a new managerial job by the back door in a supermarket, whose
managing director plays golf with his father.

(18) • Amanda has no teacher training. She has used her family connections to
help her get into the teaching profession through the back door.

• **bag :**

• **bag and baggage** − *when you mean to say with all someone's possessions:*

(19) • When Marion's lodger did not pay rent for four weeks, she threw him out
onto the street, bag and baggage.

* **a bag of bones** (informal) — *You can describe a thin person or animal as a bag of bones:*

> (20) • Before he suffered a heart attack, he was very well built. Now he is just a bag of bones.

* **be in the bag** (informal) — *it shows that you are certain about succeeding/winning:*

> (21) • Your promotion is in the bag.

> (22) • When I telephoned the office, my secretary told me that our German contract was in the bag.

• balance :

* **be hang/ in the balance** (formal) — *When there is some uncertainty about the future outcome of something:*

> (23) • When you are 55 years of age, your job security hangs in the balance.

> (24) • The re-election of our current government is in the balance at the forthcoming national election.

<u>**You can also say: remain in the balance.**</u>

• ball :

* **the ball is in your/someone's court** — *it means that it is your/someone's turn to take the next step or action:*

> (25) • I have been offered the post of senior English teacher. Now the ball is in my court.

> (26) • She has been given the opportunity of joining our club by the end of this month, so the ball is in her court.

* **get/set/start/keep the ball rolling** — *it means that you start or keep an activity going and other people may join in:*

> (27) • We have already waited for them for ten minutes. I must start the ball rolling by thanking you for coming along for this informal gathering.

(28) . If I do not return within 10 minutes from the meeting, you can get
the ball rolling with a sales software demonstration.

. **(be) on the ball** (informal) — *when you describe someone as on the ball, you are saying
that they are capable of understanding the given situation and act intelligently and quickly:*

(29) . Our new club secretary is on the ball, as our club membership is increasing
every month since he started working for the club.

(30) . Our security guard is really on the ball as recently the number of thefts has
decreased dramatically.

. **play ball (with someone)** (informal) — *when you co-operate or work with someone in
such a way that they are helped and they can achieve what they want:*

(31) . If you do not play ball with me for a joint sales venture, I will have to look
for another business partnership.

(32) . She tried hard to get me involved financially in her overseas venture but I
wouldn't play ball.

. balloon :

. **when the balloon goes up** (informal) — *when the trouble that someone is expecting
begins. It is about an expected trouble or fear:*

(33) . Our store manager is never on the shop floor when the balloon goes up.
We have to resolve the problem ourselves.

(34) . Jim often goes home late to his wife and two young children. His wife
telephoned him at work to tell him that the balloon was about to go up.

. bang :

. **bang goes something** (informal) — *It is used when something that is within reach
becomes unattainable. It simply means the end of any hopes:*

(35) . If his wife does not agree to divorce proceedings, bang goes his plan to
marry his secretary this year.

(36) . James has failed one core subject, so bang goes his promotion for at least one

****

more year.

● **go with a bang** (informal) − *it means very successful:*

> (37) ● Our summer sales went with a bang as soon as we opened
> our doors to the public.

> (38) ● Our wedding party went with a bang.

● **bark :**

● **be barking up the wrong tree** (informal) − *It means that someone has a wrong approach, or idea, or is doing something wrong:*

> (39) ● She is barking up the wrong tree, if she is hoping to marry Mr Milliner
> who lives in a great big house and drives a sport car.

> (40) ● You are barking up the wrong tree, if you think I will lend you my car.

● **beans :**

● **full of beans/life** (informal) − *You say it about someone who is full of energy:*

> (41) ● John is always full of beans despite his long illness.

> (42) ● Rose used to be full of life but recently no one knows why she is so dismal.

● **beggar :**

● **beggar belief/description** (formal) − *it is used to say that something is too bad, or very big or very beautiful, or too extreme in some way to describe it adequately:*

> (43) ● It beggars description how you got yourself in such a terrible mess.

> (44) ● The way he has behaved is so disgusting that it beggars belief.

● **bell :**

● **ring a bell** (informal) − *you can say it when something seems familiar to you, which you might have seen, or heard, etc. in the past, but is difficult to remember in detail:*

(45) • Your name rings a bell; perhaps we've met somewhere.

(46) • This bravery tale rings a bell, but I can't recall reading about it.

• **give someone a bell** (informal) — *it means to call someone by telephone:*

(47) • You must give me a bell when you have arrived at your hotel.

• benefit :

• **give someone the benefit of the doubt** — *to accept whatever someone has told you as the truth. Or that someone is innocent because you cannot prove them wrong due to a lack of evidence against them:*

(48) • His employers gave him the benefit of the doubt and did not terminate his employment contract.

(49) • The judge gave the accused the benefit of the doubt and let him go free.

• best :

• **do one's (level) best** — *when you want to say try as hard as you can or as is possible:*

(50) • You know very well how our train service is on Sundays, but I'll do my level best to be here by 10 a.m.

(51) • She did her best to qualify as a barrister.

• bitter:

• **a bitter pill (for somebody) (to swallow)** (formal) — *you say it when something is difficult to accept:*

(52) • Losing his job was a bitter pill for him to swallow.

(53) • Natasha found Boris's unfaithfulness to her a bitter pill to swallow.

• **to/until the bitter end** — *you can use it in your statement, when you mean that you will continue your efforts towards the completion of whatever must be done, irrespective of difficulties and unpleasant circumstances:*

(54) . We are prepared to fight in the legal courts to the bitter end for our human rights in this country.

(55) . I went with a friend to a party. I found myself in the company of people of whom I don't approve, but I stayed until the bitter end.

. blind :

. **the blind leading the blind** – *It is used to describe a situation in which an inexperienced person, or someone who lacks knowledge and expertise is giving advice to another person who is also of similar experience, knowledge or expertise:*

(56) . Samantha wants Ruth to teach her spoken French, but it would be the blind leading the blind.

(57) . Please don't ask me about this software. If I try to explain it to you, it would be a case of the blind leading the blind.

. blood :

. **make (someone's) blood boil** – *You can say it if someone makes another person extremely angry:*

(58) . I must tell you that what you have just said is rubbish and makes my blood boil.

(59) . These people always park their car so near to my car that I can't get out easily. Really, their selfish behaviour makes my blood boil.

. **new/fresh blood** – *when you use this idiomatic expression, you are referring, especially, to young employees who are expected to possess plenty of energy, ideas, or enthusiasm:*

(60) . To be more competitive, we must introduce some new blood in our sales team.

(61) . I'm now about to retire and no longer have the energy and vitality to compete with fresh blood.

. boat :

. **in the same boat** (informal) – *it means in the same circumstance, usually a difficult or* *problematic situation:*

(62) • We both are in the same boat, as we are unemployed and away from the comfort of our homes in another country.

(63) • Most retired people are in the same boat as far as state benefits are concerned.

• boil :

• **off the boil** — *it means something is not as good as before. It can also mean less successful than before:*

(64) • He used to be extremely quick in the ring but tonight his performance was greatly off the boil.

(65) • He is a good journalist but his article in today's Times went off the boil.

• **on the boil** — *it means very active. You can also use this expression, if someone is doing something very well or successfully:*

(66) • Despite his serious illness, his work for our charity is on the boil.

(67) • Our team is on the boil this year as we have won all our recent matches.

• bread :

• **bread and butter** (informal) — *It means someone's main source of income:*

(68) • At present, my wife's income is our bread and butter, as I'm unemployed.

(69) • Writing has been my bread and butter since I was young.

• breath :

• **a breath of fresh air** — *You can describe someone or something as such because they are more exciting, energetic or full of ideas, etc. You can also use this expression when you wish to breathe in fresh air, after being in a place where the air is unclean :*

(70) • Our new boss held a staff meeting. He is a breath of fresh air.

(71) • The lecture hall was full of students and all the doors were shut for an hour. Now we need a breath of fresh air.

- **hold one's breath** — *it is said about people who stop breathing because of anxiety, or fear, or for any other emotional reason:*

> (72) • After the interview, I held my breath hoping that I was successful.

> (73) • During the recent international crisis over Iraq, we all sat in front of a television set holding our breath and anticipating that the UN would stop war.

• **brunt :**

- **bear/take the brunt of something** — *when someone must suffer from the effects of some events, or some decision made by an authority:*

> (74) • Our central government raised income tax in order to meet pay rises for all Civil Service staff . We must bear the brunt of this tax increase from 6 April.

> (75) • Our roof took the brunt of last night's fierce storm and must be repaired today.

• **bubble :**

- **the bubble bursts** — *When something which is favourable, good, advantageous, etc. comes to an end:*

> (76) • These figures tell us that the bubble has burst, as our sales have been declining during the last five months.

> (77) • Germany's economy is no longer as prosperous as it was for many years. The bubble has burst.

• **buck :**

- **pass the buck** (informal) — *to make somebody else responsible for one's own wrong doing:*

> (78) • When dad asked him who broke the jar, my brother tried to pass the buck.

> (79) • Whenever something goes wrong, she tries to pass the buck.

• **business :**

- **mean business** (informal)- *when people are serious and business like about something:*

(80) . He was looking for you a few minutes ago. I think he means business this time.

(81) . If you can convince him that you mean business, I believe he will find a solution to your financial difficulties.

. bygones :

. **let bygones be bygones** — *this idiomatic expression is used to say forget about past differences, quarrels, or whatever happened between people and forgive each other:*

(82) . Today we met face to face since that passionate argument over politics two years ago. We decided to let bygones be bygones in our mutual interest.

(83) . Let bygones be bygones and shake hands to rekindle our old friendship, which began when we were at school so many years ago.

C

. Cake :

. **have one's cake and eat it** — *You can describe someone's desire to benefit from something/a situation without accepting its associated disadvantages at the same time:*

(1) . She wants to marry that rich old Arab in Qatar but she does not want to live in Qatar with him. Well, she wants to have her cake and eat it too.

(2) . Our local government wants to keep local library membership free of charge without increasing the council tax and without any additional money from our central government. It seems that they want to have their cake and eat it too.

. cap $\Rightarrow$ Think $\Rightarrow$ Put your thinking cap on

---

. carpet :

. **sweep something under the carpet** — *You say it when someone is hiding something*

****

from other people. The hidden thing may be only embarrassing, or even illegal:

> (3) • Some months ago the sexual harassment problem surfaced in our company. It was immediately swept under the carpet by the management and we still don't know who was involved.

> (4) • You may think that by sweeping it under the carpet the trouble will go away, but sooner rather than later your mother will come to know it.

• castles :

• build castles in the air(or in Spain) — *When someone is planning, dreaming or thinking about something unrealistic that is unlikely to happen:*

> (5) • One day I will have my own large business. His wife laughed and said, 'Don't build castles in the air as you are already 65 years of age'.

> (6) • At school, I used to build castles in Spain about becoming a judge, but when I was 18 years of age my father died and I had to go to work.

• chest :

• get something off one's chest (informal) — *when someone tells another person about something that has been causing some anxiety and by telling feels somewhat less apprehensive:*

> (7) • I haven't seen you for nearly ten days. What's aggravating you? Let's meet tonight so that by talking you can get it off your chest.

> (8) • One of my students was very much concerned about her progress. After talking to me in private, she told me that our discussion helped her get things off her chest.

• Chip:

• a chip off the old block (informal) — *when a person is very like one of their parents in personality and behaves the same way:*

> (9) • He sings and dances just like his father - a chip off the old block.

> (10) • She is a journalist on the same national daily newspaper for which her mother worked – she really is a chip off the old block.

. circles :

. **run round in circles** (informal) – *when someone is very busy doing something but is making no progress towards the achievement of some goal:*

> (11) . My wife has been running round in circles all day trying to purchase a suitable pair of shoes for tonight's party, but she returned home without any.

> (12) . It will save you from running round in circles, if you follow my instructions step by step to set up this software on your PC.

. clear :

. **clear the air** – *to remove doubts, worries, etc. by means of talking. It usually means making things easy when there are differences of opinions or tension between people:*

> (13) . Our dispute with our neighbours is still unresolved, but tonight's meeting has helped to clear the air.

> (14) . There seems to be some tension between some members of our team. Let's hope the manager can find a way to clear the air.

. **clear the decks** (informal) – *to remove unnecessary things in preparation for an activity:*

> (15) . Our front room has got so many things in it, we had better clear the decks before Joan's wedding party.

> (16) . The furniture in the staff room occupies so much space, it is better to clear the decks for the staff meeting.

. **clear the way** – *it means to remove whatever is stopping something to progress, or happen:*

> (17) . My wife's new British passport will clear the way for us to travel together to Japan.

> (18) . Our credit control checks could clear the way for your loan application to be accepted.

****

. clock :

. round/around the clock – *it means an activity is carried out all day and all night, continuously:*

(19) . Our data processing staff work round the clock as customers use the banking system 24 hours a day throughout the year.

(20) . In order to finish this project on time, we must re-organise our team activity so that we can work around the clock to complete it as required.

. cloud :

. under a cloud – *it means someone is under suspicion. It is so when other people think that the suspected person has done something wrong, or is in disgrace, or is having problems:*

(21) . Since he was caught using the Internet for his personal use, he feels that he is under a cloud and is looking for another job.

(22) . The team manager is under a cloud as this season his team has not won a single game.

. come :

. come of age – *In Britain, it means a child has grown up to be an adult. In Britain, a young person at the age of 18 is legally an adult:*

(23) . My youngest son comes of age today.

(24) . I travelled to Poland the day I came of age last year.

. conscience:

. in (all good) conscience (formal) – *when someone does something believing that the action is fair and just:*

(25) . In all good conscience, we must reinstate his contract of employment.

(26) . Mrs. Taylor worked for us for forty years and now in her retirement she needs some help. This company in all conscience cannot refuse to give her both financial and moral support.

• cry :

• **cry over spilt milk** — *when someone is wasting time regretting, or getting angry about something that has gone wrong/is broken/is lost and that they cannot do anything about it to put it right:*

    (27) • My wife has just dropped a vase and it is broken beyond repair. Well, accidents do happen at home, but there is no need to cry over spilt milk.

    (28) • We would not have lost this vital contact if we had not added extra cost items, but we cannot achieve anything now by crying over spilt milk.

• cucumber :

• **as cool as a cucumber** — *when someone is very calm and composed in difficult circumstances surrounding a situation:*

    (29) • When our car was involved in a fatal accident, we were all shocked and in hysteria. However, Karen was still as cool as a cucumber.

    (30) • During the recent house prices fall, many people with big mortgages were panic-stricken and trying to sell their properties quickly, but we were as cool as a cucumber and didn't put our house on the market.

• cuff :

• **off the cuff** — *when you make a remark, or give an opinion, or speak without any preparation:*

    (31) • Our guest speaker annoyed one of our delegates. However, he quickly apologised and added that he didn't mean to sound flippant. it was merely an off the cuff remark.

    (32) • He made an off the cuff speech on birds' migration: it was thirty minutes long, informative and entertaining.

• curtain :

• **bring down the curtain on something <u>or</u> bring the curtain down on something** (formal) — *it means to end something like a state of affairs, a programme, a schedule of work, an event, or a similar process:*

(33) • Mrs. Thatcher's loss of her job as prime minister brought down the curtain on a distinguished political career.

(34) • The closing down of our firm brought the curtain down on the car manufacturing industry in our region.

• cut :

• **cut corners** — *you can include it in your statement, when you express disapproval of someone's action of doing something with less effort, ignoring rules and generating poor results. You can also use it for people who spend less money, or time, and do not follow correct procedures and do not obey rules:*

(35) • Most retail businesses cut corners by not giving shop assistants any training and thus often staff are not able to help customers.

(36) • Our local government cut corners by not gritting the roads during winter snowfall. As a result of this policy, we have today long queues and accidents.

• the **cut and thrust (of something)** (formal) — *it means fierce competition. It can also be used to imply a lively way of doing something:*

(37) • Sometimes there is a cut and thrust battle between supermarkets that is good for consumers as prices of certain items fall.

(38) • I am in favour of inviting two politicians from opposing parties, so that we can have the cut and thrust of a debate on the economy.

• cylinders :

• **fire on all cylinders** (informal) — *it implies that someone is working as well as possible with a great enthusiasm, and energy. You can also use it to mean that a system is operating efficiently and is under full control:*

(39) • He can write such an article in a day when he is firing on all cylinders.

(40) • Our sales objective can be achieved if we fire on all cylinders.

(41) • Our department is processing sales invoices on all cylinders to send monthly

statements to all customers at the end of the month.

D

. dab :

. a dab hand (at something) (informal) — *when someone is very good at doing something:*

    (1) . Charles is a dab hand at making jewellery.

    (2) . Debra is a dab hand at hair-dressing.

. daggers

. at daggers drawn – *it means that two or more people are ready to quarrel or fight at any time if necessary.*

    (3) . Both brothers have been at daggers drawn since their father passed away recently.

    (4) . Our manager finds himself at daggers drawn with the advertising manager over too costly publicity without achieving any sales increase for months.

. look daggers at someone – *when you want to say that someone is looking at you in a very angry way or hostile manner:*

    (5) . John and I had a rousing discussion about current political issues last night. When we returned home from work, he looked daggers at me.

    (6) . At the bar, I asked for a non-alcoholic drink. As I sat to enjoy my drink, everyone looked daggers at me.

. dark

. a dark horse – *when little is known about someone who may have some qualities, skills, etc., that may surprise other people:*

    (7) . We know about our champion, but the challenger from Spain is a dark horse.

    (8) . Can you tell us something about John's social life? Well, he has been working

with us for some years, but he is a dark horse as far as his social life is concerned.

. **in the dark (about something)** – *a situation, circumstances or facts about which nothing is known:*

> (9) . Do you know who will replace our retiring manager? Well, I'm as much in the dark as everyone else. This company keeps us in the dark about staff changes.

. date

. **out of date** – *it means something is old fashioned. It also means that something is no longer valid and cannot be used legally:*

> (10) . This rail ticket is out of date sir. You can't travel using this ticket.

> (11) . My grandfather's ideas about discipline are out of date.

. **to date** – *it means until now:*

> (12) . To date, I have not received your parcel through the post.

> (13) . I'm glad to say that to date our policy is working as planned.

. **up to date** – *it means that something is completed up to the current/present time:*

> (14) . Our monthly credit payments are up to date.

> It can also imply that something is not old fashioned but modern:

> (15) . Our computer equipment is up to date – the latest technology.

. day

. **all in a day's work** – *it means part of someone's normal work. In practice it means something is not difficult to do as someone knows how to do it as part of their usual work, or they have experience of doing something in their life.*

> (16) . I'm grateful to you for your efforts to solve this problem for me. It wasn't so difficult for you, as it was all in a day's work.

> (17) . It is frightening for me to drive a car around Hyde Park Corner in London, but it is all in a day's work for Anne.

• **make someone's day** – *it means making someone happy:*

> (18) • Your bouquet of roses has made my day, thank you.

> (19) • Our daughter's telephone call from Russia made our day.

• **make a day of it**(spoken) – *it means make an enjoyable activity for an entire whole day:*

> (20) • We are going to London for a day. How nice! Make a day of it.

• dead

• **dead body** (spoken) – *when you include this in your speech, it means you are strongly opposed to something:*

> (21) • My son wants to sell our shop as a going concern over my dead body.

> (22) • My son wants to marry that young girl over my dead body.

• **be dead and gone**(informal) – *it simply means dead:*

> (23) • You hoped that by now I was dead and gone.

> (24) • She will be happy when her husband is dead and gone.

• deaf

• **fall on deaf ears** – *when someone's advice or information is ignored or not listened to by other persons:*

> (25) • In these days, too much information is available; thus parents advice
> often falls on deaf ears.

> (26) • She talked to her mother over the phone, but mother's advice fell on deaf ears.

• deep

• **go off the deep end** (informal) – *it is used when someone suddenly becomes very angry, emotional, and expresses strong feelings:*

> (27) • When Rob returned home from work, he went off the deep end as the

builders didn't come to repair his house roof.

(28) . Paul really went off the deep end when he found out that his neighbours'
dog had bitten his son.

. **in deep water(s)** (informal) – *it means someone is in difficulty or trouble :*

(29) . She found herself in deep waters when her husband had a car accident.

(30) . John has been made redundant by his employers and now finds himself
in deep waters at the age of 60.

. dig

. **dig deep (into something)** – *when someone is searching thoroughly for some
information, they are digging deep into whatever they are looking for:*

(31) . I'll dig deep into my archives for that article in which factual information
on casualties is given.

It also means to give money or something that is wanted:

(32) . Our community must dig deep for the finance needed to save our local
church from decaying.

. dressed

. **dressed to kill** (informal) – *when someone wears the kind of clothes designed to attract
attention and impress people:*

(33) . She was dressed to kill when she went to meet her new boyfriend.

(34) . Some people dress to kill when they attend job interviews. It is not always
a good idea.

. drop

. **drop off** (informal) – *it is used when someone falls into a light sleep:*

(35) . After lunch, some seminar delegates dropped off and missed the
important health and exercise hints.

(36) • I dropped off on a train journey and when the train stopped at my station, I missed it.

• drum

• **beat/bang the drum (for someone/something)** – *to try to support someone/something enthusiastically and publicly.*

(37) • You should ask your local press to beat the drum for this noble cause of helping the sick, feeble and old in this area.

(38) • Barbara is banging the drum for a new computer.

• due

• **in due course** – *you can use it to mean at the right time when it comes, not before:*

(39) • We will reply to your request for further information in due course.

• Dutch

• **go Dutch (with somebody)** (informal) – *this expression implies sharing the cost of something with somebody.*

(40) • All four of us decided to go Dutch in an Indian restaurant.

(41) • I went Dutch with my old friend when we had some drinks in a pub.

E

• ear

• **be all ears** (informal) – *it implies that you are waiting eagerly to listen to someone attentively:*

(1) • Students were all ears when the guest speaker was delivering his speech.

(2) . It has been very long since we met. Tell me all about your recent past; I'm all ears.

. **play it by ear** (informal) – *to tackle a problem or situation as it arises without a plan of action drawn beforehand:*

(3) . It is difficult to imagine how our dinner party will progress tonight - we'll have to play it by ear.

(4) . They want us to pay a deposit. I can't do it as we haven't finally decided to order it. Well, if they telephone us, I'll have to play it by ear.

. early

. **an early bird** (humorous/informal) – *it refers to a person who gets up early, or arrives early. You can also use it for someone who does something more promptly than other people and may get some advantage:*

(5) . She is an early bird this morning!

(6) . The Christmas sales start tomorrow morning. You will have to be an early bird to get a good bargain.

. **it's early days (yet)** – *You can use it to say that it is too soon to know the outcome of something, or how a situation will develop:*

(7) . It's early days yet. We don't know if our new product will be ordered by all those retailers to whom we have just sent samples.

(8) . Our security guard is alert all day along, but it's early days yet.

. earth

. **cost the earth or pay the earth** (informal) – *it means charge too much money:*

(9) . This is a beautiful dress. You must have paid the earth for it.

(10) . I'd very much like to see the pyramids in Egypt, but it costs the earth.

. **how, what, why, where, who on earth** (informal) – *this expression is used in* *a question for emphasis, when you are angry, puzzled, or unable to know an answer quickly:*

> (11) • How on earth can you afford to pay the monthly instalments for this new car?

> (12) • What on earth are you doing in my garden?

> (13) • Where on earth can you find such a loving lady?

> (14) • Why on earth did they do this to you?

• easy

• easier said than done – *it means something is much more difficult to do than it seems:*

> (15) • For some people writing a letter is easier said than done.

> (16) • Why didn't she stay with her mother-in-law ?
> That's easier said than done.

• go easy on/with something (informal) – *when you want to tell someone do not use too much of something:*

> (17) • Go easy on the printer – it's already low on ink.

> (18) • Go easy on the milk – that's all we have got this morning.

• go easy on somebody (informal) – *it means to treat somebody kindly without making things too difficult or getting too angry:*

> (19) • Go easy on Elizabeth as she has just returned to work after a long illness.

> (20) • Alf is a French student on a work experience programme – go easy on him.

• take it easy or take things easy – *when you want to tell to someone to be calm and avoid working too hard:*

> (21) • You should take it easy after a serious heart operation.

> (22) • It was a big a job that we finished on time. Now we can take things
> easy for a while.

****

You can also use this expression in the imperative when you wish to tell someone that there is no need to be so angry or upset about some occurrence:

> (23) • Take it easy, there's no need to be so emotional about it.
>   ---------------
>   ⇑

The verb is used in its base form and the sentence does not have an overt subject.

• edge

• be on edge – *when someone is nervous, uneasy, excited:*

> (24) • She was on edge when our flight was delayed for one hour.
>
> (25) • I was on edge while waiting for the outcome of my application to emigrate to Canada.

• take the edge off something – *when something is made less strong, less unpleasant, or less painful, etc::*

> (26) • The painkillers you gave me have taken the edge off my leg pain, but I'm still uncomfortable.
>
> (27) • Certainly, the piece of cake took the edge off my craving.

• egg

• egg on your face or egg all over your face – *to feel embarrassed, stupid or humiliated:*

> (28) • We hired a hall for last night's meeting, but only a few people turned up. We were left with egg on our faces.
>
> (29) • If I visit them and they already have some guests, I'll have egg all over my face.

• put all your eggs in one basket – *when you use up all your resources in one particular course of action for success and are left with no resources, if the chosen course of action fails:*

(30) • We do not supply our publications through just one sole distributor, because
we don't wish to put all our eggs in one basket.

(31) • I save my money with two different banks. I don't want to put all
my eggs in one basket.

• elbow

• give somebody/get the elbow (informal) – *both mean the same that is to be rejected by somebody:*

(32) • Sarah gave John the elbow when she won a large sum of money and
started going out with some new friends.

(33) • I went to see him last night, but I got the elbow as he was busy
finishing his project.

• end

• be at the end of something – *when there is not much left of something:*

(34) • We are at the end of our long holiday in your country.

(35) • Before she left him, she shouted, 'I'm at the end of my patience.'

• make (both) ends meet – *when somebody earns just enough money so that they can buy only the necessary things they need for their living:*

(36) • As I have only a part-time job, it is difficult to make both ends meet.

(37) • In our area, many families struggle to make ends meet.

• example

• make an example of somebody – *to punish somebody as a warning to others that they will also be punished in the same way:*

(38) • Our club management made an example of a member and expelled him from
the club for five years for making racial remarks against another member.

(39) • Our manager decided to make an example of an employee and terminated

his employment contract because he used his PC at work for private use.

. eyeball

. eyeball to eyeball (with somebody) (informal) – *when people are face to face during an angry confrontation, discussion or public meeting involving differences of opinions:*

> (40) . We have not yet spoken to that insurance agent eyeball to eyeball
> about his serious mistake.

> (41) . During our staff meeting lecturers' representatives and the college
> principal stood eyeball to eyeball on a number of staffing issues.

. be up to your eyeballs (in something) – *this expression refers to two different situations – (a) when you have a lot of work or something to handle that may be unpleasant or difficult to accomplish:*

> (42) . I'm up to my eyeballs in debt since I lost my full-time employment.

> (43) . Don't ask her to do this work for you, as she is already up to her eyeballs
> in her own work.

> *(b) It can also be used to refer to someone who is under strong effects
> of some drugs:*

> (44) . We cannot get any accurate information from him as he is drugged up to
> his eyeballs.

> (45) . Don't ask him for directions as he is already drugged up to his eyeballs.

F

. face

. disappear/vanish off the face of the earth – *when somebody disappears without any trace:*

> (1) . Wolf is not here. He must be somewhere; he just can't disappear off
> the face of the earth.

338   **Idiomatic Expressions**

****

(2) • She had a row with her mother two hours ago. Don't worry, she will return home soon, as without the money, she can't vanish off the face of the earth.

• **on the face of it** – *it means that at first glance something looks good, or whatever, but this perception/opinion may change when more is learnt about it:*

(3) • On the face of it, this equipment seems a good bargain at this price.

(4) • On the face of it, it was a straight forward job, but when we started, it took much longer than we allowed for it.

• **to somebody's face** – *when you say something to somebody directly when they are present:*

(5) • When the manager is not in the office, staff talk about his lack of managerial skills. However, no one has the courage to make that sort of remark to his face.

(6) • I'm going to see your boss and tell him that to his face.

• fact

• **the fact of (the matter) is (that)** – *this expression is used to emphasize the opposite of what has already been said:*

(7) • My wife wants to visit Paris again but the fact of the matter is that we can't even afford to travel to London from York.

(8) • It would be nice to sell all units of this product by the end of the month but the fact is, today is 25th of the month and we have sold none.

• **the hard facts** ⇒ **see hard**

• fail

• **without fail** – *it can be used for two different purposes:*

    (a) it means always:

(9) • We respond to all enquiries without fail   ⇐ always

(b) it also means someone must do something:

(10) • You must report to me by 10 a.m. tomorrow without fail.

• faint

• not have the faintest/foggiest (idea) (informal) – *when you do not know anything about something/somebody:*

(11) • Where is Daniel? Sorry, I don't have the faintest idea.

(12) • Can you please direct me to a police station? I haven't the foggiest idea.

• fair

• by fair means or foul – *when somebody uses dishonest means when honest means do not work for getting what they want:*

(13) • They are willing to succeed in this matter by fair means or foul.

(14) • He wants to cross the English Channel by ferry tonight by fair means or foul.

• a fair crack of the whip (informal) – *it means a reasonable opportunity to take part in something that may bring success, or other kinds of benefits:*

(15) • It is widely understood that for many well-paid jobs not all applicants are given a fair crack of the whip.

(16) • Virginia applied for the membership of an exclusive chess club, but some months after she felt she was not given a fair crack of the whip.

• false

• by/on/under false pretences – *someone's intention to deceive others and gain whatever they want to achieve this way:*

(17) • David was accused of getting a place on a degree course by false pretences.

(18) • A caller tried to get some business information under false pretences.

• fed

- **fed up** (informal) – *when you are bored, tired or both tired and displeased:*

  (19) • I'm fed up with loud music from next door at this time of the night.

  (20) • She was fed up with word processing all morning, so she went out for an early lunch.

• fetch

- **fetch and carry (for somebody)** – *it means doing lots of little jobs:*

  (21) • Twice a week, I fetch and carry for my grandmother as she is no longer mobile.

  (22) • Here is a small advertisement for someone to fetch and carry four days a week for an elderly gentleman who lives alone.

• few

- **few and far between** – *it refers to infrequent occurrences of an event involving a long waiting time before it happens again:*

  (23) • We close this museum during winter time as visitors are few and far between.

  (24) • I travel to work by car because public transport services between home and work are few and far between.

• fiddle

- **play second fiddle (to somebody/something)** – *to accept that you are not as important and equal in status as the other person - you are a follower, not the leader:*

  (25) • I never liked playing second fiddle to anyone and that's why I'm self-employed.

This expression can also be used for things other than people:

  (26) • Manchester and Birmingham play second fiddle to London in England.

• fight

- **fighting fit** – *it means healthy and fit physically and mentally:*

(27) • He was rushed to hospital for an emergency operation, but now he is fighting fit.

(28) • You seem to be fighting fit despite your long illness.

• **put up a good fight** – *to compete enthusiastically and with determination to succeed, or make a determined effort to succeed in achieving someone's goal:*

(29) • Our team put up a good fight against a very strong team in this competition, but unfortunately came second.

(30) • Daisy put up a good fight to win her first European race, but she was running against some very experienced international competitors.

• **finger**

• **lay a finger on somebody/something** – *when somebody touches some other person or thing, no matter how hard or soft is the touch. It usually refers to harming somebody physically in negative sentences:*

(31) • I can assure you that I never laid a finger on him.

(32) • I never laid a finger on your son; he is not telling the truth. If you lay a finger on my little boy again, I will call the police.

• **point the finger at (somebody)** – *it means blaming, or accusing somebody of doing something wrong:*

(33) • You cannot point the finger at me because I was not even in the country when the murder took place.

(34) • She pointed the finger at a shop assistant for overcharging her, without any proof to support her accusation.

• **flat**

• **flat out** (informal) – *it means doing something as fast and as hard as possible:*

(35) • We are working flat out to finish this job by tomorrow.

(36) • My wife cooked a meal flat out to get it finished before our guests arrived.

****

• fool

• make a fool of somebody/oneself – *to make somebody look silly deliberately:*

(37) • He made a fool of me by making me sing in front of the invited guests
who laughed at me.

(38) • He made a fool of her by telling her how much he loved her and then
disappeared, when she felt ill and her illness was diagnosed as cancer.

• fort

• hold the fort (spoken) – *when someone is made responsible for looking after somebody,*
doing a job or carrying on any other responsibility temporarily:

(39) • I can't close my shop for one week, but my wife will hold the fort when
I will be away for one week for a trade fair in Russia.

(40) • You can take a few days off work, I will hold the fort for you.

• foul

• fall foul of somebody/something (formal) – *this expression can be used to refer to*
somebody/something that is in trouble with the law, or an organisation, or
individual because of some wrong action:

(41) • Unfortunately, when he was only 16 years of age, he fell foul of the law
for shoplifting and was sent to a young offenders centre for six months.

(42) • Duncan fell foul of hiding his real income from the tax authorities, and
now he must pay a heavy fine as well as the unpaid tax or go to jail.

• fuss

• make a fuss or kick up a fuss (about/over) (informal) – *it implies a strong complaint:*

(43) • You ought to make a fuss about the poor quality of work and demand
at least some of your money back.

(44) • My mother is kicking up an awful fuss about her neighbours blocking
her entrance with their car.

. **make a fuss of/ over somebody** (informal) – *when too much attention is given to someone to show your affections:*

     (45) . When I was their guest, they made a great fuss of me.

     (46) . My wife always makes such a big fuss over her son-in-law who does not appreciate her kindness.

G

. **game**

. **give the game away** (informal) – *when somebody lets a secret, a trick or a plan be known to others, especially by accident:*

     (1) . When she was answering a question, she shouted angrily and her Danish accent gave the game away.

     (2) . Our local Member of Parliament wanted to announce his wedding date in The Times next month. Somehow, the local newspaper published the date three weeks before the intended publication and gave the game away.

     (3) . If you giggle, you'll give the game away.

. **be on the game** (informal) – *it means someone is working as a prostitute:*

     (4) . Many young girls from East European countries are forced by gangsters to go on the game in the West.

     (5) . How can anyone from such a respected family background have the courage to go on the game?

. **glove**

. **the gloves are off** (informal) – *when somebody is ready to argue or fight, or compete aggressively:*

     (6) . In the supermarket price war, the gloves are coming off once again.

     (7) . Our General Election to elect a central government will be held in May, but

already the gloves are off as both major political parties have begun televised campaigns.

(8) . John and Colin are about to stand in the election of a club secretary, but already the gloves are off and we can expect some heated exchanges.

. glue

. **be glued to something** (informal) – *when you are giving all your attention to somebody. or something:*

(9) . My husband spends every evening glued to his computer.

(10) . On Sundays, my wife is glued to her gardening hobby.

. go

. **as people, things, etc. go** – *when you want to compare somebody, or something with the average person, or thing, etc.:*

(11) . As footballers go, he is very good.

(12) . Just fifty pounds for this real wood table is a good bargain as real wood tables go in these days.

. **go down well, badly, etc.(with somebody) or go off well** — *this expression is used to say how well or poorly people react to someone's performance, or work, i.e., dancing, acting, or speech, etc:*

(13) . I think our guest speaker's talk and his demonstration went down well with almost all our members present tonight.

(14) . Joan's dancing performance went off well.

. goat

. **get someone's goat** (informal) *when somebody gets your goat, it implies that they irritate you very much:*

(15) . He likes to get someone's goat, as he is a troublemaker.

(16) . He got my goat when he walked out as I started talking.

• going

• a going concern – *when a business is profitable and is likely to generate more profit:*

(17) • I would like to advertise our shop as a going concern for sales as I'll be 65 years of age in six months time.

(18) • We sold our travel agency as a going concern to a big travel agency.

• the going rate (for something) – *the price of a particular type of goods or services that is widely charged at a particular time or period in a particular area of the country:*

(19) • In this part of England, retailers pay less than the going rate for shop assistants in bigger cities.

(20) • The going rate per hour for a solicitor's service is sixty pounds at present.

• good

• give as good as you get – *when during an argument, or fight you are as successful, or harmful as your opponent and well matched in the contest, etc:*

(21) • Our discussion turned into an argument, but I gave him as good as I got.

(22) • Our team is young and inexperienced at international level, but to my great surprise, we still gave as good as we got, as it was a draw.

• grab

• up for grabs (informal) – *when something is available if someone is interested in it:*

(23) • The value of this car is £20,000. It is up for grabs in tomorrow's milk race competition.

(24) • Five seats at Regents Theatre are up for grabs free of charge for the first five telephone callers on Monday morning.

• grace

• fall from grace – *this expression is used to refer to people who lost their privileges because they have made mistakes or done something that upset their superiors, the*

establishment or any other system:

> (25) • He was a senior manager. He fell from grace when he hit his managing
>   director's car in a road accident, and was made redundant.

> (26) • For three years, he was the trusted club treasurer. When the auditors
>   discovered some financial inconsistencies, he fell from grace and was asked
>   to resign.

• grade

• make the grade (informal) – *when somebody reaches the required standard to succeed:*

> (27) • This year my students performed well, as only 5% failed to make the grade.

> (28) • Unfortunately, due to illness, my son failed to make the grade in one module.

• grain

• be/go against the grain – *when something is against your beliefs, ideas, feelings, etc:*

> (29) • It goes against the grain for Muslims to eat pork.

> (30) • It goes against the grain to have to vote for the socialist party.

• grape

• on/through the grapevine – *when people come to know about something informally through friends, colleagues, etc:*

> (31) • I have just heard on the grapevine that you had a big row with the manager
>   regarding shift work last week.

> (32) • I heard through the grapevine that you have been promoted and
>   soon will be leaving our department. Is it true?

• grass

• the grass roots – *this expression is usually used to refer to people who do not make important decisions in trade unions, professional bodies and ordinary people in general:*

(33) . The Teachers' union decision to accept a management offer of a 5% pay
rise has been rejected by the union's grass roots.

(34) . The Russian Revolution started at the grass roots and finally succeeded
in replacing the monarchy with communism.

(35) . Often changes come from the grass roots and are eventually adopted by
the government* as its policy.

*government is a countable group noun because it consists of some people. It can be used
in a clause, or sentence either as singular or plural.

. grave

. **turn in his/her grave** – *it means that a deceased person would be very angry, or shocked
to hear or see what is happening at present:*

(36) . Your grandfather would turn in his gave if he saw this housing estate
built on his farmland.

(37) . Lenin, the first leader of the USSR, would turn in his grave if he knew
how his system failed.

. grip

. **come/get to grips with something** – *it means to begin to understand and deal with
a problematic situation:*

(38) . As you asked for advice, I suggest that first you should get to grips with
your cash flow problems before you apply for a further business loan.

(39) . Since she has a private lesson in Polish every week, she is getting to grips
with Polish grammar.

. ground

. **get something off the ground (also get off the ground)** – *when you put something
into operation successfully; or start something, often after some hard work successfully:*

(41) . Now it is the right time to get this project off the ground, as all essential

348   **Idiomatic Expressions**

****

tests have been completed successfully.

(42) • All design work has been completed, but without the bank loan, the manufacturing operations are unlikely to get off the ground.

• gun

• **jump the gun** (informal) – *when somebody starts doing something before the right time:*

(43) • He is very impatient and he may jump the gun, so he is not yet informed.

(44) • She jumped the gun by opening the gates fifteen minutes before the advertised time.

<u>H</u>

• hair

• **let your hair down** (informal) – *when you are relaxed and enjoying yourself without worrying about behaving in an undignified way:*

(1) • He is a very shy and gentle person and never lets his hair down at any social gathering.

(2) • I can only let my hair down in the company of a few close friends.

• halfway

• **meet someone halfway** – *to make an agreement with somebody in such a way that a compromise is reached in both parties' mutual interest:*

(3) • I'll meet you halfway, if you allow me 25% special discount.

(4) • He telephoned me to apologize for not keeping his promise. The least I could do was to meet him halfway and make another date for going out together.

• hand

• **bite the hand that feeds you** – *it means to hurt somebody who has supported you:*

(5) . I have some reservations about the way John acted tonight, but I do not wish to bite the hand that fed me sometime ago.

(6) . He was so angry with his financial backer that he has bitten the hand that fed him by refusing to be a part of his team.

. hard

. **hard done by** (informal) – *when someone thinks/feels that they have been unfairly treated:*

(7) . If someone feels hard done by, please make an appointment to see me privately on Friday afternoon in my office.

(8) . We have all received an annual bonus payment from the company, but Malcolm feels he has been hard done by.

(9) . All job applicants were interviewed fairly, but an internal candidate made a written complaint claiming that he was hard done by.

. **the hard facts** – *it means accurate information that is undeniable:*

(10) . Where were you yesterday? The hard facts are that you were seen drinking in a pub, so don't tell me that you were sick.

(11) . The hard facts are that we lost our biggest customer due to our inability to supply goods on time.

. hash

. **make a hash of something (informal)** – *when something is done badly or spoiled by somebody:*

(12) . He made a complete hash of the input data by making incorrect entries.

(13) . How well did you do at the interview? To tell you the truth, I made a real hash of it.

(14) . Have you translated that correspondence from Hungary? Yes, but I think I have made a real hash of the translation without the Hungarian- English dictionary.

350   **Idiomatic Expressions**

****

. hat

. at the drop of a hat – *it means somebody must do something immediately without hesitation:*

> (15) . You cannot expect him to join us at the drop of a hat as he has a young family.

> (16) . At work, sometimes, I must do something at the drop of a hat, even if I'm in the middle of doing something urgent.

. old hat (informal) – *it means something is out of date or old fashioned. It is usually used when you consider something with contempt:*

> (17) . His ideas are old hat because he retired nearly twenty years ago.

> (18) . It is a pity that in these days some people think marriage is old hat.

. head

. bury/hide your head in the sand – *when someone deliberately refuses to accept that a problematic situation exists; or does nothing to deal with a problem:*

> (19) . You cannot bury your head in the sand for ever. You must take some steps to save your business from bankruptcy.

> (20) . This road junction is very dangerous to motorists, cyclists and pedestrians, but our local traffic monitoring authority until now has hidden its head in the sand and refused to install traffic lights.

. go to your head – *this expression can be used to describe two different situations:*
(a) when your success in any walk of life makes you very proud of yourself and you start behaving in a way that annoys others:

> (21) . Anne's appointment as Professor of Nursing went to her head, as she hasn't been seen in the nursing staff common room since.

> (22) . James's business success went to his head. He has now joined a golf club and does not come to our rugby club for drinks any more.

(b) the way a person under the effects of alcohol may behave:

> (23) . The way she is talking, I think that drop of vodka has gone straight to her head.

(24) • It is the first time that I tried whisky and it went to my head.

• heap

• **at the top or bottom of a heap** – *when somebody is high or low in an organisational structure of hierarchy, society or any other organised system:*

(25) • Most migrants in the West are at the bottom of the full time employment heap.

(26) • At the bottom of a heap in our country are homeless people.

(27) • At the top of the heap of well paid professional people are barristers.

• heart

• **have a heart !** (spoken) – *when you wish to ask someone to be kind and show pity::*

(28) • At his age, it would be very difficult for him to find another job.
Please do not sack him. Have a heart!

(29) • Without our financial support, she cannot afford life saving medical treatment abroad for her baby son. Have a heart!

• **a heart of gold** – *when people are kind, generous, and do their best happily to help other people:*

(30) • Once I met a tall, bearded and strongly built man on a German train, but when I spoke to him, I found out he had a heart of gold.

(31) • After his work, every day he works as a volunteer at a local hospital, he drives a van for a charity and is very generous to all kinds of people. He really has a heart of gold.

• heat

• **if you can't stand the heat (get out of the kitchen)** (informal) – *it is said about someone who gets involved with some difficult activity or task. When it gets more difficult, they complain. This expression tells them either they improve their abilities, skills or whatever is needed for this activity, or finish their participation in it:*

(32) • She is a manager at a department store where there are far too many activities
to manage. Her doctor has advised her if she can't stand the heat, she should
get out of the kitchen.

(33) • He is learning judo with us, but each day it is getting harder for him and he
does not like it. Well, if he can't stand the heat now it is best to get out
of the kitchen.

• heights

• **the dizzy heights (of something)** (informal) — *it means that somebody has achieved*
a big success, or has reached an impressive position:

(34) • He had studied accountancy for five years and then worked in various
capacities in this profession until last year. This year, he reached the
dizzy heights of being a chief accountant in a large company.

(35) • My husband is a professor of computing. Well, I haven't met any body who
reached such dizzy heights in the teaching profession.

• hell

• **all hell breaks loose** (informal) — *it means sudden uproar, fighting, an ugly scene:*

(36) • It seemed so peaceful in the restaurant. Suddenly, there was a lot of noise
and then all hell broke loose and some people started punching and shouting
at each other and breaking furniture.

(37) • During the discussion, some people started arguing loudly, banging on the
desks and then all hell broke loose.

• **get the hell out of ...** (spoken/informal) — *when you want to leave a place immediately:*

(38) • We were searching for our file, when unexpectedly, we heard the sound of
footsteps; in no time, we had to get the hell out of the manager's office.

(39) • Let's get the hell out of here before we are caught by their security cameras.

• here

- **here you are** (spoken) – *this expression is used when you are giving something to someone:*

    (40) • Here you are - a nice, warm cup of Indian tea.

    (41) • Here you are sir, a memo from the managing director for an urgent reply.

• hold

- **get hold of someone or something** (informal) – *it has two meanings:*

   (a) to find somebody, talk to somebody or contact somebody:

    (42) • Where is John now? His father has been trying to get hold of him by phone since lunch time.

   (b) to find something that somebody wants:

    (43) • I would like to get hold of a copy of a good French- English & English –French dictionary.

• horse

- **(straight) from the horse's mouth** (informal) – *when information is given directly by the person who has direct knowledge of it. Or from a well-informed reliable source and thus it should be reliable:*

    (44) • Our sales figures are straight from the horse's mouth.

    (45) • This is so important for us, and thus we should get the answer from the horse's mouth.

• a dark horse ⟹ see dark

- **hold your horses** (spoken) – *when you want to say to somebody not to act hastily, but think about the situation first:*

    (46) • Hold your horses! They will not supply us with more goods, until we pay them for goods we bought from them last week.

    (47) • I suggest we hold our horses a minute and look first at their offer before rejecting it straight away.

- **horses for courses** – *For a specific task, job, assignment or for any other activity, it involves matching the person with a suitable task, job, etc. It is so because some people are better suited for a particular activity, etc. than others :*

  (48) • We could have promoted someone within our department, but we have advertised the post, as it is a case of horses for courses.

  (49) • Our staff policy is very much based on the idea of horses for courses.

  (50) • Our cricket club has over 20,000 members and different levels of membership subscriptions. Therefore, it requires a horses and courses administrative staff policy.

I

- **ice**

- **break the ice** – *when, especially, at the start of any gathering (party, meeting etc.), or a new situation someone says, or does something so that shyness and a tense atmosphere in the gathering are overcome and people feel at ease:*

  (1) • The first session of the seminar was rather formal, until the ice was broken by refreshments and a lively discussion.

  (2) • Let's break the ice by inviting that couple sitting in a corner to join us.

- **cut no ice (with somebody)** – *it means you are not impressed by somebody or something:*

  (3) • The way he dressed up cuts no ice with me.

  (4) • You can see homeless people sleeping in shops doorways, but politicians manipulate figures and tell us that the problem is less acute; it cuts no ice with me.

- **the tip of the iceberg** – *it means a small part of a much larger problem, situation, or something that is hidden or cannot be seen to its full extent:*

  (5) • What the Commission of Equal Opportunity has discovered until now about

****

inequality in the workplace is only the tip of the iceberg.

(6) • The police have arrested the gang leader, and found one million pounds in cash and a large quantity of hard drugs. The police spokesman also added, 'That's just the tip of the iceberg, and the search for other gangsters goes on.'

(7) • This is just the tip of the iceberg what he has told us so far.

• icing

• **the icing on the cake** − *it means something extra is added to an already good situation, circumstance or an activity which makes it even better:*

(8) • My parents and Jane's parents have been friends for more than thirty years. Our marriage will really be the icing on the cake for them.

(9) • We already have some good business connections in Germany, but having another distributor in Austria, which is another German speaking country, is the icing on the cake.

(10) • Our tour of France is well organised, but having a medical doctor in our team is the icing on the cake.

• idea

• **give somebody ideas or put ideas into somebody's head** − *these expressions mean:*
(a) *to give somebody hopes that may not be fulfilled.*
(b) *misguide somebody so that they do something illogical:*

(11) • I came to join the party tonight. Who gave you such ideas?

(12) • Please don't give her ideas that she can stay with us in July, as my mother-in-law will be staying with us during the whole month of July.

(13) • She wants to marry an old rich man who lives in that big house . Who has been putting ideas into her head?

• **you have no idea** (spoken) − *when you want to emphasise that something is not easy for somebody to visualize:*

(14) • I'm sorry you have no idea how difficult that journey was for me.

(15) • I think most people in this country have no idea what poverty does to

people in Africa.

. if

. if and when – *this expression is used to express doubts about the feasibility of a future event:*

(16) . If and when I ever travel to Paris, we will come to this restaurant for a meal.

(17) . It is very kind of you to invite me today. However, if and when I return to this place, I will telephone you from England to arrange for an informal meeting.

. if anything – *it is used in a negative statement to counter the idea of someone by suggesting that the opposite is true. It can also be used to give a tentative opinion:*

(18) . Well, she is more like her elder sister, if anything. ⇐ *tentative opinion*

(19) . This is not a true blue colour, if anything it is a mixture of several computer generated colours and looks like a blue colour. ⇐ *opposite idea*

(20) . I would further say that John's writing is more like his brother's work, if anything. ⇐ *tentative opinion*

. if I were you – *this expression is used mainly for advising somebody:*

(21) . Dolly, if I were you, I wouldn't invite him to my home without his wife.

(22) . If I were you, I'd have left your boyfriend a long time ago.

. if only – *It is used to express someone's wish for something to possess or happen:*

*(23) . If only I were a rich man, I'd run a charitable trust to help deprived children.

(24) . If only I'd sent her birthday greetings and some flowers, our relationship would not have been dented.

(25) . If only she had telephoned us when she arrived at the airport, we would have gone to the airport to meet her.

* if--- were in a clause representing something untrue, the verb form **were** is required in formal writing.

****

<u>If you change the order of this expression it becomes a different idiomatic expression.</u>

- **only if** (formal) — *It implies that there is only one state in which something can occur:*

    (26) • Only if the manager gives permission can we close early for the party.

    (27) • Only if the British Embassy in Turkey grants a visa is she allowed to enter the UK.

    (28) • Only if someone applies for a job by completing our employment application form is an applicant considered for a suitable employment.

• ill

- **ill at ease** — *when someone feels embarrassed and self-conscious:*

    (29) • I want to go home as I feel ill at ease in this casual outfit.

    (30) • They were ill at ease when they visited us, as we were having a meal with other guests.

• image

- **spitting image of somebody** (informal) — *when somebody/something resembles another person/something else:*

    (31) • This man is the spitting image of Tony Blair.

    (32) • She is the spitting image of her twin sister in all aspects of her character and looks.

• in

- **in that** (written) — *it means because. It is used to say for the reason that:*

    (33) • We did not write to you earlier on in that we were conducting our internal enquiries.

    (34) • I was very lucky indeed in that I had some friends in Poland at that time.

- **be in at something** — *it means somebody is present when something happens.*

(35) • I was in at the beginning of the show and left when it finished.

(36) • She was also in at the start of our group discussion.

• **be in for something** (informal) — *this expression is used when you are expecting something rather unpleasant to happen soon:*

(37) • According to the BBC weatherman we are in for a heavy snow fall and the temperature will fall below zero.

(38) • We went to this club, but we did not know that we were in for a fight and would be arrested by the police.

(39) • It looks like we are in for a nasty experience.

• inch

• **every inch** — *this expression can render two different meanings:*

(a) to mean completely:

(40) • I'm every inch innocent.

(41) • When we first met, he appeared every inch a gentleman, and after 10 years of friendship, I still believe that is the case.

(b) to imply the whole or the entire of something:

(42) • The police ransacked every inch of a flat looking for drugs but found no evidence against the suspect.

(43) • A lady doctor examined every inch of my elderly mother's body.

• instance

• **in the first instance** (formal) — *when you take the first step of a series of steps involved in a process of doing something:*

(44) • In the first instance, you should request an application form for a job.

(45) • In the first instance, I must conduct an internal enquiry.

• issue

• **take issue with somebody(about/on/over something)** (formal) — *when somebody disagrees and argues with someone else:*

> (46) • I don't wish to take issue with you about our proposal, but I must ask you to consider it again.

> (47) • He took issue with his tutor over his project assessment.

> (48) • She took issue with her girlfriend on her choice of a male companion.

• ivory

• **an ivory tower** (disapproving) — *it implies that someone's life style or work is so much different from the ordinary work or life style that these people do not understand and appreciate the problems faced by ordinary persons:*

> (49) • That management consultant lives in an ivory tower - he has no idea of the range of problems in my work, but he has come to advise us.

> (50) • Unless the chief accountant comes down from his ivory tower to learn about our current problems and difficulties, he will not approve any staff replacements.

> (51) • She was telling us about her long luxurious holiday around the world. Well, she lives in an ivory tower, and cannot imagine that we cannot afford that sort of pleasure in life.

<u>J</u>

• jack

• **a jack of all trades** — *it is said about a person who is able to do different things, but does none of them very well:*

> (1) • He is a jack of all trades and offers his services repairing all kinds of domestic appliances.

This expression can be stated as a jack of all trades but master of none:

> (2) • It is better to specialise in one particular branch of the printing industry, instead of being a jack of all trades but master of none.

• jam

• **jam tomorrow** (informal) — *when someone promises that you will get benefits, happiness or some good things in the future, but in reality it is unlikely to happen:*

> (3) • I just don't believe what the government says about motor car prices. We have been promised jam tomorrow several times before by previous governments.

> (4) • During the General Election, the Labour Party promised jam tomorrow and persuaded electors to vote for them.

• jaw

• **somebody's jaw dropped/ fell/ sagged** (informal) — *when somebody appeared shocked or surprised:*

> (5) • His jaw dropped when he had to buy such an expensive dress for her.

> (6) • Veronica's jaw sagged when she was asked to pay £120 for washing machine repairs.

• jelly

• **be/feel like jelly or turn to jelly** — *when you are nervous and your legs or knees are so weak that your body shakes:*

> (7) • When I attend a job interview I feel like jelly.

> (8) • When a policeman called at the door, she turned to jelly fearing a member of her family might have been involved in a road accident.

• jeopardy

• **in jeopardy** — *it means a dangerous situation or circumstances that may cause some harm or loss of something:*

(9) ● The current international political crisis may place our export industry
in jeopardy.

(10) ● The cancellation of those two big contracts has put our business
in jeopardy.

● jewel

● **the jewel in someone's crown** — *it means the most valuable or the best thing somebody*
possesses. It can also mean a very important success someone has achieved and they are
proud of it:

(11) ● His very successful and profitable business is the jewel in his crown.

(12) ● In my view, the jewel in any historical monuments' crown in the heart of Paris,
is the Eiffel Tower.

● job

● **do the job** (informal) — *it refers to something that can be used for doing something*
with it successfully:

(13) ● This printer should do the job.

(14) ● Use this disk drive for storing your data. If it does not do the job, let me know.

● **jobs for the boys** (disapproving) — *this expression indicates criticism implying*
that in some organisations well-paid jobs are given to relatives, friends and supporters
of people who are in high positions:

(15) ● He is now head of the Planning Division at our local Council.
How did he manage that? His uncle is the Chief Executive - jobs for the boys.

(16) ● Despite the employment laws enforced in this country, prestigious jobs are
still quietly filled through jobs for the boys.

● **just the job** (approving/spoken) — *it means something is very welcome at a particular*
time:

(17) ● It was raining, so the offer of a nice cup of tea was just the job.

****

(18) • A lady telephoned me asking for some emergency repairs. It was just the job, as I had no other work.

• jog

• jog somebody's memory – *to help someone to recall something:*

(19) • Can you please jog my memory about this offer on Monday morning?

(20) • This document may jog your memory concerning that dispute months ago.

• join

• join battle (with somebody)(formal) – *when you start fighting somebody:*

(21) • Many inhabitants of our area have joined battle with the District Hospital Authority over their proposal to close down the night time emergency unit.

(22) • Staff and students have joined battle with the college governing body over canteen facilities and charges.

• join the club – *this expression is used when you have experienced something bad and someone else has also encountered the same experience so you can relate to it:*

(23) • Why are you here at the police station? I have lost my car. Join the club!

(24) • They have offered me only a part time job. Well, join the club!

• joke

• be/get beyond a joke – *when something is no longer humorous, but a serious matter:*

(25) • I would add that your sarcastic tone towards Amanda is getting beyond a joke.

(26) • Your attitude towards our new colleague is beyond a joke.

• it's no joke (informal) – *it means a difficult matter or situation:*

(27) • Trying to arrange a home mortgage on a low income is **no joke**.

(28) • I would say bringing up a family of four for a widow is **no joke**.

- **joking apart/aside** − *it means that you are no longer saying anything funny but something serious:*

> (29) • He has been all over the world. Joking apart, he lived in France and knows enough about French cuisine.

> (30) • She thinks she is going to marry Mr. James Bond, her new boyfriend. Joking aside, he is already married and has two children.

• Jones

- **keep up with the Joneses** (informal) − *when somebody makes sure that their social status, in terms of possessions of things, friends, and achievements, remains equal to their neighbours and friends. They try to maintain their status, even if they do not have enough financial resources:*

> (31) • Since they bought a new house in a wealthy area by the sea on Cliff Road, they have spent a lot of money on a new car, a big digital television set, garden furniture and other things to keep up with the Joneses.

> (32) • We have withdrawn our golf club membership, as we were finding it difficult to keep up with the Joneses.

> (33) • Some people end up poor and in debt if they try to keep up with the Joneses, when they find it hard to make both ends meet.

• judge

- **don't judge a book by its cover** − *this idiomatic expression implies that somebody should not form an opinion about others from their appearance only:*

> (34) • He was smartly dressed in a suit and was talking fast. He gave me the impression that he was very respectable but I don't judge a book by its cover. He is a trickster.

> (35) • They looked very happy together. They must be happily married. Don't judge a book by its cover, as they are about to get a divorce.

• jump

- **a jumping-off place/point** − *it indicates a place from which you can start:*

(36) ● When I travelled from Hungary to Austria by train, I found Vienna was the best jumping-off place for touring Austria and the Slovak Republic.

● **justice**

● **do yourself justice** — *it means you must do something as well as you can to prove to other people how good, intelligent, capable or skilful you are:*

(37) ● He didn't do himself justice in this game, as he had not fully recovered from his leg injuries.

(38) ● Joan didn't do herself justice in last night's debate on social benefits.

● **justify**

● **in justification (of something)** — *when you want to give reason(s) or an explanation for something happening, or clarify why somebody has done something:*

(39) ● All she said in justification of her resignation was that she was unable to accept her new role.

(40) ● What can you tell us in justification of your actions last night?

K

● **keen**

● **(as) keen as mustard** (informal) — *this expression is used to describe someone who is very enthusiastic and wishes to do very well:*

(1) ● She joined classes three weeks after the course had commenced, but she is as keen as mustard and has already learnt what she missed.

(2) ● When he is boxing, he is rather slow in his body movements, but is keen as mustard. He loves boxing.

● **keep**

● **keep going** — *you can use this expression in two different ways:*

(a) when it is spoken by someone: it encourages somebody to carry on doing whatever they are doing:

(3) • Keep going, we're nearly there!

(4) • Your timing is perfect, just keep going at this pace.

(b) when somebody has faced hardship, or is still experiencing suffering and struggling to live a normal life:

(5) • Under these circumstances, she has no choice except to keep going.

(6) • He is very emotional since he lost his wife. Well, the best he can do for himself is to occupy his mind with something interesting and keep going.

• **keep somebody going** (informal) — *when something is sufficient for somebody until they have what is needed:*

(7) • I'm starving. Please have this packet of crisps to keep you going *till* your lunch. ----

till = until but till is informal. Usually *until* is used to begin a *clause* ↵

Until I spoke to him he ignored me completely. ↵

(8) • Sarah's fax machine is out of order. She can have our spare fax machine to keep her going for the time being.

• **for keeps** (informal) — *it means for ever:*

(9) • This dictionary is yours for keeps.

(10) • I must give this pen back to Donald, as it wasn't mine for keeps. It was only borrowed from him.

• keeping

• **in somebody's keeping** — *when something, or someone is being taken care of by somebody else:*

(11) • When we are away from our home, we leave our house front door key in our neighbours' keeping.

(12) • When we went to Paris, our son was left in his grandparents' keeping.

• **in keeping (with something)** — *something is in accordance with what is expected:*

(13) • Until now, our programme is in keeping with our planned timing.

(14) • For the quarter that has just ended, our cash flow is in keeping with our forecast.

• **out of keeping (with something)** — *this expression has the opposite meaning of the above expression — something is not in agreement , or is not suitable with what is expected in a given situation:*

(15) • The tie is out of keeping with your graduation gown.

(16) • This logo is out of keeping with the type of business you run.

• kick

• **kick the habit** (informal) — *it implies that someone has given up an addiction:*

(17) • It is not easy for an alcoholic to kick the habit.

(18) • Many smokers are unhappy about the government's policy to spend a large sum of money on advertising to persuade smokers to kick the habit.

• **kick oneself** (informal) — *when you are angry or annoyed with yourself because you have made a mistake:*

(19) • He kicked himself when the bank manager told him that his cash flow projection revealed that he did not need such a large loan.

(20) • You'll kick yourself when I tell you that your estimates do not include all essential cost items.

• **kick one's heels** — *when you are doing nothing, except just waiting for someone or something for some time:*

(21) • We arrived on time for our train but it was delayed. Therefore, we were left kicking our heels for nearly one hour.

(22) . We were kicking our heels, waiting for you to arrive.

. **kick somebody in the teeth** (informal) — *it means treating somebody unexpectedly unkindly, or not helping someone when help was very much expected:*

(23) . Our management decision to close down our section is a kick in the teeth for us.

(24) . Recently, we were led to believe that there were no financial problems. Now the company is bankrupt. We have been kicked in the teeth.

. **kid**

. **handle/treat someone with kid gloves** — *when you want to say somebody must carefully approach someone without offending them, because they are either easily offended, or they are important for whatever reason(s):*

(25) . He is our regular customer therefore, we ought to treat him with kid gloves.

(26) . Jane is my best friend's daughter. You must handle her job application with kid gloves.

(27) . I had to handle Antonia with kid gloves, when I asked her where she was yesterday all day until midnight.

. **kill**

. **make a killing** (informal) — *when somebody makes a large some of money as profit/reward:*

(28) . His software package for small businesses is very popular. He has sold thousands of copies and made a killing.

(29) . Thousands of Western companies have made a killing by supplying technology and expertise to Arab oil producing countries.

. **kill two birds with one stone** — *when somebody achieves two objectives by a single action:*

(30) . When you are at the bank, you could kill two birds with one stone and pay my cash into my account at the same time.

(31) . We killed two birds with one stone, when on our way to Edinburgh, we stopped

at Lancaster for several hours without paying any extra money.

. kind

- **in kind** — *this expression renders two different meanings in two different contexts:*

  (a) it can mean making a payment not with money but by some kind of goods or service:

  (32) • A motor mechanic serviced my car and I paid him in kind that is by installing a software package on his PC.

  (b) it also means similar treatment, doing something or answering back to someone in the same way:

  (33) • On the train, a man looked very angrily towards me, so I looked at him in kind.

  (34) • He was rude to me and I replied in kind.

- **a kind of** *(informal)* — *it implies uncertainty:*

  (35) • My wife had a kind of fear that one day someone might steal our car.

  (36) • I'm not sure about his status in our firm but he is a kind of high level executive.

- **nothing of the kind/sort** — *when you want to say that somebody or something is not at all like as it is expected:*

  (37) • We were under the impression that she would be very strict, but she is nothing of the kind. She is very relaxed and friendly.

  (38) • I was told that he was unfriendly and often rude, but he's nothing of the sort.

. knife

- **the knives are out (for somebody)** — *when a state of affairs is so unfavourable that people are looking for someone to blame for it and make them suffer in some way. This happens by removing them from their important and powerful position :*

  (39) • Our sales have been declining sharply since the beginning of the year. The board members have their knives out for the sales director.

(40) • Opinion polls are indicating a declining support for the Conservative Party. Conservative Members of Parliament have their knives out for the party leader.

• know

• **know-how (informal)** — *it means knowledge and skills that are essential for someone to possess for doing a specific task:*

(41) • I don't have the know-how to set up your network software, sorry.

(42) • Some international firms specialise in providing the know-how expertise in some specific fields, such as oil engineering and software engineering world wide.

• knowledge

• **come to somebody's knowledge (formal)** — *it means somebody finds out:*

(43) • It has come to our knowledge that you have been parking your car in our senior staff car park without displaying your car permit.

(44) • It has come to my knowledge that you have not yet paid your membership fee.

L

• Labour

• **a labour of love** — *When you wish do a hard job out of devotion or for your own satisfaction, not because it is required for a living or for making a profit:*

(1) • My mother knitted this pullover for me despite suffering from pain in her left hand. Indeed, it was a labour of love.

(2) • Daniel's regular gardening work for an elderly lady is a labour of love.

• lamb

• **like a lamb** — *it means gentle, calm and dutiful:*

(3) . There is no need to follow him like a lamb, if you are so bored in his company.

(4) . You'd obey orders like a lamb.

- **like lambs to the slaughter** — *when somebody does something obediently without being aware of the dangerous circumstances involved. Or one has no choice except to do something powerlessly knowing that it is dangerous:*

    (5) . Since we launched a joint venture, we have lost many customers. We should stop following them like lambs to the slaughter.

    (6) . I volunteered myself for this survey work in the town centre like a lamb to the slaughter, unaware that it was awkward work.

. land

- **(back) in the land of the living** — *it is used to emphasize that someone is still alive and doing fine after some health problems for whatever reasons. Or simply to emphasize the fact that someone is still living:*

    (7) . After nearly five years, she was ever so pleased to see me back in the land of the living.

    (8) . Since that accident, we were worried about you. Now we're delighted to see you in the land of the living. Well done!

- **the land of milk and honey** — *it means a prosperous country/land where living conditions are favourable. Life is very easy and people are contented:*

    (9) . Many young people in the East thought that the West is the land of milk and honey. However, when they reached it, some of them were kept in detention centres as illegal immigrants and asylum seekers.

    (10) . I would very much like to migrate to the land of milk and honey, if such a land exists on this planet.

. language

- **mind/watch your language** — *it suggests that someone should be careful when saying something, for the sake of not offending other person(s):*

(11) • Mind your language, Anne! If I spoke the same way to you, you would be angry with me.

(12) • Don't shout at me and watch your language.

• **speak/talk the same language** — *when you are able to communicate easily with someone with whom you have a good mutual understanding about life, have/share similar opinions, etc:*

(13) • I get on with my new friend very well because we happen to speak the same language.

(14) • She is at ease with me. Well, we talk the same language.

• late

• **better late than never** — *it is a saying. It means that something should happen even if it occurs after the time when it was expected to take place:*

(15) • We landed at Heathrow airport six hours late, sorry. It is better late than never, we are very happy to welcome both of you.

(16) • If she had not suffered from illness, she would have been awarded her Bachelor of Science Degree last year, but she has got it now. I'd say it is better late than never. Congratulations!

• lead

• **lead (someone) on** — *when someone deceives you by giving false hopes:*

(17) • He led us on to believe that goods would be despatched by tomorrow, so that we could make an advance payment.

(18) • The builder led us on to trust him that the job would be completed the next day, but it was three weeks ago and he hasn't returned yet to finish it.

• leaf

• **take a leaf out of (someone's) book** — *it is suggesting that someone should follow an example of good behaviour or the success of another person so that they can also do the same:*

(19) • Anjia has won the game for us. We should take a leaf out of her book and spend more time on practising techniques.

(20) • Anne, taking a leaf out of Anjia's book, has perfected her skills.

• league

• **in league (with somebody)** — *when you have joined someone or a group of people for the purpose of doing something bad secretly:*

(21) • We did not know that he was in league with drug dealers in Manchester.

(22) • She was caught shoplifting. When the police questioned her closely, she told them that she was in league with a gang of local shoplifters.

• leap

• **a leap/shot in the dark** — *when someone takes an action, makes a decision or is involved in a risky situation without any knowledge of it, and its outcome cannot be predicted:*

(23) • Since we did not know anything about the carpet dealer and his business, paying him a large deposit for the purchase of a Persian rug was a leap in the dark.

(24) • Well, as it is really hard to know exactly which is the best course of action, we just have to take a shot in the dark.

• left

• **left, right and centre (or right, left and centre)** (informal) — *it is used to emphasize that something is happening or being done in all directions, or in a large quantity:*

(25) • Since he won the national lottery jackpot, he is spending and giving away money left, right and centre.

(26) • I can't afford to give free copies of my book left, right and centre, as I'm restricted by my publishers.

• liberty

- **at liberty to do something (formal)** — *when someone is permitted or has the freedom to do something:*

    (27) • I'm not at liberty to decide about free samples, but I shall ask my manager.

    (28) • Indeed, she is at liberty to go where she wants.

• life

- **a matter of life and death** — *when a situation is very serious or urgent:*

    (29) • Please help, call the ambulance, it's a matter of life and death.

    (30) • This project must be given priority over all other tasks - it's a matter of life and and death for our business survival.

• light

- **bring to light** — *to reveal something or information for the first time to others:*

    (31) • These figures have only just been brought to light by our auditors.

    (32) • Our government's secret national pension strategy is brought to light in today's edition of the Sun. (Sun ⇒ one of the national daily newspapers in the UK)

• like

- **a likely story!** (spoken) — *it means you don't believe what someone says/said:*

    (33) • I did telephone them about the cheque. They told me it was posted last week. A likely story – ask them to issue another cheque.

    (34) • John has returned to work, as yesterday his wife was unwell. Once again, it is a likely story. We cannot pay him for yesterday.

• limb

- **out on a limb** (informal) — *when someone's ideas are not shared by other people, or somebody has done something that the other people don't like, and thus they're left in a weak position, without any support:*

(35) • A highly controversial new road scheme was approved by the committee last summer, but the Council finds itself out on a limb – residents are extremely unhappy about it and threatening further legal action.

(36) • Since he argued with the board of directors about closing down one of the factories, he found himself out on a limb and finally resigned.

• line

• **along /down the line (informal)** — *it means something happens during an activity, process or situation at some point that is difficult to predict precisely:*

(37) • She thinks that in her early life something was not right in her family along the line that had some effect on her personality.

(38) • I'm still considering all the relevant facts, but I'll decide further down the line.

• loggerheads

• **at loggerheads (with somebody)(over something)** — *when people disagree strongly:*

(39) • John Smith and Ray Robinson are still at loggerheads over the garden wall.

(40) • He is still at loggerheads with his wife over the property despite the fact that they have been separated for a year now.

<u>M</u>

• mad

• **like mad** (informal) — *it means very fast, hard, desperately etc:*

(1) • We landed two hours late at Frankfurt airport ; and I had to run like mad to catch my flight to London Heathrow.

(2) • Someone shouted fire and she ran out like mad.

• made

****

- **be made for (somebody/each other)** (informal) — *when two persons are ideally suited to each other:*

    (3) • Anne and Wolfgang are made for each other as they have been happily married for over thirty years.

    (4) • Since they met two years ago, it seems that they have been made for each other. Don't you think so?

• main

- **in the main** (formal) — *it means mostly, on the whole or above all:*

    (5) • She is, in the main, reliable and punctual.

    (6) • In the main, I agree with his research findings.

• make

- **make do(with something)** — *when you can survive with something that is not enough or is unsatisfactory:*

    (7) • When we arrived late in the night, we were really hungry, but we had to make do with just a few biscuits.

    (8) • Since she became a widow, she has learnt to make do on her pension.

- **make or break something** — *it means something that can make someone or something be either successful or a failure:*

    (9)• This business venture will make or break our relationship.

    (10) • It seems to me that this year will be a make or break year for our club.

• means

- **by all means** — *this expression is usually spoken to mean yes and allow somebody to have what they have asked for:*

    (11) • Could I use your telephone to make a local call? By all means do.

(12) • Do you mind if we share the table with you? By all means, you're welcome.

• **a means to an end** — *something that you do not like doing for whatever reasons, but you do it to achieve your goal :*

   (13) • She does not like her job any more but it is a means to an end.

   (14) • I don't like using a PC all day long for writing this book but I see it as a means to an end.

. meantime

• **in the meantime** — *it refers to the period of time that is between two times, two occurrences or events:*

   (15) • I was waiting to receive your photos from Germany. In the meantime, I sent you a small packet of some sweets by airmail .

   (16) • You wrote to us about your proposal; in the meantime our checklist will be ready to be posted to you on receipt of your proposal.

. middle

• **in the middle of nowhere** (informal) — *it is used to describe a place which is situated far from other buildings, town, etc:*

   (17) • They live in a village in the middle of nowhere.

   (18) • Some people would rather live in the middle of nowhere than in a congested and polluted big city.

. midstream

• **(halt/stop/pause, etc) in midstream** — *it means in the middle of something happening:*

   (19) • Our conversation was interrupted in midstream by an urgent telephone call from our overseas agents.

   (20) • When he saw us, he stopped his computer work in midstream and greeted us.

. mildly

● **to put it mildly** — *this expression is usually spoken. It means that something is worse than someone's telling us about it:*

    (21)● The cancellation of the French order is regrettable, to put it mildly.

                              ----

                  it really means extremely regrettable ↵

    (22)● You do look rather pale, to put it mildly. I had a serious heart operation recently.

              -----------------------------   ---

        it implies very ill ↵- speech 1   speech 2 ↵- not necessary by the same person

● mill

● **go through the mill or put someone through the mill** — *to make someone do something difficult, or put them though some difficult experience:*

    (23) ● I went for a job interview yesterday. I had to go through the mill
           during the final stage of my interview.

    (24) ● The other day we had an income tax officer to check our business records,
           and he put us through the mill.

● millstone

● **a millstone around (or round) your neck** — *it implies a problematic situation, or some troublesome responsibility that is extremely difficult to manage:*

    (25) ● Our business debts are, at present, a millstone around our necks.

    (26) ● My mother-in-law's long sickness is like a millstone round our necks.

● mind

● **bring/call something/somebody to mind** — *it can mean two things:*

    (a) to remember something/somebody:

    (27) ● I just cannot bring to mind when I posted that small packet to you.

    (c) to remind you of something or somebody:

****

(28) • Could you bring to my mind this correspondence next Monday morning?

• miss

• **miss the boat** (informal) — *it means somebody fails to take advantage of something because they were too late, and lost their chance of doing something or getting some benefit:*

(29) • I had been invited to attend a wedding party at the Dorchester Hotel, but I missed the boat, as the event took place a few days ago.

(30) • You can get 50% discount on some items today. If you don't purchase them today, you will miss the boat.

• money

• **for my money** (informal) — *it is used to say in my opinion:*

(31) • For my money, she is the best person for running our club.

(32) • For my money, Muhammad Ali is still the most famous boxer in my life time.

• most

• **at (the) most** — *it refers to an estimate of something by suggesting the biggest assessment:*

(33) • A police spokesman told the BBC that at the most 50,000 anti-war demonstrators attended the peace rally.

(34) • There are 100 seats in this restaurant, at the most.

• move

• **get moving** (informal) — *it means start doing something quickly:*

(35) • Get moving, or you'll be late again.

(36) • It's already 22.00 hours, we'd better get moving, otherwise we'll miss our flight.

• **move heaven and earth** — *it is used to emphasize that somebody does everything that* *is possible so that they achieve their objective:*

(37) • She moved heaven and earth to help her dying mother.

(38) • We moved heaven and earth to become our local council's information technology equipment suppliers.

• music

• **music to your ears** — *it indicates a piece of information or news that makes you feel very happy because for a long time you were expecting it:*

(39) • At last they have asked me to write an article for their next issue. It is music to my ears.

(40) • The postman delivered a registered letter to my daughter. Its contents were music to her ears as it was an offer of her first teaching post.

<u>N</u>

• nail

• **a nail in somebody's/something's coffin** — *it implies that something is the latest in a chain of events causing some harm to somebody, or something and that it may finally lead to the failure of somebody, etc:*

(1) • We have lost so many large customers, that the loss of this big client is another nail in the coffin of our business.

(2) • Health experts say that every cigarette a regular smoker has is another nail in the smoker's coffin.

• **on the nail** (information) — *it refers to an immediate payment:*

(3) • Some of our regular customers always pay on the nail.

(4) • When customers pay for our services on the nail, we allow them 10% discount.

• names

• **call (someone) names** — *when somebody insults another person by using rude words:*

 (5) • Sometimes children call him names because he is a quiet and shy boy.

 (6) • Do they call you names?

• **the name of the game** (informal) — *this expression refers to the most essential rule, ingredient, component or requirement for doing something successfully:*

 (7) • Young people must be advised that hard work is the name of the game for success in life.

 (8) • After five years professional dancing experience she says, 'Practising skills over a long period of time is the name of the game to become a successful dancer.'

• napping

• **catch someone napping** (informal) — *when somebody does something that you are not expecting. Their action gives them an advantage over you and you may lose something:*

 (9) • Our company has been caught napping. As a result, we could not get sole distributorship and have to be one of the two distributors in the UK.

 (10) • Our local chamber of commerce has invited all local manufacturing firms to a one-day seminar on European Union enlargement. The idea is to get ready for business opportunities, as we have no wish to be caught napping.

• neck

• **neck and neck (with somebody/something)** — *it means exactly equal, or level, especially in a competition or race:*

 (11) • All opinion polls suggest that the Labour and Conservative parties are running neck and neck.

 (12) • In the University Annual Debate, our university was neck and neck with Birmingham University.

• **stick your neck out** (informal) — *when you do or say something that has an element of risk and other people are not willing to take a risk Your action may create some problems:*

(13) ● At the risk of sticking my neck out, I wouldn't take part in signing this petition.

(14) ● I may be sticking my neck out here, but I'm willing to volunteer for guarding our club tonight alone.

● needle

● **a needle in a haystack** — *when searching for something that is almost impossible to find:*

(15) ● Searching for that document amongst this heap of files is like looking for a needle in a haystack.

(16) ● I'm afraid looking for your gold wedding ring lost by the sea will be like looking for a needle in a haystack.

● nerves

● **be a bag/bundle of nerves** (informal) — *when you mean that you are very nervous, excitable, anxious or worried:*

(17) ● Sarah lost her baby recently and at present, she is a bag of nerves.

(18) ● When she came from Poland, she was a bundle of nerves. Now she can express herself in English and feels at ease.

● **get on someone's nerves** (informal) — *when somebody or something annoys you:*

(19) ● They often get on my nerves, talking for hours and wasting my invaluable business time.

(20) ● When our telephone was in our dining room, it used to get on my nerves.

● new

● **a new one on me** (informal) — *when you have not heard about something before that may be an idea, information, etc:*

(21) ● I was under the impression that he was healthy and fit. What you have just told me about his health problems is a new one on me.

****

(22) • The Burton family no longer live in this town. Don't they? That is
a new one on me.

• news

• **be news to someone** — *this expression suggests a surprise. It is used to express a
surprise, when you want to say that you did not know about something before, and
it is the first time you have heard:*

(23) • It may be true that she has two children, but it is news to me!

• nice

• **as nice as pie**(informal) — *this expression is used for someone who you find very kind
and friendly unexpectedly. It can also be said about somebody whose present good manners
contrast with their not so good manners in the past:*

(24) • When I met her she was as nice as pie and gave me good advice.

(25) • I heard that John is rather rude and can end meetings abruptly. On the contrary,
he was as nice as pie and our meeting ended with a big smile on our faces.

• nicely

• **do nicely** — *this expression can be used to mean:*

(a) *making good progress*

(26) • His travel agency business has been doing nicely since last Easter.

(b) *something you find to be acceptable, agreeable or satisfactory:*

(27) • Shall we meet tomorrow at 11.00 hours in my office? Yes, it will do nicely.

----

it implies ⟹ I agree/ it will be a good time ↵

• nick

• **in the nick of time** (informal) — *when something happens at the very last moment,* *just before a deadline:*

(28) ● You are just in the nick of time, as you can see I'm closing the gates.

(29) ● Our train arrived in the nick of time, and we did not miss our connecting train to Stockholm.

● nobody

● **like nobody's business** (informal) — *it means very hard:*

(30) ● He is enthusiastic about his work, always working like nobody's business.

(31) ● It was a very busy day at work, so I had to work like nobody's business.

● nod

● **have a nodding acquaintance(with someone or something)** — *it means you know someone/something slightly:*

(32) ● On this street, I have a nodding acquaintance with some residents.

(33) ● We have a nodding acquaintance with a handful of people in this village.

● noise

● **make noises (about something)**(informal) — *you can use this expression in two ways:*

(a) *when someone is complaining about something:*

(34) ● He made noises about someone parked in his space in the staff car park.

(b) *when someone hints, or talks about something indirectly indicating their intention of doing it:*

(35) ● Our college management is making noises about making some members of staff redundant.

● nose

● **get up someone's nose** (informal) — *it means somebody annoys, or irritates you:*

(36) ● The way she talks gets up my nose.

(37) ● One of the delegates talked too much during group discussion. What really got up my nose in the first session was his repetition of the same idea.

● not

● **not at all** — *this expression is often used to accept thanks politely, or to agree with someone mannerly:*

(38) ● Thank you very much for your offer of help. Not at all.

(39) ● Will it be inconvenient to wait for just five minutes? Not at all.

● nutshell

● **(put something) in a nutshell** — *it means to state something clearly, and precisely by using only a few words:*

(40) ● Regrettably, I can put it in a nutshell we are divorced!

(41) ● We do have some differences of opinions on this matter. In a nutshell, we just don't get on.

O

● oar

● **put/stick your oar in** (informal) — *when during a discussion or argument you give your opinion or advice to somebody even if they have not asked you for it; and probably your contribution is not required:*

(1) ● Our group is capable of making decisions. No one asked you to put your oar in.

(2) ● He has a habit of sticking his oar in whenever there is a staff meeting.

● object

• **expense, money, etc. is no object** — *it implies that expense, money, time, etc. is not important and that someone is prepared to spend a lot of it:*

> (3) • They are always eating in the most expensive restaurants as money is no object.

> (4) • They worked on this play together for two years. For them time was no object in their interest of writing a best-seller.

• occasion

• **on occasion(s)** — *when something happens sometimes but not frequently:*

> (5) • She does on occasions drink vodka.

> (6) • We know well that on occasion he can be rude.

• **a sense of occasion** — *when you feel that an occasion is rather special:*

> (7) • Some friends, unexpectedly, visited us last Sunday evening. Their visit gave the evening a sense of occasion.

> (8) • Through the Interflora Service, my wife received some lovely flowers that gave the day a sense of occasion.

• ocean

• **an ocean of something (or oceans of something)** — *it means something in abundance (in abundance is also an idiomatic expression meaning in large quantities):*

> (9) • In China, I saw an ocean of people riding bicycles in Beijing.

> (10) • In India, there are oceans of lotus plants with flowers growing on the surface of lakes.

• **a drop in the ocean** — *it means a part or an amount of something that is very tiny. It also refers to something that is least important to influence the circumstance/situation:*

> (11) • What the suspect has told us so far, in our opinion, is just a drop in the ocean.

> (12) • How much money have you got? Only £20. This is only a drop in the ocean. You must pay us immediately £2500.

. odd

. the/an odd man out or an odd one out — *this expression can be used to express different circumstances:*

(a) when you are making pairs of things or people, and one person or thing is left over:

(13). We have sent six groups on the first coach, but this student is the odd man out. He can travel on the second coach.

(b) when a person is different from other persons, or a thing is different from other things:

(14) . Paper, pencil, ink and radio which of these is the odd one out?

(c) when a person cannot fit into a particular group with which that person is associated or any other grouping such as a local community, etc:

(15) . She is a very shy and quiet person and feels the odd one out at work.

. odds

. be at odds (with something) — *when something is not exactly the same as the other thing, when both things must match, or correspond to each other.*

(16) . Our factual findings are at odds with what was reported in the local press about expenses paid to two councillors.

(17) . His sales figures are at odds with the money paid into the bank account.

. be at odds (with somebody over /about something) — *It indicates that two or more people disagree, or quarrel over/about something:*

(18) . The Prime Minister is at odds with some senior members of his cabinet over health reforms.

(19) . Allan is often at odds with Ruth about their children's education.

. over the odds (informal) — *it means more money than you can expect for something:*

(20) . Only a few years ago, most employers paid their employees over the odds, if

they worked on Sundays.

(21) • I'm willing to pay over the odds if you can supply me with a copy of this title by tomorrow morning.

• off

• **go off** (informal) – *this expression can be used to express two different situations:*

(a) when you liked someone or something, but now begin to dislike them:

(22) • We went to the same comprehensive school, but I went off him when I found out about his shady business dealings.

(b) when food becomes rotten or perished, and it is unwise to consume it:

(23) • This chicken has gone off. We must throw it away.

• **off and on/on and off (informal)** – *it means now and again, sometimes or occasionally:*

(24) • On and off we travel to London to see our relatives.

(25) • Today, it has been raining off and on.

• Off chance

• **do something on the off chance** – *when you do something knowing that the chance of success is very small, but you still take a chance on being successful:*

(26) • I telephoned on the off chance that you might have returned from Japan.

(27) • We invited the trade minister as a guest speaker on the off chance that he would accept our invitation.

• Office

• **through somebody's good offices**(formal) – *it means with somebody's kind help:*

(28) • My wife got a part-time job in our company through my friend's good offices.

. Old boy

- **the old boy network**(informal) — *it refers to the way some people help each other. These people went to the same British private schools. Later in life, they use their influence to help each other secure high paid posts, business opportunities, etc:*

    (29) . It is not a secret that some years ago, almost all senior civil service posts were obtained through the old boy network.

    (30) . How did he manage to get such a prestigious post in the financial district of London? Through the old boy network.

. One

- **be at one (with somebody)** (formal) — *when you are in agreement with somebody:*

    (31) . After our meeting with the management, we are at one with them on staff training on the job.

    (32) . The head teacher and parents association are at one on children's road safety.

- **be (a) one for (doing) something** — *it refers to a person who likes doing something:*

    (33) . My wife is the one for enjoying her gardening.

    (34) . I have never been a great one for supporting activities.

. open

- **with open arms** — *when you are friendly and show great affection for somebody:*

    (35) . When we arrived at the airport, our hosts welcomed us with open arms.

    (36) . If we invite someone, it is our duty to receive them with open arms.

. ordinary

- **out of the ordinary** — *it means unusual, extraordinary or exceptional:*

    (37) . In my view, his reaction to what happened is not out of the ordinary.

(38) • Can I help you sir? Well, I'm looking for something a little out of the ordinary for my girlfriend.

• oyster

• the world is your oyster — *it means ample opportunities for someone:*

(39) • At the age of 22, you speak four languages, you were educated at Oxford University, and you are the son of an international tycoon - the world is your oyster!

(40) • She is young, full of vitality and is an already known film music writer. With these personal qualities and accomplishments, the world's her oyster.

P

• pace

• keep pace with (somebody/something) — *to make changes, go forward, develop, or maintain your status, progress, etc. at the same rate or speed as someone/something:*

(1) • It is difficult to keep pace with John in this race.

(2) • Nurses' salary increases have not kept pace with the salary rises of doctors.

• set the pace — *it means to give a good example, establish a high standard by doing something for other people to match it, or perform even better to make another record of success:*

(3) • He set the pace by becoming the highest paid employee in the UK.

(4) • This year, in the London Marathon, a Tunisian runner has set the pace by becoming the fastest runner in this race since this annual event started in 1981.

•on/under pain of something (formal) — *when you do something under a threat of some*

****

kind of punishment, if you do not comply with the rule(s):

> (5) • I work for an Internet services company, where all employees are on pain
>   of immediate dismissal, if they disclose any confidential data to anyone
>   who is not connected with such data.

> (6) • I must register myself with the Registrar of Data Protection by the end of this
>   month under pain of legal proceedings against me.

• **a pain in the neck**(informal) — *It means a person or thing that you find very annoying:*

> (7) • He really is a pain in the neck, as he's always grumbling to me
>   about everything in his life.

> (8) • This analytical work is a pain in the neck but it must be done today.

• pale

• **beyond the pale** — *it is used to describe someone's behaviour that is unacceptable
because it is not normal:*

> (9) • During our group discussion on immigration, Keith made some remarks,
>   which were clearly beyond the pale.

> (10) • His father was a respected member of our community, but his way
>   of life goes beyond the pale.

• part

• **part and parcel of something** — *it means an important component or prerequisite
for something:*

> (11) • Indeed, assessing students' work is part and parcel of a teacher's work.

> (12) • Developing and installing software for clients is part and parcel of
>   my overall responsibility.

• **take somebody's part** — *it implies supporting somebody, especially, during an
argument:*

> (13) • My mother always took my part when father was angry with me.

(14) • When two men were arguing with my brother, luckily, I arrived on the scene and took his part.

• **part company(with/from somebody)** – *this expression is used to express two situations:*

   (a) *when people go in different directions(formal):*

      (15) • We parted company at Stuttgard Airport.

   (b) *when people disagree, or end their relationship, partnership, etc:*

      (16) • I parted company with my business partner over a profit sharing dispute.

• particular

• **in particular** – *it can be used to express two situations:*

   (a) *when you want to say especially, mainly or notably:*

      (17) • I like meeting her in particular.

      (18) • She loves musical plays in particular.

   (b) *when you wish to say something special, definite or specific:*

      (19) • What are you doing now? Nothing in particular, just bored!

      (20) • He is writing a book. On which subject is he writing in particular?

• pat

• **a pat on the back for(doing)something** – *it means appreciation or praise:*

   (21) • She got a pat on the back from us for driving her car safely to the airport during the rush hour traffic in the London area.

   (22) • Don't you think that we all deserve a pat on the back for our hard work?

. patch

. be not a patch on someone/something — (informal) — *it means that someone or something is less good, less attractive or inferior to someone/something else:*

(23) . This car isn't a patch on our last car.

(24) . For me the coach trip wasn't a patch on our car trip, but our children thought it was fantastic.

. peg

. off the peg — *it means ready-made to wear clothes. These clothes are of average standard size, and often they do not fit every one well.*

(25) . I buy my clothes off the peg, but sometimes they don't fit me well.

(26) . It is cheaper to buy clothes off the peg, as made-to-measure clothes are too expensive for an ordinary retired person.

. penny

. the penny drops(informal) — *it implies that someone has finally understood or realized something:*

(27) . It was difficult for some of my international English speaking friends to grasp my meaning first time, but when I explained it again, the penny dropped.

(28) . It looks like the penny has finally dropped, as sales orders have started to arrive.

. picture

. get the picture (spoken) — *when someone understands something or a situation, which is being described by another person. This expression is used when someone is finding something difficult to follow at once:*

(29) . Edinburgh is the capital of Scotland and Scotland is in the UK. Do you understand now? Yes, I get the picture.

(30) . In the UK, the House of Lords is the upper chamber and the House of Commons is the lower chamber. You get the picture? Yes, it is very interesting.

- **put/keep somebody in the picture**(informal) — *when you give to someone some information about something/somebody, which they want to know:*

    (31) . Just to put you in the picture, our guests haven't arrived so far.

    (32) . We will have a new managing director tomorrow. Our management didn't keep us in the picture earlier on when changes were agreed.

. piece

- **go to pieces (informal)** — *when a person is so distressed that he/she cannot cope with day-to-day normal life situations:*

    (33) . Elizabeth went to pieces when she lost her baby.

    (34) . I have known him for a long time as an emotionally strong person, but he went to pieces when his marriage ended in divorce and at the same time his business went bankrupt.

- **a piece of cake** (informal) — *it means something is easy to do:*

    (35) . She told me that writing a short story was a piece of cake.

    (36) . The setting up of new software on my PC was a piece of cake.

    <u>**Do not use it in a negative way.**</u>

. place

- **put someone in their place** — *to make someone feel that they are not as important, clever, high in social position or rich, and thus to embarrass them:*

    (37) . Roger tried to show his cultural snobbery, but one of the guests soon put him in his place.

    (38) . He was trying to re-organise our meeting. I not only had to put him in his place, but also reminded him of the mess he had made last time.

. practise

****

- **practise what you preach** — *it implies that you do yourself what you tell to other people, so that you encourage them to do the same:*

  (39) • My doctor advises me to eat less sugar, but he takes four spoonfuls of sugar with his cup of tea. He does not practise what he preaches.

  (40) • Often ministers make public speeches in support of national health hospitals, but they do not practise what they preach – for their medical treatment, they attend private hospitals.

pull

- **pull out all the stops** (informal) — *when someone makes a determined and energetic effort to achieve their goal:*

  (41) • She pulled out all the stops to help her son to continue his university education after her husband's death.

  (42) • I had to pull out all the stops to make this business successful.

purpose

- **on purpose** — *when someone does something intentionally:*

  (43) • He spilt tea on the clean floor on purpose, knowing that it would annoy her as she had just cleaned it.

  (44) • Who broke that nice glass? Flora did it on purpose.

push

- **push one's luck** (informal) — *when someone has been reasonably successful, but tries again to be more successful by taking the risk of complete failure:*

  (45) • She has just returned from her four-week long holiday. She will be pushing her luck to ask for some time off from work so soon .

  (46) • On a television game show, he won £5000. He tried for £10,000 and lost it all, because he pushed his luck.

put

- **put somebody through it** (informal) — *when you are under some kind of control and faced with a difficult situation:*

> (47) • The interview panel really put me through it.
>
> -------------------
>
> asked some difficult questions ↵

> (48) • We were seven candidates for this post. After the preliminary interviews, one of the candidates decided to leave as he didn't wish to be put himself through it* at the final stage of job interview.

* *to put himself through it = to face difficult questioning or an unpleasant situation*

• putty

- **(like) putty in somebody's hands** — *when someone can be easily influenced and obey you, or do anything they are asked to do:*

> (49) • He thought she was putty in his hands, but she proved him wrong, as she persuaded him to move with her to her home town and find a job there.

> (50) • She is like putty in his hands. It is best for her to leave him and have her own way of life.

Q

• quantity

- **an unknown quantity** — *it means not very much is known about someone or something in terms of their nature, abilities, qualities, etc:*

> (1) • Until now, we have received only one nomination, but he is an unknown quantity.

> (2) • Our new boss is still a bit of an unknown quantity to us, as he is a very quiet person.

• quarrel

****

- **pick a quarrel (with somebody)** — *it is used to say that someone deliberately starts a fight by behaving offensively:*

> (3) • They were staring at us first and then tried to pick a quarrel with us, but we left the club immediately.

> (4) • I should not have picked a quarrel with Robin over such a small fee.

. quart

- **put a quart into a pint pot** — *when you try to put something in a container, or something that is too small for it. It means something is an impossible thing to do:*

> (5) • We were trying to move this bed into our small room; but we encountered the problem of putting a quart into a pint pot - the bed is too wide.

> (6) • I want to place all these files in this drawer of my steel cabinet. You can't put a quart into a pint pot.

. quarter

- **at close quarters** — *it means very near, or close by.*

> (7) • Do you live near Anne? Yes, at close quarters.

> (8) • At the time of the accident, I was just standing here and witnessed the accident at close quarters.

. queer

- **queer somebody's pitch (also queer the pitch for somebody)** — *when someone spoils other people's schemes, or plans, so that they cannot succeed in what they wish to do:*

> (9) • I told John that Roy would buy my car, but John queered my pitch by selling his own car to Roy.

> (10) • If you tell him that you are planning to leave this job, he could queer your pitch by telling your boss.

. question

* **call (something) into question** (formal) — *when someone wants to express doubts about something:*

  (11) • Due to cash flow problems and the bank's refusal to extend our overdraft limit, our supplies of raw materials have been called into question.

  (12) • Since he accepted a minor wrongdoing at work, his whole integrity has been called into question.

* **just/merely/only a question of (something/doing something)** — *this expression implies that something is not hard to describe, foresee, perform, do, etc:*

  (13) • I think it is just a question of time before a serious road accident happens in our increasingly busy street.

  (14) • He believes that it is merely a question of demonstrating to students all the necessary steps involved to solve this problem.

* **a loaded question** — *when someone asks a question in such a way that the person is forced to disclose some information or agree to something, etc. This way of questioning could be harmful to the person who is being questioned:*

  (15) • When answering some loaded questions, he gave some important clues for the police to investigate.

  (16) • I refused to answer some loaded questions at a disciplinary hearing without the presence of my legal representative.

* **out of the question** — *when you wish to say that something is unthinkable, impossible or not permitted by somebody in power, and there no need to discuss it:*

  (17) • Our participation in this exhibition is out of the question.

  (18) • It is quite out of the question for us to support the annual function this year.

* **pop the question** (informal) — *when you ask for someone's hand in marriage:*

  (19) • Elvis popped the question on the day he met Emily at a bus stop. He was desperate and lonely.

(20) • She almost fainted when her boyfriend popped the question.

• **a rhetorical question** — *a question that does not need to be answered by its recipient/ listener, as the speaker answers it himself/herself:*

(21) • Often politicians raise rhetorical questions to influence people; the answer given by them is most likely to be insincere.

(22) • Do I care for our national health service? Of course, I do most sincerely. This is the prime reason that I have spoken against the government so strongly.

. question mark

• **a question mark over/against something** — *when something is uncertain:*

(23) • There is still a big question mark over her trip to Ukraine next month.

(24) • He has been declared bankrupt, but there is still a question mark against millions of pounds he transferred to an unknown bank in Switzerland.

. queue

• **jump the queue** — *when you go to the front of a line/queue without waiting for your own turn:*

(25) • Some people seem to have a habit of trying to jump the queue.

(26) • Please do not jump the queue, join it.

. quick

• **to have a quick temper** — *it means a person gets angry easily:*

(27) • Can I take this chair away to my office? Well, it belongs to Susan who has a quick temper. I wouldn't touch it.

(28) • I would not have said that if I had known he had a quick temper.

• **as quick as a flash(also as quick as lightning)** — *Use it when you want to say very fast:*

(29) • As quick as a flash, she was by his hospital bedside.

(30) • An eyewitness said, 'The fatal accident happened as quick as lightning.'

• **cut someone to the quick** — *when you speak to someone unkindly, or do something bad that distresses the other person greatly:*

(31) • My wife is so sensitive that a minor difference of opinion can cut her to the quick.

(32) • He is so bigoted that he cut John to the quick.

• **a quick one** (informal) — *it means to have a quick drink:*

(33) • It is still 15 minutes before our train arrives. Let's have a quick one in that pub.

(34) • It's so nice to meet you by chance. Do you have time for a quick one?

• quite

• **quite something** (informal) — *when you want to say that something is special, very good, very impressive, etc:*

(35) • My friend's wife is quite something to look at.

(36) • The scenery is quite something, I can not remember seeing such a lovely place!

• **quite a bit** (informal) — *it implies a large number of something or a large amount of something:*

(37) • We ate quite a bit of German food in Hamburg.

(38) • We have sold quite a bit of stock recently.

• quits

• **be quits (with somebody)** (informal) — *it is used to say that two persons owe nothing to each other any more. It usually refers to money:*

(39) • This is the money I borrowed from you the other day. Now we are quits.

(40) • If you lend me ten pounds now, I will return it to you tomorrow and then we'll be quits.

• **call it quits** (informal) — *when you agree with someone to stop quarrelling. It can also be used when both sides are seen as equal, or no one owes anything to the other person:*

(41) • In a divorce case, Shirley and Richard were arguing over their property, but they finally called it quits.

(42) • At last, you have paid us in full for our goods. Let's call it quits and we're ready to supply you with our goods again.

R

• **race**

• **a race against time/the clock** — *when you have a limited time to do something in order to complete it before it is too late:*

(1) • Every month we have a race against time to complete our monthly business analysis and send it to our head office.

(2) • It was a race against time to fly from England to Russia to speak to my mother last time.

• **rack**

• **go to rack and ruin** — *when something is left to decay due to neglect(also time factor):*

(3) • People on low incomes let their property go to rack and ruin.

(4) • On that hill, there was a castle. Over the centuries, it has gone to rack and ruin.

• **rack your brain(s)** — *when you want someone to think hard about something, or think about something for a long time:*

(5) • During the interview, he racked his brains, trying to remember the answer to one of the questions on the subject he wanted to teach.

(6) • When a policeman stopped her on the motorway and asked her car registration number, she racked her brains before telling it to him.

• rain

• (come) rain or shine —*it means irrespective of weather conditions (whether rain or sun):*

(7) • After our evening meal, we always go out for a thirty minute walk, rain or shine.

(8) • When you visit us, I promise to have a long walk with you every morning by the sea, come rain or shine.

• rake

• rake over something (informal) — *when someone talks about some displeasing past experience in detail, and instead of forgetting it, they keep talking about it. It expresses disapproval:*

(9) • My girlfriend wanted me to talk about my last business failure, but I had no wish to rake over the past.

(10) • He was mistakenly arrested by the police some years ago. He often rakes over it and that annoys his wife.

• rake up something (informal) — *it is similar to the above idiomatic expression, except when somebody is mentioning the past of another person in a disapproving way:*

(11) • Some newspaper journalists seek cheap publicity for themselves by raking up some past minor wrong doings of people who are in the public eye.

(12) • Please don't rake up the past of my best friend, as we are discussing his present charity work.

• read

• read between the lines — *when something is not explicitly stated in writing, not mentioned in conversation or not shown in some situation, but implicitly stated:*

****

(13) • Diana talks about her husband a lot, but reading between the lines, I believe she is on the brink of leaving him.

(14) • My son sent us a long letter, telling us about his studies. Reading between the lines, I think he is running out of money and needs some from us.

• **read somebody like a book** (informal) – *when you understand the meaning or feeling of somebody without any difficulty:*

(15) • She says that she can read him like a book, but they often argue over simple matters.

(16) • I can read you like a book – you're in love with our cleaning woman.

• reality

• **in reality** – *it means actually or really. It is used to say that something is different from the way it seems or has been described, or what is believed by people:*

(17) • He looks happy, but in reality he is facing serious financial problems.

(18) • She acts as if she comes from high society, but in reality her father worked as a coal miner in South Yorkshire.

• realm

• **beyond/within the realms of possibility** – *it means something is not possible:*

(19) • I believe strongly, if you practise it every day until your match, a victory is within the realms of possibility.

(20) • As we have already missed the last bus, our journey back home without a taxi ride is beyond the realms of possibility.

• reap

• **reap the harvest** – *when you benefit or suffer as a result of your good or bad past actions:*

(21) • Many years ago, I started saving and let it grow in my early retirement pension plan. This year, I began to reap the harvest of this saving.

(22) • He has been smoking forty cigarettes a day for many years. Today, he reaps the harvest in the form of a serious heart operation.

• reason

• **it stands to reason (that)** (informal) — *when you want to say that any wise person, who considers it, can understand it clearly:*

(23) • It stands to reason that if you keep borrowing money from banks without the ability to re-pay it, you are most likely to be bankrupt one day.

(24) • If you don't stop drinking alcohol excessively every day, it stands to reason that you will have a heart attack one day.

• recall

• **beyond recall** — *it means something cannot be changed, returned to its original state, etc:*

(25) • I'm afraid the matter is beyond recall.

(26) • The decision made by the interview panel is beyond recall.

• record

• **(Just) for the record** — *it is used during a meeting, or in a similar situation. Someone asks the official or the person who is responsible for conducting the proceedings, etc. to write down accurately the factual information for some future reference purposes:*

(27) • Just for the record, I'll not be voting tonight.

(28) • Just for the record, I have never advised him to write this sort of nasty letter.

• red

404   **Idiomatic Expressions**

****

- **catch (someone) red-handed** — *when you find someone in the act of doing something wrong or illegal:*

  (29) • Just now, a shop security camera has caught a shoplifter red-handed.

  (30) • The landlord of a pub caught some thieves red-handed and called the police.

- **be in the red** (informal) — *it means someone has borrowed too much money from a bank, and thus owes money to the bank:*

  (31) • My bank account is in the red.

  (32) • We can't go on borrowing from a bank, as we are already in the red; and our sales figures are getting worse each day.

• regard

- **as regards somebody/something** (formal) — *it means in connection with somebody/ something or concerning somebody/something:*

  (33) • As regards John Smith, he has been transferred to our head office staff.

  (34) • As regards your latest communication, I would like to discuss it with you when we meet this afternoon.

• region

- **in the region of** (formal) — *when a price, or a cost, or an estimate is given in figures which are near to the actual figures:*

  (35) • The cost of materials and labour will be in the region of £1500.

  (36) • It will cost you somewhere in the region of £400.

• rob

- **daylight robbery** (informal) — *When somebody charges too much money for something - too high prices:*

  (37) • How much is this chair, please? £ 45. Asking £45 for this second hand chair is daylight robbery.

(38) • They are charging £20 for this shirt which sounds like daylight robbery to me.

• roof

• **go through the roof** — *it is used to state that the rate or the price of something has risen abruptly:*

(39) • This year, house prices in our area have gone through the roof.

(40) • For the first time house buyers, the best news is that interest rates have stopped going through the roof, as used to happen previously in the UK.

• **hit the roof** (informal) — *when somebody becomes very angry(and starts shouting at someone):*

(41) • Your mother will hit the roof when she finds out about your secret plans.

(42) • When she saw a large dent in the driver's door of her parked car, she hit the roof.

• **have a roof over your head** — *when someone wants a place to live:*

(43) • One of the urgent requirements for many young families is to have a roof over their head.

(44) • I have a roof over my head, as I inherited my grandfather's country home.

• round

• **round here** — *it means a place near where you live, or where you are at the present time:*

(45) • There are no public toilets round here anymore.

(46) • Well, this is a council estate. Round here, you will not find millionaires.

• rub

• **rub (someone's) nose in it** — *when you keep telling someone of their past mistakes:*

(47) • Yes, I should have turned left at that corner. Can you please stop rubbing

my nose in it?

(48) • I know I should have telephoned Alexander on his 40th birthday, but I do wish you would stop rubbing my nose in it.

• run

• **up and running** — *when something, for instance a system, is operating fully and properly:*

(49) • It will be a big relief for me when our computer is up and running again.

(50) • At present, my wife's sewing machine is not up and running.

S

• sack

• **get the sack** — *it means that you are no longer employed by your employer because you have done something which is wrong in their views and unacceptable to them:*

(1) • I will get the sack if I don't co-operate with them.

This idiom can also be stated as **give someone the sack** (informal) — *to be dismissed:*

(2) • She was given the sack because she was using the company's e-mail system for her own personal messages.

• safe

• **in safe hands or in the safe hands of somebody** — *when a person on something is being taken care of very well by somebody, some expert or authority:*

(3) • The matter is so serious that I have to contact a solicitor. Now it is in the safe hands of my lawyer.

(4) • Our daughter is with her grandparents, in safe hands, indeed.

- **play (it) safe** — *When someone is very careful and does what is possible to avoid risks:*

    (5) • If you want to play safe, don't travel to Scotland by car tonight during this heavy snow fall.

    (6) • He has recently been diagnosed with a hernia. If he wants to play safe, he should not lift heavy things.

- **salt**

- **rub salt into the wound or rub salt into somebody's wounds** — *when somebody is already in a difficult situation and you say, or do something(often deliberately) that makes the situation even more difficult (sorrowful, shameful, etc.) for somebody:*

    (7) • I was really disappointed to come last in the race, and my girlfriend keeps rubbing salt into the wound by saying that I was too fat and slow.

    (8) • For several days now, her husband has been rubbing salt into her wounds, because she didn't get the job, despite being so sure she would get it.

- **take something with a pinch of salt** — *it is used to say that you should not rely on every piece of information, as it may not be wholly true or accurate:*

    (9) • I take his information about their domestic problems with a pinch of salt, as he likes to exaggerate.

    (10) • Newspaper reports about a new friendship between Russia and the West should be taken with a pinch of salt.

- **school**

- **the old school** — *it is used to emphasize that someone's ideas or way of thinking is traditional. It does not mean traditional ways are wrong, but not as popular as they were in the past:*

    (11) • I still add someone's correct status before their surname. You may say that I belong to the old school.

    (12) • My father-in-law, as a gardener of the old school, finds some of the gardening methods, shown on popular television programmes, rather odd.

. side

. take sides (with somebody) — *when you support someone in a dispute:*

(13) . I don't like the idea of taking sides with a strong person in a dispute against a weaker person.

(14) . He took sides with me in a dispute at work.

. sight

. set your sights on something/on doing something — *when you decide that you want something and try as hard as you can to get it:*

(15) . My son has set his sights on opening another retail outlet.

(16) . They have set their sights on winning this game tonight.

. silver

. be born with a silver spoon in one's mouth (saying) – *when someone is born into a wealthy family and has had a privileged upbringing:*

(17) . She was born with a silver spoon in her mouth! What does she know about hardship?

(18) . I was born with a silver spoon in my mouth. I haven't had any problems such as those faced by people living in poor rented properties in inner cities.

. a silver lining or every cloud has a silver lining (saying) – *it means every bad or difficult situation has its good and pleasant side:*

(19) . The fall in bank interest rates in the United Kingdom is always a silver lining of the housing market.

(20) . I worked very hard on that assignment abroad. Now, they have sent me a a big cheque. Well, it proves that every cloud has a silver lining.

. sleep

- **not lose any sleep over something** –*when someone is not very worried about something:*

  (21) • He has been out of work for two weeks, but I don't think he loses a lot of sleep over it.

  (22) • French representatives have postponed their visit until next week. It is not worth losing any sleep over it, as we can wait for them until next week.

• smoke

- **go up in smoke** (informal) – *this expression can be used for rendering two different meanings:*

  (a) when your plans, wishes, etc. have resulted in complete failure:

  (23) • Since her husband lost his job, all their hopes of a long holiday by Lake Balaton in Hungary have gone up in smoke.

  (b) when something is completely burnt:

  (24) • In a few minutes, the dance hall went up in smoke; some young people could not get out of the hall to save their lives.

• song

- **for a song** (informal) – *when something is being sold very cheaply:*

  (25) • In our local newspaper, a personal computer is going for a song.

  (26) • I bought this table for a song from a market stall.

- **make a song and dance about something** (informal)(disapproving) – *when someone is very excited, very angry and complaining (fussing) about something that is not very serious:*

  (27) • There is no need to make a song and dance about coming ten minutes late as our train hasn't arrived yet.

  (28) • When we arrived at the hotel, we made a song and dance about the service, so the manager arranged a nice supper for us.

. speak

. **be on speaking terms (with somebody)** — *when you are polite or friendly enough with someone to speak to him/her, especially after a disagreement or an argument:*

    (29) . Can you give it to Colin? I can't, as he's not been on speaking terms with me since we had a disagreement during our staff meeting.

    (30) . Are you on speaking terms with James? Yes, we seldom have a quarrel.

. spend

. **spend the night with somebody** — *it means staying with somebody for a night:*

    (31) . I will spend the night with a family in Denmark.

    (32) . We couldn't find a hotel. We had to ask some friends by telephone if we could spend the night with them.

. **spend the night together** — *it has a very different meaning from the previous expression. It means staying for a night with somebody and having sex with them:*

    (33) . He expected them to spend the night together.

    (34) . She bluntly refused to accept his invitation to spend the night together in his luxury penthouse suite overlooking the River Thames.

. splash

. **make a splash** (informal) — *when someone (sometimes deliberately) does something in such a way that it attracts a lot of attention:*

    (35) . He has made a splash by winning the match for his team.

    (36) . At Frankfurt International Book Fair, Salman Rushdie made a splash by attending the event and meeting people.

. spot

. **put somebody on the spot** — *when you ask someone to answer some difficult questions,* *or do something that they don't want to, to expose themselves in a way that places them in an awkward position:*

(37) • You really put him on the spot, when you asked him repeatedly about his love affair with Elizabeth Taylor.

(38) • Mr John Major organised a cricket match for charity. However, he was not put on the spot by being asked to participate as a player.

• spur

• on the spur of the moment — *when someone does something suddenly without planning it in advance:*

(39) • I decided on the spur of the moment to attend this exhibition.

(40) • The shooting incident happened on the spur of the moment.

T

• tab

• keep (close) tabs on somebody/something (informal) — *when you always want to know what somebody or something is doing in order to control any situation that may develop:*

(1) • I like to keep close tabs on my financial circumstances.

(2) • It is hard for her to keep tabs on all aspects of her fast growing family business.

• table

• on the table — *it means a proposal, plan or an idea that is formally presented to all interested parties for their consideration, negotiation and possibly agreement:*

(3) • We have asked our management to put their salary proposal on the table.

(4) • The salary offer on the table was rejected by the union.

• talk

- **talk your way out of something/of doing something** — *when someone gives reasons or makes excuses for not doing something and thus gets out of an awkward situation:*

  (5) • She was able to talk her way out of serious trouble in a park.

  (6) • He came to work one hour late, but managed to talk his way out of losing his wage for the hour he did not work.

- **the talk of something** — *when someone or something is famous in a particular place:*

  (7) • John Smith from our town won the Nobel Prize for Peace, and now he is the talk of the town.

  (8) • Last night, Elaine won the contest to represent the United Kingdom in the Eurovision Song Contest, and overnight became the talk of the country.

. tall

- **a tall order** (informal) — *it means something is really hard to do:*

  (9) • For a retired person, an unexpected expense for house repairs is a tall order.

  (10) • When our car broke down on the motorway, it was really a tall order to to get someone to help us.

. tea

- **not for all the tea in China** — *it is used to emphasize that you will not do something even for a big gain:*

  (11) • She wouldn't accept our invitation for all the tea in China.

  (12) • Emma will not give up her horse riding hobby for all the tea in China.

. teach

- **teach your grandmother to suck eggs** — *when a less experienced person tries to advise or show a more experienced person how to do something:*

****

(13) ▪ I have been in charge of this section for ten years now, and know how to handle likely problems – don't try to teach your grandmother to suck eggs.

(14) ▪ Flora was telling my mother how to bake cakes, but she has been baking delicious cakes for thirty years – don't teach your grandmother to suck eggs.

▪ teeth

▪ armed to the teeth — *when someone is armed with some deadly weapons:*

(15) ▪ Despite his benevolent appearance, he was in reality, armed to the teeth.

(16) ▪ Our industrial park is closed to all traffic, as some robbers who are armed to the teeth are resisting arrest by the police.

▪ cut your teeth — *when you gain your early work experience that can lead to more skill learning, and acquiring more advanced knowledge about a particular job:*

(17) ▪ She has been running her business as a solicitor for a long time, but she cut her teeth at a local legal community advisory centre.

In fact, you can place an adjective before teeth, if you wish to do so:

(18) ▪ Wolfgang cut his insurance specialist teeth, when he worked for a well-established company in Stuttgart.

▪ tether

▪ be at the end of your tether — *this expression can be used to express two different circumstances:*

(a) when you feel that you cannot succeed in solving a problem, in doing something or achieving your goal any more for whatever reasons known to you.

(19) ▪ I'm at the end of my tether trying to organise finance for my son's new business.

(20) ▪ I've been under pressure of work all this week, and I really am at the end my tether. I need to rest this weekend.

(b) when someone is annoyed or disappointed by someone, or even by oneself, or angry

about something or someone, or feels powerless etc :

(21) • A Russian lady who lives in England, often reaches the end of her tether if she does not chat with some Russian women at least once a week.

(22) • Sometimes, we all reach the end of our tether in this world.

Note

The word **tether** can function both as a *noun* and as a *verb*. As <u>**a noun**</u> it means a rope or a chain that is used to tie an animal to something e.g., to a post in such a way that the animal has some freedom of movement but it cannot go very far. As <u>**a verb**</u> it means to tie an animal to something.

• thick

• **through thick and thin** (informal) — *it means through difficult times you will carry on doing something regardless of whatever problems or difficulties you face:*

(23) • She has supported her husband through thick and thin.

(24) • We remained friends through thick and thin.

• thin

• **have a thin time (of it)** (informal) — *when someone has an unpleasant time and is disappointed . In other words: when someone is facing some problems and not succeeding:*

(25) • He is having a thin time of it since he got a divorce and still has to support his children and live alone in a rented flat.

(26) • If I did something even slightly wrong, my father would give me a thin time.

• thinking

• **put your thinking cap on** (informal) — *it means to think carefully about a problem in order to solve it:*

(27) • In order to win back many of our lost customers, we'd better put our thinking caps on.

(28) • You should put your thinking cap on to see for yourself where you have gone wrong and do something about it.

• throw

• **throw /pour cold water on/over something** — *when you discourage or criticize someone, and diminish their enthusiasm for doing something:*

(29) • Whenever he told his wife about his business plan, she immediately threw cold water on it, and finally they divorced.

(30) • Our management throws cold water over any suggestions made by junior staff.

• thumb

• **under (someone's) thumb** — *it is used to say that someone is under the influence of someone else or is controlled by someone else:*

(31) • They are business partners, but John is under his partner's thumb.

(32) • His girlfriend left him as he was trying to keep her under his thumb.

• tie

• **be tied up** (informal) — *this expression is used for two different purposes:*

(a) it is used to say that you are busy:

(33) • I'm sorry, Mr Smith can't join you for lunch, as he's a bit tied up this afternoon.

(b) when you want to say something is connected with something/somebody:

(34) • He has been complaining about his health, but I think his health problems are tied up with his personal financial difficulties.

• time

- **ahead of one's time** — *when one's ideas are too advanced to be applicable or acceptable to the people of the time when one's ideas are made known to other people:*

  (35) • Charles Babbage's ideas to build a computer in 1830s were ahead of his time.

  (36) • Some of Charles Darwin's ideas were ahead of his time. (Naturalist 1809-82)

- **for the time being** — *it means for a short period of time – now but not for ever:*

  (37) • Alfred is here for the time being.

  (38) • May I leave this box here for the time being?

• token

- **by the same token** — *it is used to say for the same reason or in a similar way:*

  (39) • You must not come home too late from work every day, but by the same token, she should stop being suspicious of your actions.

  (40) • We were very pleased to have you. By the same token, we really enjoyed our stay with you and we should like to thank you.

• toll

- **take a heavy toll (on somebody/something) or take its toll (on somebody/something)** — *when an event, an action or the outcome of something has caused damage, loss, death, suffering, destruction, etc:*

  (41) • The low bank interest rate has been taking its toll on retired people who have small savings in their banks.

  (42) • I heard on BBC Radio 2 that last night's heavy floods across Europe had taken a heavy toll on people's property.

• top

- **blow one's top** (informal) — *when you become very angry with someone and shout at them:*

****

(43) • She blew her top when her husband told her about his love affair.

(44) • I never talk to him frankly because if he doesn't like the idea, he blows his top.

. torch

. carry a torch for somebody — *when you are in love with someone who does not seem to be in love with you.*

(45) • She is carrying a torch for Daniel.

(46) • When Walter was carrying a torch for Veronica, he met a beautiful young lady in a dance club and fell in love with her at first sight.

. touch

. in touch — *it means in communication with someone, by talking, writing, or by any other means of communication between people:*

(47) • It was a wonderful evening, and I promise to keep in touch with you.

(48) • It is great that we have been able to keep in touch with each other for so many years.

. tuck

. tuck in (informal)(spoken) — *when you eat greedily:*

(49) • On our arrival, our hosts provided us with free breakfast. We sat down and started to tuck in right away.

(50) • When I offered her a meal, she sat down to it and began to tuck in so fast that I couldn't believe it.

U

. umbrage

- **take umbrage (at something)** (formal) — *when often for no good reason, someone feels insulted or offended by another person:*

    (1) • He took umbrage because another guest made a remark about his country, and he left us immediately.

    (2) • I don't discuss politics with him, as he takes umbrage at other people's opposing views.

• uncertain

- **in no uncertain terms** — *it means forcefully and openly without any hesitation:*

    (3) • You must tell him what you think of him in no uncertain terms.

    (4) • We must tell them in no uncertain terms about their poor service and charges.

• uncle

- **bob's your uncle (informal)** — *when you want to say how easily and quickly something is done:*

    (5) • With your right hand, just press the left side of this mouse and bob's your uncle! It flashes.

    (6) • You must press this tiny switch twice and bob's your uncle! It's switched on.

- **like a Dutch uncle** — *when you talk to someone critically or rebuke, but kindly:*

    (7) • Why are you talking to me like a Dutch uncle? I don't have to listen to your free advice.

    (8) • When I told her that she should not have done that she replied, 'Don't talk to me like a Dutch uncle!'

• under

- **under somebody's (very) nose** (informal) — *this expression is used for indicating two different situations:*

    (a) when something is very near to you but you cannot see it:

(9) ▪ My grandfather searched the whole house for his wrist watch, but it was under his very nose.

(10) ▪ The document I have been looking for was under my nose all the time.

(b) when something happens when you are there, and you don't see it taking place, even if it is not done secretly:

(11) ▪ My pen disappeared from my desk under my very nose.

----

most likely someone has stolen it ⏎

(12) ▪ We were in our house, but we didn't know that our house was ransacked by burglars under our very nose.

▪ **under one's own steam** (informal) — *when you do something without help from other people:*

(13) ▪ I don't like travelling with a group of people, so I went to the conference under my own steam.

(14) ▪ Karen arrived in England three days ago, but she preferred to travel to York under her own steam.

▪ Understand

▪ **give(someone) to understand that ...** (formal) — *this expression is used to make someone think that... :*

(15) ▪ I was given to understand that you were sending us some samples.

(16) ▪ We are given to understand that you have received our purchase order.

▪ See ⟹ quantity ⟹ an unknown quantity

▪ unsound

▪ **of unsound mind** (especially legal) — *it is used to say that someone is suffering from* *some mental illness and is thus not responsible for their action(s):*

(17) • The barrister for the accused murderer claimed that at the time of the crime his client was of unsound mind.

(18) • The judge issued an order for a medical report to establish whether the accused was of unsound mind or not.

• unstuck

• **come unstuck** (informal) — *it can be used in two different ways:*

(a) it means something or a person has failed (informal):

(19) • Our travel plans came unstuck and we lost our deposit.

(20) • Our team came unstuck as we couldn't score a goal, and we lost the match.

(b) it means something that was fixed to another thing has become separated from it:

(21) • The plastic cover of this video tape has come unstuck.

(22) • The door handle had come unstuck.

• unturned

• **leave no stone unturned** — *when you try everything that is possible in order to achieve your goal:*

(23) • We left no stone unturned to find finance for our project.

(24) • Our fire fighters left no stone unturned to save more lives.

• up

• **be up to somebody** — *when you want to say it is somebody's responsibility to decide what to do:*

(25) • Can you do this job next? You'll have to ask my supervisor, as it is up to him to tell me what I must do next.

(26) • Shall we leave this conference now? Well, it's up to you to decide. You are

responsible for our group.

. See $\Rightarrow$ **running** $\Rightarrow$ **up and running**

. up

. on the up — *it means someone is successful or is doing well. When it refers to a thing, it means increasing or improving, developing, etc:*

    (27) **.** Well, consumer goods prices are sharply on the up again.

    (28) **.** Since she left hospital, her self-confidence is on the up.

. on the up and up (informal) — *when something or someone is becoming more and more successful:*

    (29) **.** Our sales have been up and up since last January.

    (30) **.** In the television rating of show presenters, his rating has been on the up and up since the current series started some months ago.

. up-and-coming (informal) — *it refers to someone who is likely to be successful in the future in a particular career:*

    (31) **.** She is an up-and-coming Shakespearean actress.

    (32) **.** The purpose of this exhibition is to display the work of some of our up-and-coming young artists.

. ups and downs (informal) — *it means good and bad situations as life progresses:*

    (33) **.** Well, we all have our ups and downs. That's life!

    (34) **.** This year, my business has more ups and downs than any other year.

. upon

. almost upon you — *it means something will happen in the very near future:*

    (35) **.** My son's wedding day is almost upon us.

(36) • Despite the fact that the winter season was almost upon us, it was a very
warm day in Nice, France.

• upper

• **gain, (get), have the upper hand** —*this expression means someone has or wants to have
an advantage over someone else in order to dominate a particular set of circumstances:*

(37) • They have the upper hand over me because I have already given them
that vital information by mistake.

(38) • In our dispute with our property landlord, we still have the upper hand, as
legally he can not evict us.

• **on your uppers** (informal) — *when you are very short of money, or have no money:*

(39) • I have been out of work for nearly one year, and am now on my uppers.

(40) • You can't ask him for a loan because his business has failed and he is
on his uppers.

• upset

• **upset the/somebody's apple cart** — *when you spoil, upset or throw into disorder
someone's ideas, arrangements or theory:*

(41) • The unavailability of a hall big enough to hold our general meeting in
this area has quite upset the apple cart.

(42) • Their insistent demands for full payment within ten days has upset
his apple cart.

• usual

• **as usual** — *it means something happens again like it happened previously:*

(43) • As usual, he is drunk.

(44) • He was feeling ill, but he finished his work as usual.

V

. vacuum

• **in a vacuum** — *If something happens in isolation instead of being banded together with people or things:*

    (1) • Most decisions that affect people's lives in general are taken in a vacuum by a small number of politicians.

    (2) • In workplaces in Japan, most decisions are <u>not</u> made in a vacuum, but after close consultation with the workers.

. vain

• **in vain** — *when you do something without success:*

    (3) • We really tried very hard to save his life, but all our efforts were in vain.

    (4) • We went to Holland in vain trying to purchase a new car at a comparatively lower price than in the UK.

. variety

• **variety is the spice of life** — *it is a saying which means that new and different life experiences make life more exciting and enjoyable:*

    (5) • You should travel abroad to discover that variety is the spice of life by meeting people, seeing different things and tasting local food, rather than just watching television travel programmes.

    (6) • My different jobs in so many different places both in this country and abroad have convinced me that variety is the spice of life.

. vengeance

• **with a vengeance** (informal) — *this expression has a variety of meanings including to a greater degree, violently or thoroughly:*

    (7) • If permission is granted, the project work will commence with a vengeance.

(8) ● Last night that thunder storm came with a vengeance.

● vent

● **give (full) vent to something** (formal) — *when someone expresses their feelings such as anger, strongly:*

(9) ● When she saw the mess in her garden, she gave full vent to her feelings in a fit of temper, but there was no one to see her in such a state.

(10) ● When my car was hit in the rear by another driver, I gave vent to my anger in a shouting match with the driver.

● verge

● **on the verge of something/of doing something** — *when someone is almost about to do something, or something is about to happen at any moment:*

(11) ● When we met for first time after thirty years, we were both on the verge of tears.

(12) ● When a burglar broke into her flat, she was on the verge of attacking him with a kitchen knife, but he ran away empty handed.

● very

● **before/in front of somebody's (very) eyes** — *it means something happens when you are present:*

(13) ● He was shocked to witness his house burn down in front of his very eyes.

(14) ● Before my very eyes, he hit the parked car and then tried to drive away.

● victim

● **fall victim (to something)** — *It means something is damaged, spoilt, killed or hurt by something:*

(15) ● Unfortunately, he fell victim to a gang fight and was killed.

(16) . It has been raining **cats and dogs*** in our area for a few days, and our roof has fallen victim to it.

* raining **cats and dogs** (informal) is another idiomatic expression in this sentence. It means it is raining heavily.

. view

. **in full view (of somebody/something)** — *when something happens in front of somebody or something, and it is clearly visible:*

(17) . A man was hit in his face by a flying brick in full view of us.

(18) . He was arrested by the police in a shopping centre in full view of many shoppers.

. **in view of something** (formal) — *it means considering something, or in the light of something:*

(19) . In view of your late arrival due to a national strike, you will still be paid a full day's wage.

(20) . In view of the fact that the heating system is out of order, this institute will close at 11.00 am today until next Monday morning.

. **with a view to something/to doing something** (formal) — *it means with the aim, hope, intention, purpose of doing something:*

(21) . I'm saving some money every week with a view to travelling to China.

(22) . We are decorating our guest room with a view to inviting a couple from Paris.

. virtue

. **by/in virtue of something** (formal) — *this expression is used to give a reason for doing something. It is equivalent to because of something, or by means of something:*

(23) . He was appointed to this well-paid job in virtue of his membership of a golf club, where some directors play golf with him.

(24) • She can start and finish work when she wants, by virtue of her field work as a social worker.

• voice

• **raise one's voice** — *when you are angry, you speak louder than your normal voice.*

(25) • There is no need to raise your voice to me.

(26) • Well, I don't want to raise my voice to you again. I'm only asking you to tell me to whom I should send my formal complaint.

• **with one voice** (formal) — *it means all the people in a group agree to something, or reach a unanimous*(**a** before ⇒ unanimous as u is not used as a vowel) *decision, support, etc:*

(27) • At the next meeting, our departmental representatives will speak with one voice, and will ask management for free car parking for all of us.

(28) • All parties in the House of Commons spoke with one voice on the tragic death of Diana Princess of Wales on 31 August 1997.

• void

• **null and void** — *it is used mainly in a legal sense. It means a contract, agreement, etc is no longer valid, or binding legally:*

(29) • Our solicitor has advised us that this purchase agreement is null and void.

(30) • This is merely a memorandum between you and your business partner without any witness to this statement, and thus it will be declared null and void by the court.

• vote

• **vote with your feet** — *when someone shows one's dissatisfaction with something:*

(31) • She was so annoyed by the club that she voted with her feet by cancelling her club membership.

(32) • Since they started charging for car parking, many regular customers have

already voted with their feet and started shopping elsewhere.

W

• wake

• **in the wake of something** — *when an event follows another event, usually as a result of the first event.*

    (1) • Today students all over the country are demonstrating in London in the wake of the recent government announcement to charge students tuition fees.

    (2) • In parts of Yorkshire, the flood left a trail of destruction in its wake.

• wall

• **go to the wall** — *it is often used in connection with businesses. It indicates the failure of a business often through competition, or lack of financial resources:*

    (3) • In our town, a well-known retail shop went to the wall, because a new large department store opened with a larger range of quality goods at lower prices.

    (4) • Due to high bank interest rates for borrowing money, many businesses have been going to the wall since the beginning of the year.

• wane

• **on the wane** (usually written) — *it is used to indicate someone is becoming less powerful, less important, less popular or something is becoming less common:*

    (5) • His popularity has been on the wane since a widely reported sex scandal.

    (6) • The availability of skilled traditional craftsmen has been on the wane for a much longer time than you think.

• want

- **for (the) want of something** — *it is used as a reason: to mean something is not sufficient, not enough, not available or there is a lack of it:*

    (7) • Our innovation did not result in a product for the want of financial resources.

    (8) • We didn't travel to all the places we wanted to visit in Russia for the want of both money and time.

• **wart***

- **warts and all** (informal) — *it means you accept someone or something as they are including their good and bad points, features or characteristics:*

    (9) • We welcomed them into our family, warts and all.

    (10) • She thinks that he is the man she has been waiting for, for so long, warts and all.

* Wart is a noun. It is a small lump that grows on one's skin.

• **wash**

- **wash one's hands of (somebody or something)** — *when you do not wish to be responsible for somebody or something. It can also indicate your unwillingness to take part in something or to get involved with someone:*

    (11) • If you don't listen to my honest advice, I'll wash my hands of your problems.

    (12) • When her husband, from whom she is separated, was found drunk in a public toilet, she washed her hands of him.

• **watch**

- **watch the world go by** — *when you are free and relaxed and looking at people in a public place:*

    (13) • We sat on a balcony and watched the world go by in a busy street in Paris.

    (14) • She loves watching the world go by when we are on holiday in Italy.

• **way**

- **have/want it both ways** — *when you want to benefit from two different things at the same time that is normally impossible to bind together, or achieve simultaneously:*

  (15) • You still wish to pay off your debts, as well as go on a foreign holiday trip. On your income, I don't think you can have it both ways.

  (16) • In this case, you can't have it both ways that is you must either accept the new post or stay in your current job.

. wayside

- **fall by the wayside** — *when someone or something fails, or cannot make any further progress towards the achievement of some goal:*

  (17) • Our software development project fell by the wayside due to lack of resources.

  (18) • We had started our cricket club very well, but six months after, our paid membership fell sharply and eventually the club fell by the wayside.

. wear

- **wear your heart on your sleeve** — *when you make your feelings openly known :*

  (19) • Today, he has been informed by a television company that his contract will not be renewed. I'm sure he is downhearted, but he is not the type of man who wears his heart on his sleeve.

  (20) • When Lucy heard the court's verdict that she would not get more money from her ex-husband, she cried. Well, she always did wear her heart on her sleeve.

. weather

- **under the weather** (informal) — *when you don't feel very well, but you are only slightly ill:*

  (21) • How are you this morning? I'm feeling a bit under the weather.

  (22) • I'm a little under the weather this morning, but I still came to work because we must produce our monthly report today.

. **well**

. **as well as (somebody/something)** — *this expression is used to say in addition to, or too:*

>   (23) . He has a flat in London as well as owning a big property in Dorset.

>   (24) . Daniel is coming with us as well as Adam, who will join us **later on***.

* This is another idiomatic expression (informal). It means at some time in the future.

. **wheel**

. **wheels within wheels** — *it refers to a complicated situation in which some powerful individuals have their influence and make secret deals and decision that suit them:*

>   (25) . In our large organization, there are wheels within wheels, therefore most well-paid posts are held by those individuals who know the right people.

>   (26) . I'm looking for another job, as in our company there are wheels within wheels, and it is very difficult to be promoted.

. **will**

. **with the best will in the world** — *it means someone wishes to do something or a job, but cannot do it:*

>   (27) . With the best will in the world, she could not knit.

>   (28) . With the best will in the world, he couldn't run the engineering department, as he lacked management expertise.

. **wit**

. **have/keep your wits about you** — *it means you have to be alert, cautious, and know what's going on at all times around you so that you can react to the situation:*

>   (29) . You have to keep your wits about you when you are alone on a night shift as a security guard.

>   (30) . You have to keep your wits about you when you are serving a fraudster at the cash register.

• wolf

• **keep the wolf from the door** (informal) — *it means to have sufficient money so that you can avoid going hungry or feeling poor:*

   (31) • I earn sufficient money to keep the wolf from the door.

   (32) • I work as a school cleaner and earn just enough money to keep the wolf from the door.

• world

• **on top of the world** — *when someone is very happy and well, or is very proud of oneself:*

   (33) • He is on top of the world this morning because he has won a scholarship to study law at Oxford University.

   (34) • Rachel is on top of the world since she gave birth to her first child - Alexander.

• worst

• **if the worst comes to the worst** — *it means when conditions or circumstances become unbearable, or things are too difficult, or the situation is dangerous, etc:*

   (35) • If the worst comes to the worst and our hosts don't **show up***, we will just have to stay in a hotel.

* **show up** is a phrase (informal) – *it means to arrive at the arranged time and place to to meet someone or do something.*

   (36) • If the worst comes to the worst and my husband doesn't get this job, I'll try to get a part time job for myself so that we can have some money for living.

• wrap

• **be wrapped up in somebody/something/oneself** (informal) — *when you are very busy doing something, or with someone so that you do not have the time to think about other things, people or be with them:*

   (37) • I'm very much wrapped up in my work.

   (38) • She is always wrapped up in her garden whilst her husband spends his time in the pub.

• **written**

• **be written all over somebody's face** — *it is connected with people's emotional feelings such as fear, guilt, happiness, etc which is usually seen from someone's facial expression:*

   (39) • When his mother asked him about the broken China vase, guilt was
         written all over his face.

   (40) • When she returned home after her job interview, success was written
         all over her face.

X Y Z

• **yarn**

• **spin (somebody) a yarn** — *to tell a long tale which may be untrue to somebody as an excuse for something, or just to cheat somebody:*

   (1) • He span a yarn of some domestic problems to give a reason for
        his absence from work yesterday.

   (2) • She tried to spin her boyfriend a yarn to account for not keeping a date with
        him last Saturday, but he did not believe her and went home.

• **yesterday**

• **not born yesterday** (spoken) — *It is usually said when you suspect that what someone is telling you to be untrue. It means you cannot be easily fooled, as you are not naïve.*

   (3) • You're talking nonsense. I wasn't born yesterday, you know.

   (4) • What you are telling me is **a likely story**. If you think I was born yesterday,
        you're wrong.   ------------------

idiom(spoken) – not to believe someone ↵ = ironic ⟹ the opposite of what is said

• **Z**

• **from A to Z** — *it means everything, or from the beginning to the end of something:*

   (1) • When I come I'll tell you about it from A to Z.

   (2) • Any decent bookshop will sell you an A to Z of London - a book that has all
        the names and maps of London streets.

Part 5

Writing Skills

. Introduction

'Someone somewhere wants a letter from you!'   (an old slogan used by the Post Office)

This part is divided into two chapters. These are Chapter 14 on Social Letter Writing and Chapter 15 is on Business Letter Writing.

It does not matter whether you are writing a social or business letter, you need to imagine or know the recipient, so that you have an idea what they will be thinking when they receive and open your letter. On receipt of a letter, instantly, consciously or unconsciously, the thought that often enters our mind is *what's in it for me?*

This leads to an interesting conclusion, that is, you should write it in such a way that they read the whole letter attentively, and respond to your communication positively. For instance, if it is social letter, it must create a better mutual understanding between the writer and the recipient. If it is a business letter, you want them to do business with you whether they buy from you or pay you for goods purchased from you. In both cases, it is important that you understand what the recipient wants from your letter.

. Style of Addressing People

In this day and age, formality in addressing people is somewhat relaxed, but it is still desirable that we are courteous and address people correctly. When you write to a large organisation, it is not always possible to know the name of the recipient. If you try to find the name of the person by telephone, you spend time and money on telephone charges, and they can still tell you to write to their company, or a particular department, and your letter will get there. It is, therefore, common practice to address as follows:

Salutation remark (opening remark) $\Rightarrow$ **'Dear Sir/Madam,'**, and conclude the letter with the **complimentary remark** (closing remark) $\Rightarrow$ **'Yours faithfully,'**. Usually, letters from business to business have names of individuals. In this case, it is customary to address them as follows:

Salutation remark (opening remark) $\Rightarrow$ **'Dear Mr Broomfield,'**, and conclude the letter with the **complimentary remark** (closing remark) $\Rightarrow$ **'Yours sincerely,'**. Use this complimentary remark when your salutation includes a surname or surnames. In Chapter 14, you can find salutation and complimentary remarks for informal letter writing.

The _**superscription**_ means the name and address that is written on the envelope. If you know the recipient's academic awards, titles, honours or any other distinctions, these should be included in the superscription. If it is a business letter, and you know the name of the recipient, it is polite to mark the letter for the attention of the individual by writing the name. In addition, if you know the post the recipient holds, write it as well. Here is an example:

For the attention of Mr R M Henderson MA (Brunel)
Managing Director
Henderson Films PLC
23 Bull Street
London
W1 1AA

For important letters <u>do not</u> use F.A.O.
F.A.O. stands for: for the attention of
It has **open punctuation.** This is
increasingly becoming the norm for
word processed letters.

. If it is a social letter, usually qualifications below the grade of doctor after the name are not listed. In a workplace, academic and professional awards and other distinctions awarded are important. These should be included in the superscription, if they are known to you.

. Nowadays the superscription is _**open punctuation**_ – it means <u>no</u> punctuation marks are used.

. Some women prefer not to be known as '_**Miss**_' or '_**Mrs**_'. In a business letter, if a woman does not want to state whether she is married or not, she prefers to be addressed as '_**Ms**_', e.g., _**Ms Jill Clark**_.

. In the salutation section, '_**Dear Ms Smith**_,' and in the complimentary section, '_**Yours sincerely**_,'.

. _**In important business letters**_ which are usually typed/word processed by a secretary, salutation and complimentary marks may be hand written by the person signing the letter. Often, a greeting such as 'kind regards' is also added and hand written. This is a good idea as it shows a personal touch and interest. However, it is not necessary to write it by hand. I would prefer to write these lines myself.

. If you write to _**husband and wife**_: In the salutation section say, '_**Dear Mr and Mrs Simon Smith,**_' or 'Dear Mr and Mrs S Smith,'. One initial of the husband's first name is written after Mrs as shown here. In the complimentary remark section, '_**Yours sincerely,**_'.

. For two or more _**business women**_, use in salutation section, '_**Dear Ladies,**_' and in the complimentary remark section, '_**Yours faithfully,**_'.

. For _**one woman**_ whose surname is not known to you, state in the salutation section, '_**Dear Madam,**_' and in the complimentary section, '_**Yours faithfully,**_'.

. A _**professor**_, even if he/she is a doctor and professor, 'Dear Professor Brown,". If a doctor is a surgeon, in the salutation section, '_**Dear Mr John Smith,**_' (surgeon is called Mr in the UK). In the complimentary remark section, '_**Yours sincerely,**_', as their surname is included in the salutation.

. To find out how to address people with titles such as Sir, Lord, Bishop, etc., consult a reference book.

Social Letter Writing   **435**

****

Chapter 14
Social Letter Writing

. Introduction

Social letters are written to relatives, friends and acquaintances. A get well letter is a social letter. Letters of invitation and sympathy are also examples of social letters. Social letters are informal letters.

. Stationery

Ordinary writing paper is good enough. Some people like to use *letterhead paper* designed especially for social communication. A letterhead has the name and address of a person (for business its name, address, etc.) printed at the top of their writing paper. Nowadays, for social letter writing, it is becoming acceptable to include telephone, fax and even email details in a letterhead.

Letterheads designed for purposes other than social ones have other information as well. There are local printers who can provide you with a variety of paper types, colours and designs of letterhead papers. Some letterheads for social writing include imaginative graphics.

For social letter writing, letterheads do not usually include individual names. If you correspond with friends overseas, it is a good idea to start your letterhead with your name, because it will help your overseas friends to write your name correctly. Often foreign names prove difficult to spell correctly.

Usually, printers offer *envelopes* of the same colour as the letterhead, where your name and address are printed at the left-hand top corner of the envelope, or at the back of the envelope with the message, *If undelivered, please return to: ....'*

Indeed, the use of Personal Computers has made it possible to design your own letterhead. It is not necessary to get your personalised letterhead printed. Anyway, it depends on individual preference and a willingness to spend money on one's serious interest in letter writing.

For overseas correspondence, it is a good idea to use particularly thin paper and an envelope. In the

UK, you can buy from any Post Office an *aerogramme*, which is a thin writing paper for foreign corre-spondence . It is designed to be folded and sent as a letter by air. An aerogramme has a limited space for writing, and you cannot insert any item such as a photo in it.

For many devoted social letter writers, the *presentation style* of letter writing is very important. These letter writers also pay special attention to choosing a writing instrument, such as a fountain pen and *ink* in order to match it to the paper colour. Of course, choosing the colour for paper, envelope and ink is very much a matter of individual taste. Most regular letter writers would not use pencil for writing a letter. Nor would they expect to receive a letter written in pencil.

I receive personal letters from my friends who stick pictures and similar colourful *decorative labels* on both the letter and its envelope. All these things show keen interest, mutual respect and a special kind of relationship between two correspondents.

You can also purchase ready made *cards* without any writing. These are also known as *blank-inside cards*. I find these cards very useful for exchanging messages with my friends. In a decent stationery shop, you can get well designed and attractive cards of many different styles, with or without graphic designs. These cards are not the same as holiday postcards.

It may be that your hand writing has deteriorated. In this case, it is better to type your letter by using your word processor (typewriters are almost museum pieces). Most social letter writers avoid word processing (or typing) a letter. *A word processed/typed* letter is considered as impersonal and un-friendly. If you have word processed/typed a letter, for whatever reason, it is polite to add an apology or explanation for doing so. It would be appreciated by the recipient of your letter.

The *hand-written* letter, which has indented paragraphs, is always much valued. It is worth mentioning that social letter writing, especially to friends, is a hobby that requires warmth and respect.

. Methods of Sending Letters

The traditional method of sending a letter is through the postal service in the world. Since the advent of *electronic mail*, young people are especially enthusiastic about *email*. Most serious social letter writers still use the postal system for sending letters and consider email as impersonal and unfriendly. There is no doubt about the speed of electronic mail, convenience and cost, but I would consider it only if I had to send an urgent message such as informing my friends about my arrival at their airport.

. Parts of a Letter

The visual presentation of a good written letter means that it must be set out neatly and in a logical manner. This is achieved by dividing the letter into the following sections:

. Head section – This is your printed letterhead part of the paper, followed by the date. If it is

Social Letter Writing   **437**

****

not a letterhead paper, write your address in the top right-hand corner, followed by the date. In informal letters, such as letters to your mum or dad, the address is left out altogether.

For overseas correspondence - write your name, address and date. After exchanging a few letters, you may start with the date written in the top right-hand corner. There is no harm if you start with your name and address or the name of your city followed by your country and the date. There are no rigid rules about it. It is a matter of preference. If you are using a printed letterhead for overseas correspondence, write the date beneath your printed information, in the right-hand side of the paper. If you use an aerogramme - start with the date in the right-hand corner, as there is a box for your name and address on the reverse side of the aerogramme.

- **Salutation Remark** — this is where you write, 'Dear...,' or other suitable words. This is also known as the opening section. Below you can find salutations for different relationships. It may be that a relative, boyfriend, girlfriend or even your close friend has a *"pet/nickname" name*. If so, use it in an informal letter (**Dear** *followed by "pet" name*).

- **Body Section** — this is the main part of your letter. It is divided into paragraphs. The number of paragraphs depends on the length of your letter.

- **Complimentary Remark** — this is the closing section, where you finish as 'Yours ....'. A list of complimentary remarks is given below. You can use the one you think it is most suitable for your relationship to the recipient of your letter. It also depends how you feel about the person at the time of writing.

- **Signing off** — put your signature under a complimentary remark.

- **Your Name** — There is no need to write your full name under your signature when you write to your relatives and close friends. However, if you write to someone with whom you are not on first name terms, write your name under your signature. Once you have exchanged a few letters with your *pen friends*, there is no need to write your name under your signature.

. <u>Pages</u>

Some people write on only one side of a sheet of paper. It is also perfectly acceptable to write on both sides of the same sheet of paper. When your letter has more than one sheet, it is better to number the pages, so that it is easy to read. Usually, the first page is not numbered. So, start the numbers from 2. Some people write page numbers in the centre of the page but on top of the head section. Some writers prefer to write it in the right-hand top corner, just above the head section.

. <u>Salutation & Complimentary Remarks</u>

In fact, how to begin and end a letter depends at the time of writing a letter on the following:

- . your relationship with the person
- . how well you know the person
- . how you feel about the person

The following suggestions are based on many years of letter writing experience. It is worth remembering that social letter writing is informal. Therefore, the basic rule for this type of writing is *informality*, as opposed to formality. Thus, you can use any of the following suitable remarks without any hesitations.

Relationship: Parents, Grandparents, Sisters, Brothers

Salutation Remarks: "Dear Mum,", **"Dear Dad,"**, "Dear Mum and Dad,", "Dearest Dad,",
                          "Dearest Mum,", "Dearest Mum and Dad,",
                          "Dear Brother,", "Dear John,", "Dearest Brother,", "Dearest Sister,",
                          "Dearest Sally,"

Complimentary Remarks: "Love,", "With all my love,", "With much love,", "With very
                          best wishes and love,", "With all the best,", "Lots of love,"

Relationship : Aunts and Uncles

Salutation Remarks: "Dear Auntie Barbara,", Dearest Barbara,", "Dear Uncle Tom,",
                        " Dearest Tom,"

Complimentary Remarks: "Love,", "With all my love,", "With much love,", "With very
                          best wishes and love,", "With best wishes,"

Relationship : Wife, Husband, Fiancé, Fiancée, Girlfriend, Boyfriend
----
Salutation Remarks: "Dear Frank,", "My Darling Anglika,", "My Darling John,", "Dearest Kim,"

Complimentary Remarks: "Love,", "With all my love,", "With much love,", "With very
                          best wishes and love,", "With best wishes,"

Relationship: Sons, Daughters, Nieces, and Nephews

Salutation Remarks: "Dearest Adam,", "Dear Daniel,", "Dear Rachel,", "Dearest Rachel,"

Complimentary Remarks: "Love,", "With all my love,", "With much love,", "With very

****

best wishes and love,", "With best wishes,"

Relationship: Youngsters to adults

Salutation Remarks: "Dear Mr Johnson,", "Dear Mrs Johnson,", Dear Mr & Mrs Johnson,"
When allowed to call by first name: "Dear Colin,", "Dear Mary,"
Addressing very close old family friends: "Dear Auntie,", "Dear Uncle,"

Complimentary Remarks: "Love,", "With all my love,", "With much love,", "With very
best wishes and love,", "With best wishes,"

Relationship: Very close unrelated old friends of your family -
if you call them as "Auntie", "Uncle"

Salutation Remarks: "Dear Auntie Mary,", Dearest Mary,", "Dear Uncle Tom,", " Dearest Tom,"

Complimentary Remarks: "Love,", "With all my love,", "With much love,", "With very
best wishes and love,", "With best wishes,"

Relationship: Close friends

Salutation Remarks: "Dearest Anne,", "My Dear Anne,", "My Dear Beata,",
"Dearest Beata," "Dearest Jolanta,", "Dear Ines," , "My Dear Yuonne,"

Complimentary Remarks: "Love,", "With all my love,", "With much love,", "With very
best wishes and love,", "With best wishes,", "Lots of love,"
"Kind regards and lots of love,"

Relationship: Acquaintance, or anyone with whom you are not
on first name terms

Salutation Remarks: "Dear Mr Jones,", "Dear Mrs Jones,"

Complimentary Remarks: "Yours sincerely,"

Relationship: Pen friends

Salutation Remarks: "Dear Colin,", "Dear Marketa,", "Dear Sigrid,"

Complimentary Remarks: "Yours,",
After an exchange of a few letters, you don't have to say "Yours,",
Just write:
"Best wishes,", "Kind regards,", "Best wishes and kind regards,"

. Think About the Recipient

The above information lays the foundations for social letter writing. When you write a letter, think about the person to whom you are about to write. The recipient of your letter must be pleased to receive your letter, and enjoy reading it. It is not always possible to give some good and exciting news, but the way you describe things can be interesting. Therefore, try not to impress the recipient with too many words which need explanation, but be polite and honest.

There is no need to be afraid of writing a long letter, because some people enjoying reading such letters. Usually, older people like to read and write long letters. They have time for this activity. Young people also enjoy reading such letters. Older children especially like some sort of drawing, such as a smiling face. The content of your letter will reveal how much pleasure you have had in writing it.

. Some Examples of Social Letters

(1) . Congratulations on passing exams from an uncle

---

                                                                1 Beech Street
                                                                Birmingham
                                                                B 1 17ER

                                                                (date here)

Dearest David,

I'm delighted to hear the good news that you have passed your final exams for your Bachelor of Science degree. I congratulate you whole-heartedly on your well-deserved success.

It is wonderful that you have gained an upper second class pass, which was required by the company who have conditionally offered you the post of Systems Analyst. Your achievement in the exams has met the employment condition, as well as opened the door for future prosperity. Indeed, you have gained your objectives. It is great news, as you can start your career right away with a reputable large software company. Well done!

I will return home from Switzerland next month, a few days before your double celebration party. Most certainly, it'll be a great pleasure to join you on this happy occasion.

I'm very much looking forward to seeing you all and joining the celebrations.

Love and very best wishes,

Uncle Tom

- Example 2 is another letter of congratulations to encourage or support a young person. This sort of letter may be sent to the son/ daughter of your friend, colleague, neighbour, etc.

(2) . <u>Congratulations on passing exams from a friend of the family</u>

> "The Oaks"
> 20 Star Street
> London
> SW1 1AA
>
> (date here)
>
> Dear Barbara,
>
> It is really very pleasing to hear from your mother that you have passed your Pitmans Advanced Level secretarial exams and that you're going to start a new job at our local Town Hall. We send you our warmest congratulations.
>
> You worked so hard for a long time to gain this qualification of secretarial proficiency. This is what you've always wanted, and now you have got it. Very well done!
>
> It will help you to make good progress in the future.
>
> With best wishes,

. <u>Congratulations on an engagement</u>

Examples 3-4 show two letters of congratulations. The letter in Example 3 is sent to a close friend. In this letter you can say more than just accepting an invitation for an engagement celebration party.

The letter in Example 4 is written to an acquaintance. Here the letter writer has not given any personal assessment or opinion about the engaged couple. If you know the engaged couple, you can add more to the basic letter.

(3) . <u>Congratulations on the engagement of a close friend</u>

> 10 Beech Street
> Bridlington
> Y010 2BB
>
> (date here)
>
> My Dear Jane,
>
> Thank you so much for inviting me to your engagement party on 31 May 2003. It's great news that you have become engaged to John Russell. I have known John for many years, as we both went to the same school. He is really a charming, honest and loving person.
>
> I have seen you and John happy together for nearly two years, and can say that you were made for each other. We can talk about it when we meet soon, but I must add that I honestly believe you have made the right decision.
>
> I'm very much looking forward to joining your celebration party.
>
> With very best wishes and love,
>
>

(4) . <u>Congratulations on the engagement of an acquaintance</u>

> 1 Beech Street
> Bridlingon
> Y010 2BB
>
> (date here)
>
> Dear James,
>
> I was very pleased to see your engagement announcement in "The Bridlington Times". Perhaps, one day, your fiancée will come with you to our tennis club. It would be nice to meet her with you. I'm curious to know when you will be married.
>
> Best wishes,
>
> Helen Atkinson

****

- You can send a similar letter to someone or both parties on their marriage or partnership.

. Childbirth

(5) . This is to congratulate friends on the birth of their child

1 Beech Street
Birmingham
B 1 17ER

(date here)

Dear Colin and Kay,

We were overjoyed to hear from Mrs. Smith that you had become happy parents on the arrival of your healthy baby son Alexander – you must be delighted. Congratulations!

We are very pleased to learn that there were no complications and that Kim and Alexander are both doing fine.

Once Kim and Alexander are home, one evening we will call on you to have the pleasure of seeing your lovely son with his proud parents.

With all our love and best wishes,

Dora and Dick

- If you wish to expand this letter, you can do so. For instance, you can ask them about the weight of their baby son. Of course, you can start it with *"Dearest Colin and Kay,"* if you feel particularly close to them.

. Good luck in a new job

People often change jobs. Sometimes, you feel you must wish someone good luck in their new job. The following two letters are designed to give you an idea of what you can write to a colleague with whom you have worked for a long time, or a friend, or someone in your own family.

(6) . <u>This is to wish a colleague good luck in a new post</u>

3 Beech Street
Birmingham
B11 17ER

(date here)

Dear Peter,

I have just found out from Jane that you have accepted the post of Systems
Programming Manager at People's PLC in the City, and that you will be soon leaving us.
So, at last you are successful in getting a job which you wanted for a long time. Certainly,
it is a promotion at this time in your career. Congratulations!

This is, indeed, a step in the right direction. I hope that this chance of working for an
international financial institution will give you every opportunity to progress towards
becoming Director of Information Systems. This is your final goal, and now you are
one more step nearer to it. We all know how hard you work and how much energy you
put into it. Indeed, you have done very well.

We'll miss you at XYZ , but your new work place is close to us. Once you're settled down
in your new post, we could meet, whenever possible, for lunch or a drink, as usual,
after work, in the same old place.

Do keep in touch and let me know how you are coping with your new responsibility,
and how you're getting on in general.

With very best wishes,

[signature: Robin Smith]

- The above letter is to a colleague with whom the letter writer is on first name terms, and has
  a good friendship. Therefore, the complimentary remark is used to indicate informality. The
  next letter is from an auntie.

(7) . __This is to wish a relative good luck in a new post abroad__

3 John Street
Birmingham
B4 17ER

(date here)

My Dear Roger,

Your mother just telephoned giving me the news of your success at a job interview.
I'm ever so pleased to hear that you have been promoted within the Civil Service and
that your new post will give you the opportunity of working abroad in association with the
British Trade Mission in the USA.

This is a marvellous chance for you to travel abroad, and I'm sure it will broaden your
horizons. This is what you have always wished and I'm glad you have succeeded in
doing so.

Since you were at school, you were destined for a Civil Service career, like your father.
I knew from your school days that you were a bright young man in our family, and that
you would always strive for the achievement of your goal. This new direction
will strengthen your self-confidence, and I'm pretty sure that you'll soon be making
your presence felt both in the UK and at the British Trade Mission in the USA.

It's such a long time since I saw you. I know how busy you are, but do pop in soon to
see your Auntie.

With love and best wishes,

Auntie Mary

. __Letters of sympathy__

In all our lives, there are occasions when we have to write letters of condolence, following
a bereavement. Some years ago, people used to write lengthy letters about deceased's life.
In this day and age, the tendency is to write short letters in order to covey the message of
sympathy. However, these letters are not easy to write.

You may have to write other letters of sympathy on events such as car accidents, illness, business failure, etc. The following examples illustrate this aspect of letter writing.

When writing *a letter of condolence*, it is suggested that you keep your letter short in such a way that you convey your sincere feelings of sympathy to the deceased's relatives in simple words. Any other matters should <u>not</u> be included. You may add a few words about the deceased person, if you feel that you ought to do so. It should be a hand-written letter.

(8) . <u>Letter of condolence – death of an acquaintance</u>

---

2 Kensington Place
Manchester
M1A 2AB

(date here)

Dear Mrs Jones,

I was deeply saddened to read in today's local paper that your beloved husband Lesley was involved in a fatal car accident. Lesley's sudden death has shocked my husband and I. How horrendous for you to lose him, so tragically, so young and so suddenly.

My wife and I offer our sincere sympathy on your loss.

With kindest regards,

Yours sincerely,

Peter Smith

Peter Smith

. <u>Letter of condolence – death of a close friend's wife</u>

This letter is slightly longer than the previous one. The reason is that I know how much my friend would like to hear from me, as I knew his wife well.

(9) • <u>Letter of condolence – death of a close friend's wife</u>

---

1 Beech Street
Birmingham
B 1 17ER

(date here)

My Dear John,

Last night, my mother broke the dreadful news of Jane's death over the telephone. Anne and I are shocked. I can't imagine how sorrowful you are on your beloved wife's death.
If it's any consolation, she has been finally released from her painful illness.

Anne and I enjoyed her friendship for so many years. She was always ever so kind, honest, cheerful and helpful. Jane was always very hospitable to friends and strangers. We will miss her very much.

If there is anything at all which we can do to help, please ask us without any hesitation.
We send you our deepest sympathy.
Love,

Sarah and Jack

• Example 10 contains a letter of sympathy to a colleague who has had an operation. You can write a similar letter to someone who has had an accident and is unable to work.

• **Hospital visit**

When you write to a colleague, an acquaintance, or a friend with whom you do not have a very close relationship, it is not easy to say whether you should visit them or not. The problem is that for some reasons, they may not want visitors other than their relatives and intimate friends. On the other hand, they may appreciate your visit as very few people visit them. Anyway, it is a good idea to indicate that their work has been taken care of and there is no need to worry about it. It also is advisable to add that you will be happy to help if they ask you.

(10) . <u>Letter of sympathy – a colleague in hospital</u>

> 12 The High
> Roman Road
> London
> SW1 2AA
>
> (date here)
>
>
> Dear Craig,
>
> I'm sorry to hear that you had been admitted to Chelsea & Kensington Hospital for an emergency operation, but luckily, there were no complications. It is such a big relief to learn that the operation was successful, and that you're making satisfactory progress.
>
> There is no need to worry about work, as the manager has already organised cover for you for as long as you are away due to illness. If there is anything at all which I can do to help, please let me know.
>
> I hope that you will be fully recovered from your operation soon.
>
> With kindest regards,
>
> Yours sincerely,
>
> *Arthur Painer*

. <u>Get Well Messages</u>

If a friend or relative is ill, you can send a get well message. You can buy specially designed get well cards with a variety of printed messages. It is a matter of taste and how you feel about the sick person. These cards have sufficient space to write a short personal note. So, you may send a card with your hand-written note on it. If you do send a card, it is recommended that you choose a card which does not refer to an illness on its front, as it may prove to be depressing. It is better to buy a card with some sort of alternative picture or design. If you don't send a card, you can still send a message written on a sheet of ordinary writing paper. Here are two examples:

(11) . <u>Get well message from colleagues sympathising about illness</u>

<u>Work Place address Printed</u>

(date here)

Dear James,

Here in Accounts, we are all very sorry to learn that you are unwell and wanted to let you know that we are thinking of you.
rah and Barbara are providing cover for you until you are back. Therefore, don't worry about work, just look after yourself. We will be pleased to see you back at work when you are fully recovered from your illness.

With best wishes,

Signed by colleague in Accounts

(12) . <u>Get well message to a close friend</u>

(date here)

Dear Cherie,

I met your sister by chance and she told me that you had broken your leg during a hockey match. I'm very sorry that you were hospitalised for a couple of days, but the good news is that you are back home in the comfort of your own home.

I'm sure your leg will heal soon. Don't worry too much about it, and keep yourself occupied with something interesting. Well, now you have time to read some of your favourite novels.

Knowing how much you love bright colours, I have sent you this colourful card with my get well wishes. It may cheer you up a bit. Anyway, I'll pop in over the weekend to see you and have a chat over your mother's nice cup of tea. I wish I could make tea as well as your mother. Keep smiling!

Lots of love,

Daisy

In both "get well" messages, the address is left out, because these messages are from people who know the recipient very well.

. Invitations

Nowadays, an increasing number of people send invitation cards, telephone, fax or exchange email messages. All modes of communication except the telephone still involve some writing. It also depends on the nature of the invitation. If you want to invite a few close friends for a drink in a local pub, you can telephone them. For other occasions, it is better if they have something in writing, as it is still valued. Here are three invitation letters:

(13) . Invitation to a couple overseas to stay with us

20 Crescent Avenue
Bridlington
East Riding of Yorkshire
YO16 3AB
England

(date here)

Dear Ute-Susann & Carsten,

It is very pleasing to hear that you are now happily married. We had asked you to visit us before you got married, but at that time both of you were busy organising things for your wedding celebrations. Once again, we invite you to visit us whenever it is possible. It would be a great pleasure to have you with us for at least one week, although you can stay with us as long as you wish. Our guest room is ready, waiting for your arrival.

It would be lovely to show you our area of England. Yorkshire is the largest county in England. It has many attractions including secluded bays, rolling hills, undulating moors, interesting cities, towns and villages. It has many historical places and the largest national park in England – the North Yorkshire Moors.

We live by the sea, where the air is really fresh, clean and good for your health. Our local area has cliffs by the sea, woodlands and is also well-known for all kinds of birds. We can have some leisurely walks together along the impressive and picturesque Yorkshire coastline.

We look forward to hearing from you regarding when you can visit us.

With our best wishes,

Mark and Anne

(14) . <u>Invitation to a house-warming party</u>

<u>This is a very informal letter.</u>

(date here)

Dear Jane and Jim,

Last month, we moved to our new home. It wasn't quite as simple as we thought it would be. It was rather a hectic experience, but we are glad that it's all over now. Our new address is:

> "Rose Cottage"
> 1 The High
> Ramsgate
> RM1 2TT

Telephone: 01262 888 1234   Fax: 01262 888 3456

John and I invite you to join us to celebrate the move and to toast our new home on Saturday 20 May. A bit of knees-up will kick off at about 21.00 hours. We would be delighted if you could come along! Hope to see you on Saturday.

With best wishes,

Beryl and Barry

. <u>Invitation to a Wedding</u>

If you know lots of people and can afford to invite them to your wedding party, you will most likely send them formal invitation cards. Your printer will offer you a selection of cards to choose from. In fact, you can buy already printed cards and just fill in the spaces where some information is needed.

If you wish to invite only a few close friends and relatives, you can send them a letter of invitation. Example 15 shows an invitation to a wedding party which may be used for printing formal wedding invitation cards. You can also simply write it on good quality writing paper, as an invitation to relatives and close friends. It has the same effect as the printed formal wedding card. In addition, it has a personal touch, as it is hand written, and it would be more economical. It can be prepared using a word processing software, with guests' names written in by hand.

(15) ▪ <u>Invitation to a wedding</u>

Mr & Mrs John Smith

request the pleasure of the company of

Mr & Mrs Wolfgang Kling

at the marriage of their son

Mr Colin Smith

to

Miss Kay Henderson

at the Catholic Church Bridlington

on Saturday May 20 XXXX

at 13.00 hours

Reception afterwards

at

The Carlton Hotel, Promenade, Bridlington.

2 James Street
Bridlington
YO10 1AA

RSVP

RSVP (or ⇒R.S.V.P.) is an abbreviation for the French ⇒ "Répondez s'il vous plaît."

----

please reply ↲- It is used in English.

. <u>Replying to invitations</u>

It is straightforward to accept an **<u>informal invitation</u>**. You should reply as soon as you can, so that the host has a good idea of the number of people who will participate in the event. This is illustrated below:

(16) . <u>Acceptance of an invitation to a house-warming party</u>

---

22 High Street
Scarborough
YO2 3SD

(date here)

Dear Sarah and John,

Thank you very much for inviting us to your house-warming party. Indeed, we would be ever so pleased to come. We know the area where your new house is situated very well. It is a really nice district. Well done!

Look forward to seeing you at about 8.30 p.m. on 14 May.

With our very best wishes,

Jane and Jim

- If you have **<u>to decline an informal invitation</u>** for whatever reason(s), it is important that you do so politely without any unnecessary delays. Your friendly letter will not offend them. **See Example 17**.

- If you receive a formal **<u>wedding invitation</u>**, you can send your acceptance, or refusal, on a printed card, which you can buy from a quality stationery shop. Or you may prefer to write a short note of acceptance or refusal on quality writing paper. **See Examples 18 and 19**.

(17) . <u>A letter of refusal to join a house-warming party</u>

22 High Street
Scarborough
YO2 3SD

(date here)

Dear Sarah and John,

Thank you very much for inviting us to your house-warming party. I'm very sorry that I will not be able attend it, as I have already bought my train ticket to visit my grandmother in Edinburgh.

As she is anxiously waiting for my long overdue visit, I can not give it a miss. Your social gatherings are always joyful, and I hope that you and your guests have a great time on 14 May.

When I'm back from Edinburgh, I'll ring you up so that we can arrange to meet for a drink.

With our very best wishes,

Desmond

(18) . <u>Acceptance of an invitation to a wedding party</u>

22 High Street
Scarborough
YO2 3SD

(date here)

Dear Mr and Mrs Smith,

Thank you for your kind invitation to Colin and Kay's wedding and reception on Saturday May 14.

Jim and I would be delighted to attend the celebrations and we very much look forward to congratulating you, the bride and bridegroom.

Yours sincerely,

Edna and Edward

If you have received a formal invitation in the form of a printed invitation card, it does not mean that you should reply using a similar card. A hand written letter is, in fact, a better idea because it shows your personal interest.

(19) . A letter declining an invitation to attend a wedding party

22 High Street
Scarborough
YO2 3SD

(date here)

Dear Mr and Mrs Smith,

Thank you for your kind invitation to Colin and Kay's wedding and reception on Saturday 14 May.

It is very much regretted that due to an important prior engagement arranged some time ago, we will not be able to attend.

We wish you a very happy occasion. *

Yours sincerely,

John and June

Mr & Mrs John Taylor

* You can still them send them a good luck and congratulations card with your letter or separately. It does no harm to mention this in a hand-written letter, *We wish you a very happy occasion*, or similar good luck remarks.

. Friends

Many people in the world enjoy writing to their friends. I'm one of them. These friends may be in the same country or other countries. You don't have to be a member of a pen club to have **a pen friend**. You may meet people through newspaper advertisements, travel and sometimes in public places (restaurant, etc.) or the Internet. In all circumstances, irrespective of how long you have been in contact with each other through writing, in the interest of your personal safety, you must make sure that you (especially female) have taken all necessary precautions, if you are invited by your pen friend (male) to meet up.

You may start as a pen friend, and steadily develop your friendship into a family friendship. It all depends on trust and a genuine desire to understand each other, to exchange points of view and life experiences in general. Indeed, I find letter writing a very pleasing hobby. It can brighten your day when you hear from a far away friend. It can enable you to relax, as you learn to share your feelings, etc. with your friends. Indeed, through letters, one learns that we can be united by a sense of common humanity.

(20) . <u>A letter from a friend in France</u> (A retired energetic person)

Address
in
France

dated

Dear Mark,

Thank you for your nice letter and the enclosed photo. The garden looks beautiful. You haven't changed much since we met some years ago. My enclosed snap was taken last month in Carcassonne on my way to Aix en Provence. See what happened to me? You know how thin I was! Well, that's rich French food! You may call it overeating, but I don't really eat too much.

I suppose, at some time in one's life, everyone puts on some weight. That's true! This must be the reason, I think! Don't you? That's good living! I'm not going to starve because it will not do any good to me. I have no plans to seduce anybody, not at my age, anyway!

I was supposed to visit some friends in Carcassonne, but I sprained my ankle badly and went back to my cousin's in the Pyrénées, where I came from originally. I had to rest at my cousin's home before coming back to Paris. Three days after my return, I suffered from a stiff back for two weeks. As I couldn't walk much, I read a lot, but I was anxious to move again normally.

As soon as I felt better, I booked my passage to New York, where I will be on 18 September. I'm hoping that nothing happens to me in New York. I think I'll return home totally broke as the exchange rate for dollars is too high. Who cares? You have to keep moving. *Voilà* (French), the story of my life during the summer ----.

Your own life seems less adventurous at present, but it is certainly more rewarding. You also take risks, but in a different way. I do hope that your hard work will bring positive results. How are Daniel and Adam? Are you still in touch with your friend about whom you told me some months ago?

At present, you must be feeling a little bit lonely without Anne, as she is in Russia. Like you, I enjoy looking at colourful pretty flowers. They are the symbol of harmony that seems to be vanishing from our world. Somehow, we must protect our natural environment. I do miss our 'Clamart Garden' – my family home, but I always have some flowers around me.

I may call you before leaving for the USA. Now I'm with a cheap phone company and I enjoy talking to my far away friends more than ever.

Best wishes,

Yvonne

****

(21) . <u>A letter from a friend in South Africa</u>
(A young person trying hard to build a life)

                                                          Address
                                                              in
                                                        South Africa

                                                           dated

Dear Mark,

Fondest greetings. My humblest apologies for not having written any sooner. I was wondering when I'd last heard from you and when I checked your last letter, I realised that I was, in fact, the one whose turn it was to write. So there you have my acknowledgement of guilt.

What has been happening on your side of the world?

Quite a bit has been going on here, but I don't have much time to tell you about it all. As you can see from the above address, I'm staying in a little flat in the university suburb of Rondebosch, and have been there for roughly three months. I'm looking to move at the end of the year, so if you are ever confused as to where to reach me, my parents' address is always a sure way to do so.

I promise to make my subsequent letters far more interesting and certainly longer. At the moment, work has been driving us all crazy and I have also been trying to study. My boyfriend and I broke up recently, and although it is not 'Heartbreak City', it has been a change in routine.

I've been giving some thought to my long-term future as I have very little trust in the situation here in a few years' time. It is not a place where I feel even slightly safe, or would like to see the end of my days, or my children grow up. However, there is still much to do before I can seriously contemplate a final decision of that nature.

I'm afraid I have to stop here, so I shall bid you farewell until next time. Please bear in mind that my examinations finish mid-November and I should be back to speed then, and be slightly more sociable and human!

Please write soon with all your news.

Love,

Kay

(22) . <u>A letter from a friend in Canada</u>
(Someone who is interested in the natural world)

Address
in
Canada

dated

Dear Mark,

Hello! How are you?

 Everyone and everything is fine here. There hasn't been a whole lot happening with me lately. I've just been basically existing. Doesn't that sound like the ultimate life style?

Can you believe that the present year is almost half gone? I can't. There is nothing I or any other person can do about it though, so I won't dwell on it anymore. I was listening to a really interesting radio programme this morning. The topic was the *Crop Circles*. They were saying that the number of these formations is around 3,000.   That's incredible. Don't you think so? Do you think there is another life form somewhere out there? I think there is one.

Whether or not it's Martians, I can't really say. It definitely makes a person take a look at our world. Like they were saying during this discussion, it's exciting and interesting to think that there is more out there to learn about. It is also scary because it is something new and different from what we are used to. For people who were brought up with certain beliefs, in a way it makes them re-think those beliefs. Sitting comfortably and thinking about that, if you do strongly believe in what the Bible says about God creating the earth and all life as it is today, who's to say that God didn't create any other worlds not known to us?

The Bible is man's written account of how the human race was created. Isn't it possible that other worlds' aliens have their own account of how their world and race were created?

I realise that not everyone believes in God and those that do, may have a different version (for lack of a better word) of God or some higher being. I'm not a bible reading church-goer, but I do believe there is something stronger out there.

Anyway, that is my thought venting for the day. I want to get this letter in the mail to you, so I will say bye for now, and hope that you will tell me something interesting in your next letter.

Take care,

Maya

(23) • <u>A letter to develop a friendship with someone you met on holiday</u>

Address
in
England

dated

Dear Anne and Wolfgang,

I just thought of you as I was working on my PC and vividly remembered everything about our short meeting. I decided to stop work, and write this short letter, so that I can convey my feelings to you. How wonderful it was to meet both of you!

The problem is that life on this planet is too short and we are very much involved in maintaining life. The human race is still loveable, no matter where one lives and what nationality one belongs to. Nationalities are no more than political labels, which unfortunately divide the human race and erect psychological barriers between us. Despite these artificial partitions between people of this global village, it is so enjoyable to accept people from other parts of the world and to share this short life together, whenever an opportunity for meeting arises. We should avail ourselves of life's rare chances of bringing people together, despite geographical distances, different nationalities and gender.

Indeed, our words create a world as we see it. Therefore, we should speak those words, which bring us together as the people who belong to one human race, irrespective of some apparent differences.

I send you this short letter as I feel as if I'm still sitting next to you in that café and talking to you with great enthusiasm with a view to exchanging our experiences in this present life, and indeed, sharing world heritage as well as improving our mutual understanding.

To maintain our lives on this planet, as you may remember, I work for myself as a computer programmer, and thus I can work from home. My wife has a part-time job in a department store. I thought you would like to see where we live, thus I have sent you a few snaps. These will give you an idea of our simple, but happy life style. We live in the Greater London area, just 10 miles away from Central London. We have the best of both worlds – the capital of the UK and the countryside. We consider ourselves lucky, as we are alive and healthy.

I sincerely hope that it will not be too long before I hear from you.

Kind regards and best wishes,

Yours sincerely,

Mark Shin

Chapter 15

Business Letter Writing

. Introduction

The aim of this chapter is to exemplify some aspects of business letter writing. It is not a place to discuss in detail business stationery design and style aspects, except to say that a business has its own printed letterhead paper for business letter writing and any other communication purposes. Usually a business letterhead paper has a business logo, the full address, telephone and fax numbers. It may also include some other information. Many businesses may have their full name and address printed on the envelope, with the message, 'If undelivered, please return to.....'

Business letterhead paper is official paper which should only be used for official business letter writing, that is, for dealing with business matters. Nowadays, many businesses do not send letters with day-to-day documents such as invoices, accounts statements and the like. Any generalisation of business letter writing in terms of day-to-day routine letters and important correspondence does not apply to all kinds of businesses. For instance, many firms of solicitors send a letter with an invoice to their clients. Owing to a small volume of invoices and the type of work, it appears to be important, practical and traditional for this type of business. On the other hand, a busy wholesale electrical goods firm may find it impractical and costly to send letters with its many daily sales invoices. As far as business courtesy is concerned, at one time in the business world, it was almost universal to enclose a compliments slip with day-to-day correspondence (e.g. a sales invoice), but it is less common than it was some years ago because of the increasing cost.

__A compliments slip__ is a small piece of paper which contains a complimentary remark and the company's name and address. It is similar in style to that of the letterhead. The complimentary remark is 'With compliments' or 'With our compliments'. Sometimes, it is also used to write a short note and send it with some other business documents.

Some businesses keep *__copies__* on files of all correspondence for a specified period for the purpose of internal department communication, and to prove that action has already been taken.

Some firms, particularly small concerns, consider copies of letters unnecessary, if they are not part of accounting records for tax purposes. However, it is wise to keep copies of letters that you think may be required as evidence in any legal dispute.

. Letter Format

It is possible that your company has a business letter format. If so, you are expected to adhere to it. However, there are the following three formats:

Blocked Format	Semi-blocked Format	Indented Format
. all lines start at left-hand margin	. date and references start at right-hand margin	. paragraphs are indented by some spaces
		. the entire layout may follow either blocked or semi-blocked format

. Examples of Letters

It is of paramount importance that the writer should have precise ***factual information*** relating to the letter being written. In order to establish all facts, it may be necessary to check all relevant records, telephone conversations or seek information and advice from any other colleague(s) who might have dealt with the matter before.

Depending on the nature of the business and the content of the letter, the writer should use ***the English language style*** that is most suited, and which matches the knowledge and understanding of the recipient. It is wasteful and confusing to the recipient if you use too many words and jargon/technical phrases or local expressions.

 It should go without saying that ***plain English*** is preferred by most people. Of course, if you are a biologist writing to another biologist, your language will include technical phrases, which will not alienate the recipient. On the other hand, if you use technical words which are commonly used in your trade, and write long and verbose sentences, you can easily confuse the recipient who does not possess the knowledge of your trade or profession. Likewise, if you oversimplified your writing, the recipient may feel patronised. Therefore, the best idea is to use plain English, that is to use appropriate words and short sentences that make the point directly, clearly, accurately and briefly. [Note: Plain English is not for toastmasters.]

. Salutation & Complimentary Remarks

If you know the title (Mr/Mrs/Miss/Ms/Dr....) and surname, use an appropriate salutation and complimentary remarks as shown in Appendix 1, otherwise:

> Salutation: "Dear Sir/Madam,"   Complimentary remark: "Yours faithfully,"

Sign it and underneath write your name. Under your name write your job status. If your company has its own style, you must adhere to it.

(1) . Enquiring about supplies

Letterhead
Business name and address etc.

date here

Sales Manager
XYZ Limited
12 London Road
Birmingham
B1 2BB1

Dear Sirs/Madam,

I understand that your company is the sole distributor for the W WW Publications, which we are interested in stocking.

I would be grateful if you would provide me with a current catalogue of WWW Publications, and a retail price list. Please could you also send your trading terms and conditions, together with your discount rates for bookshops, and credit account opening information by return of post.

Yours faithfully,

John Smith
Manager

. In Example 1, the idea is to obtain some relevant information on WWW Publications only. You are not interested in some other products which XYZ Limited may stock. Thus, the opening paragraph refers only to the publications from one publishing house.

. In case you decide to take this matter further, relevant commercial and payment information is requested in the second paragraph. There is no need to give any information on your business, as in the second paragraph the nature of your business is already stated -bookshop.

. If you wish, you can add 'With good wishes' on a separate line above the complimentary remark.

(2) . <u>Opening a credit account</u>

<u>Letterhead</u>
<u>Business name and address etc.</u>

date here

Mr R M Henderson
Sales Manager
XYZ Limited
12 London Road
Birmingham
B1 2BB1

Dear Mr Henderson,

Thank you for your letter of 12 June. We would very much like to stock some of the items listed in WWW Publications current catalogue. We are pleased to send you the following two business contacts whom you can approach for references about our company:

. Mr H N Roberts, Manager, Hope Bank PLC, High Street, Rugby, RB1 2NW

. Miss A Johnson, Credit Controller, ABC PLC, Tree Street, White Cross Reading , RE1 2BC

We await your reply and look forward to doing business with you to our mutual interest.

Yours sincerely,

John Smith
Manager

In Example 1, credit facilities were requested. Now you have decided to open a credit account at XYZ Limited. Since XYZ does not have a formal form for this purpose, you must send two references. One of these must be your business bank where your current business account is operated
from. Example 2 illustrates how to write this simple letter.

(3) . <u>Confirming the opening of a credit account</u>

<u>Letterhead</u>
<u>Business name and address etc.</u>

date here

Mr John Smith
Manager
Vision Bookshop
3 Kensington High Street
London W11 4MN

Dear Mr Smith,

<u>Reference: Current Account Number: 00123</u>

We are pleased to confirm that your credit account number is **00123** and that your monthly credit limit is **£1,500**.

At present, we do not accept payments by BACS (Bankers Automatic Clearing System). Therefore, all payments should be made by cheque within thirty days from our invoice date.

Yours sincerely,

Doris Day
Miss Doris Day,
Credit Control Manager

In the above letter, the essential information is given in paragraph 1, so that the trade between these two businesses can commence. In the second paragraph, a polite advance notice is given so that the supplier is not approached for BACS method and delaying payment. Many smaller businesses find BACS expensive. There is no need to add any further information.

(4) . Accepting a quotation

Letterhead
Business name and address etc.

date here

Mr M R Dodd
Director
Dodd Building Services(London) Limited
1 Camden High Street
London NW1 7 AX

Dear Mr Dodd,

Reference: Q123908

Thank you for your quotation for replacing the existing flat roof of our office extension at the above address. We are pleased to accept your quotation for the following work:

. to strip off the existing felt and decking
. to re-board the roof with 18 mm plywood
. to re-felt using 2-layers of built laid bonded hot bitumen, finish lay green mineral
. to supply and fix new wooden fascia to all three sides of the roof
. to re-fix all gutters
. to dispose of all waste materials

We understand that the work will commence at about 7.30 hours on 20 July. The job will be completed within three days. If there are any changes due to severe weather conditions before starting the work, you will contact me immediately, so that we can make some other arrangements to complete this job satisfactorily without any unnecessary delays.

The total cost for all materials and work is £3,500 plus 17.5% VAT. This price includes five years guarantee of labour and materials, if within five years any part or the whole flat roof need any repairs or replacement. The total price three thousand and five hundred pounds plus VAT is payable on the day, when the job is satisfactorily completed as per your quotation and this letter. If you accept the content of this letter, please sign and date the attached and return it to me.

Yours sincerely,

Carl Duncan

Carl Duncan
Purchasing Manager

. The acceptance of a quotation forms the basis of an agreement between two parties. Thus, it is advisable to clearly state the nature of your purchase, prices, terms and conditions. Without clear understanding of what is agreed, there can be some problems later on. Therefore, it is important to write a precise and concise letter stating all key points.

. In Example 4 above, the bullet-pointed list of items gives a job specification (nature of purchase). These are the things that must be done.

. The next paragraph relates to the date when the work should commence, days to be taken to complete the work and any problems that may arise because of unpredictable weather conditions.

. In the last paragraph, the price is written twice – in both numbers and words. The guarantee is underlined and payment time is stated with the payment condition. Finally, the recipient's attention is drawn to the attached copy of the letter which must be signed and dated by the recipient and returned to the writer.

. If a quotation is about a complex job or some expensive purchase, such as a property deal, it is worth paying a fee to a solicitor, so that the purchase agreement has a proper legal format.

. <u>Rejecting a Quotation</u>

The buying department may receive a number of quotations. Often many buyers do not write to prospective suppliers whose quotations are rejected, because it is both time consuming and costly. On the other hand, some buyers feel that it is in their business interests to acknowledge all quotations and inform each supplier why their quotation was unacceptable. By using this approach one can also avoid receiving further telephone calls, letters or even salesmen's visits from all those prospective suppliers of goods and services, enquiring and trying to negotiate about the outcome of their quotations. It is suggested that you write a letter to all prospective suppliers on the following lines:

. start by acknowledging the receipt of their quotation, and state the quoted price for the proposed goods and service.

. give your reason for finding their quotation unacceptable.

. tell them that at some point in time in the future you will contact them for some quotations.

Example 5 contains a letter rejecting a quotation. The tone of this letter is friendly, but its message is dismissive.

****

(5) . <u>Rejecting a quotation</u>

<u>**Letterhead**</u>
<u>**Business name and address etc.**</u>

date here

Mr M R Dodd
Director
Dodd Building Services(London) Limited
1 Camden High Street
London
NW1 7 AX

Dear Mr Dodd,

<u>**Reference: Q123908**</u>

Thank you for your quotation of £3,500 plus 17.5% VAT for replacing the existing flat roof of our office extension at the above address.

We are very sorry to inform you that we feel that your price is in excess of what we have budgeted for this work.

Once again, we thank you for sending us the quotation and giving us the opportunity to consider it with great interest. We assure you that whenever we need similar repairs to our office properties in the future, we will approach you for a quotation.

Yours sincerely,

Carl Duncan

Carl Duncan
Purchasing Manager

. <u>Sales Letters</u>

Sales letters are not easy to write, yet many people consider them as junk mail and

468   **Business Letter Writing**

****

put them into the waste paper basket without opening them.

. <u>Different Forms of a Sales Letter</u>

The prime purpose of a sales letter is to persuade the recipient to buy some products or services offered by the writer of the sales letter. For instance, a small hand written duplicated note from a window cleaner, offering his services, pushed through the letterbox, is a sales letter. When you receive through the post a large white envelope containing a letter and some glossy leaflets from a large insurance company, it is also a sales letter. The range of sales letters is very large indeed. A sales letter may be disguised as an invitation, which is well designed and printed in colours on glossy paper. For instance:

> "An invitation to wine and cheese party and witness the launch of a new
> and exciting BMW business car at our purpose-built showroom in your town ...."

In some sales letters, some ridiculous claims are made. For instance, 'the most attractive place in the world', 'the cheapest and best', and similar phrases. You should describe your products or services in words which give correct factual information, and ensure that your products or services can match their descriptions and stand up to close scrutiny. Here are two examples of

sales letters – (6) . Sales Letter 1 and (7) . Sales Letter 2:

- Example 6 contains a sales letter about specialist bilingual dictionaries from Germany. In its opening paragraph, the writer has introduced the business as the sole distributor of these dictionaries. The writer has not given any other information about other business activities, because the main purpose is to sell these dictionaries.

- In the middle part of the letter two products are listed and their vital book information is given. The prospective customer is provided with two information sheets on these two products. These information sheets contain concise and precise information, and no wild claim is made about the products being introduced.

- In the next paragraph, the importance of these products is highlighted, but not over-stated.

- In the last paragraph, the writer expresses an appreciation in anticipation of an order by any of the four modes of placing an order.

This is a simple and honest sales letter. It informs the recipient about two products, from whom and how to purchase them. Its approach is friendly and its tone is polite. It is precise and concise.

(6). <u>Sales Letter 1</u>

<u>Letterhead</u>
<u>Business name and address etc.</u>

date here

DR R Angus
University Science & Technology Library
Newland University
Newland
NEW1 6AB

Dear Dr Angus,

<u>Specialist bilingual dictionaries from Germany</u>

We are pleased to inform you that we are the sole distributors of reputable comprehensive specialist dictionaries from Germany:

. Dictionary of Engineering & Technology - Wörterbuch der industriellen Technik,
                                        Englisch -Deutsch
 Ernst Richard, ISBN 3-87097-162-2, 6th edition 2000

. Data Systems and Communications Dictionary –
                     Wörterbuch der Daten-und Kommunikationstechnik
                       Deutsch – Englisch and Englisch – Deutsch
 Brinkmann, Karl-Heinz / Blaha, Herbert F. ISBN 3-87097-206-8, 6th edition 2002

Further information on each of these dictionaries and their prices is given separately on the enclosed two information sheets.

These dictionaries are indispensable for communication between the English and German speaking countries in the field of science and technology. Indeed, they provide authoritative coverage of science and technology subject areas in depth.

We would greatly appreciate your order by post, fax, email or telephone, and look forward to hearing from you in due course.

Yours sincerely,

Mrs Anne Arniticheva,
Library Supplies Co-ordinator
A.D.R.(London) Limited

(7) . <u>Sales Letter 2</u>

<u>**Letterhead**</u>
<u>**Business name and address etc.**</u>

date here

Mr G Spencer
Proprietor
Linden Hall Nursery
Linden Hall
YO1 8LH

Dear Mr Spencer,

I visited your nursery last Sunday afternoon, as we were in your area. It is, indeed, a large nursery, as you have a wide range of all kinds of indoor and outdoor plants, shrubs, bushes and gardening accessories. At your cash desk, four persons were dealing with customers payments, and all chargeable amounts were worked out without the aid of any calculating machine. Customers paid by cash and transactions were completed without receipts given to customers. In fact, there was a long queue of customers, including myself, waiting to pay for their purchases.

I do not see anything wrong with this system, but I thought I should write to inform you that we have developed our computer based cash register and management system. This system has been supplied to many retailers, and our clients include a number of nurseries in the UK.

Once you have initially invested in this reliable, accurate and fast system, you will soon experience fast cash handling, dealing with credit card transactions, issuing sales receipts, improved and timely ordering of stock items, regular management reports, customer satisfaction and an increase in sales. After some time, the financial benefits will become apparent, as the cost of overall business administration will decrease gradually.

Our system is guaranteed and we service it on a regular basis. I would be happy to introduce you to one of our clients in the nursery business, and they would be happy to discuss our system with you.

Our systems consultant and a demonstrator can visit you at your earliest convenience and give you a demonstration without any obligation.

I look forward to hearing from you.

Yours sincerely,

Alan Jolly,
Managing Director

- The communication approach in this letter is based on an observation. The first paragraph makes it clear.

- In the second paragraph, Linden Hall nursery's current system is <u>not</u> criticised. Here, the writer has briefly mentioned the product which was supplied to nurseries in the UK.

- In the third paragraph, a link is created between an initial investment in this system and some key benefits without too much unnecessary emphasis.

- In the fourth paragraph, an assurance is given to the prospective customer in terms of the guarantee, service and a reference so that the recipient takes a keen interest in the letter and the product.

- In the next paragraph, the recipient is invited to see a demonstration of this system at the recipient's own place without any obligation.

Like the sales letter in example 6, it is a simple, precise and concise letter. It does not make any wild claims about the system being offered for sale.

. <u>Money Matters</u>

For whatever reasons, sometimes customers do not pay for goods or services purchased, but continue sending orders. In the interest of your business, you do not wish to upset them, but at the same time you must get your payment from them before they even go bankrupt.

- In Example 8, the writer acknowledges the order from a customer, but politely and firmly rejects it. The idea is to refer to the order number/ reference and in simple words tell them the reason for not passing this order for completion.

  In the second paragraph, the recipient is reminded of the terms and conditions of trade. Here the writer firmly informs the recipient that the order will be kept on file for only ten days. It is also stated that within this period, payment should be made, so that it can be processed.

- Example 9 is concerning a request from a customer to increase the existing credit limit. Since the customer's sales account shows that they have not paid for goods supplied two months ago, and have already bought goods equivalent to the agreed credit limit, it is not your company's policy to increase credit limit in such circumstances.

There is no need to tell them something which does not sound right, when a polite and sympathetic reply is sufficient. However, tell them that you still value their orders, and you will continue to supply goods within the existing credit limit.

(8) . <u>Declining a sales order</u>

<u>**Letterhead**</u>
<u>**Business name and address etc.**</u>

date here

Mr J M Simpson
Buyer
Bow Electronics Ltd
12 Clapham Common
London
SW12 8 VC

Dear Mr Simpson,

Thank you for the order number A 00234 received today. Regrettably, your account is already two months overdue. Furthermore, you have already purchased goods equivalent to the agreed monthly credit limit of £5000.

In accordance with our terms and conditions of trade, we would very much appreciate your cheque for £5000 before we can complete this order. We will keep this order on our pending file for ten days. We hope that within this time you will be able to send us a cheque. As soon as we have received your cheque, we will release this order for completion.

Yours sincerely,

Bruce Butler

Bruce Butler
Credit Control Manager

- It is generally understood that it is worth asking for a discount. Example 10 exemplifies the content of a letter asking for a discount.

- In the opening paragraph, the writer thanks the suppliers for sending them a copy of their current catalogue, and shows an interest in their goods.

- In the next paragraph, the writer tells them what they will buy immediately, and that they purchase IT products on a regular basis. It is better not to place too much emphasis on future purchases, because it may look as if you are trying to stress this point in order to get a discount. It is a good idea to ask for a particular percentage discount rate. If you don't, they may suggest a rate which may be lower than you would like to have, and that may be their final offer. See Example 10 on the next page.

(9) . <u>Declining a request for increasing credit limit</u>

<u>Letterhead</u>
<u>Business name and address etc.</u>

date here

Mr A K Brown
Proprietor
Brent Bed Manufacturers
Industrial Park
Brent
BR1 9 MM

Dear Mr Brown,

<u>Account No. 0786</u>

Thank you for your letter of 10 June, asking us to increase the credit limit from £5000 to £7500, and informing us about your company's capital investment and expansion plans.

As a small company, we do understand and appreciate your current difficulties and commitments. Indeed, we have a number of our own commitments to meet. Like yourself, we also operate within the financial constraints and cash flow problems.

In fact, you have already bought goods equivalent to the agreed credit limit, and the account is already two months overdue. It is our company policy, in line with general practice in the manufacturing industry, that no credit extension is granted when the account is already 60 days overdue.

Under these circumstances, regrettably, we are unable to increase your credit limit on this occasion.

Yours sincerely,

Tim Clark

Tim Clark
Credit Controller

---

(10) . <u>Asking for a discount</u>

<u>Letterhead</u>
<u>Business name and address etc.</u>

date here

Mr P N Smith
Sales Manager
London PC Centre
12 Old High Street
London
W11 7CC

Dear Mr Smith,

Recently we received your product catalogue together with your price list, for which we are grateful. It is really good to know that you have a wide range of IT products.

We are a large commercial IT training provider in this area of London. We do buy IT products, on a regular basis, for both our training requirements and administrative purposes. At present, we would like to purchase four Deskjet 999 Cxi printers. According to your price list, the total gross cost will be £ 1,050 plus VAT @17.5%.

We usually get 25% discount on all our IT supplies. If you would like to match this rate of discount, we would be pleased to place an order immediately.

We look forward to hearing from you in due course.

Yours sincerely,

Dr Frank Nödel
Director

. <u>Employment Matters</u>

It is really important to give serious thought to what you should say in your letter of employment and CV(Curriculum Vitae). A well-written letter of employment and CV can get you an interview, but cannot guarantee that you will be successful at the interview. However, your letter of application clears the first hurdle for you, if you get a call for a job interview. Therefore, it is important to prepare both the letter and the CV with great care and thought. A well-written letter does not mean a letter composed as a super literary piece of writing, but simple, polite, clear and concise that gives correct information. Here are some examples to help you develop your own style of presentation of your application for a job.

. A CV or *Résumé*

A CV is also known as a *résumé*. A CV will be read by a number of people. Each person will make an observation. Therefore, you should design a CV that keeps selling your attributes. Your attributes include your abilities, qualifications, experience, ambitions and personal qualities related to a particular job. It also includes your potential that can be developed further in the job or by means of further education and training. The best way to prepare your CV is to develop a personal data bank for collecting all information about yourself. Example 11 lists items on which you should start collecting information for your CV. As you gain more experience, you may need more headings to build up your up-to-date CV.

(11) . <u>Personal data bank for preparing a CV</u>

Personal Information

Title (Prof/Dr/Mr/Mrs/Miss/Ms) -- ------------

First Name(s) -- Surname--------------------------------------

Address --

Telephone (home) --------------------- Telephone(work) ----------------------- Fax--------------------

Email --

Date of Birth ------------------- Place of birth --- --------------- Age at last birthday --------------------------

Nationality ------------------------------ National Insurance No.--------------------------------

Gender --------- Marital Status -------------------- Children -------------- Age(s) ----------------------------

Current Passport ---------------Driving Licence----------------- Health.--------------------------------

Next of kin --------------------- Telephone -------------------- Fax ----------------- Email------- ---------------

(11) . <u>**Personal data bank for preparing a CV**</u> (cont. from last page)

Education & Training

School (from age 11 in the UK) --

Qualifications gained with dates --

College/University attended (start from the last course/ qualification gained include professional training	Date	Course(list subjects)	Qualification gained
	-------	----------------------	----------------------
		------------------------------------	--------------------
		------------------------------------	--------------------
		------------------------------------	--------------------
		------------------------------------	--------------------

Membership of Professional bodies	Date	Methods of Joining Exams passed/ exempted	Level of Membership
	-------	----------------------------	----------------------
		------------------------------------	--------------------
		------------------------------------	--------------------
		------------------------------------	--------------------

Employment History (start from your most recent job)
------------------------------- --

Employers	Start date	End date	Job title and brief description	Salary & reason for leaving
-------------	----------	----------	------------------------	--------------------

****

(11). <u>Personal data bank for preparing a CV</u> (cont. from last page)

Any publications

Describe some other aspects of your current job or previous jobs which you initiated or developed leading to improved efficiency, better working environment, increased profitability, etc.

Objective (describe in a few words how you can make a contribution)

Interests & Hobbies (clubs, societies, charity work, etc.)
-------------------------   ---------------------------------
 ----

Any accomplishment from the age 11 at schools/college/university/ sport
----

Any special aptitudes/skills that can be developed at work and is useful to employers
----

References

Usually a minimum of two references are required. These are your last and present employers. If you are still a student, give the names of your present tutor and the head of department. Your tutor can advise you about this matter. It may be that you worked for many years for just one employer, and left school/college many years ago. In this case, give references from the same company where you were employed. You must ask for permission before listing them as your referees. Give full name, status, address, telephone (and fax) number and email address (if any).

. <u>CV Styles</u>

There are a number of ways to draw up your CV. In fact, some companies offer a commercial service for preparing your general CV, which you can circulate to prospective employers and employment agencies. This service is not recommended in this book. If your letter of application and your performance at the interview do not match it, you will be very disappointed after the interview. A general CV may not have the specific information for a particular post or it may have too much information. If so, it will be difficult for the reader of your CV to pick out the relevant information from it. This will not help you to get an interview. Therefore, it is strongly suggested that you are write your own CV.

Once you have your personal data bank, you can use it to write your CV. From your personal data, you can extract the relevant information for a CV for a particular job. If you want to compete successfully with other applicants, you must write a CV that meets the requirements of the job for which you wish to apply. It is worth knowing that a style of CV for a young person will not be suitable for someone who has been working for some years, and may have changed jobs many times.

It is best to use quality white paper of A4 size. It must be typed/word processed on one side of the page only. Allow left and right margins, as well as at the top and bottom of the page. It is a good idea to avoid excessive use of underlining, or similar emphasis, as some people do not like it.

- Example 12 illustrates a CV drawn for a young graduate applying for the post of a graduate trainee. The style is known as *historical*. It gives information in a chronological order. It is most suited when someone's career or work experience is unbroken. Therefore, this style is ideal for young people, as it shows continuity since they left school. It is also suitable for people who have not changed jobs over many years of their lives, because it reveals their career progress and continuity. The CV must be sent with a covering letter, only when you are looking for employment.

- If you are responding to an advertisement to fill a vacancy, you must apply for this vacancy in accordance with the prospective employers' rules. It may be that you have to fill in a formal application form and send it with a letter of application. It is strongly recommended that a letter of application is short and precise. It must not be more than two pages. Usually, prospective employers set the size - A4 one page, one side only.

- Example 13 contains a letter of application written by an applicant to send with the CV shown in Example 12.

(12). <u>A CV for a graduate</u>

<u>Personal History</u>

<u>Title:</u> Miss   <u>Status:</u> Single

<u>Surname:</u> Scott   <u>Other Name:</u> Jane   <u>Date of Birth:</u> 12.12.1980   <u>Age:</u> 21 years

<u>Address:</u> 23 Home Street, London NW1 1BN   <u>Telephone:</u> 0123 456 987

<u>National Insurance No.</u> ABC/1334/ABN   <u>Driving Licence:</u> Full UK <u>Passport:</u> Full UK

<u>Health:</u> Excellent   <u>Next of Kin:</u> Mr and Mrs Scott (parents) at the address shown above

<u>Objective</u>

A graduate trainee appointment in IT field. I possess BSc(Hons) Degree in IT and some part-time work experience. I can quickly learn and contribute towards the IT team work at Goldsmith Retail Stores.

<u>Education</u>

1991- 98	Green Comprehensive School, Camden Town London NW1 2BB
1998 –03	Newland University Bristol BR1 6FD

<u>Qualifications</u>

1996	GCSE in English Language (B), Maths (A), Computer Studies (A), Physics (C), British Constitution (B)
1998	A Levels in Computer Studies (A), English (B), German (C)
2003	BSc (IT), second Class Honours, Newland University

<u>Work Experience</u>

1991– 03   Part-time weekend, Shop Assistant, Foods & Drinks Store
Camden Town London NW1 1SD
Duties included filling of shelves, stock checking, checkout help and stock taking

2003-to-date Part-time weekend, Shop Assistant, Friendly Stores
Newton Street, Bristol BE3 5AC
Duties included filling of shelves, stock checking, and checkout help

<u>Interest & Hobbies</u>

I played hockey at school and university.
I held the post of chairman, IT Society at Newland University

<u>Reference:</u>

Dr Peter Sellers	Miss J Smith
Head of Computing School	Store Manager
Newland University	Foods & Drinks Store
Bristol	Camden Town
BR1 6FD	NW1 1SD
Tel: 0126 44445	Tel: 0207 444 1234

(13) . <u>**A letter of application for a trainee job from a graduate**</u>

23 Home Street
Bristol
BR1 9AS

(date here)

Miss M B Jones
Personnel Manager
Goldsmith Retail Stores
Paddington
Peterborough
PE1 4AA

Dear Miss Jones,

I have been informed by our Graduate Employment Officer at the University of Newland that annually you recruit some newly qualified graduates. This year, I completed my BSc (Hons) degree in IT. I would very much appreciate it if you would consider me as a candidate.

I am particularly interested in joining your company as I have had some part-time experience working in the retail business. During the last six years, I worked for two major retail stores in London and Bristol. This experience has given me some working knowledge of big store operations and the important role played by IT in the smooth running of a large retail store.

On my IT degree course, I have experienced theoretical computing and IT knowledge, and acquired some software development skills. I believe that my training at your company will enable me to extend my knowledge and skills as well as to take part in developing software for the company quickly.

 I enclose a copy of my CV and hope that you will grant me an interview.

I look forward to hearing from you.

Yours sincerely,

Jane Scott

****

- The above letter is from a graduate who has just completed her course of study. Jane Scott's chosen career has not begun yet. Therefore, it is more appropriate to call her CV 'Personal History'. This CV format is most suited for someone who has not had much work experience. In your letter of application, avoid the use of long and complex expressions as simple and direct sentences will convey your meaning more clearly.

- In this application, it is relevant to list all part-time jobs. It does not matter if they are not related to the work you are seeking now. If you had any additional duties, over and above your normal responsibilities, you must state them. Part-time work shows your motivation to work as well as some experience of the world of work.

- The section on interest and hobbies is essential. You can call it 'Other Information', or give it another title. However, it is important to say something about your activities other than just learning to gain a qualification. This section reveals your social and sports activities, and gives an idea of any sign of leadership. Applicants who show signs of leadership and team work have something extra to offer. If you did not take part in any sports or societies, you could still mention something like gardening, charity work, etc.

- The lack of space in this chapter does not allow me to discuss another type of CV known as *functional* and a cover letter, except to add that this type of CV is most suited for an applicant who has had varied experience and held a number of posts over some years. The functional CV can also be called *'Career History'*. To write a functional CV, you still have to extract data from your personal data bank. When listing work experience in your CV, break it down into some functions. The following is a part of a functional CV:

Major Experiences during the last ten Years

Store Manager - 1999 –2001   World PLC , Kings Road, Chelsea, London W1 2SS
Under my control, the sales increased from £14 - £17 millions during the last three years.

Sales Manager - 1997- 99   Home Stores PLC, High Street, Nottingham NO1 3CV
Manager   I was responsible for 'Northern Sales Regions'. My sales team had twenty sales representatives. I re-organised our sales and goods delivery procedures that led to an increase in sales. Our sales steadily increased by 20% under my supervision.

--------- cont.

Most employers will ask you to fill in an application form. It is important that you fill it. A CV and a letter of application are sent together when you are directly approaching a prospective employer for a suitable job. If you are granted an interview, it is highly likely that you will be asked to fill in a form.

. <u>Holiday Arrangements</u>

Holiday booking is fairly easy. Sometimes it can lead to serious problems due to a lack of clarity of information given by either party. It is, therefore, suggested that you give and receive precise written information prior to agreeing the terms and conditions of your booking.

(14) . <u>A letter to the manager of a hotel for holiday arrangements</u>

Your name
and
full address

date here

The Manager
Bridlington Hotel
Promenade
Bridlington
Y016 4 AA

Dear Manager,

I write to enquire whether you have accommodation for five nights for four persons. I list our requirements:

. Arrival on Saturday 11 June xxxx (early in the morning).

. Departure on Thursday 16 June xxxx.

. Accommodation in a large en suite bedroom which should have one double bed and two single beds. This accommodation will be for my wife, myself and my two sons 7 and 10 years of age (two adults and two children). We would prefer an en suite room on the front side of your building and located on the first or second floor. It must <u>not</u> be next to the lift or a staircase. The room must have a colour television set and its use must be included in your rates. Please inform us if the room is equipped with tea/coffee making facilities.

. If you do not have a large en suite bedroom for a family of four, then I would be interested in two small adjoining/connected rooms, one must be an en suite bedroom providing their total cost for five days does not exceed the cost of one large en suite bedroom, as long as they have the same facilities as outlined above.

Cont. on page

Business Letter Writing 483

****

(14) .A letter to the manager of a hotel for holiday arrangements (cont.)

Cont. from page

. We will arrive at 3.30 hours at Edinburgh Airport from London Heathrow Airport.

   . Can you please tell us the best way to travel from the airport to your hotel.

   . Will we be able to have access to our room as soon as we arrive early in the morning? If not, when can we do so ?

By the time we arrive at your hotel, our children will be rather tired, and therefore, we would very much appreciate your help if we could occupy our accommodation on our arrival, or as soon as it is ready for us. If we have to wait for some time before our room is ready:

   . Will it be possible for us to relax in your reception area until our accommodation is ready for us, and buy our breakfast at your hotel? If so, please inform us of the cost of breakfast per person. Will it be English breakfast or continental?

. We would also need breakfast during our five nights' stay.

   . Can we please book our evening meals on a day-to-day basis, when we are staying with you?

If for some unknown reason(s), I have to cancel the booking, please tell me:

   . How long notice should I give you without losing my deposit?

   . Are there any recreation facilities for children at the hotel or near the hotel?

I would be grateful to hear whether you can accommodate us. If so, please send me your rates, how much deposit you would require, and how you would like to be paid, together with the other information requested above.

I look forward to hearing from you in due course.

Yours faithfully,

(signature)

John R Smith

This is not really a social letter. It is better to word process/type it and write your name below your signature; otherwise, print important information such as date of arrival. For salutation and complimentary remarks, see Business Letter Writing in the next chapter.

(15) . <u>A letter to the manager of a hotel for further information</u>

Your name
and
full address

date here

Mrs Anne Blair
Manager
Bridlington Hotel
Promenade
Bridlington
Y016 4 AA

Dear Mrs Blair,

Thank you for your letter of 15 May in response to my enquiry of 10 May. I am pleased that you have provisionally booked for my wife, myself and my two sons one large en suite bedroom which has two single beds and one double bed for five nights, from 11 June to 15 June inclusive, leaving on 6 June. It is good to know that a full English breakfast is included in the rates you quoted, and we can book our evening meals each morning, if we wish to do so.

I'm glad to learn that on our early morning arrival, we can stay in your reception area, if our accommodation is occupied by some other guests until 11.00 hours. We can also buy either English breakfast or continental breakfast. I understand that 20% of the total cost is payable as a deposit on booking, and that it can be paid by cheque or by a credit card (visa card only).

I should be grateful if you would answer the remaining point raised in my last letter concerning cancellation notice without losing the deposit.

On receipt of your prompt reply, I should be able to decide about my booking and inform you without any delay. Thanking you in anticipation of your prompt reply.

Yours sincerely,

John R Smith

In summary, business letter writing is for the purpose of achieving business objectives. The personal letter writing is an excellent way of keeping in touch with friends. It creates mutual understanding, removes prejudices between young and old, man and woman, especially of different cultural and religious divides across the world. It gives considerable pleasure when you send or receive a letter.

Remember ⟹ _Someone somewhere wants a letter from you!_ ⟸repeat

Glossary

A

absolute adjectives – adjectives which exist in their basic form only. e.g. $\Rightarrow$ wrong.

abstract nouns – nouns that are used for concepts, which have no material existence, e.g. $\Rightarrow$ anger.

active clause – a clause in which the action or doing of something is taken by the agent (subject), e.g. $\Rightarrow$ John is writing a letter.

active participle – the **-ing** form of a verb in the continuous, used after **be**, e.g. $\Rightarrow$ I am reading.

active verb (or Active voice) – when the subject performs the action or experiences the state or condition, e.g. $\Rightarrow$ I write a letter.

adding relative clause – it is separated off from the main clause by two commas. It gives some additional information about the headword, e.g. $\Rightarrow$ Frank, *who is Elina's friend*, is

working abroad.   **relative clause** ↵

adjective – a word that modifies/qualifies the meaning of a noun, or pronoun, e.g. $\Rightarrow$ she is **kind**.

adjective phrase – a phrase which has an adjective in it, e.g. $\Rightarrow$ she is very beautiful. In this sentence: very beautiful $\Rightarrow$ adjective phrase **and** the headword $\Rightarrow$ beautiful $\Rightarrow$ adjective.

adjunct (adverb) – an adverb or phrase that adds meaning to the verb in a sentence or part of a sentence, e.g. $\Rightarrow$ he screamed loudly. Here, loudly $\Rightarrow$ adverb is acting as an adjunct and adds meaning to the verb scream. An adjunct shows degree (extent to which something happened), manner or place.

adverb – the most common function of an adverb is to modify the main verb in a sentence, e.g. I can do it *easily*. easily $\Rightarrow$ adverb.

adverb phrase – it can be an adverb on its own e.g. ⇒smoothly. It can also be part of a phrase, which has an adverb as its headword (see ⇒headword), e.g. very abruptly ⇒ very ⇒headword.

adverbial clause – in a complex sentence, it modifies the main clause, e.g. I will talk to you when I meet you tomorrow. An adverbial clause is joined to the main clause by the conjunction ⇒ when.

adverbial element (or phrase) – a part of a sentence which gives the least compulsory information in a sentence, e.g. ⇒ I wrote this letter in a great hurry.

adverbial element ↵

agent – in an active clause/sentence, the subject is doing the action. It is known as the agent, e.g. ⇒I write it. Here, agent ⇒ I. In a passive clause, an agent comes after *by*, e.g. The letter is signed by *Anne*.

agreement (or concord) – it is a rule in accordance with the verb form which is agreed with the subject and number of the subject (singular/plural), e.g. ⇒ she sings. On the other hand, e.g. ⇒ they cry.

apostrophe – a punctuation mark, e.g. ⇒ Joan's father is a phrase in which the apostrophe is placed between Joan and s to indicate the possessive case. For other usage, see punctuation.

apposition – when in a sentence or clause, two *noun phrases* come one after the other and both refer to the same thing, then phrases are in apposition, e.g. ⇒ *Mr Brown, our director*, is retiring today.

article – there are two types of articles: *a* and *an* ⇒ indefinite article and *the* ⇒ definite article.

aspect – there are two verb aspects: progressive aspect, e.g. ⇒ I am writing and perfect aspect ⇒ I have written. These two aspects can be combined together, e.g. ⇒ she has been living in the UK.

asterisk '*' – it is a star symbol used as a punctuation mark to indicate the omission of letters, the importance of a particular word , a reference or a footnote at the bottom of the text, or elsewhere.

attributive adjective – it comes before a noun or clause, e.g. ⇒ my **new** car has arrived.

auxiliary verb – a small number of verbs such as *be, will, have* are used with ordinary verbs, such as *work*. These are divided into modal and primary auxiliaries. See ⇒ modal.

B

bare infinitive – verbs without the particle *to* e.g. ⇒ talk . Bare infinitive is the base form.

base form ,(*root form* or *stem*) – verbs as listed in a dictionary, e.g. ⇒ walk

brackets – in the British English for writing purposes the round brackets ( ) which are known as parentheses are used. They indicate alternatives, include abbreviations or show additional information.

C

cardinal numbers – a whole number, e.g. ⇒ 1,2,3.

classifying relative clause – it describes the head noun in the main clause by its nature or type. It does not have commas around it, e.g. ⇒ she likes John *who is very intelligent*. John ⇒head noun.

clause – it is a group of words containing a finite verb, and any other verb complement, e.g. ⇒ he went home early tonight. See ⇒ main clause and see ⇒ independent clause.

clause elements – there are five clause elements: subject, verb, object, complement and adverbial. A clause may have some or all of these elements.

colon ':' – a punctuation mark. It is used for different purposes.

comma ',' – like the full stop, it is a common punctuation mark. There is a tendency to use too many or too few commas despite the fact that it is well documented and understood.

comparative clause – this is used to express comparison, e.g. Anne is less interested in eating out *than her husband*. It is introduced by the subordinators *than* or *as*. It is a subordinate clause.

comparative form of adjective – for comparing two things or people, e.g. ⇒ he is older than me. old ⇒ adjective and older ⇒ comparative form (oldest ⇒superlative form).

complement – a noun or adjective phrase that follows a linking verb, e.g. ⇒ she is the *champion*.See ⇒ copula verb and **see** ⇒linking verb

complex sentence – in a complex sentence, one clause is a main clause, with one or more subordinate clauses, e.g. ⇒ I telephoned my wife when I arrived at Heathrow Airport. Main clause ⇒ underlined.

compound sentence – a compound sentence has at least two clauses of equal status which are joined together with a coordinating conjunction, e.g. *he lives downstairs* and *I live upstairs*.

compound word – it is composed of two or more words, e.g. mother-in-law.

concord - see ⇒ agreement.

concrete noun – a tangible thing that can be seen or touched is a concrete noun, e.g. ⇒ book.

conjunction – a conjunction functions as either a coordinating or subordinating conjunction, and joins clauses, e.g. ⇒ when in: I will meet you *when* you are upstairs.

coordination of phrases – it means joining together two phrases or clauses of the same status.

coordinator – a coordinator is a coordinating conjunction, e.g. ⇒ *and*, *but*, *or*. It joins clauses of the same status.

copular verb – it links the subject with a complement. The basic linking verb is '**be**'. There are only a few copular verbs. These include *be, appear, become, seem*.

countable noun – it has singular, and plural forms and can be preceded by a determiner such as *the, a, an, every, many, one, two, three, four*, etc.

<u>D</u>

dash '-' – a punctuation mark. It is used for a variety of purposes.

declarative (sentence/statement) – its order is: subject ⇒ verb ⇒ verb complement (if any).

declarative structure – it means the structure of a declarative sentence or statement.

defining relative clause – see ⇒ identifying relative clause.

definite article – see ⇒ article.

degree (adverb of) – a word such as *very, rather, somewhat*, **quite**, *pretty*. It shows the extent of quality, e.g. ⇒ she is very clever. Here, very ⇒ adverb of degree.

demonstrative pronoun – it is used to refer to a particular person, or thing, e.g. ⇒ *this* is a car. Other demonstrative pronouns are *that*, *these* and *those*. These are also demonstrative determiners.

dependent clause – it cannot stand alone, e.g. ⇒ *when I gave him a cup of tea*, he drank it fast.

determiner – a simple word that is placed before a noun phrase, e.g. ⇒ this.

direct object – I gave students passes. In this sentence: passes ⇒ direct object because the direct effect of the verb *gave* is on passes. In the same sentence: students ⇒ indirect object because the indirect effect/ secondary effect is on students.

direct speech – the exact words of the speaker which are enclosed within the quotation marks, e.g. ⇒ ' We were aware of your financial problems,' said the chairman. It is quoted in someone's words.

dummy subject – when the word *it* or *there* is used in the subject position and does not relate to any specific thing, e.g. ⇒ **It** appears she is late again. It is also known as an empty subject. It is used because it is needed in the subject position.

E

embedded prepositional phrase – prepositional phrases are embedded in the noun phrase, e.g. ⇒ you spoke to Rachel about her journey. In this sentence: [Rachel about her journey] ⇒ noun phrase   and [about her journey] ⇒ prepositional phrase

empty subject – see ⇒ dummy subject

empty verb – *have* is the most commonly used empty verb but there are other empty verbs, e.g. ⇒ take, give, do. We use them as: *give* an example, *have* tea. In these examples, the action is indicated by the nouns *example*, and *tea*.

exclamation mark – it is a punctuation mark represented by ! e.g. Cheers! It is a terminator.

F

finite clause – He walks to work. In this clause, the verb walk is marked for tense ⇒ present tense. When in a clause the verb is marked for tense it is called a finite clause.
See ⇒ non-finite clause.

finite phrase and finite verb – a finite verb or finite phrase such as *talk, went, was going, will be* are finite verbs and finite phrases. These are marked for tenses, e.g. ⇒ he is singing a song. In this clause, the finite phrase is singing and is marked for tense ⇒ present continuous.

****

footnote – it is a punctuation mark. It is written below the text to give further information.

formal style – it is used in official and important situations. It often indicates a distant than a close relationship. It is very correct in both writing and speech.

fraction – a number which is not a whole number, e.g. ⇒ half, two-thirds, four fifths.

full stop – it is the most commonly used punctuation mark. In the USA it is called a period.

future (tense) – it is a state or action that will take place in the future, e.g. ⇒ I will come. It is formed by ⇒ auxiliary verb (will or shall) + bare infinitive verb.

future continuous(progressive)– it expresses a state or action that will continue in the future. It is constructed as ⇒ shall/will + participle –ing form, e.g.⇒ *I will be thinking of you*.

future perfect – it refers to our thinking in the future and then looking back when something will be completed at a specific point in the future, e.g. By next Friday, I will have met him in Paris. It is constructed as ⇒ will/shall + have + past participle

future perfect progressive – it is as future perfect, but the action. or state of something continues in the future, e.g. Next month, you will have been studying at the university one year. It is constructed as ⇒ will/shall + have been + participle –ing form.

G

gender – in English the gender classification is: feminine ⇒ woman , masculine ⇒ man, and neuter ⇒ artefacts/things such as radio.

genitive case – it shows possession . It is a noun in its possessive form, e.g. John's car.

gerund – When a participle verb formed with *-ing* is used in a clause or a sentence as a noun, it is known as a gerund, e.g. *Dancing* is her favourite hobby. In this sentence, dancing is a gerund.

grammar – it has rules for combining words together for a meaningful communication in spoken and written language.

H

headword – it is a main noun or pronoun in a phrase, clause or sentence, e.g. ⇒ a **bundle** of files.

****

hyphen '– ' – it is a punctuation mark. It is used either to join two words together or to split the word at the end of a line of print.

I

identifying relative clause – its purpose is to identify the earlier noun in the main clause, e.g. ⇒ The young man **who is smartly dressed** is my son.

idiom or idiomatic expression – it is a group of words. Its meaning is different from the meaning of individual words forming the idiomatic expression. They are listed in alphabetical order in Chapter 13.

imperative mood – it is a command and an order. It can also be a polite order, e.g. ⇒ *forgive me.*

indefinite article – see ⇒ article

indefinite pronoun – a word which does not refer to any particular person or thing, e.g. ⇒all

independent clause – see ⇒ main clause

indicative mood – when we make a statement, ask a question or state a fact, e.g. ⇒ I'm here. See ⇒ moods.

indirect object – see ⇒ direct object

indirect speech – it is not in the words of the speaker but its meaning is reported in our own words, e.g. ⇒ I said she told me about her love affairs.

infinitive – it is the base form of the verb. e.g. ⇒ **go**. See ⇒ base form and bare infinitive (without the participle to-) as shown in a dictionary.

infinitive clause – it has an infinitive verb, e.g. We **walk** every evening. I wanted **to go**.
                                   bare infinitive ⌐   to-infinitive ⌐
infinitive particle – see ⇒ particle

inflection – it means changing the ending or spelling of a word in accordance with its grammatical function, e.g. ⇒ She studies French. The verb 'study' is inflected to match the present tense of its subject.

informal style – the use of the English language in social circumstances, e.g. both ⇒ spoken and written communication between relatives and friends.

ing- form – when **-ing** is added to a verb and used as a participle, or gerund e.g. ⇒ write⇒writing.

interjections – a minor class of word. Used for expressing feelings, e.g. ⇒ *Gosh!*

interrogative pronoun – what and which are used with nouns to ask questions, e.g. ⇒*Which* book was it?

intransitive verb – it does not take an object or complement, and it can stand alone, e.g. ⇒ I talk.

inversion – it occurs when the regular word order is changed to form a question, e.g. ⇒ has she finished that job? In this sentence: the subject *she* has changed (inverted) place with the auxiliary verb *has*.

irregular verbs– they do not follow the pattern of adding '-ed' to form the past tense, e.g. ⇒ begin: its irregular past tense ⇒ began.

L

linking verb – see ⇒ copular verb

M

main clause – any clause which can stand alone is a main clause, e.g. ⇒ I walk. It stands alone as a meaningful clause or a short sentence.

main verb – it is the finite verb in the main clause, e.g. ⇒ When the doorbell rang, I *opened* the door.

manner – it is the adverb of manner. It tells us *how* something happened, e.g. ⇒ she cried *loudly*.

modal (auxiliary verb) – these are auxiliary verbs, e.g. ⇒ can, could, may, might, etc.

modify (modifier) – it means giving further information about a word or phrase, e.g. It is a *tall* tree. 'tall' modifier is an adjective, but functioning as a modifier. It gives further information about ⇒**tree**.

moods – see ⇒ indicative, imperative and subjunctive entries.

N

non-finite clause – it has a to-infinitive form verb, ⇒ We asked them *to return* our camera.

noun – it is a name given to a person, place, object, etc., e.g. ⇒ John, London, Book ....

noun (nominal) clause – it can act as the subject, object or the complement of the main clause, e.g. ⇒ He thought *that she was not at home*. Here, the noun clause is acting as an object.

noun phrase – it has a noun or pronoun as its headword, e.g. ⇒ I wanted John *as our leader*.

O

object – it comes after the verb in a clause, e.g. ⇒ this is Andrew. object ⇒ Andrew.

object complement – it comes after the verb in a clause, e.g. ⇒ we all paid her **our** respects.

object predicate – see ⇒ object complement.

ordinal numeral – it refers to the position of something in a series, e.g. ⇒ he was in *third* place.

ordinary verb – there are thousands of ordinary verbs, such as ⇒ go, run, jump, write, etc. Auxiliary verbs are not included in ordinary verbs. See auxiliary and modal Verbs.

P

participle – it is a non-finite verb form. It ends either with *–ing* or *-ed*. See ⇒ present and past participle.

participle clause – it has a participle verb form in it, e.g.⇒ *Coming* to London, we were late.

particle – it is the word *to* with the base form of the verb, e.g. ⇒ to run.

particles class – it is a minor word class, e.g. ⇒ she *fell off* her bicycle on the road.

passive – in a passive clause/sentence something is done to the subject (agent), e.g. ⇒ the report *is being typed*.

passive verb (or passive voice) – when the subject is affected by the action. The passive

494   **Glossary**

****

voice involves the use of the **auxiliary verb.** For instance, the house **is** occupied. here is ⇒ auxiliary verb.

past continuous/progressive – it expresses what was happening at some point in time in the past, e.g. ⇒ I *was working* in London.

past participle form – Regular verbs: it ends in **–ed**. Irregular verbs: it ends in some other ways. e.g. ⇒eaten, drunk, etc. In the perfect it comes after 'have, e.g. I have *finished* it.

past perfect – it is formed with 'had' and a past participle e.g. ⇒ she *had received* my letter.

past perfect continuous/progressive – it is formed with 'had been' and active participle, e.g. ⇒ We *had been dancing* all night. Here, *dancing* ⇒ active participle.

past simple – it is the past tense, e.g. ⇒ they *returned* home. It tells what happened or existed at a particular time (then) before the present time (now).

perfect – it expresses action completed by the present, or a particular point in the past or future. It is constructed with 'have' with the past participle of the main verb, e.g. ⇒ *I have left* (present perfect), *I had left* (past perfect), and *I will have left* (perfect future).

perfect aspect –it is the underlined in: She *has been living* in Germany. See ⇒ aspect.

performative verb – it means the action it performs, e.g. ⇒ *I accept*. The action ⇒ accept.

person (singular and plural) – first person ⇒ **I, we**. Second person ⇒ **you**. Third person ⇒*he, she*, *it, they*.

personal pronoun – I, you, he, she, etc.

phrasal verb – it is a verb combined with an adverb or a preposition, e.g. ⇒ fall off, break down, etc.

phrase – a word or some words, e.g. ⇒ rubbish, a white elephant. There are five types of phrases: verb phrase, noun phrase, adjective phrase, adverb phrase, and prepositional phrase.

plural – it means more than one, e.g. ⇒ a song is the singular form but songs ⇒ the plural form of the noun.

possessive determiner – it is a possessive pronoun, when it replaces a noun, e.g. ⇒ this is *my* car.

possessive pronoun – mine, yours, ours, etc. This coat is mine. Possessive pronoun ⇒*mine*

predicate – in a clause, it is the verb element and any other elements that follow the verb, e.g. ⇒ England <u>is the largest part of the UK.</u> The underlined part is the predicate.

prefix – many words can be created by adding the beginning to a word, e.g. ⇒ *un*necessary. It is *un* + *necessary*. See ⇒ suffix.

preposition – a class of word, e.g. ⇒ over, since, for. Also more than one word, e.g. ⇒ instead of.

prepositional idioms – it is the preposition used with an idiom, e.g. ⇒ *at heart*.

prepositional phrase – it is the preposition plus a noun or an adverb e.g. ⇒ in our school, over there.

prepositions of relationships – express a variety of relationships. Most common are time and place.

present continuous/progressive – it is the present tense that shows the action is continuous.

present participle form – it is the part of the verb which ends in *–ing* , e.g. ⇒ missing, crossing, etc.

present perfect – it indicates that the action or state was complete in the near past up to the present time, e.g. ⇒ The parcel has arrived.

present perfect progressive – an action or state in the past which continues up-to the present time, e.g. ⇒ it has been raining. It is formed as: have/has + been + active participle.

present simple – it is the present tense, e.g. ⇒ I work. It expresses a current action or state.

pronoun – a word used instead of a noun or noun phrase, e.g. ⇒ *You* are kind.

Q

qualify – see ⇒ modify

question – it is a sentence for asking a question, e.g. ⇒ What's wrong with you?

Question tag – a short question at the end of a statement, e.g. ⇒ She loves him, doesn't she?

question word – these are what, when, where, who, whom, which, how, whose, why.

R

reciprocal pronoun – it is used to express mutual relationships, e.g. ⇒ they love *each other*. There are only two reciprocal pronouns each other and one another.

reflexive pronoun – it refers to the subject, e.g. ⇒ They can do it *themselves*. I do it *myself*.

regular verbs – they change their forms in the past by following a set pattern of *–ed ending*, e.g. ⇒ verb 'help' its regular past tense form ⇒ 'helped'.

relative adverb – where, when and why are used in relative clauses as relative adverbs, e.g. ⇒ the house *where* I was born.

relative clause – it modifies a noun, e.g. ⇒ the salesman *who talked too much*.

relative pronoun – it links a subordinate clause to a main clause, e.g. ⇒ it is not me *who* hit first.

S

s-form of the verb – it is the inflected form of the bare infinitive. It is formed with either *s*, or *es* added, e.g. ⇒ he *runs*. Here *s* is added. She *cries*. Here, cry is inflected by *es*.

sentence – a sentence is the largest syntactic unit which has at least one clause.

simple tense – it is without the auxiliary verb, e.g. ⇒ I go.

singular form – it means one thing only, e.g. ⇒ noun 'man' refers to only one person/man.

slang style – it is an informal way of speaking used between a specific group of people, e.g. ⇒ criminals.

split infinitive – the placing of a word or words between the *to* and the *verb* creates a split infinitive.

standard English – a form of the English language that is nationally used. Speakers of other languages learn standard English. For instance, broadcasting services use standard English.

statement – it is a declarative sentence which gives information. It is not a question.

structure - for our purpose, it means the way some words are arranged in accordance with the rules of grammar, e.g. ⇒ I went there.

style – it is a distinct way of doing something, e.g. writing or speaking in the language context. There are many styles. For instance, various styles are imposed on the use of idiomatic expressions.

subject –in a sentence, it comes before the verb, e.g. ⇒ he writes a letter. he ⇒subject/agent.

subject complement – in a clause/sentence it comes after a linking verb. e.g. ⇒she appears *calm*.

subject element – it precedes the verb in a clause. It is the agent of an active clause, e.g. ⇒ I'm writing this text. Here, I'm ⇒ **subject** or subject element. It is also the agent of this active clause.

subject position – it is the first element in a clause, e.g. ⇒ she loves you. subject ⇒ begins the clause.

subject predicate – see ⇒ subject complement

subjective pronoun – *I, you* (both singular and plural) , *he, she, it, they* and *we*. They occur in the subject position in a clause.

subjunctive mood – it indicates possibility, uncertainty, wish, etc., e.g. ⇒ she wanted a baby.

subordinate clause – it supports the main clause. See ⇒dependent clause

subordinator – in a complex sentence clauses are of unequal status. We use a subordinator (**when** ...) to join two clauses of unequal status.

suffix – words can be created by adding **an ending** to a word, e.g. ⇒ soft + *ly* = *softly*.

superlative – the form of an adjective for comparing three or more things, e.g. ⇒ highest, tallest (adjectives).

T

taboo style – use of swear words.

tense – it is a form of the verb which indicates when the action of the verb occurs, or the state affected by the verb, e.g. **I talk** ⇒ present tense and **she cried** ⇒ past tense. It is marked for present and past only.

to-infinitive – it is a verb form which is preceded by 'to', e.g. to run, to sign, to smile.

to-infinitive clause – see ⇒ infinitive clause.

transitive verb – it cannot stand alone and it is followed by an object, e.g. ⇒ she *rang* the <u>bell</u>.

       object ⤶

U

uncountable noun – it has only one verb form. Some uncountable nouns are only plural such as jeans, e.g. ⇒ **a pair of jeans**. On the other hand, some uncountable nouns such as **space** are only singular, e.g. ⇒ There **wasn't much space** in the room. When an uncountable noun is the subject, the verb is singular, e.g. ⇒ Some *money is* in Euro currency.

unclassified style – no restriction is imposed on the use of some idiomatic expressions.

V

verb – doing, action/state word. It is the most important part of speech, e.g. ⇒ she *loves* her children. Without the word *loves* which is a verb, the sentence will not make any sense.

verb aspect – see ⇒ aspect

verb element – it is the focal point of a clause, e.g. ⇒ she <u>has completed</u> her assignment. In this sentence, the underlined element is the verb.

verb phrase – it is an ordinary verb, e.g. ⇒ run, have gone, etc. it may also have an auxiliary verb and other words, e.g. ⇒ will go, had gone away.

verbals – these are derived from verbs but are <u>not</u> used as verbs, e.g. ⇒ it was a *horrifying* scene.

voice – see ⇒ active verb (voice) and passive verb (voice).

vocabulary – it consists of words, e.g. all words in the English language.

W

wh-question – it is the question which begins with a question word, e.g. ⇒what, where., etc.

word class – it is another name for parts of speech, e.g. ⇒ noun, adjective, etc.

Index

****